The Microsoft® SQL Server™ Survival Guide

JIM PANTTAJA

MARY PANTTAJA

BRUCE PRENDERGAST

WILEY COMPUTER PUBLISHING

John Wiley & Sons, Inc.

New York • Chichester • Brisbane • Toronto • Singapore

Picture two kids who hear talk about a company, software, and SQL at the dinner table, in the car, in a kayak, sitting on the sofa on a Sunday morning. They did both leave home, but it was to go to college and study . . . computers. At least that's what they tell us . . . .

To Erin and Jonathan who keep us going.

M and J

For this shared toil, a special dedication to dearest Dianna.

B

Publisher: Katherine Schowalter
Editor: Theresa Hudson
Managing Editor: Angela Murphy
Text Design & Composition: North Market Street Graphics

Library of Congress Cataloging-in-Publication Data:
Panttaja, Jim and Mary.
     The Microsoft SQL Server survival guide /
   Jim Panttaja, Mary Panttaja, and Bruce Prendergast
        p.   cm.
Includes index.
ISBN 0471-12743-4

Printed in the United States of America
10 9 8 7 6 5 4 3 2 1

C O N T E N T S

Foreword   ix
Preface   xi

PART ONE   SQL SERVER VERSION 6

Chapter 1   SQL Server Overall Architecture

SQL Server Engine   2
  Physical Disk Storage   3
  Mapping of Logical to Physical Layout   3
  Maintaining Logical Object Design   4
  Managing Multiple Users   4
  Managing Network Connections   5
  Parsing of Transact-SQL   5
  Analysis of Queries: Optimization   5
  Transmitting Data to the Client   6
  Logging Changes   6
  Transaction Management   7
  Locking Pages and Tables   7
  The SQL Server—A Busy Guy   8
DB-Library   8
Net-Library   8
Open Database Connectivity (ODBC)   9
Open Data Services (ODS)   9
Enterprise Manager   10
SQL Executive   10
SQL Distributed Management Objects (SQL-DMO)   11

Chapter 2   New Features in Microsoft SQL Server Version 6

Transact-SQL Features   13
  ANSI Standard Features   13
  T-SQL Enhancements   16

Performance Enhancements   19
   Performance   19
   VLDB Issues   22
Enterprise Database Product   22
   Centralized Administration   22
   Replication   26
   Messaging   27

Chapter 3   Core Technology Issues

Locking   31
   Basic Locking Principles   32
   Locks on SQL Server   33
   Viewing Locks   39
   Keys to Planning   40
   A Conclusion   40
Query Processing   41
   Translating the Query   41
   Optimization Phases   42
   Query Optimizer Processing Strategies   47
   Optimizer Tools, Statistics, and the Distribution Page   53
   User Tools, Query Plan Maintenance   55
Communicating with SQL Server   59
   Using DB-Library with SQL Server   60
   ODBC   64
   Extending SQL Server with Open Data Services   67
Very Large Database Issues (VLDB)   71
   Scalability of Hardware   71
   Symmetric Server Architecture   72
   A Distributed Operating System   73
   RAID0, RAID1, and RAID5   74
   Parallel Processing   74
   Lock Management   75

PART TWO   PROCESS, ARCHITECTURE, AND IMPLEMENTATION

Chapter 4   Project Life Cycle

Disciplines, Skills, and Tasks   78
   Disciplines   78
   Skills and Tasks for Each Discipline   81
   Roles and Responsibilities   93
Timing   94
   Iterative and Parallel Development   96
   Project Management Sequencing   98

Management Issues   110
   Opportunities   110
   Responsibilities   112
Standards   113
   Architecture Standards   113
   Programming Standards   114
   User-Interface Standards   125

Chapter 5   Application Architecture

Tiered Architecture   128
   Two-Tiered Architecture   128
   Multitiered Architectures   129
   Open Servers   130
Client/Server Architectural Model   131
   Connection Management   132
   Error Handling   136
   Data Access   139
   Data Validation   143
   Transaction Management   145
   Concurrency Control   148
   Distributed Processing   150
   Security   151
Replication   153
   Distributed Data Overview   153
   Overview   154
   Models   156
   Planning   158
   Making It Work   163
   When It Doesn't Work   164
   Tuning Replication   168
Messaging   169
   MAPI 1.0   169
   Windows NT Mail   171
   SQL Mail   175
   Automated Backup Using Alerts, E-Mail, and Tasks 180

Chapter 6   Database Design

Overview   183
Identifying Needs   184
Creating the Logical Design   185
   Entities, Attributes, and Relationships—Step 1   186
   Business Functions and Rules—Step 2   190
   Performance Requirements—Step 3   192
Building the Application   193
   Creating Tables   194

Creating Indexes   206
Planning Capacity   214
Tuning the Application   216
Modifying Design: DSS versus OLTP   216
Denormalization   217
Tuning Indexes   226
Placing Objects   227

Chapter 7   Coding Techniques

Simple SQL Techniques   229
Simple SELECT   229
Correlated SELECT   229
Nested SELECT   230
INSERT . . . VALUES   230
INSERT . . . SELECT   230
Simple DELETE   231
Referencing Another Table with DELETE   231
Simple UPDATE   232
Referencing Another Table with UPDATE   232
Checking for Duplicates   233
CASE   233
GROUP BY   235
Cursors   240
Dynamic EXECUTE in a Stored Procedure   242
Dynamic EXECUTE with Cursor   242
Neat SQL Tricks   243
Difference Operations and Outer Joins   243
Cross Tabulations   244
Creating Serial Numbers in an Existing Table   247
Managing Serial Numbers   249
Code Generation Techniques   250
Generation Techniques—SQL to Create SQL   250
Generation Techniques—SQL to Create C   251
Handling a Hierarchy (Bill of Materials)   253
Stored Procedures   255
Stored Procedure Syntax   255
Output Parameters   256
Giving Help for Stored Procedures   256
Using Temporary Tables in Stored Procedures   256
Stored Procedure Transaction Error Handling   258
Triggers   259
Trigger Syntax   260
Trigger Guidelines   260
Verifying the Presence of Foreign Keys   261
Cascading Delete Trigger   262
Imposing a Business Rule on UPDATE   262
Changing the Primary Key Trigger   263

RAISERROR   264
   RAISERROR with the sysmessages Table   264

Chapter 8   **Technical Discourses**

Transaction Design Discussion   267
   A Logical Unit of Work   267
   Implementation Issues   268
   Transaction Solutions   270
Relational Thinking, Relational Processing   272
   Relational versus Procedural   273
   An Example   273
   Mentoring and Rules of Thumb   276

PART THREE   OPERATIONS

Chapter 9   Infrastructure

Network Models   279
   OSI Model   279
   IEEE Models   280
   Interface Models—NDIS and TDI   280
   Routing Models—MUP and MRP   282
Network Protocols   285
   Data Link Control (DLC)   285
   NetBEUI Frame (NBF)   286
   NWLink   291
   TCP/IP   297
   Choosing a Protocol   309
Interprocess Communication   309
   Server Message Blocks   310
   Named Pipes   310
   NetBIOS   311
   Remote Procedure Calls   311
   Windows Sockets   312
Network Support with RAS   312
   RAS as a SLIP Client   313
   RAS as a Software Router   313
   RAS as a NetBIOS Gateway   314
   RAS Security   315
   RAS and the Internet   316
File Systems   318
   FAT   319
   HPFS   320
   NTFS   320
   Security   321
   Fault Tolerance   324
   File System Issues   326

Managing Users 328
  Special Groups 328
  Local Groups 329
  Global Groups 331
  User Manager for Domains 331
Managing Windows NT 333
  Domains 333
  Server Manager 334
  System Management Server 336

Chapter 10   Operations

Installation 341
  Accounts 341
  Character Sets 342
  CHKUPG 343
  Environment 343
  Service Pack 343
  Sort Orders 345
  Replication 345
  When the Installation Fails 347
Server Management 348
  Devices 349
  Configuration 349
  Security 352
  Error Recovery Issues 363
  Problem Resolution 366
  Special Databases 368
  Starting the Server on System Boot 369
  SQL Server Limits 371
Database Management 371
  Tools for Loading Data 371
  Managing Users with Groups 374
  sp_dboption 376
  DBCC 379
Backup and Restore 396
  DUMP DATABASE Statement 396
  LOAD DATABASE Statement 397
  DUMP TRANSACTION Statement 397
  LOAD TRANSACTION Statement 398
  DUMP/LOAD Schemes 399
  Backing Up Using Operating System Commands 401
  Backing Up the Master Database 402
  Warm Standby 402
  Disk Mirroring 403
Appendix 404
Index 425

F O R E W O R D

SQL Server has become the most popular SQL database system, with 3,000 more today than yesterday. It is popular because it is extremely easy to install and use for client/server and Internet computing. SQL Server's tight integration with NT platforms and tools makes it a pleasure to use. In fact, SQL Server is so easy to use that it makes it really easy to make mistakes.

The Panttajas have been working with SQL Server since its beginnings on OS/2. They built a thriving consulting business helping small and large companies deploy new client/server applications as well as downsize from mainframes. They watched SQL Server move to NT and evolve into the centerpiece of Microsoft BackOffice.

This book records what they've learned. It summarizes their design guidelines, their favorite tips and tricks, and their project management advice. *The Microsoft SQL Server Survival Guide* is full of useful information gleaned from years of experience, watching hundreds of projects go through their growing pains.

Much of the book is dedicated to a SQL Server-centric view of project management, database and application design, system administration, and operations. These are the areas where most projects (using any tools) make their biggest mistakes. This book gives practical and concrete advice on each of these areas, which is useful for SQL Server projects, and is equally applicable to most other projects.

The Microsoft SQL Server Survival Guide assumes you have a rudimentary knowledge of SQL and NT—it is not a tutorial for novices. Rather, it is a survival guide for someone who has worked with other systems, or has worked with SQL Server, and now wants to get past the basics. The book contains many how-to sections that take you through design, programming, installation, and operations tasks. These sections often have performance guidelines that tell you about the good points and caution you about things that have unexpected behavior. Years of experience are hiding in this book. It contains nuggets that you would learn the hard way otherwise.

You will really like SQL Server as it continues to evolve. The newest version includes Internet support, distributed transactions, and data warehousing tools, and even easier administration and programming environments with C++ and Visual Basic. As always, the next release is even more exciting. But, SQL Server has a very rich functionality today. You will find this book a welcome companion to the product's reference manuals. Together, they should help you design exciting new applications.

JIM GRAY
Microsoft Research

P R E F A C E

Historical Perspective

Relational database management systems (RDBMS) were initially proposed over 25 years ago. The first commercial products didn't show up on the market until about 15 years ago, and sometime in the last decade these products finally won over the data management market. Today, the majority of database application development is done using RDBMS.

SQL Server was first introduced by Sybase in 1987. Sybase then teamed up with Microsoft to introduce SQL Server on OS/2. Over a number of years, Microsoft took on ever-greater responsibility for SQL Server development on its own platforms. In 1994, Sybase and Microsoft agreed to end the joint development of SQL Server. Although Microsoft had clearly put its own imprint on SQL Server release 4.21, it wasn't until the release of SQL Server Version 6 that it clearly outlined the direction that Microsoft will take to create enterprisewide database solutions.

SQL Server Version 6 offers significant enhancements in system administration tools, and these enhancements allow it to run large enterprise systems. SQL Server Version 6 is also an evolutionary product, building on the solid and successful existing features and behaviors of the SQL Server. Existing queries and applications will easily migrate to SQL Server Version 6. In many cases, they will experience improved performance with no software changes.

SQL Server was already a complicated product. These new features add to that complexity. In the past, a developer needed access to a great collection of experience and folklore in order to be successful with SQL Server. The goal of this book is to provide the lessons that we have learned from implementations of SQL Server to help you avoid some of the common (and not so common) mistakes that affect most projects.

Target Audience

This book is not intended as a replacement for the existing manuals. When you start with SQL Server Version 6, you will certainly need access to other materials for details of the syntax and semantics of the Transact-SQL language and specifics about the use of tools.

This book has grown out of several needs:

1. *The SQL language, SQL products in general, and SQL Server in particular often present a number of alternate ways to get a job done.* With experience, you learn which ways work and which don't; you learn which are efficient and which aren't; and you learn which are extensible, and which aren't. For existing features, or new twists on old features, we present concepts and usage developed from our experience.

2. *Key technical problems and how to solve them.* When application designers architect an application solution, there are a number of issues that must be addressed. These include locking, transaction management, and concurrency control. Understanding the syntax is not enough. The designer has to understand the implications of each alternative.

3. *Key new features and how to utilize them.* When will it make sense to use these features, and how should an application designer take advantage of them? This is especially important when dealing with replication.

Working with relational database management systems often requires a different way of thinking about problems. This book presents those different ways of thinking.

How to Use This Book

The book can be used in a number of different ways:

♦ A developer new to SQL can benefit from reading the book cover to cover.

♦ A database developer wanting to learn more about a specific topic can pick the appropriate chapter and dive in.

♦ An experienced programmer looking for a specific technique (perhaps how to write a trigger that propagates changes made to primary keys) can use the index and find the appropriate section.

Topics are treated so they can stand alone as much as possible.

Organization

The book is made up of three parts:

1. *SQL Server Version 6:* Introduces the overall architecture, features of SQL Server Version 6, and core technical issues associated with SQL Server.

2. *Process, Architecture, and Implementation:* Presents the details of developing and deploying applications based on SQL Server: project lifecycles, architecture, database design, and coding.

3. *Operations:* Presents the Microsoft infrastructure and operation of a SQL Server system.

Chapter Number	*Purpose*
PART 1: SQL Server Version 6	
Chapter 1 Overall Architecture	Offers a discussion about the basic client/server architecture of the SQL Server and the core functionality internal to the server.

Chapter 2
New Features of
  Microsoft SQL Server
  Version 6
	Reviews the new technical features of the SQL Server.

Chapter 3 Core Technology Issues	Reviews core technical issues inherent in application development with SQL Server. These issues determine how you should design and develop systems: locking, query optimization, communicating with SQL Server, and very large database issues.
PART 2: Process, Architecture, and Implementation	
Chapter 4 Project Lifecycle	Explains the disciplines, skills, and tasks that make up the project life cycle when developing client/server applications with SQL Server. What are the different sets of knowledge (disciplines) needed to develop an application? What are the specific skills? What are the different tasks? When should they be done?

Chapter Number	Purpose
Chapter 5 Application Architecture	Discusses application architecture for client/server. In particular it focuses on what we believe are the key architectural issues in designing a client/server application. Topics discussed include tiered architecture, the key architectural issues, replication, and messaging.
Chapter 6 Database Design and Implementation	Discusses logical and physical database design as it applies to SQL Server. It then describes the impact of decisions made during logical and physical database design on system performance.
Chapter 7 Coding and Code Management Techniques	Presents specific techniques for writing code using the various features of SQL Server. Sample code is included throughout this chapter. Topics covered include triggers, stored procedures, neat SQL tricks, use of surrogates, cursors, use of temporary tables, and use of GROUP BY.
Chapter 8 Technical Discourses	Presents two key aspects of relational database development that are usually misunderstood: transaction management and relational vs. procedural processing.
PART 3: Operations	
Chapter 9 Infrastructure	Describes the interaction between a SQL Server and the other aspects of a network and operating system. Specifically addressed are network issues, operating system interaction, file systems, and administrative tools.
Chapter 10 Operations	Discusses a number of important operational topics, including installing SQL Server, administering the server, administering a database, use of the log threshold manager, and other operational details.

About the Authors

As you read through the Microsoft SQL Server Survival Guide, you'll probably notice that the three authors have different concerns and styles. Mary Panttaja comes from a management and application background and likes to start with methodology. Her special interests are project planning, application architecture, solution design, and technical appropriateness.

Jim Panttaja is more of a systems person. With 20 years of experience in the computer field, he concentrates on large database systems, primarily in the areas of performance evaluation, tuning, and training. He's also interested in the practical aspects of coding, and the source of many of the neat tricks you'll find in the book.

Mary and Jim Panttaja are the founders of Panttaja Consulting Group, Inc. PCGI is a client/server consulting company specializing in consulting, training, and outsourcing for client/server development projects. They have been specializing in client/server development since 1988.

Bruce Prendergast is a large-scale systems architect whose computer career started in the 50s and who believes that the computer industry really started in November 1992 with the announcement of the Digital Alpha. He is an independent consultant who enjoys teaching advanced programming at the University of California, Irvine.

Throughout the book, our goal is to record the folklore and our experiences so that your experience with SQL Server will be vastly improved. Think of this book as a consultant in your pocket without the expense. Good luck with SQL Server Version 6.

Acknowledgments

Terri Hudson, our editor at John Wiley & Sons.

Judy Bowman, our co-author on another project who contributed to the chapter on Database Design.

Tom Bondur of *SQL Forum Journal*. Tom used to "book" Mary and Jim when he coordinated client-site training at Sybase, and more recently has published our articles in SQL Forum Journal.

Karl Fischer, former editor of *SQL Forum Journal*.

Valerie Anderson, Jim and Mary's first contact at Sybase, and now a member of the Panttaja Consulting Group, Inc. board of directors.

Stacey Burch, Jim and Mary's first contact at Microsoft when they began teaching classes.

Gary Voth, Group Product Manager at Microsoft for Database and Development Tools.

Jim at Samba Java for letting us linger over our dessert and cappuccino with a stack of pages and a red pen.

Jonathan Vaughan of Chase Manhattan Bank. Jonathan encouraged us to put together a set of guidelines for using SQL Server. That's where the book started many years ago.

Bruce—thanks for helping us pull this together.

The entire staff of Panttaja Consulting Group, Inc. They all had to put up with this project. Especially our VP and General Manager, George Loyer, who bore the brunt of putting up with this project, and Russell Barber and Patrick Wright, who reviewed many of our articles before they went off to the publications.

M and J

A very special thanks to my editor Terri for suffering through the problems of a new writer. To Jim and Mary, a heartfelt thanks for not giving up on me.

B

Chapter 1 is based on previously published material found in *Relational Database Journal*, article entitled "Roles of the SQL Server," January/February 1994. Used with permission.

Chapter 2 is based on previously published material found in *SQL Forum Journal*, article entitled "Top Ten Mistakes Using SQL Server—Log Management Mistakes," Volume 2, Number 6, November/February 1994, and article entitled "Top Ten Mistakes Using SQL Server—Transaction Design Mistakes," Volume 3, Number 2, March/April 1994. Used with permission. *Sybase Magazine*, article entitled "Locking Behaviors and Why They're Important," Summer 1994, Sybase, Inc. Used with permission. *Relational Database Journal*, article entitled "RDJ Advisor—The SQL Server Response," August/October 1993 and November-January 1994. Used with permission.

Chapter 8 is based on previously published material found in *SQL Forum Journal*, article entitled "Defining and Using Useful Indexes," Volume 1, Number 5, September/October 1991, article entitled "Top Ten Mistakes Using SQL Server," Volume 2, Number 2, May/June 1993, and article entitled "Top Ten Mistakes Using SQL Server—Mistakes Three and Four," Volume 2, Number 4, July/August 1993. Used with permission.

Chapter 9 is based on previously published material found in *Sybase Server Magazine*, article entitled "Hot SQL Techniques," Fall 1994, Sybase International User Group Inc. Used with permission.

SQL Server Overall Architecture

The term *SQL Server* is sometimes used to refer to a family of products. Technically, SQL Server refers to the server itself, or the relational database engine. Other SQL Server-related capabilities are described later in this chapter. The following components make up the family of products known as the SQL Server and are illustrated in Figure 1.1.

- *SQL Server Engine* is the RDBMS controlling all database activities.
- *DB-Library* is a programming interface callable from C or Visual Basic.
- *Net-Library* is a lower-level interface that is accessed by DB-Library. This allows programs written using the DB-Library interface to ignore network specific issues.
- *Open Database Connectivity (ODBC)* is another programming interface, callable from C. Many database products allow access via ODBC. This grants a single application program access to different data sources via a single interface.
- *Open Data Services* is an application programming interface that allows the developer to extend the capabilities of SQL Server by creating extended stored procedures and by creating server-based applications.

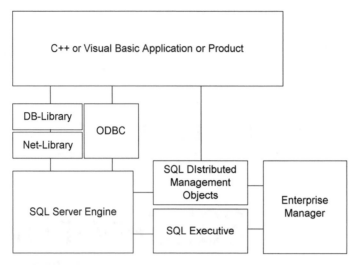

FIGURE 1.1 Components of SQL Server.

- ♦ *Enterprise Manager* is a graphical tool that facilitates the administration of one or more SQL Servers on a network.
- ♦ *SQL Executive* is a Windows NT service that manages replication and allows the scheduling of time-dependent administrative functions.
- ♦ *SQL Server Distributed Management Objects* is an object-based application programming interface that supports the development of administrative applications in C++ or Visual Basic.

SQL Server Engine

The *SQL Server Engine* is the **RDBMS** controlling all database activities. It runs on the server machine, processes all requests from client applications, and ensures the recoverability of the data.

Microsoft SQL Server 6 differs significantly from Sybase's SQL Server and from other relational database management systems. In particular, Microsoft's SQL Server was designed to exploit the core services of Windows NT. SQL Server takes advantage of Windows NT services in its implementation of security, system administration, thread management, scheduling of threads, memory management, and I/O.

The SQL Server can be viewed as a single process that executes on the server machine. Because of the Windows NT design, multiple NT threads are used. This is somewhat different from other relational database management systems where multiple processes and services may be required. The server does take advantage of the native thread-level multiprocessing available in Windows NT. The SQL Server has the following responsibilities:

- ◆ Physical disk storage
- ◆ Mapping of logical design to physical layout
- ◆ Maintaining logical object design
- ◆ Managing multiple users
- ◆ Managing network connections
- ◆ Parsing of Transact-SQL
- ◆ Analysis of queries: optimization
- ◆ Transmitting data to the client
- ◆ Logging changes
- ◆ Transaction management
- ◆ Locking pages and tables

Many of these roles will be found in other RDBMS, although the specific implementations will be different. In the following sections, we describe some of these responsibilities of the SQL Server.

Physical Disk Storage

Disk space is allocated to the SQL Server by the SQL Server *system administrator* (A SQL Server login called *sa*). This disk space is allocated as SQL Server *devices*. These devices correspond to Windows NT files. When SQL Server is installed, three SQL Server devices are created: *master, MSDBdata,* and *MSDBlog*. The system administrator can also allocate additional devices at a later time. Databases are allocated to these devices by the system administrator, and the SQL Server stores system tables, user data, and indexes in these databases.

The devices that are allocated are completely controlled by the SQL Server. The only reason you may want to access the files directly would be as an alternative to SQL Server backup capabilities. *SQL Server provides online backup and recovery capabilities. In some instances, it may be more convenient to stop the server and use operating system utilities to back up the devices that comprise the Server.* After the system administrator has specified which devices a given database should be placed on, there is seldom any reason to pay attention to the physical storage except to note how much space is available.

SQL Server provides the ability to mirror a device. With *device mirroring,* any data which SQL Server writes to disk will be written to both devices. If there is ever a failure on either the primary device or its mirror, the SQL Server will notice, stop using the failed device, notify the system administrator, and continue processing. All of this without any required intervention from a system administrator.

Mapping of Logical to Physical Layout

The SQL Server provides the mapping from logical objects in the database to physical disk locations. As designers and developers using a relational database management system, we view all data as residing in tables with index structures for those tables. But the SQL Server is storing all of the data on data pages on disk. The SQL Server provides this mapping automatically.

SQL Server stores all data on disk in 2K pages. These pages are written to the devices allocated for a database. When a row is inserted, updated, or deleted, the SQL Server determines which page or pages are impacted and makes the appropriate changes. Although it is possible to determine which pages a given object is on—and which object is on a given page—this is rarely necessary.

The server also handles the maintenance of all indexes. As rows are inserted, updated, or deleted, entries are added to or deleted from the index structures. All page splitting and freeing of data and index pages are handled automatically. When a page is almost empty, the last row is moved to an adjacent page if possible, and the page is freed. The mapping of our logical layout to the physical data storage (pages) is handled entirely by the SQL Server.

Maintaining Logical Object Design

When we define the objects in the database, the SQL Server keeps track of the object definition in system tables. The SQL Server knows what is in the database and how the objects relate to each other.

Every database contains a set of tables that record the description of all of the objects in the database, the *system catalog*. The catalog records all of the columns of a table, including their datatype and size; permissions associated with each object; the text used to define views, stored procedures, rules, defaults and triggers; and descriptions of all of the indexes.

The SQL Server documentation describes these system tables and their interactions. In addition, the SQL Server includes system-stored procedures that retrieve the definition of a given object from the system catalog.

Managing Multiple Users

A SQL Server is a single process managing multiple clients in the computer operating system. Some other relational database management systems generate server processes for each user/client. Internal to the SQL Server process is a control structure for each connection that a user application is holding. SQL Server makes efficient use of Windows NT threads for controlling the execution of multiple threads. This allows parallel processing of queries.

The SQL Server uses control structures to manage the requests of each connection and to schedule the work required by that connection. This mechanism allows for a very fast context switch from one connection to the next and for the efficient execution of the server. The SQL Server maintains locks on pages or tables to keep transactions from interfering with each other. We will discuss this in greater detail in Chapter 3.

The additional resources required to support more users are typically quite small. Approximately 50 to 60K is required for each additional user—plus any additional cache required.

Commonly referenced data pages are maintained in *cache* (memory) saving subsequent reads. This also enables the server to combine several logical writes into one physical write. The SQL Server writes log pages to disk whenever a transaction is committed. The data pages may not be written to disk until much later. The writing of log pages at commit guarantees recoverability. Data pages are only written when there is a checkpoint operation or when the page is aged out of cache.

Managing Network Connections

Each connection from a client application is managed within the SQL Server. For each connection, the server knows its current context and the location of the client. Data rows and messages are sent to the appropriate client application based on the client's requests. SQL Server can even operate in mixed network environments where different clients are using different network protocols. For more information on network protocols, see Chapter 9.

Parsing of Transact-SQL

In some ways this is the most obvious requirement of a RDBMS: to parse the SQL language and translate it into executable code.

When a client program sends a batch to the SQL Server, the server checks the syntax of the batch, then checks to see whether all referenced objects exist. If either the syntax is invalid or a referenced object does not exist, the batch is not executed. If the SQL text passes these two tests, it is translated into an intermediate form and the next task of the SQL Server is to optimize the query.

Analysis of Queries: Optimization

Extracting data from a relational database is a very complicated process. A wrong decision about the sequence of obtaining the data can be disastrous (slow). It is the job of the optimizer to analyze the query and decide how to do it.

The SQL Server optimizer considers the query structure, the structure of the tables, the indexes that exist on the tables, and statistics (showing the distribution of data) in order to determine the best query plan. All of these items are critical to determining the best query plan.

The SQL Server converts the query into an internal tree structure. This allows a number of apparently different, but in fact comparable queries to be optimized in the same way. Differences in order of tables in a FROM clause, or differences of comparisons in the WHERE clause will not impact the query optimizer.

The SQL Server then uses cost-based algorithms to consider various combinations of indexes and orders of accessing tables to determine the query plan that requires the least number of physical and logical I/Os. The use of index statistics allows the SQL Server to make accurate predictions of the number of I/Os for various candidate query plans. In addition, there are a number of special cases of SQL syntax that the SQL Server detects. The server generates a query plan and makes an executable version of the query implementing that plan.

Transmitting Data to the Client

The SQL Server executes the query plan and extracts the data from the database. It uses *tempdb*, if necessary, for work space (sorting, grouping, and temporary tables). The server then packages the data and sends it across the network as soon as data is ready. The server and the client keep track of where they are in the transmission of data to the client.

Logging Changes

The SQL Server logs all data modifications that are made in the database. The log is in a table called *syslogs*. The log is for the SQL Server's use. You cannot read it. All INSERTs, UPDATEs and DELETEs are logged. In addition, transaction activity (BEGIN TRANSACTION, COMMIT TRANSACTION, ROLLBACK TRANSACTION) and space allocation are also logged. The log is a physical log, recording the actual data changes made. It is not a logical log. It cannot be used to provide an audit trail of changes made for application purposes. If you need that type of audit trail or journal, the application must provide the log with triggers, stored procedures, or application logic.

The log is used for three purposes:

1. Transaction rollback.
2. Recovery any time the server is restarted—to ensure that committed transactions are present on the server, and uncommitted transactions are not present.
3. Incremental recovery using transaction log dumps.

The transaction log contains the data image in *before* and *after* states. In an INSERT entry in the log, the new row is recorded in the log. In a DELETE entry in the log, the old row is recorded in the log. In an UPDATE entry, either the whole old and new rows or just the data changed is saved in the log (depending on the specific UPDATE that is done). For more information on the use of the transaction log, see Chapter 3.

Transaction Rollback

If a transaction should fail or be rolled back by the application, the server uses the log to recover the data to the original state.

Recovery

If the server processing is interrupted, the log is used to ensure that modifications that were committed are written to the database, and that modifications that were not committed are not in the database. This is possible because the transaction log contains the before and after versions of all rows modified by the transaction.

Incremental Recovery

If an administrator performs *transaction dumps* (incremental backups of the log), they can be used to do an incremental recovery of the database following media failure. A full database dump may take a long time. It may not be practical to do a dump database as often as you would like to minimize the possibility of lost transactions. A transaction dump only dumps the transaction log. This can then be used in conjunction with a previous full database dump.

Transaction Management

An application submits data modification statements (INSERT, UPDATE, and DELETE) to the SQL Server. The application either includes transaction management statements (BEGIN TRANSACTION, COMMIT TRANSACTION, and ROLLBACK TRANSACTION) or else it expects that each individual data modification statement will be a transaction by itself. If any statement in a transaction fails, or if the transaction does not get to the COMMIT TRANSACTION statement, then the SQL Server rolls back the entire transaction.

From the perspective of the application, the transaction is *atomic;* that is, either the entire transaction is completed or no part of the transaction is completed. The SQL Server implements this transaction behavior.

Locking Pages and Tables

The SQL Server allows many users to simultaneously access the same database. It is critical to isolate transactions being done by various users to ensure that one user does not read another user's uncommitted transactions. The SQL Server locks either pages or entire tables, depending on the query plan for the transactions. *Exclusive locks* are held until the end of the transaction. *Read locks* are usually held only long enough to read the page, and are then released.

It is possible to control the holding of read locks to have them held until the end of the transaction as well, so that all of the rows read are consistent from one point in time. For more information on locking, see Chapter 3.

The SQL Server—A Busy Guy

The SQL Server acts like an operating system within an operating system, plus database-specific functionality. It serves in all of these roles to provide an efficient, dependable execution environment as the hub of a client/server system.

In addition to the SQL Server Engine and all of its responsibilities, there are other components of the SQL Server product. They are covered in the remaining sections of this chapter.

DB-Library

The DB-Library is a set of functions callable from third-generation programming languages (3GLs) that provide access to the SQL Server functionality. Visual Basic and C are examples of the more popular 3GLs. DB-Library provides functions for submitting queries to the SQL Server and processing the results.

Most client applications use the DB-Library to communicate with the server. The DB-Library functions communicate with the server using a protocol called *Tabular Data Stream* (TDS). This protocol allows queries to be sent to the SQL Server. When the results of queries are returned, the TDS includes descriptive information as well as the data. Using DB-Library calls you can determine the shape of the results, including column names and datatypes. This protocol is the core of client/server communication.

Net-Library

Net-Library is an interface component of the server, as well as a set of *Dynamic Link Libraries* (DLLs) available for use on client machines. The Net-Library is a set of libraries provided by Microsoft. They are required by a client application to connect to the network when using DOS, Windows, or Windows NT. When running a DOS, Windows, or Windows NT application that accesses the SQL Server, the user's PC must have the appropriate network Net-Library available. Similar to the server-side Net-Library, the Net-Library on the client side isolates the client application from all network interprogram communication (IPC) or network protocol concerns.

If the application is a DOS application that is not Windows based, then the machine must have the appropriate terminate and stay resident (TSR) Net-Library. If the application is Windows, or Windows NT based, then the appropriate DLL must be present.

On the server, the Net-Library is a network interface to communicate using a given network IPC interface. All of the network-specific considerations are isolated in this layer. SQL Server includes support for named pipes, TCP/IP sockets, SPX, and Banyan Vines. Some of these IPC mechanisms can be used with multiple network protocols. Named pipes, in particular, can be used with NETBEUI, NWLINK, SPX/IPX, and TCP/IP. SQL Server can utilize these different IPC mechanisms simultaneously, allowing client applications using different network protocols to all communicate with the same SQL Server. For more details, see Chapter 9.

Open Database Connectivity (ODBC)

SQL Server provides a second set of functions called Open Database Connectivity (ODBC)—see Open Database Connectivity in Chapter 3—which support accessing the SQL Server using C, Visual Basic, or Access. Microsoft proposes that ODBC is a standard database interface. A number of different database engines already support this interface, and ODBC interfaces are provided by third parties for other database engines. Using ODBC, a developer can write a program that works against several different database management systems (DBMS). In addition, developers of third-party development tools can provide support in their products for ODBC. When this happens, a developer can develop an application using a development tool (like Microsoft's ACCESS), and have it work against several DBMS. Like DB-Library, Microsoft's implementation of ODBC uses TDS to communicate with SQL Server.

Open Data Services (ODS)

Open Data Services (ODS) is the interface in the SQL Server between the server itself and the net-libraries. In addition, ODS is a set of function calls contained in a DLL that can be used by an application developer to implement an open server—an application that appears on the network to be a server—and can interact with client applications developed using either DB-Library or ODBC. ODS can also be used to extend the capabilities of a SQL Server by creating extended stored procedures.

For an open server developer, the ODS is a set of C functions allowing developers to create an application that appears to a client application as a server. The client application can interact with the open server using DB-

Library calls or ODBC. ODS provides the SQL Server with thread creation and pooling capabilities. Because of this, open server applications can take advantage of these same capabilities, allowing developers to create open server applications that can take advantage of symmetric multiprocessor systems and that support multiple network protocols.

Among other uses, developers can create open servers that provide gateways to DBMS and access to other system services (e.g., sending mail). It is often complicated to write open servers that serve as gateways to other DBMS, and they typically must be purchased from third-party vendors. Open servers that interface using stored procedure interfaces (such as the mail server) are fairly easy to write. If a developer creates an open server providing access to a mail system, stored procedures on the SQL Server can then send a stored procedure request to that open server whenever an important event occurs (e.g., when inventory is low). Note that SQL Server includes a built-in interface to Messaging Application Programming Interface (MAPI), so it is not necessary to use ODS to provide access to MS Mail. See the Messaging section of Chapter 2 and Chapter 5 for more information.

By creating extended stored procedures in ODS, a developer can augment a SQL Server with additional functionality. This functionality is executed as if it were a SQL Server stored procedure, but it is really a function in a DLL.

Enterprise Manager

The SQL Server Enterprise Manager is a graphical tool that facilitates administration of one or more SQL Servers on a network. You can use SQL Server Enterprise Manager to administer databases, objects, logins, permissions, and all of the contents of a SQL Server. In addition, the Enterprise Manager allows you to schedule activities, establish alerts, transfer objects across networks, and manage replication. For additional information about operations activities, see Chapter 10. For additional information about replication, see Chapter 5.

SQL Executive

SQL Executive provides sophisticated scheduling capabilities. It is an essential part of the replication capability provided in SQL Server. SQL Executive allows you to schedule various administrative tasks, such as backups and DBCC. It is a separate Windows NT service that is accessible from the SQL Enterprise Manager.

SQL Distributed Management Objects (SQL-DMO)

Distributed Management Objects (SQL-DMO) are objects that provide a programming interface to SQL Server management functions. You can access them on Windows 95 or Windows NT. The objects can be accessed via programs written in Visual Basic or C++. SQL-DMO allows you to develop sophisticated administrative applications. The Enterprise Manager takes advantage of SQL-DMO to obtain its information.

2

New Features in Microsoft SQL Server Version 6

Microsoft SQL Server 6 includes many important new features. The enhancements can be grouped into three key areas:

1. *Transact-SQL language.* These include features specified in the ANSI standard. They also include significant enhancements to existing features.
2. *Performance enhancements.* Some of the enhancements will improve the performance of existing applications without any changes to the application code. Others allow improvement when the application programmer includes hints for the optimizer in the Transact-SQL code. Improved support for multiprocessor environments has been included, as well as improved support for very large database (VLDB) environments.
3. *System administration.* One of the biggest deficiencies in relational database products has been in the area of tools that allow convenient management of a network containing multiple servers. Microsoft has included a number of tools and services that allow a company to develop and manage an enterprisewide distributed database. This enterprisewide database can consist of many SQL Servers, with some

data replicated from one server to several others. The database can be managed from one machine running the Enterprise Manager. These enhancements have allowed SQL Server to become a true enterprise-database product.

Transact-SQL Features

Microsoft SQL Server Version 6 adds a number of enhancements to the Transact-SQL language. New features have been added which are already part of the ANSI standard. Of notable importance is the introduction of the CASE statement which can be used anywhere an expression is to be used. This feature is ANSI SQL-92 compliant and helps to move Microsoft SQL Server closer to ANSI SQL standards.

Some of these new ANSI standard features are already found in other relational database products such as numeric datatypes and a subset of the ANSI standard integrity enhancement feature. Other features such as CASE expressions have not been extensively implemented elsewhere.

Enhancements to the already useful Transact-SQL extensions pioneered by Microsoft and Sybase include extensions to stored procedures, text and image datatypes, and new global temporary tables.

ANSI Standard Features

New Datatypes

A number of new datatypes have been added in order to provide support for the ANSI standard. The new datatypes include two exact numeric datatypes, and new syntax for float, character, and variable length character data types.

Decimal and *numeric datatypes* have been added and support storage of exact numeric values. This feature provides support for exact calculation of decimal numbers, with precision of up to 38 digits (28 digits by default). Decimal can be abbreviated as *dec*.

An option is now allowed for the *float datatype*. This allows you to specify how many digits of precision you would like to have maintained. The number is placed after the datatype name in parenthesis. An example would look like:

```
CREATE TABLE testing (a float(8))
```

This example specifies that the column should have at least eight digits of precision. In SQL Server, a precision of seven or less will be stored in four bytes, and is equivalent to a column of datatype *real*. A precision of 8 to 15 digits will be stored in eight bytes and is equivalent to a column of type *float*. Also added in this release is the datatype *double precision*. This is equivalent to the standard float in SQL Server.

New syntax has also been added. The syntax does not add any new datatypes. Datatype synonyms for ANSI compatibility offer alternate and standard spellings of the datatypes as shown in Table 2.1.

In addition, datatype names are now case insensitive, regardless of the sort order defined for the server.

Identity

A new attribute has been added for columns of type *integer* (tinyint, smallint, or int), *numeric* (with scale of 0), or *decimal* (with scale of 0). This attribute will maintain a unique value for the specified column. Whenever a new row is inserted with INSERT, SELECT INTO or bcp, a new unique value is automatically generated for this column. There are options available to override the system-generated value. This is a significant improvement over previous releases, where an application was required to generate unique numbers if a surrogate key was desired.

CASE Expression

Within any expression in Transact-SQL, you can now include a *case expression*. This expression is conditionally evaluated to yield a value. Many queries that required either a very complicated expression or multiple queries in past releases can now be easily, clearly, and efficiently implemented using case expressions.

```
SELECT Name = name,
       "Object Type" =
    CASE type
            WHEN 'U' THEN 'User Table'
            WHEN 'S' THEN 'System Table'
            WHEN 'TR' THEN 'Trigger'
    END
FROM sysobjects
```

However, the full import of the CASE statement is really not understood until a code fragment from the Transact-SQL reference manual[1] is examined where the use of the CASE expression reduces the number of passes made on the database.

TABLE 2.1 New Syntax and ANSI Equivalent

New Syntax	Equivalent
character	char
character varying	varchar
char varying	varchar
binary varying	varbinary
integer	int

```
UPDATE employee_salaries
     SET salary =
           CASE
                 WHEN (review = 4 AND
                        (DATEDIFF(month, hire_date, GETDATE()) > 18))
                        THEN salary * 2
                 WHEN (review = 3 AND
                        (DATEDIFF(month, hire_date, GETDATE()) > 18))
                        THEN salary * 1.6
                 WHEN (review = 2 AND
                        (DATEDIFF(month, hire_date, GETDATE()) > 18))
                        THEN salary * 1.2
                 ELSE salary
           END
```

Performing the same update without the use of the CASE expression would require three UPDATE statements with WHERE clauses and hence three independent passes over the table. See chapter 7 for more examples using CASE expressions.

Cursor Support

Previous versions of Microsoft SQL Server have included cursor support—but only client-side cursors. Although client-side cursors are a useful feature, the addition of standard server-side cursor support in Version 6 is significant.

It is important to use set-level operations to work on your data whenever possible. Sometimes that is not practical. In such cases cursors allow you to step through your data a row at a time in order to process it. Although you will most often work through the rows one at a time—moving forward through the result set—SQL Server also supports FETCH PREVIOUS operations with the ability to fetch any given row in the result set.

When you fetch a row, you will usually fetch the column values into variables in Transact-SQL. You can use those variables in other queries, and you can UPDATE or DELETE the current row within the cursor. Chapter 7 includes examples using cursors.

Integrity Enhancement Feature

SQL Server pioneered support for a programmable server. This support includes *triggers,* which were often used to ensure referential integrity across primary and foreign keys. With Version 6, there is now another way to enforce referential integrity as well as other constraints that were previously implemented with triggers.

When you declare a table, you can declare constraints as well. You can also add constraints after the table has been created. These constraints may be restrictions on individual columns, they may constrain values among multiple columns in a row, or they may limit the values in one table based on values in another table.

There are four types of table constraints that can be enforced and six types of constraints that may be enforced at the column level, as shown in Table 2.2.

How to best use constraints is described in Table 2.3.

Referential constraints are created with the *foreign key constraint*. In this version of SQL Server, only one style of foreign key constraint is supported (denial). Other forms still must be implemented using triggers. *Intrarow constraints* allow you to limit the values in one column with respect to other columns in the table; for example, you can specify that the termination date must be greater than the start date.

Domain constraints limit the values that may appear in a given column. This could previously be implemented with rules. *Entity constraints* ensure that only one row appears in a table for a given individual. A database designer enforced this prior to Version 6 by creating a unique index. You can now identify a *primary key constraint* or a *unique constraint* which will automatically build a unique index. *Don't confuse this with the stored procedure sp_primary key, which only provided documentation of which columns comprised the primary key.*

T-SQL Enhancements

In addition to the ANSI standard features added to Transact-SQL in Version 6, Microsoft has included other enhancements. SQL Server has always supported features that allow database and application designers to create a significant part of their applications on the server. New extensions to stored procedures extend this capability.

Local and Global Temporary Tables and Stored Procedures

An application can create local and global temporary stored procedures and global temporary tables in addition to the local temporary tables that have been supported in the past.

TABLE 2.2 Table and Column Constraints

Constraints	Table Level	Column Level
Primary key	Yes	Yes
Unique key	Yes	Yes
Check	Yes	Yes
Foreign key	Yes	Yes
Null	No	Yes
Default	No	Yes

TABLE 2.3 Demonstrates How to Best Use Constraints

Integrity Type	Constraint	Other Implementations
Entity	PRIMARY KEY, NULL, UNIQUE	UNIQUE indexes Identity datatypes
Referential	REFERENCES, FOREIGN KEY	Triggers Stored procedures
Domain	NULL, DEFAULT, CHECK	Datatypes Rules Defaults User-defined datatypes Triggers Stored procedures
User Defined	REFERENCES, FOREIGN KEY, CHECK	Rules Triggers Stored procedures

A local temporary stored procedure, once created, can only be accessed by the connection (session) that created it. This allows an application to dynamically create a procedure needed for some specific task. This procedure is not visible to any other connection, and it will be dropped when the connection is closed. To make a stored procedure temporary, use the # character as the first character in its name.

A temporary table or a temporary stored procedure can be made global by beginning its name with two # characters. A table or stored procedure created in this way is visible to all other connections. It is dropped when the creating connection is terminated. If some other process is using it and if the creating connection is terminated, the object is not dropped until that other process finishes its current access (that is, if another process is selecting from it—as soon as the select statement is finished).

Global procedures and temporary tables are powerful in applications that need multiple connections, where communication among those connections is useful.

Text and Image Datatypes as Parameters

Text and image parameters can be declared for stored procedures, making procedures useful for dealing with these datatypes.

RAISERROR

Version 6 extends the capabilities of the *RAISERROR* statement. Error messages can now be saved in a table (sysmessages). In addition, they can include formatting of arguments specified on the RAISERROR statement. This allows an application to store a set of messages in the database. In previous versions the message string had to be specified on the RAISERROR statement, and therefore often appeared in application code. Allowing the string to be stored in database tables means that you can manage the text in the error message without having to touch application code.

Messages generated with **RAISERROR WITH LOG** will create an event for the Event Manager subsystem of the SQL Executive. This event can be used to invoke a task or send a message by e-mail or a pager to an operator. The WITH LOG parameter is required for severity codes 19 through 25, and can only be issued by the *sa*. These codes are fatal errors and the client connection will be terminated after receiving the message. Severity codes 0 through 18 may be used by any user and do not require the WITH LOG parameter.

Execute Enhancements

The *EXECUTE* statement can be used to execute a SQL statement that is dynamically created at execution time. This execute-immediate capability allows you to create a string based on the results of other queries and then execute the resulting string. Among other things, this allows you to dynamically decide which table to query from based on the results of some other query, or to pass a stored procedure a parameter that is an object name in the database so that it can dynamically take some action against that table. To perform UPDATE STATISTICS on all user tables, the following procedure could be used. This procedure not only illustrates the use of a CURSOR but also the use of the EXECUTE statement.

```
DECLARE my_cursor CURSOR FOR
     SELECT name FROM sysobjects WHERE type = 'U'
     FOR READ ONLY
OPEN my_cursor
DECLARE @my_table VARCHAR(30)
FETCH NEXT FROM my_cursor INTO @my_table
WHILE (@@fetch_status <> -1)
BEGIN
     EXEC('UPDATE STATISTICS ' + @my_table)
     FETCH NEXT FROM my_cursor INTO @my_table
END
CLOSE my_cursor
DEALLOCATE my_cursor
```

Encryption of Stored Procedure Text

In previous versions of SQL Server, the stored procedure text was saved in the syscomments table. It was possible for someone to query this table and see the text of the stored procedure. This may have been inappropriate for security reasons or because the code was proprietary. One alternative was to delete the text. Removing the text caused problems later if you wanted to recreate the procedure or if you wanted to move the database to another server.

Version 6 allows you to specify that you want the stored procedure text encrypted in the syscomments table. You cannot retrieve the text after it has been encrypted, but it can be used by SQL Server when a server is upgraded and needs to recreate the stored procedure.

Statement Enhancements

The UPDATE statement has been enhanced to allow the setting of variable names in the SET clause. This allows you to select the new value for a column into a variable at the same time you are updating the column in the table.

The INSERT and UPDATE statements can be used to set a column to the column's default value.

Performance Enhancements

Performance

A number of enhancements have been made to the SQL Server that will improve performance. Some of these enhancements will take effect without any action on the developers' part (such as improvements in the optimizer and parallel scan capabilities). Other enhancements are provided as new syntax, or hints that you can specify to the server.

Parallelization

Beginning with Version 6, SQL Server is able to take advantage of multiprocessor hardware to provide responses to a single query more efficiently. Version 6 scans tables and indexes in parallel. The sp_configure Advanced Options can be used to set RA (read ahead options) which are set *on* by default. The SQL Server anticipates which pages will be needed and prefetches them in some cases (asynchronous read ahead). This will improve the performance of individual SELECT, CREATE INDEX, DBCC, DUMP, and LOAD statements. In addition, searched UPDATE and DELETE statements may be improved.

Backup can now be accomplished using up to 32 tape or disk devices. These devices are written to simultaneously.

Multiple load operations using either BCP or SQL Enterprise Manager can be executed simultaneously, improving loading time for a large load.

Optimizer Improvements

The following optimizer enhancements may improve the performance of an existing application without any modification to the application required:

1. *Subqueries:*   Optimization has been greatly enhanced on this release. This may be a significant improvement for some applications that have used subqueries extensively.
2. *Query optimizer:*
   - May traverse an index in reverse order.
   - May use an index to satisfy an **ORDER BY DESCENDING** clause.
   - Will consider using an index to satisfy a query with **DISTINCT** in it.
   - Now uses 64-bit integers in doing its cost analysis. This allows it to more accurately analyze and compare query plans.
3. *Index statistics:*   Have been improved to include multiple density values for composite indexes. This will allow the optimizer to more accurately analyze which index will be most efficient in satisfying a query.

Optimizer Tuning

What You Used to Be Able to Do

Previous versions of **SQL Server** provided two techniques for giving advice or hints to the **SQL Server** about how to choose a query plan:

1. *SET FORCEPLAN ON:*   Told the optimizer to process the tables in the order that they appear in the **FROM** clause.
2. *Force index:*   Allowed the application programmer to place index *ids* following the table name in the **FROM** clause in parentheses, instructing the query optimizer to use the specified index to access that table.

What You Can Do Now

Version 6 significantly enhances this ability to provide hints to the query optimizer. In addition to **FORCEPLAN** and force index, an application developer can now do the following:

1. *Specify multiple options* in the **FROM** clause to specify what query plan should be used and what locking options should be taken.
2. *Specify by index name.*
3. *Indicate no locks* will be obtained for the query, and exclusive locks from other processes will not block this query using a **SELECT** statement.
4. It is also possible to specify for a given query whether you want *page locking* or the *entire table locked.*
5. You can also specify on a **SELECT** that you want to obtain an *update lock.* This lock precludes any simultaneous access by someone who wants to modify the page or table but allows others read access.
6. On a **SELECT**, you can specify that you want the optimizer to optimize *access to the first row,* as opposed to optimizing the entire query processing time. This may be useful in applications where it is important to return some of the rows as quickly as possible, even though the **SQL Server** will take longer to deliver the entire result set.

7. *Tune lock escalation* can also be specified. These options are set using sp_configure. While processing a query that requires page locks, the query optimizer will (by default) escalate to a table lock when it has obtained 200 locks on a given table for that query. This is done to try to reduce the overhead, and to avoid deadlock that might occur if several processes each locked many pages.

8. *Set the minimum and maximum number of page locks* that should be allowed before escalating to a table lock, as well as a percentage of the number of pages that must be locked before a table lock is obtained.

Update in Place

Under certain conditions, an update to a row can be executed in place (the row is replaced) without having to perform a DELETE and an INSERT operation. This is a true *update in place* and is the fastest method for update because it eliminates the need to adjust nonclustered indexes twice. On previous releases this would only happen when a single row was updated. It is now possible to perform an update in place on multiple rows. For an update in place to happen in a multiple row update, the following must be true:

◆ The columns appearing in the SET clause must not be part of a clustered index.
◆ The table must not have a trigger for update.
◆ The table must not be marked for replication.
◆ The columns being set must not be part of a unique index.
◆ If a column being set is part of a nonunique nonclustered index, it must be fixed length.
◆ The table must not have any timestamp columns.

For more information on update in place and for information on the requirements for single row updates being done in place, see the *Microsoft SQL Server Transact-SQL Reference* manual.

DBCC and DISK RESIZE

Numerous new DBCC commands have been added. The most interesting are DBCC SHRINKDB and DBCC SHOW_CONTIG, which will shrink a database and assess the amount of object fragmentation. DBCC UPDATEUSAGE is also interesting since it fixes the problem of inaccurate reporting of space used with sp_spaceused.

Device resizing (expansion) can now be done with the DISK RESIZE statement. The command can be used on any database device including the MASTER device. To expand a device:

```
DISK RESIZE name = logical_device_name, size = final_size
```

For more information on these commands see Chapter 10.

VLDB Issues

One of the major focuses of this version of SQL Server has been to provide improved support for very large databases (VLDB). We are often asked to assess the suitability of SQL Server for various database projects. We recently had someone ask us if SQL Server could handle their requirements—the most significant of which was support for a 64Mb database. SQL Server has always been quite appropriate for databases up to about 10 to 100Gb. At that point SQL Server has run into various limitations and performance problems. This version of SQL Server addresses many of the limitations that started to appear as a database grew larger than about 10Gb.

Many of the optimizer improvements previously listed are aimed at the VLDB market, especially the improved index statistics, optimizer hints, and control over lock escalation.

The ability to read ahead and to do simultaneous access of data and the index for a single query will improve performance for queries against large tables.

One of the most significant problems with VLDBs has been simple administrative tasks. They simply took too long. The new parallelization techniques apply to database dumps, loading, and to DBCC scans; hence large databases are now easier to administer. Using up to 32 devices significantly improves performance of DUMP.

Enterprise Database Product

Centralized Administration

It is difficult to manage a large number of servers. The stand-alone server is the exception in an enterprise application. Server administration has traditionally been done manually—the system administrator is required to log onto each server for maintenance.

In today's databases, servers still require hands-on maintenance. Standard procedures such as database and transaction dumps, updating statistics, data distribution, and general task scheduling are manually performed by each administrator. And don't forget the setup and installation responsibilities. Microsoft SQL Server 6 provides a number of tools that provide centralized administration.

Installation of SQL Server can be a major issue for a large number of servers. With Version 6, unattended setup for SQL server is now supported. As an example, SQL Server can now be installed with:

```
setup /t IniFilePath = filename
```

Where *filename* is the path to a setup initialization file with a fully qualified name and an .INI extension. Unattended installation of SQL Server is only supported for local installations. A discussion on creating and using the setup file can be found in Microsoft SQL Server, SQL Server Setup manual in Appendix B.

Remote installation of SQL Server is interactive only and done by selecting REMOTE from the *Microsoft SQL Server 6.0—Option* screen of SQL Server *Setup*. Installation will be interactive after completing the dialog box.

Management Tools

Database administrators are not typically set up with the tools that are necessary for management, and if tools are provided, they typically do not offer the capability to build custom and automated administrative tasks. Database servers need to be self-monitoring and self-managing. Operators should be able to automate administrative tasks that can occur during nonbusiness hours or must occur on a regular basis.

When the proper SQL Server tools do not exist, management of SQL Server can be extended with the addition of tools tailored for unique requirements. Even though SQL Server tools are easy to use and can seamlessly manage multiple servers from a single interface, an occasional requirement can develop for a custom tool. The ability exists to create custom administrative tools that satisfy both individual tastes and needs with the use of OLE and Visual Basic for Applications (VBA).

A lower-level interface is provided as well with the OLE automation interface to all administration features. This interface is available by using the VBA from Visual Basic or from Excel. We illustrate this lower-level interface with a program fragment where we perform an UPDATE STATISTICS for all tables in a database. The following code fragment in VBA illustrates performing UPDATE STATISTICS on all the tables on the server *MyServer*.

```
DIM MyServer As New SQLServer

Set MyServer = CreateObject ("sqlole.SQLServer")
MyServer.Connect "labdog", "sa", ""
For Each MyDatabase In MyServer.Databases
      For Each MyTable In MyDatabase.Tables
            MyTable.UpdateStatistics
      Next
Next
Set MyServer = Nothing
```

In the code example, default collections are used. To perform the same function on a specific table, use a form like:

```
SQLServer("SERVER").Databases("pubs").Table("authors").Index("PK").UpdateStatistics.
```

Take-Charge Management

Proper administration should be proactive and not reactive. The all-too-typical situation of placing a call to the system administrator when the transaction log is full cannot be tolerated. In a proactive environment such as Version 6, the administrator can be notified by e-mail or pager that the transaction log has exceeded a threshold. The system can then dump the transaction log and notify the administrator of the success or failure of the operation. The ability to manage the system with e-mail/pager notification and automatic task scheduling for either normal maintenance or contingency situations is essential for successful enterprise management.

It is no longer sufficient to view a SQL Server as an isolated component within an enterprise's network. As the capabilities of relational database management systems have increased, so has the importance of the servers to the enterprise. With this release of SQL Server, Microsoft has made significant improvements in the ease of administering a network of multiple SQL Servers and has provided essential components required in an enterprisewide database strategy.

The most visible administration tool is the *SQL Enterprise Manager.* This graphical Windows NT tool allows an administrator to manage all of the SQL Servers on the network. Servers may be placed in groups for ease of management. One logon allows access to all of the servers. It allows access to all of the objects on all of the servers on the network and provides for monitoring and control of those objects. The administrator now has the necessary tools to centrally manage an enterprisewide distributed database management system.

Finally, a significant new capability in this version of SQL Server is data replication—the ability to automatically copy data as it is modified to another server. This capability is integrated in the SQL Server, SQL Executive, and SQL Enterprise Manager of SQL Server. The Enterprise Manager, together with the SQL Server Engine and the SQL Executive, are the essential components that support scheduling of tasks, replication of data, handling of events, and logging of alerts.

Enterprise Manager

The SQL Enterprise Manager is the graphical user interface of the Distributed Management Framework to the SQL Server Distributed Management Objects (DMO). DMO is the interface which stands between the graphical interface and the SQL Executive or SQL Server Engine. This interface gives the user the capability to *drag and drop* objects and operates much like the Windows NT File Manager. Management tasks are now very easy to use, with object properties able to be set directly. In addition, permissions, new accounts, data transfer, BACKUP, and BCP are just some of the tasks which can be accomplished in the SQL Enterprise Manager without the use of Transact-SQL. Operators are no longer required to a have knowledge of Transact-SQL.

Access to another server is no more difficult than selecting the icon. An additional level in ease of use is achieved by placing servers in groups. The SQL Enterprise Manager combines all the functions of the former graphical tools SQL Administrator, SQL Object Manager, SQL Server Transfer Manager, and Transact-SQL into one interface, allowing administrators to remotely manage, monitor, and control collections of distributed database servers.

Distributed Management Objects—an OLE Automation Layer

SQL Server Distributed Management Objects is an intervening software layer which gives the user graphical interface access to the SQL Executive or the SQL Engine. It also provides the same intervening interface for Visual Basic or Excel between SQL Executive or the SQL Engine. This capability gives the system administrator the necessary tools to design custom support and maintenance applications.

SQL Executive

The SQL Engine and the SQL Executive form the heart of Version 6. The SQL Executive, through the Scheduling Engine, controls four managers:

1. Replication Manager
2. Task Manager
3. Event Manager
4. Alert Manager

With these managers SQL Executive manages the SQL Server infrastructure while the SQL Engine manages the data (see Figure 2.1).

The Alert Manager, Event Manager and Task Manager are all components of the SQL Executive and work in concert with each other. The *Event Manager* captures events and passes them to the *Alert Manager.* The Alert Manager then screens those events and when necessary takes whatever action has been deter-

SQL Enterprise Manager	OLE Automation
SQL Server Distributed Management Objects (SQL-DMO)	

SQL Executive	SQL Server Engine
Replication Manager	
Task manager	
Event manager	
Alert Manager	

FIGURE 2.1 SQL distributed management framework.

mined. If in addition to sending an e-mail or pager message an action is to be performed, the *Task Manager* is notified. The Task Manager then schedules the required task which can be a Transact-SQL script, a Windows NT command-shell script, or a VBA (see OLE Automation) application. The SQL Executive then calls the appropriate subsystem (VBA, SQL Engine, Windows NT Command) with the task information. A completion status is then returned to the Event Manager, which could quite possibly start another cycle.

With the SQL Executive it is now possible to have automated control of remote operations as well as auto server restart, unattended backup, log threshold management, remote performance monitoring, event logging, and administrator paging and alerts. An extensive audit trail is maintained of all activities. Not only has Microsoft defined the *programmable* server, it has also defined the *manageable* server.

When Version 6 is installed, the SETUP program will automatically create the MSDB database used by the SQL Executive for scheduling management. The new database consists of a 2Mb MSDB Database and a 1Mb MSDB Log on the same device as the *Master* database. Found within the new database are the tables:

sysoperators	Operator work schedules, e-mail names, pager number, and so on
sysalerts	User-defined alert information
systasks	User-defined task information
syshistory	Historical information including success/failure status
sysnotifications	Activated alert information including operator name, notification method, and so on

Replication

Replication is a new feature of Version 6. With replication, support is now available for a range of organizational models. One model to consider for the enterprise is the separation of an online transaction environment from decision support systems. Another model to consider is the decentralization of data, which normalizes the workload across multiple servers with a resultant reduction in network traffic.

Replication will take additional resources. The server must have a minimum of 32Mb, 32-bit ODBC must be installed, and additional mass storage devices may be needed by the server for the distribution database. Resources of replication subscribers must also be evaluated.

Metaphors

Replication uses an easily understood metaphor of a *publisher* who publishes articles and a *subscriber* who may subscribe to all or none of the articles. With centralized management of the network and the necessary privileges, a server can be forced to subscribe—a *push*—and a subscriber may browse published offerings and subscribe—a *pull*. Articles may be databases, tables, or segmented tables. Triggers and constraints are only enforced on the publisher and the published articles are considered read only. A SQL statement or stored procedure is constructed by the Replication Log Reader to re-create changes at the subscription server.

Synchronization of a new subscriber is required. The synchronization may be manual, automatic, snapshot, or not done at all. After synchronization, replication may be continuous, at specific intervals, or not at all.

Models

There are four basic models for replication:

1. Single publisher–multiple subscribers
2. Single publisher using a separate distribution server
3. Multiple publishers–single subscriber
4. Multiple publishers–multiple subscribers

Which role a server plays in the replication helps determine the architecture. A publisher could be a subscriber; in fact, if the articles are the same, the server is considered to be a *distributor*. If, on the other hand, there is only one subscriber and many publishers, then this architecture lends itself very well to defining activities such as corporate-rollup for such things as locally maintained customer lists, business order processing, or warehouse inventory maintenance of autonomous business divisions. Illustrations of business models using replication can be found later in this book in Chapter 5.

Messaging

MAPI

Messaging Application Programming Interface Version 1.0 (MAPI) is a messaging architecture that has been added to Version 6. Two service-provider interfaces have been provided: e-mail and pager. Version 6 has paging implemented as sending e-mail to a *pager-provider*. Good examples of messaging might be a trigger sending mail when a particular event has occurred or a mail message from **SQL Enterprise Manager** indicating that the batch was completed successfully.

A protocol must be followed to start a MAPI-client session which includes a password. Sending a message is implemented with the use of extended procedures which use the MAPI 1.0 Service Provider Interface. Use of a MAPI-extended procedure is illustrated with:

```
xp_sendmail 'user1', @query = 'sp_configure'
```

This statement mails the current SQL Server configuration to *user1*. What is important to note here is that any result set could be mailed. Sending daily reports to department managers is a good example of combining mail with task scheduling.

Messages will not be lost with MAPI 1.0. The architecture includes a messaging subsystem which is part of the operating system. This messaging subsystem provides spooling similar to that found in a printer subsystem and is service-provider independent. The messaging subsystem will provide *store* and *forward* services, which are vital when a service provider is off line.

OLE Automation

In Version 6, SQLOLE or Distributed Management Objects (DMO) has been implemented as more than 40 server objects with more than one thousand properties or methods (see Figure 2.2). Server objects expose their properties and methods for manipulation by OLE controllers, in this case either with Visual Basic or Excel. Access to these objects is with Visual Basic for Applications (VBA), the common scripting language of Visual Basic and Excel. These objects expose all administrative functions in a consistent format. When the user double clicks on an icon in the SQL Enterprise Manager, what is actually taking place is OLE *in-place activation*. This allows an application program to set properties and use methods of DMO. As an example, consider this Transact-SQL statement:

```
EXEC sp_dboption pubs,'single user', true
```

The corresponding program fragment used from either Visual Basic or Excel which sets the property *SingleUser:*

```
SQLServers("SERVER").Databases("pubs").DBOption.SingleUser=True.
```

SQLOLE does not support data access, the Data Access Objects (DAO) of VBA. VBA functions using DMO will only return a single value, not a result set. VBA functions using DAO will return a result set. With SQLOLE, the administrator now has a programmable tool for SQL Server management.

With the use of OLE and OLE Automation, system management is significantly simplified. Control of management functions is as simple as an OLE drag and drop. In-place editing is available with DMO acting as an OLE automation server. In using VBA to control DMO objects, a management interface can be tailored to individual needs or tastes as desired. Integration with the system is seamless. VBA was previously used in this chapter to set properties of objects. But it can do more than this. It can be used to create objects such as SQL Server database devices.

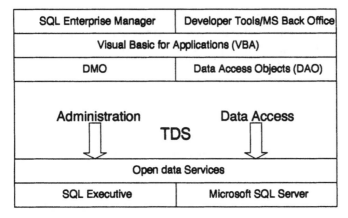

FIGURE 2.2 SQL DMO architecture.

Removable Media

With Version 6, databases can now be published. The removable media may be a floppy, Write Once Read Many (WORM), Magna-Optical (MO), or CD-ROM. But just don't run out and buy the latest technology. The removable media must be in the Windows NT Hardware Compatibility List (HCL), that is, supported by Windows NT.

The database created is read-only and cannot be modified. Microsoft has reduced the minimum database size to 1Mb, so that a *removable media database* will fit on a floppy. There are stored procedures and special procedures which must be followed for creating a removable media database.

    sp_create_removable   dbname, syslogical, and so on
    sp_certify_removable   dbname

Unified Logon

Administration of Version 6 has been integrated with Windows NT administration. With the new Enterprise Manager, multiple SQL Servers can be maintained. Selecting a server is nothing more than clicking on an icon. To do this, however, trusted connections must exist between the SQL Servers on different systems and if any of the servers are in a different Windows NT domain, domain trusts must exist between those domains. Microsoft defines a unified logon as *one logon for access to all resources*. Trusted connections are by definition unified since the Windows NT domain logon will be used for all access. Trusted connections are also a requirement of replication.

During installation, SETUP will prompt for the Windows NT Administrator password. With the trusted domain model for Windows NT, the Windows NT Administrator is also a SQL Server Administrator. The SQL Server Administrator is now a member of the Domain Administrators Group and has system administration privileges on all servers in the domain in addition to all servers in trusting domains. For a further discussion of trusts and domains, please see Chapter 9.

Notes

1. *Microsoft SQL Server, Transact-SQL Reference,* CASE expression, Microsoft Corporation, 1995.

3

Core Technology Issues

In this chapter we will discuss some of the core technology issues that affect decisions that you must make when you design and deploy SQL Server applications. It is necessary to understand how the server is architected and how it processes data and data requests.

The issues of *locking, optimization,* and *connectivity* (DB-Library, Net-Library, and ODBC) are pervasive components of the SQL Server architecture that are core to how you should build applications. This chapter will help you understand why your applications behave the way they do. These behaviors are not something that you control (for the most part). You have to understand them to design optimal application architectures that use the server's natural behaviors to good result.

The discussion of *very large database* (*VLDB*) issues highlights some of the key issues that affect our systems as our databases grow ever larger.

Locking

The *locking behavior* of a database engine is usually considered to be an internal and very technical issue, and therefore is left for consideration only after a project is in trouble. For most applications, the SQL Server controls which locks are used and when they are used. Since the server takes care of locking automatically, developers get the sense that they don't have to consider locking behavior. This is a bad idea. There are new features that allow developers to actually define the chosen locking behavior of a SQL Statement. Some developers will use these features to establish the specific locking that they want in all cases. This is not always a good idea either. A developer should be certain to understand the locking behavior of the server, whether taking the defaults, or completely controlling the locking.

In reality, the locking behavior of a database engine is critical to most everything in an application development environment. A technical leader in every IS department must thoroughly understand it. This technical leader must chart the way for all developers of the system with regard to styles of database usage: reading, writing, and transaction management. These activities should be managed in a systematic and thoroughly defined way. This is especially critical for Online Transaction Processing (OLTP) systems that expect large volumes of transactions and/or large numbers of users.

Casual regard for the importance of locking results in performance degradation, deadlocks, and potential failure of an application to deploy.

Basic Locking Principles

Locking is a way of controlling access to data in a multiuser system. If the system were single-user, you wouldn't need locks. Locking is required in multiuser systems as one of the mechanisms to ensure the atomicity, consistency, isolation, and durability (ACID)[1] properties of transactions.

When a user needs access to locked data, success is dependent on the activity and the type of lock that the server has placed on the data. If the style of access needed is not allowed (prevented by the lock), the process will simply wait for the release of the locks. Deadlock is an exception that we will discuss later.

ACID Properties

A *transaction* is a series of actions (INSERT, UPDATE, or DELETE) that have the following ACID properties. A number of mechanisms in relational database management systems insure these properties. These mechanisms include *locks*, the *transaction log*, and *recovery algorithms*.

Atomicity: Either all of the transaction's changes are present in the database, or none of the transaction changes are present in the database.

Consistency: The transaction must reflect a correct set of changes within the database. This reflects business rules that may have been implemented using declarative referential, triggers, or transaction logic (the use of BEGIN TRANSACTION, ROLLBACK TRANSAC-TION and COMMIT TRANSACTION within the application). Locks are part of the mechanism used to implement this in the SQL Server.

Isolation: It must appear that for any pair of transactions, one transaction is executed completely, then the other. This is implemented by the SQL Server using locks.

Durability: Once a COMMIT TRANSACTION has been executed for a transaction, the changes must be present, even if the server fails. On SQL Server, this is true unless there is a media failure. In the case of media failure, it is still possible to recover under most circumstances if you have planned ahead.

Transaction Implications of Locks

Locks are implemented to insure isolation of transactions. That's good news and bad news. The good news is that the transactions are isolated. The bad news is that other transactions may be waiting on the completion of this transaction. Once an exclusive lock is obtained for a process by the server, it is held for the duration of the transaction.

It is essential, in constructing applications, that the developer does the following: Determine the minimum amount of work for a transaction, insure that transactions lock as little as possible, and COMMIT the transaction as soon as possible. You should work to ensure that only pages are locked, and that you don't get and hold locks on tables that are not really critical to the transaction.

Locks on SQL Server

Locking Isolation Levels

There are three isolation levels supported by SQL Server. The purpose of isolation levels is to specify how this transaction interacts with other transactions running at the same time. The application may select one of these three isolation levels for the connection using the SET ISOLATION LEVEL command. The application may also choose an appropriate isolation level for a given SELECT statement using optimizer hints (see the Optimizer Hints section later in this chapter).

These isolation levels only affect the behavior of SELECT statements. The locks for data modification statements will be covered later in this chapter.

READ UNCOMMITTED allows the maximum concurrency; that is, it has the least impact on other users. READ COMMITTED reduces concurrency somewhat, but avoids the possibility of reading changes which have not yet been committed. REPEATABLE READS allows for much less concurrency. It is more likely to block or be blocked by concurrent access to the same data.

1. *READ UNCOMMITTED:* This isolation level allows one transaction to read modifications made by another transaction that have not yet been committed. Using this isolation level will probably improve performance for some applications, but an application may read changes made by transactions that were not (and may never be) committed. Microsoft warns that it is possible to get various error messages (605, 606, 624, or 625) while using this isolation level. If your application encounters these errors, you must resubmit your query or transaction. This option is rarely needed, and for many queries may give inconsistent results. We recommend against its use in most queries or applications. The optimizer hint NOLOCK is equivalent to this isolation level.

2. *READ COMMITTED:* At this isolation level, a transaction can only read the rows changed by another transaction after that other transaction has committed. This is the default behavior on SQL Server. This isolation level precludes what are often termed *dirty reads,* by insuring that one transaction cannot read the uncommitted changes from another transaction. This isolation level does not guarantee repeatable reads.

3. *REPEATABLE READS or SERIALIZABLE:* This isolation level ensures that inside a transaction, running the same query twice will yield the same answer (repeatable reads). It also ensures that while a query is running other transactions will not modify some of the rows that this query is reading. In particular, the following query will yield a result that is consistent.

```
SELECT sum(amount) FROM account
```

At the other two isolation levels, it is possible that another transaction can modify multiple rows in this table while the query is running. With READ COMMITTED, you may get a result that is inconsistent. With READ UNCOMMITTED, you may include changes that are not yet committed or you may get an error.

Although REPEATABLE READS guarantee the greatest consistency of data, they also hold their locks for a longer time (all shared locks are held for the duration of this query, or for the entire transaction if the application explicitly starts a transaction). This reduces concurrency. REPEATABLE READS is equivalent to using SELECT with HOLDLOCK on all of your queries.

Classes of Locks

SQL Server obtains three classes of locks: *shared, update,* or *exclusive* locks. The class of lock is selected based on the operation that the SQL Server is about to perform for the user. The purpose of the locks is to prevent conflicting actions by other transactions. For example, if one transaction is modifying data, an exclusive lock is held so that no other transaction can read the data until the first transaction is done.

Shared Locks

When reading pages, SQL Server obtains *shared locks*. In general, SQL Server holds shared locks only while the page is being read, and immediately releases them. Each subsequently required page is locked, read, and the lock is released. This model is used for all SELECT statements, unless it is a SELECT HOLDLOCK or the transaction is SERIALIZABLE (see section on Isolation Levels in this chapter). SELECT HOLDLOCK or SERIALIZABLE transactions will hold the shared lock for the duration of the SELECT statement's execution, or, if the SELECT is embedded in a transaction, it will hold the lock until the completion of the transaction. When data is locked with a shared lock, other readers can share the lock; that is, obtain a shared lock for their process on the same data. Any data modification statements will be blocked.

Exclusive Locks

Exclusive locks are used whenever data is being modified (INSERT, UPDATE, or DELETE). Exclusive locks are held until the end of the transaction (this is how locks are used to ensure the isolation part of the ACID properties). When data is locked with an exclusive lock, no other process may obtain a lock of any kind on the locked data.

Update Locks

An *update lock* is obtained when a process is executing an UPDATE against the data. An update lock is similar to a shared lock. Most UPDATE statements are implemented by obtaining an update lock, reading the page, then obtaining an exclusive lock and making the change. While the update lock is held, other shared locks are allowed, but no exclusive (or update) locks are allowed.

Specific Locks Held

SQL Server locks *pages, tables,* or *extents.* A *page* is 2048 bytes, and the basic storage unit for all server data. The locks held are dependent on the query plan that is being used to satisfy the query, and the isolation level that is applied for this query. Pages are locked when the query plan indicates that an index is being used to satisfy the query. *Tables* are locked whenever a table scan is used to access the table for a change (INSERT, UPDATE or DELETE). *Extents* (sets of eight pages) are locked when additional space is being allocated by the server. (There are some exceptions; see the Optimizer Hints later in this chapter.)

The following are the lock types that the SQL Server will hold:

1. *Shared page lock:* Other shared locks are allowed, but no exclusive locks are allowed on the page or table.
2. *Exclusive page lock:* No other locks are allowed on this page. No table locks are allowed on the table.
3. *Update page lock:* Other shared locks are allowed, but no exclusive (or update) locks are allowed on the page or table.
4. *Shared table lock:* Other shared locks are allowed, but no exclusive locks at the table level, or individual exclusive page locks within the table.
5. *Exclusive table lock:* No other locks are allowed at the table level, or on any page within the table.
6. *Shared intent lock (table):* This lock indicates that at least one page in the table has a shared lock. This lock is recorded as a convenience for the server. It does not imply any additional locking beyond the page lock that is held. It makes it easier for the server to determine whether a specific table lock is allowed for some other process. In particular, no exclusive table lock would be allowed.
7. *Exclusive intent lock (table):* This lock indicates that at least one page in the table has an exclusive lock. This lock is recorded as a convenience for the server. It does not imply any additional locking beyond the page lock that is held. It makes it easier for the server to determine whether a specific table lock is allowed for some other process. In particular, no other shared or exclusive table lock would be allowed.
8. *Exclusive extent lock:* This lock indicates that an additional extent (eight pages) needed to be allocated for this object.

Blocking Example

When one transaction has a lock that is in conflict with a request from another user, the second user waits. Consider the following example:

```
User 1 -    BEGIN TRAN
            UPDATE WHERE id = 'xxx'
User 2 -    UPDATE WHERE id = 'xxx'
```

User 2 waits until User 1 issues a COMMIT or ROLLBACK. In this case, if you looked at the results of EXEC sp_who, you would see the row for User 2 would have an entry in the *blk* column indicating User 1's block. The SQL Server will do nothing to resolve this conflict. The server will block User 2 until User 1 issues a COMMIT or a ROLLBACK.

Deadlock Example

If two transactions each hold a lock on a page that the other transaction wants, then there is a *deadlock*. Although SQL Server automatically detects this case, and rolls back one of the transactions, deadlocks should still be avoided. Often, when there is a deadlock, the application that owns the rolled back transaction will rerun the transaction. This reflects wasted effort by the server (and possibly other blocking). You can do much to minimize the threat of locking and deadlock:

♦ Shorten transactions and transaction times.
♦ Use the resources in the same sequence in all transactions where possible.
♦ Minimize indexing (and therefore index locking) on vulnerable tables.

Without analysis, deadlocks will surprise you when you start to test or deploy with many users. Testing with few users will not usually illustrate the deadlock problem.

```
User 1 -    BEGIN TRAN
            UPDATE WHERE id = 'xxx'
User 2 -    BEGIN TRAN
            UPDATE WHERE id = 'yyy'
User 1 -    UPDATE WHERE id = 'yyy'
User 2 -    UPDATE WHERE id = 'xxx'
```

In this case, the SQL Server will pick one of the two users and ROLLBACK that transaction.

How the SQL Server Determines Whether to Obtain a Table Lock or a Page Lock

The lock strategy for a given query is determined when the access strategy is set for the query. The SQL Server locks tables if the server must scan the table to satisfy the query for INSERT, UPDATE, DELETE, or SELECT HOLDLOCK. The SQL Server locks pages if it is using an index to satisfy a query for INSERT, UPDATE, DELETE, or SELECT HOLDLOCK. It also locks pages when doing a SELECT without HOLDLOCK.

Page Lock Escalation

When a single command obtains more than 200 page locks against a single table, the SQL Server obtains a table lock. If the SQL Server were to continue obtaining more page locks for this one command, the likelihood of a conflict, including a possible deadlock, increases. You can change this 200-page lock threshold using the sp_configure stored procedure to set the *LE threshold maximum*, *LE threshold minimum*, and the *LE threshold percent*.

Optimizer Hints

In the SELECT statement, it is possible to provide hints to the SQL Server concerning what locks it should obtain to satisfy a query. These hints allow you to adjust the default behavior of the SQL Server. The optimizer hints are placed after the FROM clause of a SELECT statement, and only affect that SELECT statement. For example, the following query specifies that no locks should be obtained in satisfying the query. This may result in *dirty reads:*

```
SELECT * FROM titles (NOLOCK)
```

Table 3.1 shows the hints that affect locking.

Special Locking Situations

In addition to INSERT, UPDATE, DELETE, and SELECT statements obtaining locks, there are other statements that will acquire locks. You need to pay attention to possible conflicts when considering running the following commands:

1. The CREATE CLUSTERED INDEX statement obtains an exclusive table lock. Any user accessing this table will be blocked until the statement has finished executing.

TABLE 3.1   SELECT Statement Hints That Affect Locking

Hint	*Action*
NOLOCK	This specifies that no locks should be obtained for this query. This allows dirty reads, that is, reading pages that may have been changed by an as yet uncommitted transaction. This is equivalent to the **READ UNCOMMITTED** isolation level.
HOLDLOCK	This specifies that any shared locks obtained for this query should be held for the entire transaction. If this statement is not in a transaction, then the locks will be held for the duration of the statement. This is equivalent to the **REPEATABLE READS** or **SERIALIZABLE** isolation level.
UPDLOCK	This specifies that the SQL Server should obtain update locks instead of shared locks in executing this query. These update locks will be held for the duration of the transaction. If this statement is not in a transaction, then the locks will be held for the duration of the statement.
TABLOCK	This specifies that the SQL Server should obtain a shared table lock for this table. It should hold this lock until the end of the statement. If HOLDLOCK is also specified (or the REPEATABLE READS isolation level has been set), then the table lock will be held until the end of the transaction.
PAGLOCK	This specifies that the SQL Server should obtain shared page locks for this table. This will be true even if the optimizer is doing a table scan to satisfy the query.
TABLOCKX	This specifies that the SQL Server should get an exclusive table lock for this table. This lock will be held until the end of the transaction. If this statement is not in a transaction, then the locks will be held for the duration of the statement.

2. The CREATE NONCLUSTERED INDEX statement obtains a shared table lock. Any user executing a data modification statement against this table will be blocked until the statement has finished executing.

3. The UPDATE STATISTICS statement also obtains a shared table lock. Any user executing a data modification statement against this table will be blocked until the statement is finished executing.

Viewing Locks

sp_lock

The *sp_lock* stored procedure can be used to view the locks currently held on the server. With no parameters, all locks currently held by the server are displayed. If a system process id (spid) is passed as a parameter, all locks held by that process are displayed.

On one connection:

```
use pubs
go
begin tran
update titles set type = 'aaa'
update publishers set city ='xxx' where pub_id = '1389'
select * from titleauthor holdlock where royaltyper = 10
go
```

On another connection run the following to find out what locks are held by process number 10.

```
sp_lock 10
go
```

Results:

```
spid    locktype             table_id      page         dbname
------  -------------------- ------------  -----------  ----------
--
10      Ex_table             112003430     0            pubs
10      Ex_table             192003715     0            pubs

(1 row(s) affected)
```

Translating the table_ids:

```
select object_name(112003430)
select object_name(192003715)
go
```

Results:

```
publishers
titles

(1 row(s) affected)
```

A page number of zero indicates a table lock.

Enterprise Manager

Currently held locks can also be viewed using the Enterprise Manager. Select from the menu: Server, Current Activity, then choose the Object Locks tab. For each connection, you graphically view the locks held and whether there are any blocks.

Keys to Planning

Make sure that your change requests (INSERT, UPDATE, or DELETE) are using indexes.[2] One way to determine whether indexes are being used is to review the query plan.

Minimize the number of modifications in a transaction. Determine whether multiple modifications are really dependent on each other. If not, make them separate transactions.

Use a stored procedure for your transaction. This ensures that your transaction is as short as possible by eliminating the network communication, parsing, and optimization.

Some transactions cannot be defined ahead of time. They must be dynamically generated in the application. In this case, you cannot use a single stored procedure. If it is not possible (or practical) to put your transaction in a stored procedure, at least make sure that it is completed in a single batch. Again, this will eliminate any network communication time from the transaction.

If you are using a third-party application development tool, make sure that you understand how the tool is processing transactions. When using some development tools, each change may be submitted as a separate batch. You may have to override this default behavior in order to minimize the duration of transactions (and hence locks).

A Conclusion

Knowledge, planning, and study can help. What will help even more is to design a systematic way of processing all data manipulation statements. A defined protocol can give developers proven tools and methods with which to implement their transactions and greatly improve the rate of success for deployment of new systems, which, of course, will reduce costs. This is one of the many topics for which the consideration of client/server systems (client, network, and server) changes the way we should construct applications. The old ways will not work. The new ways are a challenge, but one that can be understood and used (see Chapter 5).

Query Processing

The SQL Server processes SQL statements submitted by a user. Its goal is to create an efficient execution plan. There are a number of phases that the SQL Server goes through to generate this execution plan. The query is parsed, then standardized or normalized, and finally optimized. Optimization is the process of building an execution plan that will use the least system resources (see Figure 3.1).

Translating the Query

Parsing

The *parsing* process prepares the query for normalization. Syntax is scanned and the query is broken down into components which are recognizable by SQL Server. The resulting clauses or phrases are stored in a structure called a query tree (see examples following).

Normalization

In *normalization,* the overall strategy is to *flatten*[3] the query tree. At this level it is done by analyzing the query mathematically since relational databases are set-theoretic. Flattening the query tree is to break conjunctive selects down into cascading selects and the selects are then moved down the tree to reduce the number or rows returned. The flattening process also moves projects (SQL Projections) down the tree to eliminate the return of unnecessary attributes. Additional flattening will convert BETWEENs to >= and <= or flatten a subquery into a join if possible.

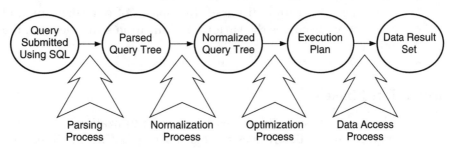

FIGURE 3.1 The optimizer and the overall plan.

The query tree is optimizer input. To see what one looks like, we define some tables with a query and several versions of the query tree.

Employees	*Projects*	*Tasks*
E_Num(PK)	P_Num(PK)	E_Num(FK)
E_Name	P_Name	P_Num(FK)
		T_Title
		T_Time

A SQL query is submitted:

```
SELECT E_Name
FROM Employees E, Projects P, Tasks T
WHERE T.E_Num = E.E_Num
AND T.P_Num = P.P_Num
AND E.E_Name <> 'A. Programmer'
AND P.P_Name = 'SQL SERVER'
AND T.T_Time = 12 OR T.T_Time = 24.
```

The initial query tree is shown in Figure 3.2.

Although not completely optimal, an improved version is shown in Figure 3.3. Note how the flattening process changes the query tree.

Optimization

During the optimization, SQL Server tries to find the best access path to satisfy the query. The optimizer has knowledge of the tables, their indexes, the size of the tables, and the distribution of values within the indexes of the table. It will consider many different access strategies (including some that may not have occurred to you).

Implementation of any strategy by the query optimizer is cost-based. It will construct an execution plan based upon the least cost in terms of disk accesses. It uses statistical data to evaluate different alternatives. The query optimizer may choose to do a table scan instead of using an index if it thinks that the table scan will be more efficient.

The next section discusses the phases of optimization, and the following section discusses the various optimization strategies that the query optimizer uses.

Optimization Phases

There are three main phases to query optimization. The number of tables within a query determines the tasks performed in the different optimization phases.

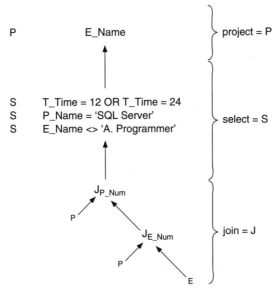

FIGURE 3.2 Query tree from SELECT statement.

Number of Tables	Single	Multiple
Query Analysis—Phase One		
Analyze the query for search arguments	Yes	Yes
Locate disjunctions (qualifications with OR clauses)	Yes	Yes
Locate join clauses		Yes
Index Selection—Phase Two		
Useful index ranking	Yes	Yes
Match search arguments to indexes	Yes	Yes
Find best index for each join clause		Yes
Join Selection—Phase Three		
Permute tables and indexes for join order evaluation		Yes
Evaluate reformatting strategy		Yes

Query Analysis—Phase One

Phase one of the SQL Server query optimizer is to analyze the query. The query is scanned and broken down into clauses from which the optimizer attempts to identify *search arguments, OR clauses,* and *join clauses.*

Search Arguments

Search arguments will limit the search and will be an exact match, a range of values, or conjunctions joined with an AND. The following rules are observed for identifying search arguments during the query scan:

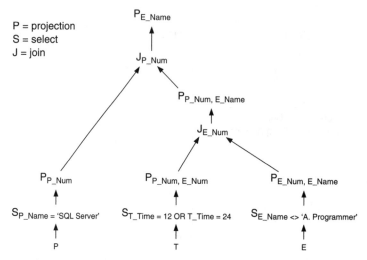

P = projection
S = select
J = join

FIGURE 3.3 Rewritten query tree showing the moving down of SELECTS.

- Search argument format: <column> <inclusion operator> <column> [AND . . .]
- Common operators might be: BETWEEN, LIKE, =, <, >
- All columns of the search argument clause must be in the same table.
- A Search argument must be conjunctive, that is, all terms are linked with an AND.

Examples:

```
Description = 'gadget'
250 < QuantityOnHand
Description = 'gadget' AND Warehouse = 'SpitBrook'
```

When analyzing the clauses, the following rules will identify arguments which are *not* search arguments, that is, they do not limit the search. Comparisons that are not search arguments may force a table scan. However, if there are other search arguments, then the query could still take advantage of an index for that clause. So the presence of one of these doesn't imply that an index won't be used for the query—it just won't be used for that clause.

- Comparisons between columns. *QuantityShipped = QuantitySold.* Since both columns are in the same table, an index is not meaningful.
- Computations before data access. A good example is *MonthlyRent* * 1.2 > 1500 where the data must be retrieved and the calculation done before the comparison is made. The use of a function on the column is another example.
- Each of the following operators will not limit a search and may force a table scan unless another index is available or this index is used in another clause: NOT, NOT IN(), !, and <>.

Some nonsearch arguments can be converted to search arguments. SQL Server converts BETWEEN clauses to clauses using <= and >= during the normalization phase discussed previously.

If a clause contains LIKE and the first character is a constant, then it may be converted to search argument form. name LIKE 'part%' becomes name >= 'part' AND name < 'paru'.

Sometimes you can apply simple logic to convert a clause to search argument form. If for example, the value is numeric, then $A <> 0$ could be changed to $A > 0$ if negative values do not exist in the table.

OR Clauses

As part of the analysis phase, the optimizer recognizes OR clauses. A SELECT with an OR clause is an OR statement and is the equivalent of a UNION. ORs and INs will be processed in the same manner. The optimizer does this by converting IN clauses to OR clauses.

```
SELECT*
FROM authors
WHERE au_1name IN ('James', 'Hemingway')
```

becomes

```
SELECT*
FROM authors
WHERE au_1name = 'James' OR au_1name = 'Hemingway'
```

Index Selection—Phase Two

In order to understand how index selection works, we need a brief introduction to indexes (for more information, see Chapter 6). SQL Server supports two types of indexes: *clustered* and *nonclustered*. A *clustered index* has data stored at the *leaf* level in sorted order. A *nonclustered index* has *pointer pages* at the leaf level. A clustered index is termed a *sparse* index, since at its lowest level there is a pointer to each page of data. A nonclustered index is termed a *dense* index, since at its lowest level, there is a pointer to every row of data. You can have at most 1 clustered index per table, and up to 249 nonclustered indexes.

If you do not have a clustered index on a table, then that table is a *heap*. All news rows will be inserted at the end of the table. The data pages of a table are linked together in a linked list.

The optimizer has a number of choices in determining how to find the results of a query. The first approach is that it can do a *table scan*. To do this, the first page is found, and then all of the data pages of the table are read, following the pointers that link them together.

Figure 3.4 shows a clustered index on a table.

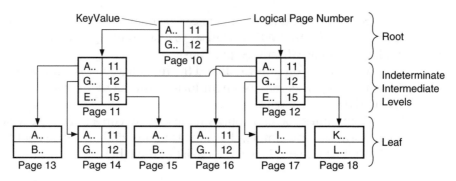

FIGURE 3.4 Clustered index detail.

If there is a clustered index or a nonclustered index on the table, and the optimizer finds at least the first column of the index in a search argument in the WHERE clause, then the row can be found by starting at the root of the tree and navigating down the tree to find the row or rows that satisfy the query.

There are a number of special cases where the optimizer does not necessarily have to identify a search argument in order to consider taking advantage of an index. For advice on what to index, see Chapter 6.

Optimizer Index Selection

During this phase, the optimizer evaluates indexes, looking for the fastest access. The most obvious candidate for using an index is when there is a search argument that includes at least the first column of an index. For example, if there is an index on last name and first name, then the optimizer would consider using that index when it encountered a query with the following search argument:

```
AND lastname ='Smith'
```

Using the index would probably require that the Server look at fewer data pages than doing a table scan.

Search arguments are not the only thing that will cause the optimizer to consider a given index. If the server is asked to count the number of rows

```
SELECT count(*) FROM authors
```

it may choose to read all of the leaf pages of a nonclustered index. That will be more efficient than doing a table scan.

Join Selection—Phase Three

Candidate indexes for a *join selection index* are all indexes which follow the previously outlined rules. The *join analysis* (see following) will select the most useful index and the best strategy for join clauses. The selection will be cost-based and its goal is the least I/O. Included in the factors will also be cache size.

Query Optimizer Processing Strategies

Table Scan and Index Analysis

The query optimizer can always use a *table scan* to process a query. It considers various indexes that exist and the table, and attempts to find an index that will allow it to process the query with the least I/Os. In order to evaluate the cost of an index, in considers the following values that it has available in the index statistics:

Density   The average percentage of duplicate rows. A unique index will have a density of 1/number of rows in the table, and is highly selective.

All density   For composite indexes, the density is available for each index segment. For a three-column composite index, density is available for the first column, the first and second columns combined, and for all columns combined. This is a new feature of Version 6 (see the DBCC SHOW_STATISTICS section later in this chapter).

From the index statistics and, if necessary, the densities, the optimizer calculates how selective a given index is for this query. Selectivity can be expressed as the ratio of the number of rows accessed to the total number of rows in the table. Low selectivity may return many rows while high selectivity will return very few rows. With index statistics, the optimizer knows (or has a very good estimate) how many rows will match the clause. This is particularly important when evaluating a nonclustered index.

When Isn't an Index Used?

♦ If there is no index, it must do a table scan.
♦ If the table is small, the optimizer may decide that it is faster to use a table scan.
♦ If the nonclustered index is not very selective, the optimizer may decide that a table scan will be faster.
♦ An index might not be used when there are no statistics, or when the statistics aren't being used. This occurs when:

    1. A local variable is used, since the value is unknown when the optimizer is evaluating query plans.
    2. UPDATE STATISTICS have never been run, and there were no rows in the table when the index was created.
    3. Under some circumstances, the optimizer can't evaluate the value being compared to the column. This may happen if the datatype of the column is different from the datatype of the value to which it is being compared.

With an index and no statistics, the optimizer assigns default values for selectivity. Having no statistics can be a major factor in rejecting an index. The optimizer makes the following assumptions about selectivity when statistics are not available or cannot be used.

Operator	Default Selectivity
=	10%
Closed Interval (e.g., BETWEEN)	25%
Open Interval (e.g., >)	33%

If there is an equality match on all of the columns of a unique index, it realizes that at most one row will match.

OR Processing Strategy

An OR clause is resource intensive since each component is a SELECT statement and the result is equivalent to a UNION statement. For this reason, each column component of an OR clause should have an index. If all columns have an appropriate index the optimizer will consider the *OR* strategy. Otherwise, it will do a table scan. (The optimizer will convert an IN clause to an OR clause.)

For the *OR* processing strategy, all columns must be in the same table or it is considered to be a *join*. The *OR* processing strategy will build a dynamic index in *tempdb*. The dynamic index is initially built as a work table with row identifiers for all qualifying rows. The rows are sorted with all duplicates removed. The resultant dynamic index is then used to retrieve rows from the actual table (see Figure 3.5).

The optimizer may elect to do a table scan even though both OR components have an index. If the optimizer thinks that it is faster doing a table scan to satisfy one of the components of an OR, then it will do all of the comparisons in a single pass of the table scan. If any portion of the OR clause causes a table scan even though an index is available, the table scan will be used in the execution plan rather than the *OR* processing strategy.

Join Order Strategies

There are only two strategies for a *join:*

1. Nested iteration of *joins.*
2. Reformatting (occurs when no useful index is available). In this case, it is still doing nested iteration—joining through the various tables. It just decided that it would be more efficient to build an index on the innermost table.

For either type of *join,* the optimizer evaluates various possible join orders. Although it will not necessarily consider all possible orders, it generally does a good job at determining an optimal order.

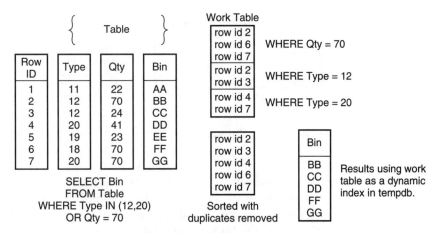

FIGURE 3.5 An example of OR processing strategy.

Join Nested Iteration Strategy

For a join strategy, only one index per table is used. The outer table will typically be the only table for which an index is used to match a search argument. The optimizer will typically use an index to get to the corresponding rows in the next inner table. If no index exists or the index is not usable, then the *Reformatting* strategy may be used. In this strategy, the optimizer creates a temporary index on the table (usually only on the innermost table in its join order).

The optimizer evaluates the number of tables, indexes, joins, and number of rows to determine the optimal order for the nested iteration (see Figure 3.6). The iteration proceeds as follows:

> For each row in the outermost table:
>> Find every qualifying row in the next outermost table.
>> Determine whether the matching row meets the WHERE criteria.
>> For each qualifying row:
>>> . . .
>>> For each qualifying row in the innermost table:
>>>> Solve constant query.

JOIN Reformatting Strategy

The *Reformatting* strategy is considered when there is no useful index on the innermost table. The optimizer sorts data and creates an index in a temporary work table at run time.

The query:

SELECT account.name, mytable.number
FROM account, mytable
WHERE account.number = mytable.linkkey

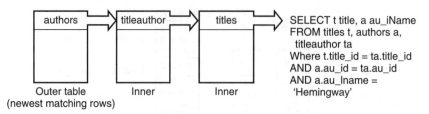

FIGURE 3.6 Nested iteration in Pubs database.

produced the output below. Figure 3.7 shows output that was obtained by selecting *Query Options* from the top tool/bar in ISQL/w and selecting *Show Query Plan* from the dialog box. If additional detail is needed, then also select *Display Show Plan* from the bottom tool/bar.

There may be occasions when it is desired to override the *JOIN* reformatting strategy. To do this use the Transact-SQL statement SET FORCEPLAN ON. *However, FORCEPLAN is not a recommended procedure. You are asserting that you are smarter than the optimizer. You also have the problem that the optimizer changes with each SQL SERVER update, and your technique may fail on a later version.* If you do use **FORCEPLAN**, it will force the optimizer to pro-

```
STEP 1
The type of query is INSERT
The update mode is direct
Worktable created for REFORMATTING
FROM TABLE
mytable
Nested iteration
Table Scan
TO TABLE
Workable 1
STEP 2
The type of query is SELECT
FROM TABLE
account
Nested iteration
Table Scan
FROM TABLE
Worktable 1
Nested iteration
Using Clustered Index
```

```
STEP 1
The type of query is INSERT
The update mode is direct
Worktable created for REFORMATTING
FROM TABLE
mytable
Row estimate: 0
Cost estimate: 0
Nested iteration
Table Scan
TO TABLE
Worktable 1
STEP 2
The type of query is SELECT
FROM TABLE
account
Row estimate: 10000
Cost estimate: 8432
Nested iteration
Table Scan
FROM TABLE
Worktable 1
JOINS WITH
account
Row estimate: 10000
Cost estimate: 79829
Nested iteration
Using Clustered Index
```

FIGURE 3.7 Show Query Plan, Show Query Plan with Display ShowPlan.

cess joins in the same order as they appear in the FROM clause. If you're still not satisfied, then you have several alternatives:

- ♦ Evaluate the current indexes and create new ones if necessary.
- ♦ Use UPDATE STATISTICS to update the respective distribution pages for current indexes. If the distribution pages are out of date, then the optimizer may not be making good choices.
- ♦ Force the use of different indexes[4] in your query with the INDEX = (*index_name|index_id*) (id 0 = table scan, id 1 = clustered index, id 2–250 = nonclustered indexes). Either an index id or an index name can be used as illustrated:

SELECT au_1name
FROM authors (INDEX = aunmind)
WHERE au_1name = 'White'

Special Optimizer Strategies

Aggregates

Aggregates include COUNT, SUM, MAX, MIN, and AVG and are always done in two steps as the following query plans indicate. The extra step is the presentation of the information and not another scan of the table. Note in the following examples, that when you select MIN, and there is an index on that column, the query optimizer can use the index to find the minimum. It can also use the index to find the maximum. The third example demonstrates that if you select both in the same query, the optimizer chooses a table scan. Some queries and their respective query plans are shown in Figure 3.8, which illustrates aggregate query plans where an index is available.

A *covering index* is ideal to use for an aggregate. A covering index is a nonclustered index that contains all of the columns required to fulfill this query. When there isn't a WHERE clause and there is either a clustered or a nonclustered index, then processing starts at the leaf level. When a nonclustered index covers the query, the root is accessed and the leaf level scanned.

Consider the following query and its query plan:
SELECT COUNT(uid) FROM sysobjects.

```
STEP 1
The type of query is SELECT
Scalar Aggregate
FROM TABLE
sysobjects
Nested iteration
Index:ncsysobjects
STEP 2
The type of query is SELECT
```

```
STEP 1                          STEP 1                          STEP 1
The type of query is SELECT     The type of query is SELECT     The type of query is SELECT
Scalar Aggregate                Scalar Aggregate                Scalar Aggregate
FROM TABLE                      FROM TABLE                      FROM TABLE
authors                         authors                         authors
Nested iteration                Row estimate: 1                 Nested iteration
Using Clustered Index           Cost estimate: 48               Table Scan
STEP 2                          Nested iteration                STEP 2
The type of query is SELECT     Using Clustered Index           The type of query is SELECT
                                STEP 2
                                The type of query is SELECT
                                Scalar Aggregate
                                FROM TABLE
                                authors
                                Row estimate: 1
                                Cost estimate: 48
                                Nested iteration
                                Using Clustered Index
                                STEP 3
                                The type of query is SELECT
```

SELECT MIN (au_id)   SELECT MIN (au_id), MAX (au_id)
FROM authors   FROM authors

SELECT MIN (au_id), (SELECT MAX (au_id)
FROM authors) FROM authors

FIGURE 3.8 SELECT aggregate example.

If you do this in the master database, it uses the nonclustered index on *name* and *uid*. This is a little surprising, but it works because the nonclustered index has an entry for every row in the table. The answer to this query can be found by reading the leaf level of the nonclustered index, since *uid* is in that index. You actually get the same query plan for SELECT COUNT(*) FROM sysobjects, since it can just count the number of leaf entries in the nonclustered index.

ORDER BY

The *ORDER BY* clause is usually resource intensive. Even though front-end applications can sort the data, it is best done on the server. If you want the rows in a given order, you will ask the server to do it (and maybe, just maybe, there will be a nifty index, and the server won't have to do a lot of work). If you then decide (after the rows are on the client), that you want another order—you can sort them on the client rather than selecting them again from the server.

A work table will be created if the ORDER BY column does not match an index. The optimizer may not create a work table if the index on the ORDER BY column is clustered or if a nonclustered index covers the sort column (and if it decides to use that index).

GROUP BY

The optimizer will always create a work table for a *GROUP BY* clause, even if an index exists. A table scan will be used to create the work table if no index is present or there is no WHERE clause. The GROUP BY operation is resource intensive, but is still an operation which should be done on the server. If you can use a GROUP BY on the server, it will likely *dramatically* reduce the number of rows in the result set. A server is a great place to do this summarization. It is resource intensive—but it is often exactly what you want.

Views

Views are useful to the SQL Server user. However, they present problems to the optimizer. A view masks the underlying database structure from the user. When using the view for data access, the user may request information from a view even though there may be a much simpler data access path. The optimizer ends up joining the table to the view as illustrated in Figure 3.9.

We'll create a view as:

```
CREATE VIEW view1 as
SELECT *
FROM Inventory, Division
WHERE Inventory.FK_Div_No = Division.Div_No
```

We'll do two queries as shown in Figure 3.10, one using the view and one referencing the table directly. We get back different query plans and one will be a join even though the result sets are identical and all the data comes from one table.

The server can't make an assumption that it can ignore the join even though you may know a more efficient query.

Optimizer Tools, Statistics, and the Distribution Page

Each index within SQL Server has a distribution page if there were rows in the table when the index was created or if the object owner or dbo does an **UPDATE STATISTICS** (see following, User Tools). The distribution page stores the statistics for the index. Executing **UPDATE STATISTICS** will update this page. You may query the *distribution* column in *sysindexes* and if there is a zero there, then no statistics have been recorded. It is now possible with ver-

PK			PK		FK	
Div_No	Div_Name		Part_No	Description	FK_Div_No	Quantity
1	div_1		1	Desc_1	1	10
2	div_2		2	Desc_2	2	20
3	div_3		3	Desc_3	3	30
			4	Desc_4	1	40
Division Table			5	Desc_5	2	50
			6	Desc_6	3	60
			Inventory Table			

FIGURE 3.9 Views.

STEP 1
The type of query is SELECT
FROM TABLE
division
Nested iteration
Table Scan
FROM TABLE
Inventory
Nested iteration
Table Scan

SELECT Description,
Quantity from view1

STEP 1
The type of query is SELECT
FROM TABLE
Inventory
Nested iteration
Table Scan

SELECT Description,
Quantity from Inventory

FIGURE 3.10 Query plan differences with a view, same result set.

sion 6 to view the distribution page using **DBCC SHOW_STATISTICS** (see User Tools). If this page is not kept up to date, then the optimizer will probably make a poor choice when considering index usage.

Statistics are stored as an *even* distribution. The data is divided into n equal steps with each nth value recorded. The density (average number of duplicates) is stored in the leftmost column. To compute the distribution page steps, the number of index keys and the key size must be known.

♦ (Page size, 1962 bytes)/(key size) = Number of index keys per distribution page.
♦ Number of distribution steps per distribution page = Number of index keys per distribution page –1.
♦ (Index keys –1)/(distribution steps) = Index keys per step.

For example, consider a table with the 22 rows as shown in Figure 3.11. Assume that the key values are 245 bytes long. In that case, the SQL Server can only maintain eight values on the distribution page. The SQL Server breaks the table into seven pieces. It then places the eight values (note it includes the min and the max in this case) into the distribution. From this distribution page, the optimizer can conclude that a where clause like **WHERE** key **BETWEEN** 19 and 26 would return about 3/7 of the rows. It could also conclude that a where clause like **WHERE** key > 200 probably would return few rows (it can't assume that no rows will match, since some rows may have been inserted since the distribution page was updated).

The optimizer has two other tools to work with in creating an execution plan, *selectivity* and *density*. *Selectivity* is the ratio of the number of estimated rows that qualify to the total row count expressed as a percentage.

Density is the average number of duplicates in the index. This value is used in joins to determine how many rows will match a given value. It is expressed as a percentage. If all the non-null values are the same, the density is 100. If it is a unique column, then the value is $1/N$ (where N is the number of rows). Determining the density with **DBCC SHOW_STATISTICS** is discussed

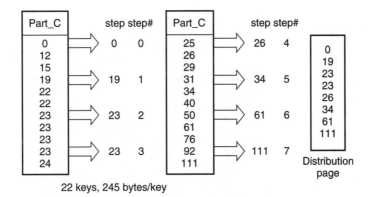

22 keys, 245 bytes/key

FIGURE 3.11 Distribution page detail.

below. The output of the distribution page has the density for the columns (see the DBCC SHOW_STATISTICS section below).

User Tools, Query Plan Maintenance

DBCC SHOW_STATISTICS

The DBCC SHOW_STATISTICS statement displays the index statistics for an index. This is not necessarily something that you should view for every index. However, it can be quite informative, especially when you have a query that does not seem to be using an appropriate query plan.

First, you can see when the statistics were last updated. For some indexes, the statistics need to be updated regularly. These are indexes where the skew (distribution) of the data changes regularly. An index on social security numbers probably doesn't need to have its statistics updated regularly, since the distribution of values probably are fairly constant over time. On the other hand, a table with an index on completion date probably needs to have its statistics updated weekly or daily, since the distribution of values is changing constantly (today, there is no data with a completion date of tomorrow).

Next, the command displays the number of rows in the table, and the number of steps in the statistics. Then the density for the index, and the *all density* for the first column, the first two columns, the first three columns, and so on are displayed. The all density reflects the average number of duplicates if a query specifies an equality match on the first column only, or the first two columns only, and so on.

In the following example (from the authors table, aunmind), there are two all density values. To find how many duplicate rows exist, calculate *row count*percentage*. The calculation for the following output (23 * .047259) is 1.08, which says that on average, there will be about 8 percent duplicate rows (or, more accurately, on average a query for last name will return 1.08 rows).

The output from DBCC SHOW_STATISTICS (authors, aunmind)

```
STEP 1
The type of query is DBCC_CMD
Updated              Rows       Steps       Density
------------------   ----------  ----------  ------------------------
Jun 7 1995 2:39PM 23 22 0.0396975
(1 row(s) affected)
All density               Columns
-------------------       ------------------------------
0.047259                  au_lname
0.0434783                 au_lname, au_fname
(2 row(s) affected)
Steps
------------------------------------------------
Bennet
Blotchet-Halls
Carson
DeFrance
del Castillo
Dull
Green
Greene
Gringlesby
Hunter
Karsen
Locksley
MacFeather
McBadden
O'Leary
Panteley
Ringer
Ringer
Smith
Straight
Stringer
White
(22 row(s) affected)
```

DBCC TRACEON

SQL Server has four flags which may be used for analyzing index selection and *join* clauses. These are the *DBCC TRACEON/TRACEOFF flags* as shown in Table 3.2.

Partial DBCC trace flag 302 information is shown for the query below. Not all of the output is given, but enough is shown here to illustrate how the optimizer attempts to make decisions based upon different costs. Reviewing this output may be useful if the optimizer is not using an index that you expect would be useful. By reviewing the output, you can observe which search arguments it considered, and how many rows it thought would match. This output is quite cryptic, and should probably only be reviewed when other attempts to understand the plan have failed.

```
DBCC TRACEON(3604, 302)
go
SELECT title
FROM titles t, titleauthor ta
WHERE t.title_id = ta.titleauthor_id
AND ta.royaltyper > 50
```

Partial trace 302 output

```
********************************
Leaving q_init_sclause() for table 'titles' (vamo 0).
The table has 18 rows and 3 pages.
Cheapest index is index 0, costing 3 pages per scan.
********************************
Leaving q_init_sclause() for table 'titleauthor' (varno 1).
The table has 25 rows and 1 pages.
Cheapest index is index 0, costing 1 pages per scan.
********************************
Entering q_score_index() for table 'titleauthor' (varno 1).
The table has 25 rows and 1 pages.
Scoring the search clause:
AND (!:0xf08de2) (andstat:0xa)
 GT (L:0xf08dc2) (rsltype:0x38 rsllen:4 rslprec:10 rslscale:0
 opstat:0x8)
   VAR (L:0xf08d58) (varname:royaltyper right:f08da8 varno:1
   colid:4 colstat:0x8 coltype:0x26 colen:4 coloff:-4 colprec:10
   colscale:0 vartypeid:7 varnext:f08cd4 varusecnt:1 varstat:90
   varlevel:0 varsubq:0)
   INT4 (R:0xf08da8) (len:4 maxlen:4 prec:2 scale:0 value:50)
Cheapest index is index 0, costing 1 pages and generating 8 rows per scan.
 Search argument selectivity is 0.330000.
********************************


********************************
Entering q_score_join() for table 'titles' (varno 0).
The table has 18 rows and 3 pages.
Scoring the join clause:
AND (!:0xf08dd6) (andstat:0x2)
 EQ (L:0xf08d22) (rsltype:0x2f rsllen:255 rslprec:6 rslscale:0
 opstat:0x0)
     VAR (L:0xf08c66) (varname:title_id right:f08cd4 varno:0 colid:1
     coltype:0x27 colen:6 coloff:-1 colprec:6 colscale:0 vartypeid:102
     varnext:f08b48 varusecnt:1 varstat:84 varlevel:0 varsubq:0)
     VAR (R:0xf08cd4) (varname:title_id varno:1 colid:2 coltype:0x27
     colen:6 coloff:-2 colprec:6 colscale:0 vartypeid:102 varusecnt:1
     varlevel:0 varsubq:0)
Unique clustered index found--return rows 1 pages 2
Cheapest index is index 1, costing 2 pages and generating 1 rows per scan.
 Join selectivity is 18.
********************************
```

TABLE 3.2 DBCC TRACEON/TRACEOFF Flags

Flags	Purpose
302	Optimizer index selection information
310	Optimizer *join* analysis output
3604	DBCC output is sent to the screen
3605	DBCC output is sent to the *errorlog*

SET Statement

The SET statement affects the behavior of a connection. Table 3.3 shows how SET statements cause the server to change its normal behavior or to provide extra information about the processing of commands across the current connection.

TABLE 3.3 SET Commands That Provide Additional Information about Information Within a Connection

SET Commands	Purpose
SET NOEXEC	Executing the SET statement with the NOEXEC parameter compiles a query plan but doesn't execute the query. This allows you to examine query plans without actual execution. To use this feature execute SET NOEXEC ON on the connection (from ISQL/w or other tool). To allow queries to execute, issue SET NOEXEC OFF.
SET PARSEONLY	The syntax of a query statement can be checked without generating a query tree or an execution plan. Use it as a tool for query building. To use this feature execute SET PARSEONLY ON. Use the OFF parameter if normal query processing is desired.
SET SHOWPLAN	This statement generates a description of the query processing plan and immediately executes the plan unless the NOEXEC feature is ON. To use this feature execute SET SHOWPLAN ON. It can also be used from ISQL/w by selecting the *plan* from the command button at the bottom left of the ISQL/w screen.
SET STATISTICS IO	If this feature is enabled, it displays the number of scans, the number of logical reads (cache pages accessed), and the number of physical disk I/O reads for each table in the query. To enable this feature execute SET STATISTICS IO ON. To disable it, use the OFF parameter.
SET STATISTICS TIME	When set, displays the time in milliseconds required to parse and compile each command. This feature is enabled with SET STATISTICS TIME ON. The parameter OFF disables this feature.

Show Query Plan (ISQL/W)

This ISQL/W feature is activated by selecting the *wrench* from the ISQL/W toolbar, and then selecting *Show Query Plan* from the dialog box. The output is not as comprehensive as SET SHOWPLAN, but both SET SHOWPLAN and *Show Query Plan* may be used simultaneously.

Stats_Date( )

This a new system function which tells you the last time the index statistics for a given table was updated. On previous releases this was a serious problem—there was no way to know when the index statistics had been updated. For regularly updated tables, an UPDATE STATISTICS is needed periodically. Good examples of indexes which should be updated regularly are indexes on date-time columns or columns that are surrogate keys. This function requires two parameters, the **object_id** of the table, and the **index_id** of the index. The following example obtains the last date that index statistics were updated for all of the indexes on the sales table:

```
select stats_date(id,indid)
FROM sysindexes
WHERE id=object_id('sales')
AND indid != 0
```

Update Statistics

Update statistics recalculates the steps in the distribution page. Using UPDATE STATISTICS *table_name* will update the distribution statistics for all indexes on the table. Updating the distribution page for a single index is done with UPDATE STATISTICS *table_name index_name*.

Updating of statistics can also be done from Enterprise Manager. When a table is selected in Enterprise Manager, from the tool/bar select *Manage,* select *Indexes,* select *Distribution,* and then select *Update* from the command button at the bottom of the dialog box. You have the choice of making this a batch job and updating all statistics on the table or only one.

Communicating with SQL Server

SQL Server must be used in conjunction with other development tools to create an application. In order to access your server, you will either write your own programs using the DB-Library or ODBC APIs, or you will use products that provide an interface using these APIs. We start this section with discussions of DB-Library and ODBC programming. We then introduce Open Data Services (ODS). This is another API that allows you to extend the capabilities of your client/server environment by writing servers, or providing additional functionality that can be called from your SQL Server.

Using DB-Library with SQL Server

DB-Library is the C-language native API for SQL Server and is a component of the Programmer's Toolkit found in the single-user license version of SQL Server. DB-Library utilizes the data stream protocol *Tabular Data Stream* (*TDS*), used by Open Data Services for SQL Server and SQL Server for the most efficient communication. DB-Library also offers specialized support for bulk copy and two-phased commit between multiple servers.

Setup

DB-Library *Setup* will install the following files in *<drive:>\SQL60\DBLIB\LIB*. *These are the client-side files required for DB-Library application development.*

BLDBLIB.LIB	Borland large-model DB-Library static library for MS-DOS.
BMDBLIB.LIB	Borland medium-model DB-Library static library for MS-DOS.
MSDBLIB3.LIB	DB-Library import library for Windows.
NTWDBLIB.LIB	DB-Library import library for Win32.
RLDBLIB.LIB	Large-model DB-Library static library for MS-DOS.
RMDBLIB.LIB	Medium-model DB-Library static library for MS-DOS.
W3DBLIB.LIB	Old DB-Library import library for Windows. (Use MSDBLIB3.LIB, not W3DBLIB.LIB.)

Dynamic Link Libraries

DB-Library uses Dynamic Link Libraries (DLLs) to provide an efficient run time environment. The architecture isolates the application program from different network protocols by using Net-Libraries. Net-Libraries are DLLs tailored to a specific network protocol. When the requesting DB-Library application opens a connection to the server with **dbopen,** the appropriate communication DLL is determined and loaded. This allows an application to be dynamically deployed against different network protocols. For MS-DOS, a terminate and stay resident routine (TSR) is used rather than a DLL and is limited to one active TSR being loaded at any given time. NET-Library supports Named Pipes, TCP/IP Sockets, DECnet, SPX, and VINES IP (see Figure 3.12).

DB-Library on NT

The use of DB-Library for C with Windows NT is unusually appealing in that the full resources of the Win32 API are available to the application developer. Full utilization of multiprocessor capabilities are available with multiple asyn-

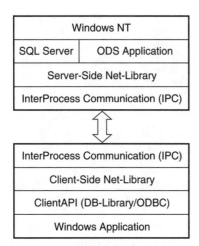

FIGURE 3.12 Net-Library/DB-Library Architecture.

chronous threads executing in support of a query. Numerous Win32 features of Windows NT such as *memory files* (virtual ram files which may be shared), synchronization with a *mutex* (exclusive ownership), signaling with a *semaphore* (controlling queue levels is one use), and locking of program resources with *critical section* are some of the tools available for use in mission-critical applications. Programming resources of this type are only available in DB-Library for C and not DB-Library for Visual Basic.

DB-Library—Simple Example

Communication between SQL Server and DB-Library is done with the following steps:

1. Connecting to SQL Server
2. Sending Transact-SQL statement in a buffer to SQL Server
3. Processing the results, if any are returned
4. Handling DB-Library and SQL Server error messages
5. Disconnecting from SQL Server

With these steps in mind, a successful DB-Library application requires the following:

1. An understanding of a DB-Library program structure
2. The ability to handle errors and still maintain concurrency
3. An understanding of the behavior of SQL Server
4. A thorough understanding of the client-side programming language

DB-Library provides the services to open connections, format queries, send query batches, and retrieve results. A typical structure of a DB-Library application is found in the example.

```
dbinit( )                              Initialize DB-Library. Can only be called once
        dblogin                        Allocates a LOGINREC structure for use in
                                         dbopen
              dbopen( )                Allocates and initializes a DBPROCESS
                                         structure
                  dbcmd( )             Add text to the DBPROCESS structure
                  dbsqlexec( )         Sends as batch, the text to SQL Server
                        dbresults( )               Initialize query result
                                                     processing
                        dbbind( )                  Bind column data to
                                                     variables
                        dbnextrow( )               Obtain a row
                        <process>
            dbclose( )                 Closes and frees DBPROCESS structure
dbwinexit                              Terminate DB-Library usage
```

The DB-Library function dbnextrow is procedurally oriented and will read a row directly from the server. There are other options, including routines that provide support for client-side and server-side cursors.

DB-Library Bulk Copy Service

DB-Library also provides a set of functions that can be called to do bulk copy. SQL Server does provide bulk copy services at both the command and graphical interface levels; however, both of these interfaces are limited in that the data must be in either a fixed format file or a file with fixed delimiters. The DB-Library special library provides tools which can be used for tailoring specialized bulk copy applications whose data format don't meet the contraints of the bcp command-line and graphical utilities.

DB-Library Two-Phase Commit Service

Application updates can be coordinated between multiple servers with the DB-Library two-phase commit service. One server is declared to be the *commit server* for distributed transactions and is the record keeper which provides a single point for recording that a commit has occurred. If any server participating in the two-phase commit transaction is unsure of the outcome, it can verify the state with the commit server. Even though there are multiple servers involved, the distributed transaction is treated as a single transaction. *In all systems, two-phase commit has performance, locking, and concurrency problems and should be used sparingly if at all.*

The application opens a session with each server, executes the update commands, and then prepares to commit the transaction. The application executes at each server a *Begin Transaction, Transact-SQL statements,* and a *Prepare Transaction.* In the first phase, all servers agree to commit and in the second phase they all commit. If an error occurs between phase one or two, all servers interrogate the *commit server* to see if the transaction should be committed or canceled. If any server fails before the *Prepare Transaction,* the transaction is rolled back. The problem becomes very complex when the commit service fails.

DB-Library with Visual Basic

In SQL Server Version 6, the DLL W3DBLIB.DLL has been replaced with the DLL MSDBLIB3.DLL. This is the DLL which maintains the DB-Library connection for Windows and is the same DLL used with the VBSQL.VBX of Visual Basic. (A VBX is unique to the Visual Basic 3 16-bit architecture, and will be replaced with an OCX in the Visual Basic 4 32-bit architecture.) The VBSQL.VBX module is based upon a subset of the DB-Library and is another component of the Programmer's Toolkit found in the workstation version of SQL Server. Visual Basic for DOS is supported with the VBDSQL.QLB module.

Visual Basic stands between Microsoft Access and Microsoft C in functionality. It is a higher level language than Microsoft C and is correspondingly easier to use. With that comes certain risks. Not all Visual Basic programmers understand SQL Server, and since they are used to dealing with a procedural language, they think procedurally and build less-than-optimal applications (see Chapter 8, Technical Discourses).

There are certainly fewer performance issues with VBSQL (DB-Library for Visual Basic), than with those of ODBC involving coding technique; however, a bad design will always be a bad design.

The following example is a typical program structure used by the Visual Basic VBSQL.VBX module to communicate with SQL Server.

```
SqlInit$()                       Initialize DB-Library for Visual Basic
     SqlOpen%()                  Allocate and initialize a SQL Server connection
          SqlCmd%()              Add Transact-SQL to the command buffer
          SqlExec%()             Send the Transact-SQL statements to SQL Server
              SqlResults()           Get a result set
                 SqlNextRow          Get a row
                    SqlData()        Get data from each column
     SqlClose()              Close a connection
SqlWinExit()               Inform DB-Library that the application is about to
                           exit
```

This communication mechanism is synchronous when using the *SQLExec* command performing the combined duties of *SQLSend, SQLDataReady,* and *SQLOk.* SQL Server communication becomes asynchronous when these commands are used individually in lieu of the *SQLExec.*

We have been discussing DB-Library for the Visual Basic application. The Visual Basic programmer actually has other options for communicating with SQL Server.

1. The default database communication path for Visual Basic is the Jet engine of Access which uses **ODBC** from the *DeskTop Driver Set* (see following section). There is extra overhead with Jet-ODBC and it is slower.

2. Another option for the Visual Basic programmer is to bypass the extra overhead of Jet and connect directly to ODBC (see following section). ODBC applications are more difficult to program because all drivers are not written to the same API or SQL conformance level, and the application program must provide the missing functionality.

3. The third option is to use VBSQL.VBX which has a performance very nearly equal to DB-Library since it uses the DB-Library DLL.

ODBC

While DB-Library is an interface that provides an interface only to SQL Server, ODBC provides a single-user common client interface to numerous databases in a heterogeneous database environment. ODBC has become an industry standard for interconnecting databases and is based upon the Call Level Interface (CLI) of the SQL Access Group (SAG). The interface, being vendor neutral, allows client applications to access, view, and update diverse and multiple databases stored in a variety of personal computer, minicomputer, and mainframe DBMSs. ODBC was designed to allow application developers to decide between using the least common denominator of functionality across DBMSs or exploiting the individual characteristics of specific DBMSs. The major advantage of using the ODBC interface is that the developer can write one set of source code, change the ODBC driver (or change the driver *handle* in the application), and have the application talk to a different DBMS.

Microsoft has licensed the OBDC specification to Visigenic, Inc. for use on Unix platforms and numerous other companies have released ODBC products. ODBC may also be found in Visual C++ 2.0 and Visual Basic 3.0 Professional Edition. The ODBC SDK 2.0, designed for use on Windows NT or Windows 3.1, is available on the MSDN-II CD-ROM, which includes both 16- and 32-bit versions. Products such as Microsoft Excel and Microsoft Access contain the *Desktop Driver Set,* a suite of ODBC drivers.

The ODBC architecture includes a very rich API, a driver manager which the API calls (isolating the application from the drivers), and drivers written to API and SQL grammar conformance levels. The ODBC SDK includes the ODBC Spy tool which is used for application emulation and the tool ODBC Test which is used to test driver conformance level.

To provide the vendor neutral environment, ODBC is defined with three levels of API (application program interface) and three levels of SQL grammar conformance. A unique benefit of this approach is that applications can communicate with diverse databases, each having varying dialects of SQL, and yet the application developer uses only ODBC SQL. The SQL driver has the responsibility of converting the ODBC SQL to the SQL of the proprietary database. If the ODBC driver doesn't recognize the SQL command, (such as SQL Server *USE*), then the ODBC driver forwards the SQL directly to the data source in what is called *pass-through.*

This database independence is possible only with compliance to the API and SQL Grammar conformance levels. Driver writers are encouraged to support the Level 1 API (at a minimum); however, not all ODBC drivers support the same level of interoperability. Proper API and SQL Grammar conformance levels are a major issue. Features such as a scrollable cursor, retrieving or sending parameters, or browsing a connection for information *are not required to be supported by the ODBC API conformance level for Visual Basic or Access even though the language, SQL Server, or the ODBC driver may provide functionality beyond the required conformance level.*[5]

Typical ODBC Usage

An application allocates an environment and then connects to a data source. A statement is allocated, prepared, and executed. The results are returned and the program ends each transaction by either committing it or rolling it back. How the processing is accomplished will determine the system response time. *The functional structure of the order in which ODBC functions are called can cause the programmer to think in* procedural *rather than* relational *terms.*

Both the ODBC API and ODBC from the *DeskTop Driver Set* are illustrated in Figures 3.13 and 3.14. Visual Basic or Access may use either one.

ODBC Implementation Considerations

If the application requirements include features that are not provided with the selected ODBC driver in an interoperable environment, then a decision must be made as to whether or not to provide the missing functionality. For example, the datatype *timestamp*, which is used as a tool to enforce concurrency, is

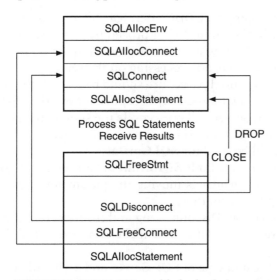

FIGURE 3.13 ODBC API, usable by both Access and Visual Basic.

OpenDatabase
   Database.CreateDynaset
     Dynaset.MoveNext
       Dynaset.Fields
   Dynaset.AddNext
   Dynaset.Update
   Dynaset.Delete
   Database.ExecuteSQL
Database.Close
	Set MyWorkspace = DB Engine.Workspaces (0)
	Set MyDB = MyWorkspace.Databases (0)
	Set MyQuery = MyDB.CreateQueryDef (" ")
	SourceConnectStr = "ODBC;DSN =..."
	MyQuery.Connect = SourceConnectStr
	MyQuery.ReturnsRecords = True
	My Query.SQL = "sp_who"
	Set MySet = MyQuery.OpenRecordSet()
	For I = 0 to MySet.Fields.Count-1

Visual Basic	Access

FIGURE 3.14 ODBC from the DeskTop Driver Set (Jet) for both Access and Visual Basic.

only available as a datatype in Extended SQL Grammar. If the selected driver does not support Extended SQL Grammar, then another means must be used to control concurrency.

The design issues can become exceedingly complex when the API and SQL Grammar conformance levels are not known in advance to the application developer. In this case, the developer will use the **SQLGetInfo, SQLGetFunctions,** and **SQLGetTypeInfo** functions which returns over seventy values of driver specific information. The application then makes a decision about the features to support at execution time. If the driver is available during application design, the ODBC Test tool can be used to evaluate driver conformance levels.

ODBC Performance Issues

Performance can be an issue with ODBC usage as a SQL Server interface. Keep the following issues in mind in order to maintain an efficient application:

◆ Programmers developing an ODBC interface will tend to have a procedural programming background. Using procedural processing rather than set processing techniques will have a negative impact on system performance. Wherever possible, do processing on the server.

◆ Whenever possible, a stored procedure should be used. If the statement is dynamic and used in a loop then **SQLPrepare** followed by **SQLExecute** should be used. SQL Server will precompile the statement and cache it so that it need not be recompiled on each pass of a processing loop.

◆ **SQLBindCol** should be used for **SQLGetData.**

◆ For input parameters use both **SQLBindParameter** and **SQLPrepare.** Another solution to consider is moving the parameters to a work table and do a batch update from there.

◆ Maintain the connection. Disconnecting and reconnecting can be expensive in terms of resources. Of course if the connection isn't being used, then terminate it.

◆ Fetch the data in the datatype of SQL Server and do it with a block fetch, **SQLExtendedFetch.**

♦ Only use canonical SQL Server functions.[6] As an example, if an Access application has a statement that reads, ". . . where value = Date( )", then the complete recordset will be moved to the client for processing since **Date( )** is a valid Access function, but not a valid SQL Server function.

♦ When the application starts, cache static catalog information obtained with **SQLGetTypeInfo.**

♦ Evaluate scrolling very carefully. Backward scrolling in ODBC is resource intensive. Consider using the new scrolling features of SQL Server. A viable option might be to move the data set to the client and do the scrolling there.

♦ Positioned updates and deletes will be faster on some databases. For SQL Server, if possible, make sure that you understand the rules for update-in-place, and that most of your updates meet these rules.

♦ Don't use the functions **SQLTables, SQLColumns,** or **SQLPrimaryKeys** unless absolutely necessary. If you do need to call them, then cache the information.

Extending SQL Server with Open Data Services

Unlike DB-Library which allows the developer to design client applications that share a common client protocol, *Open Data Services* (*ODS*) allows the developer to create server applications which communicate with a common server protocol. ODS supports many types of client applications running on a variety of operating systems and includes support for simultaneous client connections over several types of local area network protocols (see Figure 3.15). ODS is a component of the Programmer's Toolkit provided with the workstation version of SQL Server. ODS is a licensed product and the user must have a separate ODS run-time license for each server on which the ODS application will run. Licenses for embedded copies of ODS are also available to application vendors.

Extended Stored Procedures and Remote Stored Procedures

ODS is a server-based Microsoft API used for creating two types of applications. In addition to server applications, ODS can be used to extend features of the SQL Server by directly adding *extended stored procedures*. Extended stored procedures are functions written in C and compiled and linked into DLLs. They can execute any functionality you can develop in C. These extended stored procedures can be used to expand SQL Server functionality. Adding an extended stored procedure is illustrated with:

```
sp_addextendedproc 'xp_proclist', 'xp_dll'
```

For example, SQL Server triggers can be used to initiate extended stored procedures as the result of an update. In an inventory application, a trigger using

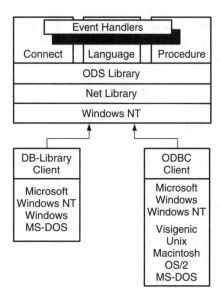

FIGURE 3.15 ODS architecture.

an extended stored procedure could start an inventory reorder or another user application. The event which caused a trigger has now linked the SQL Server to an application rather than to another SQL Server function

Triggers, stored procedures, or batches can execute a *remote stored procedure*. Remote stored procedures allow a client on one SQL Server to execute a stored procedure on another SQL Server without establishing a connection to that second server. *Remote procedure* calls may be initiated by a client or a server. When SQL Server receives a remote procedure call from a client which specifies a server name that refers to an ODS server application, the request is forwarded to the ODS application. Any returned data will be returned by the ODS application and is then forwarded to the client application. The returned output parameters from the remote stored procedures can be used in subsequent statements.

Another example is the stockbroker who must constantly monitor particular security issues. Continual querying (polling) will be expensive in terms of both client and server resources. System performance can be improved significantly if a trigger is defined which would activate an extended stored procedure which would send a message or initiate an external process whenever the security issue price is changed by a percentage.

Remote stored procedures can be used to capture specialized data. Data may be returned as the result parameter of a remote stored procedure. An example is maintaining the current value of a currency in a currency-exchange application. An automated approach is to have SQL Server call a remote stored procedure to obtain the current currency value. This technique provides an almost instantaneous update transparent to the user with the single value being returned as a return parameter of the remote stored procedure. In this application, SQL Server has the unlikely role of being a client.

Using ODS to Create a Server Application

ODS can also be used to create a server application which looks like a SQL Server on the network. Both SQL Server and ODS support the same data stream protocol, Tabular Data Stream (TDS). This means that an ODS application will be a server to the client and could in turn be a client of SQL Server. Client communication will be with DB-Library except for gateways which might use the ODBC Gateway driver.

An ODS application can run as a server process functioning as a gateway in a three-tier system interfacing to other databases. The ODS data source may be a relational or a nonrelational database. The ODBC architecture has API and SQL conformance standards which enable an application to interface more than one database simultaneously. ODS gateways, however, generally do not support the exact same features as SQL Server. This standard SQL Server ODBC driver expects all SQL Server features to be supported and would not work transparently in a gateway environment. The ODS gateway driver for ODBC is designed to specifically connect ODBC client applications to gateway applications. (There are other gateway products which allow various DBMSs to appear to any TDS client as a TDS server, often like a SQL Server).

The ODS ODBC driver is a three-tier version of the SQL Server ODBC driver, designed to connect to a back-end data source via an intermediate ODS gateway. Only ODBC can be used in a heterogeneous environment. DB-Library is proprietary to SQL Server and VBSQL. VBX uses the DB-Library DLL. It is also designed to adapt to the features of the back-end data source. As with most ODBC applications, additional functionality can be provided by the developer at the client level.

However, a gateway server need not be used to connect to only foreign databases. A gateway server can be used for pass-through to SQL Server for either a security or auditing applications. Clients must make a direct connection to the ODS server application and the ODS server application must be configured to connect as a client of SQL Server.

Building the ODS Application

The ODS API consists of C functions and macros used for creating applications. The API includes an ODS library which is the layer between Net-Library and three classes of event handlers: *connect event handler, language event handler,* and a *procedure event handler.* Programming an ODS application is not unlike programming Windows events. There is an event for many DB-Library commands. Table 3.4 shows the DB-Library calls that interface to an ODS server application and the specific event that is the result.

NT, and hence SQL Server, is scalable from Intel CISC processors to MIPS or DEC Alpha RISC processors. This is possible since all common code of the operating system is written in a high-level language. Hardware interfacing is with HAL, the Hardware Abstraction Layer. The ODS Library is a complete client manager. ODS handles all the complexities of managing and communicating with multiple clients. An application handling many clients will have many instances of an event handler, each with their own thread. Thread pooling is used to accommodate a large number of clients. With multiple threads, ODS is able to take advantage of the multiprocessor capabilities of Windows NT.

Stubs enable the developer to define their own data management routines in response to events when developing remote stored procedures. The developer determines what data should be returned to a client or what action should be taken for an event and writes code for that event. There is no need to worry about blocking other clients with protracted processing; however, the developer will have to provide an appropriate protection mechanism for global parameters.

A Sample ODS Gateway Application

An ODS server is used differently than an extended stored procedure where the client connects to SQL Server. For an ODS gateway server, the client application connects directly to the ODS application.

Microsoft provides a sample gateway application in the Programmer's Toolkit provided with the workstation version of SQL Server. This sample gateway may be customized, but since the purpose of a gateway is for pass-through of information, very little customization will be required. The only modifications possible are to the resources DLL, which consists of four files and ODBC.INI. As in most ODBC applications, missing functionality is usually provided by the application.

ODS server applications and SQL Server databases communicate on the network using remote procedure calls.[7] Connection to Open Data Services is also done with remote procedure calls using protocols which support either *named pipes* or *sockets*. (A *local pipe* is used if ODS and SQL Server are on the same computer.) The connection is made from an installable NET-Library

TABLE 3.4 Building an ODS Application

DB-Library Call	*ODS Event Activated*	*Description of Event*
dbcancel	srv_attention	Interrupt request
dbclose	srv_disconnect	Disconnect request
dbopen	srv_connect	Connect request
dbsqlexec	srv_language	Language request
dbrpcsend	srv_rpc	Remote stored procedure request

after ODS listens for connection requests (from clients and from servers) on multiple network protocols simultaneously.

ODS Security

Security is handled by using the technique of *impersonation* for access to Windows NT facilities. The ODS application can issue the Win32 API function **ImpersonateNamedPipeClient** and the ODS application then assumes the access privileges of the requesting client. Security can be implemented by creating a unique key in the Windows NT Registry and assigning access privileges to it. While impersonating the user, the ODS application attempts to access the key previously placed in the registry which then determines the user's authorization.

Installing the ODS Server

Registering an ODS server application as a gateway server for SQL Server is illustrated with:

```
gateway -rregistry_key_name -sservername
```

Clients of ODS servers which are not gateways will use the normal client driver for ODBC. Any client application which can connect to SQL Server can connect to an ODS server application.

Registering a server is illustrated by:

```
sp_configure 'remote access", 1
reconfigure with override
sp_addserver SERVNAME
```

Open Data Service server applications can also be installed as a Windows NT service that responds to Windows NT commands such as *net start, net stop,* and *net pause.* Windows NT services must use the Win32 API to register with the Service Control Manager.

Very Large Database Issues (VLDB)

Scalability of Hardware

The Very Large Database (VLDB) of yesterday is the commonplace database today. The business community today uses systems described as Online Transaction Processing (OLTP), Online Analytical Processing (OLAP), and Decision Support Systems (DSS), all of which have a voracious appetite for data. These systems are either doing or are expected to do in the very near future tasks that were only theoretical a few years ago. Keeping all transactions on line for the last eight years, data warehousing, and mining data for hidden demographics or buying patterns are some examples of the applications for large databases. As we write this, we are familiar with SQL Server applications with 100Gb of data.

The adoption of object-oriented technology by the software community has rapidly escalated software functionality, and the spiraling hardware performance curve has helped to fuel this demand. An example is the Alpha chip by Digital, which uses Microsoft Windows NT as the host operating system for SQL Server. The performance of this chip is currently in the 300 Mhz range and is scalable to 750 MHz. Now what is really exciting is that SQL Server, which can support databases in the 50Gb+ range, sells for less than $1,000 without client licenses. The cost of a four-processor 325 MHz DEC Alpha 210 with 512Mb of memory and 50Gb of hot-pluggable SCSI disks can be contrasted with a recent advertisement:

> For Sale: CRAY X-MP Supercomputer. 5 years old, original cost $12 million. With all support equipment, ready to use. Asking $30,000 or best offer.
>
> —*Atlanta Journal and Constitution*

If you want to review current Transaction Processing Council (TPC) benchmarks, you can go to the TPC web page at http://www.tpc.com. These benchmarks give you one way to compare different platforms and RDBMSs. The summary report for some benchmarks is available on the web page.

As Windows expands, SQL Server may be moved to other Windows NT platforms with little effort.

Windows NT will soon expand beyond multiprocessing. Within the recent past, Microsoft has signed a contract with Digital Equipment Corporation (DEC) to license the clustering technology of OpenVMS. This seems ideal for the distributed Windows NT architecture. This is the missing link in the Microsoft architecture. Clustering will give automatic system fail-over. Currently there is software fail-over in different software subsystems within Windows NT, an example being the Primary Domain Controller (PDC) failing over to a Backup Domain Controller (BDC), which is transparent to users. There is also software and hardware RAID technology available for Windows NT which provides redundancy for disk subsystems. Clustering completes the Windows NT architecture.

Symmetric Server Architecture

Microsoft SQL Server has a distinct advantage over those DBMSs which include operating system functionality. Microsoft SQL Server cooperates very closely with Windows NT and does not attempt to micromanage operating system functions. In a multiprocessor environment, scheduling of work on other processors is done by the Windows NT operating system and not by the SQL Server.

Database vendors today claim support for symmetric multiprocessors (SMP), and then proceed to bind a process to a CPU. Resources are consumed by threads, not by processes (a process is the overall task with a unique memory space and threads are the constituents of this process), so there is no guarantee that the processor load will be balanced. It may be multiprocessing with different tasks (processes) on different CPUs, and it may even be a SMP in a loose sense. These processes are then faced with the problem of interprocess communication since each process runs in its own address space; however, interprocess communication can still be accomplished with shared memory. Within Windows NT, and hence within SQL Server, thread execution is scheduled by the operating system and interprocess communication problems are minimized.

Unlike database management systems which use a dedicated transaction processing monitor and micromanage the operating system, Microsoft SQL Server does not attempt to usurp scheduling management functions of the operating systems, but instead uses them to its advantage. The Symmetric Server Architecture (SSA) of Microsoft SQL Server schedules threads, not processes, on a processor basis. Multiple threads for a single SELECT statement may be simultaneously running on more than one processor. Note that each of these threads, while on different processors, have the same address space and interprocess communication does not exist since the threads occupy the same address space. Interprocess communication is now simplified. SQL Server is able to manage this multitasking environment with Win32 features such as *Mutex, Mutant* (rather fun names), *Critical Section* (resource lock management), and *Semaphore*. A *Mutex* controls exclusive access to kernel objects and a *Mutant* controls access to either kernel or user-mode objects.

We see that the design of SQL Server has addressed three major issues for scalability:

1. *Processor loading:* Threads are scheduled on a processor basis by Windows NT so effective load balancing occurs. This does not happen when processes are bound to a unique CPU.
2. *Interprocess communication:* This problem doesn't exist since all threads have the same address space.
3. *Minimized system overhead:* Threads are scheduled by the Windows NT operating system at the behest of SQL Server, but since the threads all have the same address space and are elements of the same process, there is minimal system overhead.

A Distributed Operating System

Windows NT is not a monolithic operating system. In fact, you might call it a distributed operating system. For example, there is the WINS server for NetBIOS name resolution. It can be on a different computer in the domain, and not the SQL Server computer. The same is true for SNA server and the Systems Management Server (SMS). Even SQL server can have a separate distribution server for replication. And of course we can't forget the Primary Domain Controller (PDC) and the Backup Domain Controllers (BDCs). Optimal performance of SQL Server is possible when SQL Server is on a Windows NT system which is running no other subsystems. If SQL Server is placed on a node which functions as a Primary Domain Controller (PDC) or Backup Domain Controller (BDC), then performance will not be optimal since there will be significant context. The only context switching in a dedicated SQL Server environment when placed in a resource domain will be with kernal service requests or those activities directly supported by SQL Server, such as replication.

RAID0, RAID1, and RAID5[8]

The *Symmetric Server Architecture* (*SSA*), of Microsoft SQL Server includes software support for RAID0, RAID1, and RAID5, which are striping, mirroring, and striping with parity. Another alternative is RAID5 defined at the hardware level. RAID5 defined at the hardware level is a very attractive storage medium, since disks are hot-pluggable.

When defined as a part of the Windows NT system, striping will be used transparently by SQL Server for backup and restore with loading now done in 64K units to improve performance. However SQL Server gives the administrator the capability to manage SQL Server stripe sets. This is illustrated with:

```
DUMP DATABASE pubs to diskdump1, diskdump2, diskdump3, diskdump4
```

The SQL Server administrator now has three choices:

1. Transparent striping at the hardware level (SCSI RAID5 Array)
2. Transparent striping at the operating system level (Windows NT)
3. Managed striping to SQL Server dump devices

For managed striping, the *sysdevices* table is used to locate devices in a stripe set with the number of threads determined by a configuration parameter. The default setting is 5 with a maximum of 32 backup threads.

Parallel Processing

The Symmetric Server Architecture (SSA) for SQL Server includes parallel read-ahead buffering. Multiple read-ahead threads can be scheduled on different processors for RAID5 storage arrays or stripe sets. Parallel read ahead can be used for:

◆ Scanning the leaf level of an index
◆ A table scan (no index used)

♦ Reading a text chain
♦ Scanning consecutive data pages for a range (index used to locate starting point of range)

Performance of queries in DSS will improve when pages are read from disk. Speed of all operations will improve for such operations as using a table scan, DBCC operations, UPDATE STATISTICS, text/image operations, and SELECTs in which an index is not used.

Read Ahead can be managed. The *sp_configure* option **show advanced options** can be used to set read ahead parameters. Table 3.5 shows the parameters for the Read Ahead default configuration values.

An administrator should have a thorough understanding of these parameters before attempting to make any configuration changes. In the default values listed in Table 3.5, the 5 worker slots times the 3 worker threads equals support for 15 concurrent Read Ahead (RA) scans. Defining too many concurrent scans *will defeat the purpose of RA*. Read Ahead is not done automatically on a table scan but only after the systems notes that a scan is in process and may initiate an additional thread.

Lock Management

Lock escalation can be a problem on a large database. In prior versions of SQL Server, when a process obtained more than 200 locks, the lock type was escalated to a table lock and all other users were locked out. This is a very untenable situation for a VLDB. With Version 6, locks can now be managed.

♦ No locking will occur if the database is set to *read-only* or *single user* mode.
♦ Escalation to a table lock may be based upon a percentage of the table size.
♦ Minimum and maximum values before escalation may also be set. The *sp_configure* option **show advanced options** can be used to set lock escalation parameters as shown in Table 3.6.

TABLE 3.5 The Parameters for the Default Configuration Values for Read Ahead Processing

Name	Minimum	Maximum	Configuration	Run Value
RA cache hit limit	1	255	4	4
RA cache miss limit	1	255	3	3
RA delay	0	500	15	15
RA prefetches	1	1000	3	3
RA slots per thread	1	255	5	5
RA worker threads	0	255	3	3

TABLE 3.6 Default Lock Configuration Values

Name	Minimum	Maximum	Configuration	Run Value
LE threshold maximum	2	500,000	200	200
LE threshold minimum	2	500,000	20	20
LE threshold percentage	1	100	0	0

Notes

1. Jim Gray and Andreas Reuter, *Transaction Processing Concepts and Techniques* (Morgan Kaufmann Publishers, 1993).
2. Jim Panttaja, "Defining and Using Useful Indexes", *SQL Forum*, Sept./Oct., 1991.
3. M. Tamer Ozsu and Patrick Valduriez, *Principles of Distributed Database Systems*, Chapter 8, "Query Decomposition" (Englewood Cliffs, N.J.: Prentice-Hall, 1991).
4. We only recommend that you force the use of specific indexes as a tool in investigating a problem query. In most cases, there are other actions you can take to insure the use of the appropriate index. Some of the steps you can consider are updating statistics, making sure that the appropriate index really exists, making sure that you are using the same datatype in your queries, and minimizing the use of variables in your where clauses.
5. Microsoft ODBC 2.0, Programmer's Reference and SDK Guide (Microsoft Press), pp. 12–14.
6. The Date( ) function is valid in Access and not SQL Server, so SQL Server will return the record set to Access for filtering rather than just returning a result set.
7. Microsoft SQL Server, Programming Open Data Services, pp. 144–145.
8. Other RAID implementations are only intermediate solutions and are not commonly used.

Project Life Cycle

The software development endeavor is a complex one. Traditionally the industry has evolved methods and structures with which to understand, organize, and control the development process. Many of these techniques and structures continue to be useful and important while developing with the client/server architecture supported by Microsoft's SQL Server Version 6. Out of existing strategies and methods, the industry has evolved successful implementation methods and ways of structuring the vast number of technical disciplines involved in the new architectures.

An implementation methodology must map and organize the key elements of project development: technical capabilities, technical facilities, personnel, and time. It needs to define a clear sequence of steps, a complete list of deliverables, explanations of how, explanations of why, guidelines for controlling the process, and a complete descriptive structure of the system. This chapter will not provide a complete presentation of a methodology, but will attempt to outline some of the issues that must be addressed.

We will discuss four major elements:

1. *Disciplines:* Consider the technologies involved in client/server development and the use of these technologies.

2. *Timing:* Applies the concept of time to the process under discussion as project management sequences with an emphasis on the advantages and challenges of iterative development.
3. *Management issues:* What is involved in controlling the process?
4. *Standards:* With respect to process and the software deliverables.

This is not intended to be a thorough discussion of any of these topics, but an introduction to lay the groundwork for understanding the complexities of the platforms and processes involved in **SQL Server** development.

Disciplines, Skills, and Tasks

Disciplines, skills, and tasks are a structured way to look at the myriad complex technologies and issues that are involved in the development process. One of the problems with this environment is its extreme complexity. Client/server was not designed to make the software engineer's or administrator's job easier. (It enables complex, distributed systems based on heterogeneous platforms.) Much of the information available is from vendors and clarifies a particular topic or product. For someone new to the environment, it is almost impossible to distinguish how the technologies relate to each other, much less how to use them. Not every technology is required (or desired) in each implementation effort.

Disciplines

A *discipline* is a group of tightly related technologies which provides a portion of a client/server system or of the client/server development process. They are used to group the technologies we encounter in the marketplace (shows, vendors, magazines). A detailed understanding of each of these disciplines is required to sort out which are important to your process and your system. As you evaluate new technology you can better understand where the value lies, and how you might make use of a particular technological innovation. Remember, this is just a way of looking at technology and as technology changes, though the technique still applies, the details will change.

In addition, these disciplines help us to categorize skills and tasks. There is an enormous set of skills required to accomplish the detailed tasks involved in the development and support processes. These disciplines help us to view the skill sets and tasks required. As you adopt a technology, you must acquire the knowledge to use that technology through additional personnel or training. *Training and continuous acquisition of new skills is a critical component of the corporate investment.*

The disciplines group into three principal arenas: *infrastructure, software development,* and *support and control.*

Infrastructure Arena

Infrastructure includes the technologies that are required to provide the underlying structure and architecture for a physical system. The structure of your developed system is based on the architecture and services that you install as the backbone. This can vary from simple two-tiered client/server (database server, network, and client application as shown in Figure 4.1) to a much more complex architecture with transaction monitors, complex communications, replication, and a more extensive array of services (see Figure 4.2 for an example). The number and nature of the products used will be dependent on the tasks you wish to accomplish with your systems. As the capabilities increase so does the complexity.

Disciplines associated with infrastructure include:

♦ Hardware
♦ Operating systems
♦ Networks
♦ Network operating systems
♦ DBMS
♦ Data warehouses
♦ Communications
♦ Web and internet services
♦ Other purchased services

These are the primary underpinnings of a complex system. You may have more than one version of each of these in a hetergeneous collection of clients and servers. That is what makes client/server and the concept of open systems so challenging.

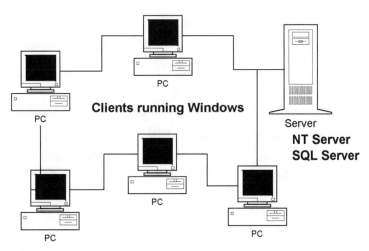

FIGURE 4.1 Two-tiered client/server system.

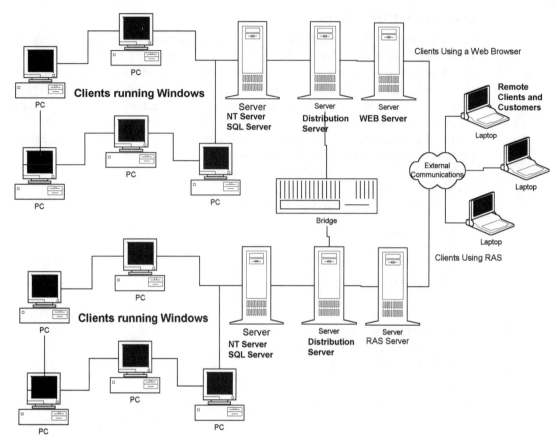

FIGURE 4.2 A more complex client/server system.

Software Development Arena

This arena includes those technologies that are part of the specific system or application development cycle. They contribute directly or indirectly to the development process. These disciplines have dynamically changed the process of building software in the last decade.

Disciplines associated with software development include:

♦ Database management systems (DBMS)
  ♦ Relational database management systems (RDBMS)
  ♦ Object-oriented database management systems (OODBMS)
♦ Graphical user interfaces
♦ Object-oriented technology
♦ Client/server development: cooperative processing
♦ Analysis and design
♦ Programming

Many of these are recognizable from reading the media and listening to vendors. Some are not. Cooperative processing architecture is a field that is sorely neglected by many vendors. (How do you make it all work together?) As you evaluate a new technology, you must understand how it explicitly comes to bear on the development cycle. There are many aspects to each discipline and it is critical to understand how it applies directly to the project life cycle.

Support and Control Arena

Many new technologies and new versions of old technologies are used to support the development process. All of these technologies have always been a part of the development process. Because the platforms and technologies used for development have changed, the techniques and tools for support have changed as well. Project management and control are very critical elements in the success of a project. These disciplines need particular attention if you are to be successful.

Disciplines associated with support and control include:

♦ Project management
♦ Development methodologies
♦ Documentation (user and internal)
♦ Version control and configuration management
♦ Testing
♦ Technical review
♦ Deployment and distribution

Many of these disciplines are well established, but need adjusting to deal with new design concepts, methods, and new technologies.

Skills and Tasks for Each Discipline

While not providing a complete enumeration of all possible skills and tasks involved in the development of a client/server system, we will briefly discuss some of the skills for each of the disciplines. A map can be constructed of the relationship of disciplines, skills, tasks, and time (see Figure 4.3). This is the basic project plan, a musical score for your client/server orchestration.

A *skill* is something that someone on a project must possess. That is, you must hire or train a person to accommodate each skill required by your system. A complete understanding of the disciplines and skills allows you to plan training and hiring. In addition, disciplines and skills are selectively enhanced by the adoption of tools or methods purchased or developed.

There are some standard *tasks* that must be accomplished for many of these disciplines. They deal with acquiring the hardware or software, understanding it, and getting ready to use it (research, training, evaluation, acquisi-

Arena: Software Development
Discipline: Relational Database
Skill: Performance Tuning
Task: Design and Test the Indexes

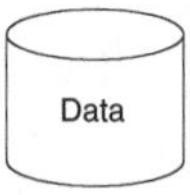

FIGURE 4.3 Hierarchy of disciplines, skills, and tasks.

tion, installation, and operational management). In most systems, you must first understand the current systems architecture with respect to the discipline. To plan for the future you must study the discipline and the marketplace, evaluate products, choose a product solution, and train personnel. You must acquire the item and install it. It is important to understand your system requirements within the constraints of your process or organization. It is not necessary to understand all of the possible technologies to construct a small discrete system.

For example, we have all heard of object-oriented technology. We think we need it. We try to get it. But, what are we getting? Object-oriented technology is not something you buy. It is a large, complex array of technologies, tools, and skills that apply to different aspects of software analysis, design, and implementation. It is not enough to know that you want to adopt object-oriented techniques. You have to understand how they apply to your process and which elements of the technology you want to adopt.

Hardware

The *hardware* required to support a client/server installation is quite extensive. In the early phases of this market it was called *downsizing* because it was viewed as a way to move off the mainframe onto smaller, less-expensive hardware. In reality, costs can go up or down. In all cases, the promise of open systems is that you can interoperate various systems of various sizes. Everything in the system can be right-sized for your requirements.

Hardware, of course, includes computers of various sizes—servers and client hardware. It also includes network hardware and protocols, interfaces between networks (routers and bridges), externally supplied network services (T1, ISDN, and so on), printers, fax machines, storage devices (disks, optical devices, jukeboxes, and tape drives), modems, and memory configurations (solid state memory). The list is endless and getting longer.

Skills for the hardware discipline include:

♦ Hardware installation
♦ Hardware integration
♦ System administration
♦ Routing and communications for LAN/WAN
♦ External communications

Operating Systems

Operating systems are the core software platform on which you will build your system. It is a more important decision than the hardware in many cases. It is critical that you understand the functionality and interoperability of the various operating systems. In addition, existing requirements and established protocols can create limitations in operating system choices.

Skills for the operating systems discipline include:

♦ Operating system installation
♦ System administration
♦ Monitoring
♦ Security
♦ Performance and tuning

Networks and Network Operating Systems (NOS)

The basis of client/server architecture is the *network* and the software ability to parse application logic into multiple processes that can be deployed on various platforms connected by a network. Networks are the hardware and software that enable communication between systems. They provide communication, messaging, security services, and location transparency (see Figure 4.4).

Skills for the network discipline include:

♦ Network installation
♦ Network operating system installation
♦ System administration
♦ Security
♦ Interoperability
♦ Performance and tuning
♦ External communications (Internet, Web, and so on)

Data Management Systems

Most client/server systems use a *relational database system* for primary data storage. This is the current leading technology for managing data. While its success has been a key factor in the success and growth of client/server computing, it is not an architectural requirement for client/server computing. Some client/server systems can be deployed without database management at all. In the future, we may see the growth of other primary data management systems including object-oriented databases.

Understanding, installing, programming, and managing a relational database system like SQL Server will be one of the major focuses of the development process.

Skills for the data management discipline include:

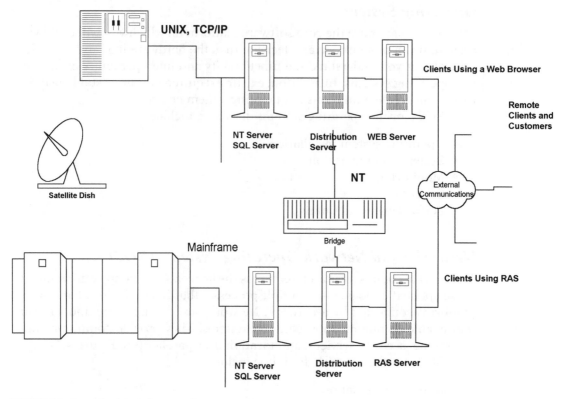

FIGURE 4.4 Complexities of networks.

- ♦ Entity/relationship analysis and design
- ♦ Data normalization
- ♦ RDBMS installation
- ♦ RDBMS programming
- ♦ SQL standard
- ♦ RDBMS performance and tuning
- ♦ RDBMS system administration
- ♦ All of the above for other DBMS

This discipline contains vast areas of required expertise and much of the training and experience base must be vendor-specific. A detailed understanding of the behavior of the system's optimizer and transaction management behavior is critical to writing successful SQL in an application.

Graphical User Interfaces (GUIs)

The deployment of applications in client/server is often associated with *graphical client applications*. The advent of stronger graphical development tools has moved client/server strongly in the area of graphical applications. Figure 4.5

shows an example of a typical GUI. Not all client/server application development is graphical, because there is still a strong contingent of batch and report processing that is not user-interface based. Most user-interface software constructed is graphical and based on Windows 3.1, Windows 95, Macintosh, UNIX Motif, OS/2, and other contenders. Some applications are required to run on more than one graphical operating system. This places additional design and implementation constraints on the application.

The graphical development platform is a critical decision factor based on the hardware and operating system requirements for users. This is a large and complex discipline, usually requiring new training and new tools. There are management and design issues associated with graphical user interfaces, including graphical design, user interviews and reviews, iterative development, and usability. Design methods associated with these aspects are variously named, but deal with the constant (and historical) issue of accurately understanding the user's requirements and desires and correctly reflecting them in software design. New methods are possible because of the power of the current graphical application development tools. It is possible to build versions of the software and allow constant and frequent review by the user to improve and expand the design of the software. This development has led to improved software deliveries though the development cycle is more complex to manage.

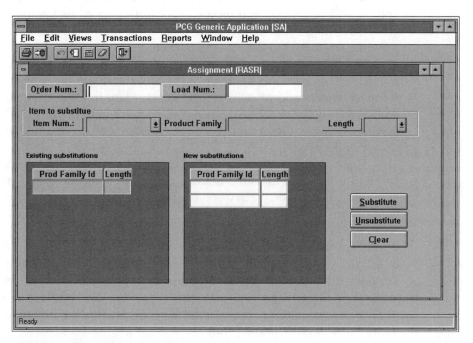

FIGURE 4.5 Illustration of a GUI.

Skills for the graphical user interface discipline include:

♦ Graphical user interface design
♦ Graphical user interface implementation
♦ Cross-platform design and implementation
♦ Iterative development
♦ User interview techniques
♦ Usability testing
♦ Graphic design
♦ Joint application development (JAD)
♦ Rapid application development (RAD)

Object-Oriented Technology

Object-oriented (*OO*) *technology* is another discipline that has become associated with client/server development, though they are independent technologies. Object-oriented technology applies to many areas of the software development cycle. It can be used in analysis, design, and/or implementation. It is not required to use the technology in all software development phases to take advantage of it in any one of the phases.

Object-oriented technologies deserve a thorough study to understand how they can be utilized by your development process. Key aspects of OO include classes and objects, inheritance, structures, polymorphic behavior, and more. Understood and used well, object-oriented technology can provide great advantages, but it is a technology that requires serious investment in training, study, and in gaining experience.

In addition to understanding object-oriented technology itself, there are special techniques and systems required to manage the corporate use and reuse of objects and object-based systems. Planning and designing for reuse and managing the successful reuse of classes is a new and different task in corporations, sometimes requiring new development groups and management responsibilities.

There is one more use of the term objects—*distributed objects*. A distributed object architecture defines the style, standards, and protocols for communications and behaviors between distributed software components. OLE 2.0 and CORBA are contending standards in this area. Application developers can reuse objects (often referred to as *software components*) provided by vendors in their applications and can construct reusable distributed objects to build client/server applications that are more distributed and segmented. This provides interoperability throughout an application's environment and provides the application developer with expanded capabilities in the reuse of developed and vendor-supplied complex objects. This is a new area of development that will grow in the future.

Skills for the object-oriented discipline include:

- ♦ OO analysis
- ♦ OO design
- ♦ OO implementation
- ♦ OO to entity/relationship conversion
- ♦ OO object management process
- ♦ OO database management systems
- ♦ Distributed objects
  - ♦ OLE 2.0/COM
  - ♦ CORBA
  - ♦ OpenDoc

Cooperative Processing

The heart of client/server development is the concept of *cooperative processing*. The key to client/server architecture is the support for the parsing of applications into discrete processes that communicate with each other through *messaging protocols*. These application partitions can be individually deployed on appropriate hardware and operating system platforms that provide communication through a network. In addition, these systems are created to provide *open interoperability*. That is, the ability for the layers of products to communicate through industry standards that are used among vendor's products.

The simplistic version of a client/server system is a single-server application (often a relational database system like SQL Server) and a client application (often a Windows application). Even in this simple version of a client/server system, one can discern the advantages of the client/server architecture and the advantages that one can derive from using a very task-specific operating system like Windows on the client and NT on the server. In addition, the hardware can be application-specific and can be scaled appropriately at every point in the process.

One of the difficulties in deploying systems on this architecture is understanding the implications of the internal capabilities and behaviors in the systems being deployed. For example, it is critical to understand the connection, locking, and communication behavior of a server to properly implement the communication to it from a client application. When you design a client/server application you must choose (design) how, when, and where to program any particular behavior. It is necessary to *design* these cooperative processing elements of your applications. This design work is very reusable throughout a system. Failure to design these cooperative elements usually leads to serious failures in the production application.

Classical (if you can use the term classical for a concept that is barely a decade old) client/server deployment is two-tier. This means that we have a client application communicating directly with one or more server applications. In this architecture, each application process is parsed into two components (or tiers), part of which is executed on each tier. There has been a movement in the industry to define a more distributed architecture. In a multitier environment much of the business logic of the application is moved to a third middle tier. The concept is used to create application and database independence in the business logic.

Skills for the cooperative processing disciplines include:

♦ Two-tier client/server
♦ Multitier client/server
♦ Open servers and gateways
♦ Transaction analysis and design
♦ Performance and tuning

Analysis and Design

Analysis and *design* have always been components of the development process. The nature of analysis and design has changed over the years. Analysis and design techniques need to be applied to all of the software component architectures and the system specifications at all levels: the enterprise, the application domain, the database, the processes, and the user interface. Various methods of analysis and design are appropriate for client/server. Experience, appropriateness, and technical capabilities should be used to choose methodologies. Don't be afraid to use more than one. Application components are very different and different analysis and design methods may be appropriate.

It is important to try to identify a primary design methodology with which everyone is familiar—the development team, management, and the user community. It is possible to build a primary and unifying model of the system to guide and control the development processes.

One of the most important tools for analysis, design, and testing is reviewing the system with the user. *User review* needs to be institutionalized as a technique for understanding and designing a system. To accurately reflect the business requirements of a system, the users should be involved throughout the analysis and design of the system. This is accomplished with joint application design sessions and one-on-one interviews and reviews. This provides a method of assurance that you are building the correct system.

Skills for the analysis and design disciplines include:

♦ Entity/relationship analysis
♦ Structured analysis
♦ State/transition modeling
♦ Object-oriented analysis
♦ Object-oriented design
♦ Business expertise
♦ Facilitation (JAD)
♦ Rapid application development (RAD)
♦ Software design
♦ User review

Programming

The number and types of languages and development environments is growing. You should try to restrict the number of languages and environments that you use to the minimum that will support your needs. The system's chosen operating systems, development, and database platforms will dictate the particular implementation methodologies (languages and development environments).

We must acknowledge that the nature of programming has changed. It is not a procedural and linear process anymore. Object-oriented language development requires a more sophisticated level of design when architecting reusable software components. A project plan must make allowances in the development methodology, sequencing, and timing to successfully support the development of reusable software components.

Skills for the programming discipline include:

♦ 4GLS
♦ 3GLS: C, C++, COBOL,. . . .
♦ Scripting languages
♦ Macro languages
♦ Software design
♦ Software implementation
♦ Design, development, and management of reusable components

Project Management

Project management is the most important aspect of software development. As a discipline it comprises many, many skills. Because the technology is so complex, it is requisite that a client/server project manager be quite technically experienced. He or she must understand the reality of the development process and must be able to understand the problems and solutions proposed by the staff. A client/server project has an enormous number of small and complex tasks that must be organized and integrated. The development schedule must be flexible and must be *juggled* (this is a technical term!) at regular intervals. Technical expertise is required to allow a manager to be successful in these maneuvers.

Project design is the task of deciding how to organize the development cycle and how to structure the dynamic dependencies inherent in the project. These stem from the complex development environment, the high level of user involvement, the quick turnaround for any given single task, the skills of the development team, and the constraints imposed by the organization or technical environment. A manager can only microschedule within a short time frame. Some tasks, or iterative development processes, can barely be scheduled at all, but will be timeboxed; that is, "We will continue with this cycle for a certain number of days/weeks/months." What a developer will be doing on a given day in the future will depend directly on how today's work is going and where it leads.

Project control (the desired result of project management) requires detailed reporting and analysis to understand progress, direction, and productivity of the project. Scheduling is not useful without tracking and analysis. The loop of information back to the developer about his work must be completed to steer the project team on the correct course. The project manager has the hardest job on the team. It requires skill and experience for success, as illustrated in Figure 4.6.

Skills for the project management discipline include:

♦ Personnel management
♦ Communication skills
♦ Negotiation skills
♦ Project design
♦ Technical design and implementation
♦ Scheduling
♦ Tracking
♦ Reporting
♦ Juggling

Development Methodologies

Methodologies are reusable systems that contain lists of tasks, deliverables, sequences, explanations, examples, and tools. To improve development cycles over a period of time it is necessary to evolve strong reusable methods for accomplishing tasks. Key areas for systematization are the development process itself, testing, and designing. Methods are used to enable a group to produce consistent and high-quality results. The best methods come from

FIGURE 4.6 Juggle everything, and predict the future. . . .

experience, and it is important to remember to reuse what works and throw out what doesn't. Methods need to evolve and they need to be constantly reviewed for continuing applicability.

Many methods have been developed to support analysis and design methodologies: entity/relationship, structured (data-flow diagrams), object-oriented, and so on. Choosing and institutionalizing one or more of these systems (with tools, training, and support) can vastly improve productivity and quality.

The development process itself is a prime target for a methodology. In the client/server area, it is of utmost importance because of the complexity of the development process. Many projects fail because too many of the required skills and tasks were unknown to the planners of the development cycle. This is an expected problem when addressing a new technology. It is necessary to train or buy experience when planning first projects in client/server, or it is necessary to allow for the fact that you are learning and to make management and corporate allowances for that. Most organizations allow for some leeway and freedom on a small first pilot, but then expect the next "real" project to be in full control. This usually isn't the case. A method should constantly evolve with the tools, technologies, skills of the participants, and previous experience.

Skills for the development methodology discipline include:

♦ Know-how in developing a client/server system (experience)
♦ Development methods
♦ Testing methods
♦ Analysis methods
♦ Design methods

Documentation

Documentation is an important underpinning of the development life cycle. At every step, the document is the tie that binds one state of the process to the next. It is very important to insist that documentation must be done, and to create standards concerning when, where, and how it should be done. When designing documentation systems look at the system as a whole and how the documentation will consistently flow from phase to phase, from analysis through design through implementation. Never consider a document as an isolated component, but as part of a consistent thread of information about the growing detailed knowledge that is being developed. Build systems that implement this thread (connection) between all of the documents. Our methodology uses an object model as a key, primary, and unifying design document. Such a unifying model will hold the map to all other design documents and tie them back to the abstract business model developed in the analysis phase.

The discipline of user documentation has changed with the advent of graphical user interfaces for our end-user applications. We are required to write manuals, but more importantly, we are required to embed context sensitive online help into our systems. Technical writers are ever more in demand, and have to possess new skills for developing effective help systems.

Skills for the documentation discipline include:

- ♦ Analysis documentation
- ♦ Design documentation
- ♦ Software documentation
- ♦ User documentation
- ♦ Technical writing
- ♦ Document management

Version Control and Configuration Management

Version control and *configuration management* are standard disciplines that must move to new technology platforms. They need to be developed before a project begins, or immediately thereon. *Librarianship* is a term used for the responsibilities of organizing, filing, archiving, and restoring of documents, software, and systems. It is often neglected and is always critical when a major system fails.

Configuration management is more important than ever in the client/server environment. Any given client/server system has a complex pattern of hardware and software interoperability. Changes in any given piece can cause a system to fail. Tracking the correct combinations of operating systems, networks, databases, tools, and interoperability layers is complex and technical work, and much has to be done to control this environment.

Skills for the version control and configuration management disciplines include:

- ♦ Librarianship
- ♦ Documentation version control
- ♦ Software version control
- ♦ Configuration management

Testing

Testing is a major set of tasks that come in many flavors. Complex systems require varying types and scopes of testing. Each software element must be individually tested (unit tested) for accuracy of performance and robustness. Each element must be tested for usability. In addition, subsystems and entire systems must be tested as a whole. Testing must pertain to usability, data manipulation accuracy, behavior correctness, robustness, and consistency.

Many tools exist to assist us in these processes. In addition to tools, testing requires discipline, method, measurement, tracking, and consistency.

Skills for the testing discipline include:

♦ Design test systems
♦ Testing and reporting
♦ Fault tracking and repair
♦ Usability testing
♦ Unit testing
♦ System testing

Technical Review

It is critical to have a *technical review process* in your software development cycle. It enables early checking and testing of methods and techniques and keeps everyone on a similar development tack. It also provides a mechanism for a more experienced developer to guide a less experienced developer. The junior developer can learn by reviewing the experienced developer's code and by having his or hers reviewed.

Skills for the technical review discipline include:

♦ Evaluation methodologies
♦ Standard procedures
♦ Facilitation of meetings
♦ Mentoring
♦ Problem resolution

Roles and Responsibilities

Many *roles* and *responsibilities* must be covered even on a small project. Team members may play multiple roles, that is, take responsibility for multiple facets of the development process. The term *wizard* refers to those very experienced people who can solve problems quickly. These environments are so complex that much time can be saved by identifying an expert or wizard in these areas to use until you have acquired such expertise on the team. The most important job is to identify the disciplines your system will encompass, the skills required, and the tasks that need to be accomplished. Map those skills to the available team—find out what you are missing before you begin. Figure out where and how you are going to obtain those skills.

Infrastructure Roles

♦ Hardware system administrators
♦ Operating system administrators
♦ Network administrators
♦ Database administrators
♦ Interoperability wizard
♦ Performance and tuning wizards
♦ Communications administrators

Software Development Roles

- ♦ Project manager
- ♦ Technical manager
- ♦ Technical reviewers
- ♦ Database designer
- ♦ Database builder(s)
- ♦ Database performance and tuning wizard
- ♦ Application designer
- ♦ Application builder(s)
- ♦ Application tuning wizard

Support and Control Roles

- ♦ Librarian
- ♦ User Representative(s)
- ♦ Quality assurance (tester)
- ♦ Technical writer

Timing

A task is an action item that is part of a skill set within a discipline. The development process incorporates an enumerated list of tasks (what to do) and those tasks are scheduled and accomplished over a period of time. There are an infinite number of ways to organize the tasks over time. Most of those ways will lead to failure.

Many issues are involved in organizing tasks:

- ♦ Task dependencies
- ♦ Availability of staff with the correct skills
- ♦ Requirements for deliverables
- ♦ Creating proof-of-concept solutions
- ♦ Prototyping
- ♦ Iterative design loops
- ♦ Risk management

In addition, there are usually corporate or organizational requirements to prove progress and to confirm delivery dates and estimates. All of these factors bear on the organization of time and sequence that will be useful in the development life cycle.

Much has been made of changing styles of management in software development. A phased waterfall approach was replaced by one or more *spiral* technologies in the fashion of development. A traditional waterfall development methodology steps through rigorous phases which have finite deliverables. No application code was written until the entire system was completely designed and specified. Once coding began, no design changes were allowed. Large systems were developed using this approach, but the final application often did not meet the system's goals, which changed after the analysis was complete. Iterative, or *spiral*, development methods allow the system to be designed, implemented and tested by producing ever-improving versions of the software. This has been enabled by the great improvements and power in development languages and tools.

In reality, complex software development uses aspects of both styles. Complex systems must step through a series of design, implementation and test phases, but must use iterative (spiral) development techniques in key phases of the development cycle. Rapid application development (RAD) is a set of techniques for very rapid deployment of relatively small and discreet applications. To use RAD you must already have a corporate infrastructure and an architecture of reusable components must be in place. In addition, RAD is most effective on small to moderate projects (maximum of four to six experts and four to six months) or modules of a larger system. When a system is larger than this, management and corporate requirements usually demand that the project is constructed in a phased approach keeping many of the productive elements of RAD.

Most development methods for large projects (or for inexperienced development groups) use a series of phases which each have a specific list of tasks and deliverables that progress toward project completion. Many tasks can be moved from one phase to another if you understand the dependencies involved. The complete list of tasks involved must include the construction of a complete infrastructure for client/server systems and establish the reusable systems and components required to build subsequent applications with rapid techniques. The use of defined sequences of tasks does not imply that everything is 100 percent complete before you move on or that one cannot return to a previous phase task on a given area of the application if that is required. In fact, if the analysis information proves not to be complete, it is a *requirement* that you pass through the analysis and design phases on that piece of the application to make sure you've covered the bases and documented the new information.

Many of the tasks in the development plan require iterative development processes and make use of *timeboxing* (limiting the development process or the number of iterative loops by fixing a time to quit). Not all processes can be timeboxed. Some things (such as building the triggers) have to be complete. But the overall scope of a project, the effort devoted to user review and design, the effort devoted to analysis, can and must be limited to a reasonable and cost-efficient expenditure.

Another key reason for phasing the development cycle is to meet organizational requirements for reporting on progress and expenditures. Some projects are by nature fairly large, and it is necessary to track the ratio of effort to progress (work to percent complete) and to re-evaluate estimates during the life cycle of the project. Phases should be designed to do this. They should group tasks into meaningful, dependent phases that provide a point of delivery (not necessarily formal). At these moments, it is possible to take stock of progress and with increased knowledge make predictions on the costs and risks of subsequent phases of the project.

It is also important to assess and document risk at each of these points in the project life cycle. Risk is the existence of the unknown—unknown business problems, unknown technology, unknown solutions, or unknown user requirements. These are things that have no currently known solution and have the possibility of becoming large problems or time sinks. We call them *black holes*. Just identifying them gives your estimates and projections new meaning because you can allow for the fact that some of these things will take a significant amount of time.

Once your infrastructure is in place, new applications or changes to existing applications can be managed within a rapid development framework. The extensive learning and experience developed in creating a complete client/server infrastructure will give you the experienced team required to build a system much more quickly at each subsequent turn.

Iterative and Parallel Development

Goals of Iterative Development

Iterative development is a process of building something, holding user and technical reviews, and improving and extending it based on the review feedback. Then you go through the cycle again until the result is close enough to be effective, you run out of time, or it's perfect! This is often represented as a protyping method of development, but in reality, for the current state of the art of software development, the entire life cycle proceeds in iterative stages.

Iterative development is used because it produces better and more applicable software solutions. The user community is not involved only once at the beginning and once at the end when they are delivered software. They are a continual part of the process. This process, while challenging to manage, produces software that is more precisely what the user requires at the time of deployment. Many strategic systems that are being developed cannot be completely defined by the user before development starts. New business systems and strategic solutions are invented and created through this partnership of the developer and the business user.

Iteration is applied at many levels to the development life cycle. First, a large system should be modularized as much as possible. If it is possible to deploy part of a system, the system should be broken down into smaller applications that are delivered in sequence. Sometimes you can deploy the inventory system before you deploy the sales or shipping systems. This allows you to pass through the entire life cycle of software development for each module with all of the reusable components and experience gained on the previous module. Iteration leverages learning and gets a team up quickly on the entire process, as shown in Figure 4.7. In addition, you only have to train one division of the corporate users at a time.

In addition, each task accomplished throughout the life cycle has its own iterations: development, test, review, development, test, and review. But it can't go on forever. It is necessary to stop at some point. The total time is dictated by business implications, cost-effectiveness, timeliness, and efficiency. *The design, development, and testing cycles of software development are actually one single stage of iteration towards a more perfect solution. Delineation of phases in this period of the life cycle are done for business and management reasons: risk control, cost control, cost projections, and management review.*

Parallel Development

Parallel development is the ability to move forward on more than one tactical front (area of development) at a time. At a minimum, there are five fronts on which effort needs to be made simultaneously:

1. Infrastructure
2. Support and control
3. Database implementation (software development)
4. User-interface applications (software development)
5. Batch components (software development)

While development on these fronts interacts and shares information, there are vast areas in which they are independent of each other. Understanding dependencies or, more importantly, finding nondependencies is one of a manager's key tools in creating a project plan or schedule. Finding and creating paral-

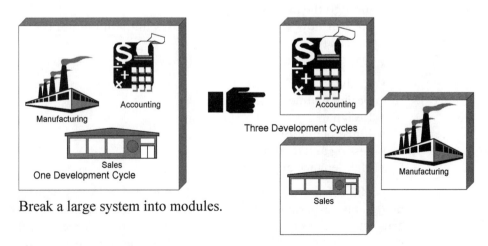

Break a large system into modules.

FIGURE 4.7 Iteration leverages learning.

lelism in the life cycle can improve delivery schedules by allowing more people to be put on the project. Experience improves this ability.

Project Management Sequencing

This is not a complete, detailed task list for client/server development, but a suggested way to break the tasks into meaningful phases and a suggested starting list. Detailed task lists will vary depending on the software tools and platforms you use. It is important to structure tasks to support these key development requirements:

1. Task dependencies
2. Estimating future costs
3. Deliverables
4. Constant forward progress
5. Proof of progress and concepts
6. Iterative development
7. Risk assessment
8. Available staffing

We will enumerate many of the tasks involved for the database implementation side of a client/server system. These tasks are pertinent to building a database system with **SQL Server**. There are many other tasks dependent on the application architecture and tools involved in your process. These phases and their contents are relatively arbitrary. There can be fewer phases. In a small project, design, development, and testing can be one iterative sequence. With a very experienced team and a relatively small project, the entire process can be collapsed into a rapid application development process. Larger projects and less-experienced teams will benefit from a more structured way of stepping through the process.

We will now go through the phases and enumerate the tasks involved. The phases are:

♦ Specification
♦ Analysis
♦ Design enumeration
♦ Design
♦ Implementation
♦ Testing and deployment
♦ Maintenance and support

These lists are a general guide. They evolve every day with new tools, technology, and experience. They illustrate a method using seven distinct phases. This set of phases and tasks applies to a moderate or large project that is a first project to formally adopt and use client/server, object-oriented development, and a new client/server infrastructure. It will accomplish the development of the infrastructure and architecture creating a reusable corporate architecture which will allow for more rapid development in subsequent projects.

THE ALEXANDER MANUFACTURING PROJECT

The Alexander Manufacturing Company manufactures widgets. It is a subsidiary of a large corporate entity. Over the last ten years the parent company has supported all of the subsidiaries on a large centralized mainframe. The subsidiaries are spread over a large geographic area and use wide-area network technology for communications. Two years ago, the mainframe became overloaded as the subsidiaries grew. In addition, the mainframe was considered to be too expensive. The Alexander Manufacturing Company was told that it had eighteen months to remove all of its systems from the mainframe. This action would save Alexander Manufacturing $350,000 per year and would free the mainframe for other growing corporate requirements.

Specification

A *specification phase* is designed to define the business problem to be addressed and the enterprise and system components involved in the process. Statements of business problems should address existing systems, business processes served, goals of a new system, project parameters such as expected costs (investment) and expected time of delivery, and the who's who of corporate involvement (user community, financial sponsor, information systems sponsor, likely development team, and so on).

Infrastructure

♦ Analyze hardware systems and requirements.
♦ Analyze architectural requirements.
♦ Review platform possibilities.

Software Development

♦ Define business requirements.
♦ Define business goals.

Support and Control

♦ Review staffing requirements.
♦ Identify management.
♦ Define management expectations.

THE ALEXANDER MANUFACTURING PROJECT (CONTINUED)

The MIS director of Alexander Manufacturing (AlexMan) determined that the systems should be redeployed on client/server. The MIS group consisted of two system administrators and three developers. Half of these services supported the work done on the mainframe. The other half supported the user systems and small spreadsheet applications.

The MIS director, the CFO, and the COO of AlexMan worked to define the business case for the project. They produced preliminary reports on costs, savings, and benefits of a new system. The administrative group started to accumulate information on hardware, system requirements, and possible platform choices. The MIS director identified a leader from the parent organization to hire or borrow for the duration to help manage the project and together they defined potential staffing requirements and solutions. They produced an estimate of costs for the next phase and a detailed list of risk factors that they could envision.

The documents produced were presented to a steering committee from the parent company and partner companies for review, risk assessment, recommendations, and approval for moving into the next phase. Once approved, the project was on its way.

Analysis

The *analysis phase* of a project is designed to capture a high-level picture of the business problem at hand, define the scope or extent of the problem to be addressed, and create a model of the business problem from the standpoint of the business and/or users of the system. This business model should enumerate all entities (or objects) and all processes (or methods) required for the system. In addition, many of the tasks involved in the design, selection, and installation of infrastructure items must begin here.

There are three areas of work to be done at this moment:

1. Infrastructure documentation and conceptualization
2. Enterprise or system analysis
3. Conceptualization for support and control systems

These areas of work are all iterative using joint application development (JAD), research, interviews, and review.

Infrastructure

♦ Proceed with hardware research.
♦ Select development tools.
♦ Select relational database platform.
♦ Design primary architecture.

Software Development

♦ Define the mission of the system to be deployed.
♦ Define the mission of the project.
♦ Compile key word list.
♦ Conduct joint application development sessions.
♦ Create an enterprise model.
♦ Research and document user scenarios.
♦ Document list of tasks the system should support.
♦ Perform OO analysis.
♦ Publish data dictionary.

Support and Control

♦ Conduct risk assessment.
♦ Select system software.

♦ Create a training plan.
♦ Prepare estimates for design enumeration.

THE ALEXANDER MANUFACTURING PROJECT (CONTINUED)

The group had no experience with client/server and hired an outside consulting firm, Consultants R Us (CRU), to lead the entire organization through the process. The first action was a joint application development (JAD) workshop that lasted three days. It included the heads of all of the major departments in the corporation (Sales, Manufacturing, Shipping, Inventory, and Production Planning), major users, and the MIS staff. This group became the primary review committee. The CRU lead analyst led the meeting jointly with another senior analyst. The attendees learned about the process they were about to go through and then proceeded to create the following design documents: illustration of the business; business object model; key terms definitions; goals of the new system; and lists of key tasks to be supported by the system. They also made estimates/guesses about the final costs of the system and came to an agreement that the system was possible and critical and that they should move forward.

The analysis team proceeded modeling the system with user interviews and questionnaires. In addition, the review committee met periodically to review the designs, answer questions, and keep the analysts on track.

The administrative group proceeded with hardware and operating system platform research and testing. At the end of this phase they had a fairly complete idea which platforms they would choose. A preliminary physical architecture design was produced with cost estimates for implementation. In addition, this group began a checklist of risk factors to append and share with the other groups.

The manager of the project began to choose and develop a design team, put management tools in place, and plan for training. At this time the system had a preliminary architecture and scope (size and areas of responsibility). An estimate was made for the costs of the next phase.

The steering committee met to review all of the reports and plans. They were concerned about the growing complexity of the system and their lack of client/server development experience. They cautioned the group to carefully track risk factors and make sure they were getting experienced help where needed. They were particularly concerned about the cost overruns they had heard about in software development for client/server. They stressed that they wanted to the team to develop strong controls to measure and track their progress. As the next design phase started, they wanted regular reports on progress and costs.

Design Enumeration

Design enumeration is a phase designed to help scope the total size of the project at the earliest moment. It is properly part of the design task, but focuses on enumerating the nature and number of each software element to be constructed. This enumerated list combined with a complete list of global tasks gives the best possible opportunity to estimate the total cost of a system. Of course, every step forward will get more accurate numbers (you'll really have it down when you finish!), but this phase is deliberately separated from the design phase so as to know how many software objects need to be designed, and therefore how much design time is needed. Any decisions need to be considered tentative and changeable but with experience you should be able to be relatively accurate.

The use of object-oriented implementation technologies will change this and subsequent phases significantly. If you need to design reusable objects and architectures, you will have to allow for this here and in the design phase as a separate and ongoing set of tasks, some of which can only be completed after prototyping (a major design phase task) and more complete system design. But if you know it is coming, you can allow for it in your estimates and planning.

Infrastructure

♦ Purchase or acquire infrastructure components.
♦ Complete training sequences for all components.
♦ Install all infrastructure components.
♦ Install all tools.

Software Development

♦ Extend the business object model or enterprise model.
♦ Review reusable components already developed.
♦ Document business rules.
♦ Design cooperative processing model.
♦ Iterate enumeration of each task to be supported by the system.
♦ Tentatively design implementation model for each task (user-interface objects, stored procedures, 3GL components, and so on).
♦ Establish programming standards.
♦ Database:

Translate business object model to preliminary database implementation.

Define table volumes.

Define datatypes.

Design and implement domains (defaults, rules, and user defined datatypes).

Build preliminary database.

Compile preliminary test data.

Design a data conversion process for existing data.

♦ Applications or user interface:

Enumerate and rate for difficulty all user-interface components.

Estimate effort and time to design each component.

Identify trouble spots.

Design prototype.

Prepare window flow diagram or hierarchical map of the application.

Establish user-interface standards.

♦ Batch or task components:

Enumerate and rate for difficulty all user batch or task components.

Estimate effort and time to design each component.

Identify trouble spots.

Support and Control

- ♦ Implement technical review.
- ♦ Implement project management.
- ♦ Select supporting software.
- ♦ Design testing systems.
- ♦ Implement the development environment.
- ♦ Modularize the system.
- ♦ Sequence modules.
- ♦ Sequence design phase.
- ♦ Prepare estimates for design.

THE ALEXANDER MANUFACTURING PROJECT (CONTINUED)

At this point the project was in full swing. Besides the MIS group and the user community, four experienced application designers were added to the team. The MIS group focused on the data model, database design, and associated issues. In addition, they documented the complex batch requirements with which they were so familiar. Another complexity they addressed was the problem of moving from the old to the new system (transferring data, running in parallel, and cutting over).

The design team worked extensively on building the architectural infrastructure (cooperative processing model, development standards, and reusable components) and the design of application components to support the user scenarios developed previously. At the end of this phase they had a detailed design of the number and nature of application components and could more accurately size the design and implementation process.

The administrative group began the process of acquiring and installing the infrastructure. This was a slow process in a manufacturing plant. Several false starts were made with network hardware decisions to optimize speed and minimize maintainance of the system. The administrative group went to appropriate training for administering and tuning their systems.

The management group finalized the selection of programming and management tools; made plans for testing the systems; managed the coordination of technical reviews, user reviews, and meetings. They worked on modularizing the system and decided on a system by functional area (Sales, Manufacturing, Shipping, Inventory, and Production Planning). They realized that they could not switch any of the functional areas over to the new system independently. Because of the tight integration of their information, the switch from the mainframe would have to be done all at once. The addition of experienced team members helped reduce the risk factors somewhat. The modularization was still a great asset. Each of the modules had its own production schedule and user group, and could be managed independently. This reduced contention and improved parallelization on the project.

All groups produced a list of risk factors that they had identified: potentials for network failures; a new area of the business that was not fully understood; a technical complexity with bar code readers integrated with the Windows applications; and so on. Management was concerned with the likelihood that the application was so large that they would need more developers and began a plan for integrating more members into the team.

With a detailed list of the bill of materials (identification of all software components) for the system and a complete list of other global tasks required, the team was able to jointly develop a detailed estimate for the design phase. In addition, they made some preliminary guesses at the cost of implementation. When they finished they were concerned about how big it was but pleased to note that their estimate had only grown about 40 percent. They also believed that with all of the information they had developed that their new number was much more accurate.

The steering committee approved the budget for the next phase.

Design

The *design phase* includes designing all of the software elements and systems, databases, and infrastructure support. One of the key tasks is prototyping key aspects of the application. Prototype all aspects of the application that have risk associated with them: they need lots of user review; the users are sensitive to their applications; the technical problems are not understood; you are going to use many versions of this solution; you haven't built anything like this; you don't understand the business problem; the users are defining the solutions to their problems as they go; and so on. Design other things on paper or not at all, only enumerate them.

During the design phase much of the database implementation is completed. The database implementation should always be somewhat ahead of the user interface and task programming if possible. This makes the other lines of development easier and more productive.

Infrastructure

◆ Continue installation of infrastructure.
◆ Support the new environment.
◆ Tune the environment.
◆ Plan for installation and support for deployment.

Software Development

◆ Document cooperative processing solutions.
◆ Implement cooperative processing solutions as required.
◆ Database:

Categorize all transactions the system will support.

Implement domains.

Implement business rules.

Define trigger model to be used.

Iterate implementations of the database.

Compile test data.

◆ Applications:

Review reusable components.

Design inheritance hierarchy.

Design each ancestor.

Extend and maintain the window flow diagram.

Design key windows.

Prototype key application areas.

Design user documentation.

Address and resolve all difficult problems.

Finalize (as much as possible) reusable framework and reusable components.

♦ Batch or task components:

Design each report.

Design each batch/task.

Address and resolve all difficult problems.

Support and Control

♦ Implement version control.
♦ Implement testing software.
♦ Implement testing systems.
♦ Implement application repository.
♦ Modularize the system.
♦ Sequence modules.
♦ Sequence implementation phase.
♦ Conduct technical reviews.
♦ Implement project management.
♦ Prepare estimate for construction of all elements.

THE ALEXANDER MANUFACTURING PROJECT (CONTINUED)

The administrative group now had the complete development environment installed and was ready to support it. In addition, they were finishing their plans for final installation of the production system. They had a noncritical path for the installation of extensive connectivity hardware throughout the factory and started early so that it would not become a critical path.

The design team broke up into groups for each of the functional areas. The prototype was specified. All areas of the application that entailed risk were chosen to be included in the prototype. This included application areas that had technical difficulties, usability problems, components for users with specialized requirements (difficult users), things that hadn't been tried before, components that would be reused extensively, or new technologies. The prototype was essentially starting development early on those things that may need more time, research, or testing. In addition to the prototype, the functionality and definition of all of the application components was detailed. This entailed documentation, research, and technical review. All of the application modules were defined in story boards that could be reviewed by the users in great detail. Design groups met with the user community at least weekly.

A technical leader was identified to design, integrate, and control the reusable components for the application. She worked with all of the design teams throughout this phase to design components that would work for all of the application modules.

The database design team delivered ever more accurate implementations of the database. Changes that came out of design work were worked into the database design and it was redeployed regularly. All of the transactions (INSERT, UPDATE, DELETE) were defined and studied to optimize their design for performance and concurrency. Test data was generated for use by the prototyping team.

Except for system testing, the management team was in full swing. All developers were delivering product, prototypes, and design documents on a regular basis. Coordination of resources was a major task. Regular user reviews were scheduled, along with technical reviews and management meetings. Systems were developed to minimize meetings for status only. E-mail and voice-mail were used for that extensively.

At the end of the phase, the steering committee and the user community were invited to a demonstration of the prototyped systems. Everyone was jazzed at the progress the entire organization had made. The steering committee approved the budget for the next phase. The implementation budget had to go to a higher authority—the CFO of the parent company. This caused a three-and-a-half-week delay when the project was without budget. Some of the outside contractors had to be sent away for three weeks, which was problematic—would they be there when things started up again? The internal folks struggled to keep things going. All worked out, but it was decided that next time the phase would be planned in such a way as to consider a possible funding delay. This could be done by producing the estimate for the next phase before completing all of the design work. It was judged that this could be done by leaving wrap-up design work and documentation until after the estimates. This work would occupy everyone while the funding process was taking its appointed time. All phase-completion periods are planned this way now.

Implementation

Implementation is the phase where most of the construction and unit testing is conducted. It is a continuation of what has been happening in the preceeding phase. In a prototyping environment, it is very difficult to draw lines between design, implementation, and testing. The general focus changes gradually from conceptualizing the application to constructing it. In the middle of each phase you can recognize where you are, but at the edges it is very arbitrary where you draw the line. The key difference between design and implementation phases is that during implementation you know *how* you are going to build the system, while in the design phase you are trying to figure that out.

It is critical to understand that each of these tasks is iterative and will require complex scheduling with regard to user reviews, technical review, and the number of iterations required to get satisfactory results.

Infrastructure

♦ Continue installation of infrastructure.
♦ Support the new environment.
♦ Tune the environment.
♦ Plan for installation and support for deployment.
♦ Design system administration systems.
♦ Begin installation for deployment.

Software Development

♦ Write user documentation.
♦ Test the system.
♦ Database:

Create indexing strategies and implement indexes.

Monitor index effectiveness.

Iterate implementations of database as required by changes.

Compile volume test data.

Write the required triggers.

Write the required stored procedures.

Test all components.

♦ Applications:

Implement inheritance hierarchy and reusable components.

Maintain window flow diagram.

Implement all windows and user-interface components.

Implement all transactions.

Test each component.

♦ Batch or task components:

Implement data conversion.

Implement each report.

Implement each batch/task.

Test each component.

Support and Control

♦ Maintain application repository.
♦ Provide librarian services.
♦ Sequence testing phase.
♦ Begin subsystem testing as soon as possible.
♦ Maintain project plan.
♦ Conduct technical review.
♦ Implement project management.
♦ Prepare estimate for testing and deployment.

THE ALEXANDER MANUFACTURING PROJECT (CONTINUED)

This phase was a continuation of the design phase. All of the systems were constructed and tested. Constant user reviews were continued throughout the phase. Users were used to test certain applications as well.

A problem arose. Developers indicated to their management that they were done with a certain portion of the application. When the manager put a user to work testing it, it would crash more often than rarely. It was discovered that the developer had a different meaning for the word *done* than the manager. The amount and nature of the testing that the developer was expected to do had not been clearly defined. The group met and carefully defined the amount and nature of the testing that the developer was expected to do before declaring a component done. This improved the quality of the deliveries. It was also decided that the developer should fix any code problems immediately (as opposed to putting them on a list to be fixed later). This made the developers a little more sensitive to leaving problems in their code, and they were more likely to remember the coding situation than if it had been left until later.

Database tuning began at this time using the applications and stored procedures being developed. Final projections on database sizing were used to finalize the order of the final production hardware.

The management group put together a small team of junior developers and users to execute testing of subsystems (integrated components) as they came together. This provided usability testing (did the users like it?) and preliminary testing of robustness and accuracy. The testing tool allowed them to begin to develop regression testing scripts that could be amalgamated later for a complete regression testing system.

The implementation phase was reviewed by the steering committee in the middle of the process. Though costs were fairly in line with estimates, the time schedule had slipped. The CFO was quite concerned with the slippage and questioned whether the team had really improved its estimating capabilities so that the new schedule was accurate. The group reviewed the information being used to make the judgments and determined that it was as good as they could do. The good news was that though early components had run over, the last three delivered components had come in under their estimates. Everyone noted the concern and the system development proceeded. Of course, turning back at this point was hardly an option. They were not failing, nor excessively over budget. The user community was very pleased with the applications they had seen.

Testing and Deployment

Testing and *deployment* can vary in formality. Thorough testing should be employed throughout the implementation phase. Developers should each have a method to test their portion of the application before it is considered done. Systems and subsystems should be tested as soon as they are ready. Corporations requiring a formal testing phase need to document and standardize tools, processes, and results tracking. Regression test suites should be constructed to enable rapid regression testing at each new release of the product. Testing in this environment is complex. It will involve a set of tools to test the different types of software and system components involved.

Infrastructure

♦ Support the environment.
♦ Tune the environment.
♦ Prepare installation for deployment.
♦ Implement system administration systems.
♦ Build delivery system.
♦ Test delivery system.

Software Development

♦ Unit test each component.
♦ Conduct system and subsystem testing.
♦ Finalize all documentation.
♦ Fix problems.
♦ Consolidate and document reusable software components.

Support and Control

♦ Track problems.
♦ Collect enhancement requests.
♦ Provide librarian services.
♦ Evaluate project.
♦ Conduct technical review.
♦ Implement project management.

THE ALEXANDER MANUFACTURING PROJECT (CONTINUED)

This phase really began during the implementation phase as application components became available. As lead developers finished their components, they were assigned to formalize the testing of other components. Some developers were no longer needed and were put on other projects. A small team of senior testers and user testers was developed to integrate and use the test suites. The developers still on the project were assigned problems to fix and reintegrate into the application. User documentation was completed and tested along with the usability testing.

The technical leader studied the final application and extracted from it the best and most reusable components for inclusion in the growing reusable framework. As available, the team reviewed and/or helped improve the framework architecture.

The administration group finalized testing of the installed hardware and then began deploying the application for testing over the network. They also finalized the development of the support structure of the system: deployment, backup/recovery, helpdesk services, and technical firefighting.

The core MIS team moved the system through the cut-over procedures and brought the system up. The old system was still in place. Another pass of testing ran as if the system was up. There were some difficulties. When those were addressed they went through the process again, and brought the final system up for parallel execution with the old system. This proceeded with only a few data glitches that the programmers were able to fix as the system moved forward. After eight weeks of parallel processing, it was felt that the system was stable.

Key developers were available for emergency repairs throughout this period, and they had some long days of trouble with some of the batch processes. One key user also had serious problems which took days to trace to an unusual setting in their Windows environment. A new system was developed to test differences (diffs) in the .ini files on Windows clients.

Management produced wrapup reports. The project had gone 18 percent over budget and was delivered 12 weeks later than originally planned. The system also produced a corporate reusable hardware and software architecture which the company feels it can leverage throughout the parent and peer subsidiaries.

Maintenance and Support

Maintenance and support of existing applications are ongoing tasks. How they proceed depends on the corporate model for these activities. In more formal organizations, the entire process is passed from the development team to a support group. This requires high quality and formal documentation and controls. In some organizations, the development team continues to support the software. If this is the case, you must allow for it as the team is assigned new projects. Proper preparation throughout the development life cycle insures the groundwork for the continued support and enhancement of a system.

THE ALEXANDER MANUFACTURING PROJECT (CONTINUED)

The original AlexMan organization was not very big. It was basically a support organization. With this success under their belts, the MIS group began to have designs on building other systems to enhance the business capabilities of the company. As they tried to do so, they were hampered by the fact that they only had one team to support the new application and develop new systems. With the staff reduced to the internal group, they did not have enough bandwidth to engage new opportunities. Management was able to go to the parent company and the steering committee and convince them to hire new staff to support the application, so that the entire company could leverage the investment in education, experience, and skill of the development team. Over a period of time, they created a small, highly talented swat-team of developers that is used to kick-start development efforts throughout the company.

This was a successful project. At least, that's how the story goes. Client/server projects can be successful, but they need constant care and attention, a lot of talent, some experience, and dedication to the end results.

Management Issues

Software development is a difficult process to manage, and always has been. It has become increasingly more difficult with the advent of client/server. Corporations have been sold on how easy it is to deploy systems and are therefore not amenable to investing an adequate amount of resources in the project.

Proper investment in adequate, high-quality management is the most powerful investment a development organization can make. The highest leverage in software development is an investment in management skills and tools.

Project management will probably take between 10 and 15 percent of the time for everything else. Unless a project is very small (fewer than three developers), a project will gain from a full-time project manager. If it is large (more than six developers), think about more management or at least break the group into teams with team leaders.

There are several key tasks that must be accomplished by project management:

- ♦ Create an effective schedule.
- ♦ Keep developers productive.
- ♦ Understand technological problems and roadblocks.
- ♦ Help developers to keep moving.
- ♦ Juggle what really happened as opposed to what you planned to happen.
- ♦ Move quickly.

One of the most critical issues is that the project manager must be technically oriented. It is not possible to manage in this environment without a thorough technical understanding of the primary platforms and development issues. Good technical skills along with good problem-solving skills will lead to expeditious and accurate decision making. A project manager must also understand the business reasons for software. Software is not just an interesting technical challenge—it is a business tool. A manager must understand the financial importance and cost efficiencies required to make a software organization support the business goals of a corporation.

Opportunities

Management is full of opportunities. A manager's job is to manage a team that delivers a high-quality product at a reasonable price. Like a pilot, a manager has to be ready, able, and willing to make course corrections on a moment's notice to ensure timely delivery of the system. Opportunities are those points where something is not optimal (sometimes something's *really* wrong) and a correction can improve effectiveness of the team. It is paramount that a manager search out, recognize, and act on these opportunities.

Problems in the project life cycle come from varying sources. In all cases, they require management to comprehend, analyze, predict, resolve, and act. In the software development area, a project can fail for many reasons:

1. The software does not work as required.
2. The software was not completed in the time allowed.
3. The software doesn't meet technical specifications for speed, architecture, usability, and so on.
4. The software's specifications were wrong or have changed.

Review this list of opportunity identification questions and see if you can find a next step or resolution:

Wrong Staff

Is the developer on the task skilled enough?

Do we have a more able developer?

Could someone else be more effective? How would that affect the project?

Can the original staff be put on a more effective task for their capabilities?

Inadequate Training

Have we provided adequate training?

Can we stop and get the training now to get up to speed?

How would that affect the project?

Can we get a mentor for the developer to speed up the process?

Wrong Timing

Would this task be easier or more effective at another time in the sequence?

Is a required predecessor not yet complete?

Wrong Solution

Is the design of the solution being implemented the best and most efficient solution?

Is it the one that was designed?

If there an inferior solution that is sufficient and can be done in time?

Wrong Estimate

Does the estimate correctly reflect the component requirements?

Do the lead developers concur with the estimate?

Why is the development going over the estimate?

If the overage is appropriate, can we explain it and document new estimates?

Changing Specifications

Are we doing more than we originally planned?

Are we doing a more user-friendly but more costly solution?

Do we have information which was not available or accounted for in our estimates?

Did we forget that there were cost constraints at some point in our process?

Look for what's going wrong during the development process. Something is *always* going wrong somewhere.

Responsibilities

When building project plans and implementing a project, it is important for all team members to know what their responsibilities are and how they are to proceed when they encounter a problem. A list of responsibilities and guidelines for processes are an important part of the agreement between management and the development team.

A sample list of responsibilities for the developer responsible for implementing each software component during the implementation phase follows:

Review and amend (if necessary) the component design.

Review and amend (if necessary) the component estimate.

Prepare a component work plan.

Obtain management and technical sign-off for the work plan.

Coordinate with other developers as required.

Construct the component.

Unit test the component.

Document the component.

Maintain design documentation.

Obtain technical review and sign-off for the component.

Keep accurate record of effort (hours) and progress (percent complete).

Make regular reports on progress to management.

Notify management of unsuspected problems.

The management responsibilities for the same phase include the following:

Assign and schedule all tasks.

Track effort and progress on a weekly basis.

Generate reports on effort and progress on a weekly basis.

Provide appropriate technical review personnel on a timely basis.

Obtain resources for developers on a timely basis.

Coordinate requirements from the customer.

Provide all required reports to customers.

Evaluate effort to progress ratios for management adjustments:

Appropriateness of developer training

Appropriateness of design

Appropriateness of estimate

Appropriateness of scheduling or sequencing

Notify customer in the case of any failure of effort to progress.

Standards

Standards are an important part of developing a corporate methodology. There are many areas that can be standardized, including coding, naming conventions, and interface standards. Architectural and cooperative processing standards are difficult to develop but are the most important standards for insuring the successful deployment of client/server systems.

Architecture Standards

There are key architectural issues that are critical to the successful deployment of a client/server solution. If a corporation or project team does not knowledgeably design solutions for these technical issues, the likelihood is that the application can fail for any number of reasons.

A client/server technical issue is one where the client, the server, and the communication between them affects the *usability* of an application, the *control* that the programmer has over the application, and the *performance* of the application. For example, how should we validate data in a SQL Server application? Tools are available from the server and the client development environment. Which should we use? And when?

One of the most critical areas in an online transaction processing (OLTP) application is the execution of transactions. Transaction management is the heart and soul of an OLTP system. You also may have problems of size: hundreds of users and thousands of transactions. It is critical that a programmer (and a corporation) understand the implications of transactions and the locks that the Server uses to manage them. Once you have understood the issues and how the tools work, you can design reusable solutions that can deliver the quality of usability and performance required by your system.

Developing corporate standards around these issues is vitally important. Imagine that you have an OLTP system being developed by *n* programmers, and you have not created a standard for how to implement data modifications. They each develop their own style, some better and some not so good. You have *n* styles. As you go into production, the performance of the application is not adequate and the system generates deadlocks. How do you fix this? Whose transactions have caused the problem? The problem transactions might have been adequate by themselves, but they interact poorly with the other programmer's transactions. The problems could be widespread throughout the application and very difficult to fix. Planning ahead and designing architecturally correct solutions always pays off.

The key issues are connection management, error handling, data access, data validation, transaction management, concurrency management, distributed processing, and security. A more detailed presentation on each of these topics is included in Chapter 5.

Programming Standards

Programming standards are guidelines for programmers. They allow us to present a standard look and feel to our code. More importantly, they provide standards for usage. Standard coding practices improve the structure and organization of code, allow the developer and the maintenance developer to more easily read the code, and remove confusing or obfuscating inconsistencies. Programming language standards are much easier to develop than architecture standards and are usually the first place that corporations approach standardization. Architecture standards are much more important to the success of a project than the coding standards. But coding standards are still very important.

Standards are created for language usage, naming standards, code layout, documentation, and usage. Standards are often particular to a specific language, though many of the standard issues can be addressed at a general level.

General Programming Standards

General programming standards can be applied to various languages and are not specific to any given language. The next sections show examples of the types of standards you can create. Each corporation, development team, and environment would extend and customize these to meet their corporate requirements.

Formatted or Structured Code

All program code should be formatted, or structured, to make the program control of flow clear. It should be easy for an outsider to read the code and follow the flow.

Tab refers to one indent (or one TAB). As different editors treat a TAB differently, replace each TAB with the actual ASCII value of three spaces.

General rules:

Indent one tab space (defined as three spaces) under every IF/BEGIN, FOR, DO, WHILE (or similar construct).

For long conditional sections or loops, or for nested conditionals or loops, add a short comment following the terminator for the conditional or loop specifying what IF, FOR, DO or BEGIN it belongs to. ELSE statements may require additional comments during complex logic.

Naming Conventions

Each language will have its own naming conventions. However, some principles do apply. Different combinations for mixed case and underscores are used for each language. It is most important that language usage be consistent, not that it exactly follows one of these sets of rules. The goal is to create a consistent environment with consistent indicators, structures, and documentation to improve productivity of programmers. Examples follow:

- Use no underscores with mixed case.
- For mixed case languages, within a variable or object name, uppercase the first letter of each word (GetItemTag, AssignSeqNum).
- Use underscores with all lowercase.
- Separate prefixes from names with underscore _ characters (r_rulename, ud_datatype).
- Within a variable or object name, break up whole words with underscores (f_this_function, g_global_variable).
- Where possible, favor whole names over abbreviations for the significant part of a name. That is, abbreviate the prefix (g for global, f for function) or type (int for integer, char for character), but leave the name whole (Patrick instead of PTK, Jellyfish instead of JFSH).

Comments

All major processes within a program should be commented with a comment header, and important single commands should be as well. See under the appropriate sections for the particular language you are using.

General rules:

- *Every* individual or stand-alone piece of code (function, stored procedure, or trigger) should have a header specific to its type of object and the language you are working in.

♦ Comments are written for any developer who maintains your code. Write concisely but liberally about what is about to happen and why.

♦ In between minor processes—simple function calls, variable initializations—add blank lines (one or two) to add breathing room to your code. This should also be done in between SQL SELECT, INSERT, UPDATE, and DELETE statements.

♦ Include comments to identify modifications made to the code. Include the date of the modifications.

Documentation

This document is mainly about formatting and documenting source code at the source. Documentation deliverables for a project are addressed only secondarily. In most cases, there should already be standard templates for those.

All of the following language software components should have a documentation format as well as coding standards:

♦ C or C++

.c files

.h files

Function header for C functions

♦ Other 3GL languages: COBOL, Fortran, Pascal, and so on

♦ Other object-oriented languages: Smalltalk, C++, etc.

♦ TSQL

Triggers

Stored procedures

SQL batch files

♦ DOS Batch files

♦ UNIX script files

♦ Development environment languages (Visual Basic, for example)

Event header scripts

Object functions

Global functions

Transact-SQL

The primary language used to program SQL Server is Transact-SQL (T-SQL). Transact-SQL is an extended SQL language based on the ANSI Standard. The language includes all statements required for creating objects [Data Definition Language (DDL)], manipulating data [Data Manipulation Language (DML)], logical constructs, specialized functions, triggers, stored procedures, and remote procedure calls. Within the SQL Server environment, it is a full-programming language.

All of the SQL Server–based functionality created for an application will be written in Transact-SQL; therefore it is an important language for which to impose programming standards.

Formatting and Structuring Code

These are example rules for formatting and structuring your Transact-SQL code. Feel free to adjust them to your requirements.

- Variables should all be declared and initialized at the beginning of a batch.
- Code should be structured so that control of flow within the code is easily readable from the structure.
- Code is structured by indenting one tab space (defined as three spaces) following each IF or BEGIN.
- *Structuring DECLARE statements:* There are two acceptable alternatives to DECLARE statements as shown in Figure 4.8.
- *Structuring SELECT statements:* Because a single SELECT statement can include a number of clauses (WHERE, HAVING, ORDER BY, GROUP BY) it is important that structure be maintained within each individual SELECT (see Figures 4.9 and 4.10).
- On creating a subquery for a SELECT, there are two acceptable alternatives for structuring the subquery dependent on the length of the subquery SELECT statement (see Figure 4.11).

```
A DECLARE is used for each variable.


DECLARE @log_seq_no          tinyint

DECLARE @log_seq_last        smallint


A single DECLARE statement can be used for a series of variable type declarations.


DECLARE @log_seq_count       tinyint,
        @scale_segment_no     tinyint


In all cases the variables and datatypes are left-aligned as shown in the above examples.
```

FIGURE 4.8 Structuring the DECLARE statements.

Place the SELECT statement itself at the leftmost position.

Indent subsequent lines of the SELECT columns and other lists to a common indent.

```
SELECT cli.lsp_species_group_code,cli.lsp_grade_group_code,
       cli.diam_range_code, cli.conf_line_grade_seq_no
```

Left align all other SQL keywords (except AND and OR) associated with the SELECT under the SELECT.

```
SELECT @lsp_grade_code = lsp_grade_code,
       @gross_segment_diameter = gross_segment_diameter
FROM   segment_to_confirmation sc, grade_map gm
WHERE  sc.certificate_key = @certificate_key
```

FIGURE 4.9 Structuring the SELECT statement.

♦ If providing aliases for table names, generally limit these to no more than three characters.

Each project should define standard aliases for each table.

Avoid the use of a preface of *temp* for working tables maintained in the permanent database.

For multiple joins to one table (selfjoins), use aliases with a number or role name.

♦ When aliasing table names, the alias (as opposed to the full table name) should be used exclusively and consistently throughout the T–SQL statement.

Structuring INSERT statements are shown in Figure 4.12.

Structuring UPDATE statements are shown in Figure 4.13.

Structuring DELETE statements are shown in Figure 4.14.

All IF statements require BEGIN and END, even if there is only one statement between them (see Figure 4.15).

♦ BEGIN and END keywords are left-aligned with the keyword they are associated with (IF, ELSE, WHILE).

♦ Nested conditions or long BEGIN-END structures should have a short comment following each END indicating which structure they apply to.

When structuring the FROM clause, try to list the tables in a logical sequence.

When structuring a WHERE clause, try to order the joins by table, so that it is easy to read the join sequence. List the joins at the beginning of the WHERE clause. List all the domain restrictions (**column = "constant"**) or (**column = @variable**) or (**column in (set)**) at the **end** of the where clause.

Right-align all AND and OR underneath the WHERE clause, so it is clear they belong to that WHERE clause. With any combined use of AND and OR, parens () should be used to explicitly identify associations.

```
SELECT  @lsp_grade_code = lsp_grade_code,
        @gross_segment_diameter = gross_segment_diameter
FROM    segment_to_confirmation sc, grade_map gm
WHERE   sc.certificate_key = @certificate_key
  AND   sc.scale_ticket_no = @scale_ticket_no
  AND   ( sc.log_seq_no = @log_seq_no
   OR   sc.scale_segment_no = @scale_segment_no)
```

FIGURE 4.10 Structuring FROM and WHERE clauses.

Naming Conventions (Specific to T-SQL)

By definition, an object name in T-SQL must:

♦ Be between 1 and 30 characters in length.
♦ May contain a character # which precedes a name that denotes a temporary table or temporary stored procedure. Temporary table names must not exceed 13 characters including the # sign.

Standards are as follows:

♦ All T-SQL keywords/statements should be typed uppercase (SELECT, INSERT, CREATE, DROP).

Follow all these stipulations for the SELECT in the subquery, so it is clear what belongs to the subquery

and what belongs to the outer query.

```
SELECT titlename

FROM    titles

WHERE   author_id in ( SELECT author_id

                         FROM    authors

                         WHERE   date_hired > getdate() )
```

Have the subquery string out on one line under the WHERE clause.

```
SELECT titlename

FROM    titles

WHERE   author_id in

        (SELECT author_id FROM authors WHERE au_id = '1')
```

FIGURE 4.11 Structuring a subquery.

♦ All object names in **SQL Server** should be lowercase and should not begin with an underscore. This includes databases, user names, and all object names, except as previously noted.

♦ Avoid, where possible, abbreviations for object names—sales_tracking instead of sls_trk. However, also avoid names that are excessively long.

Comments

Header comments should be aligned left. Block comments embedded in code should be indented with the section of code where they are used.

Documentation

♦ Triggers and stored procedures each carry a document header section which should be filled out when the object is created and updated each time it is modified.

♦ Large blocks of comment text, in a header or embedded in the code, should be introduced and ended by a single line of *s, followed by a blank line.

```
/*********************************************************
This is the header section for the . . .
*********************************************************
```

Always list the columns to which data is being added for a given INSERT.

List the table name being inserted into on the line with the INSERT.

Place the parenthesis at the beginning and end of the list on separate lines below and above the list itself. Multiple columns may be listed on one line.

Left-align the VALUES list with the INSERT statement. If three columns are listed on the first line, the first line of the VALUES list should have the first three values being inserted, and so on.

```
INSERT tickets
    (
    column1, column2, column3,
    column4, column7, column9
    )
VALUES
    (
    value1, value2, value3,
    value4, value7, value9
    )
```

If a SELECT is included in the INSERT, left-align the select with the keyword INSERT, and follow the stipulations for a SELECT listed above.

```
INSERT tickets
    (
    column1, column2, column3,
    column4, column7, column9
    )
SELECT column1, column2, column3,
       column4, column7, column9
FROM   old_tickets
WHERE  . . .
```

FIGURE 4.12 Structuring INSERT.

♦ Block comments for a trigger or a stored procedure should follow the AS keyword.

```
CREATE PROC p_authors_insert
AS
/***********************************************************
Procedure Name: this is the name of the stored
                procedure in the database
Date Created:   date when first submitted to server
.........
***********************************************************/
```

♦ Trigger headers and comments:

> The comment header for a trigger should have, roughly centered on the first line, the table name and action which fires the trigger. Again, this should go after the AS keyword. The header should include a listing of each event in the trigger. The text of each of these event comments is repeating with the code of each event. The order that

Left-align all keywords associated with the UPDATE statement. Left align object name lists to the same column.

```
UPDATE   contract
SET      date_expired = getdate()
FROM     contract cnt
WHERE    cnt.date_created = getdate()
```

If multiple columns are being updated at once, left-align each column name and assignment with the topmost column and give each its own line.

```
UPDATE   contract
SET      col1 = val1,
         col2 = val2,
         col3 = val3 . . .
```

If a subquery is included in the WHERE clause, follow the stipulations for structuring a SELECT provided above.

FIGURE 4.13 Structuring UPDATES.

Left-align all keywords associated with the DELETE under the DELETE keyword.

```
DELETE   titles
FROM     titles ttl, authors au
WHERE    ttl.author_id = au.author_id
```

If a subquery is included in the WHERE clause, follow the stipulations for structuring a SELECT provided above.

FIGURE 4.14 Structuring DELETE.

```
        IF ( condition1 )

    BEGIN  /* Condition 1 */

            IF ( condition2 )

            BEGIN /* Condition 2 */

                    SQL statements for execution...


            END /* Condition 2 */

            SQL statements for execution


    END /* Condition 1 */
```

FIGURE 4.15 Structuring IF statements with BEGIN/END.

the validations are listed here should be the same order that they are executed in the trigger.

The text of comments should list, briefly, the validations being performed and the actions taken in each case. Again, these are repeated in the trigger header.

```
CREATE TRIGGER ti_authors
AS
/**********************************************************
                    Author INSERT
- Disallow insert if the inserted author_id does not exist in
title_authors. RAISERROR and ROLLBACK.
**********************************************************/
```

♦ Stored Procedure header:

The following comment header should be filled out and incorporated into every stored procedure.

```
/**********************************************************
Procedure Name:      this is the name of the stored
                     procedure in the database
Date Created:        date when first submitted to server
Original Programmer: developer's name
Last Updated:        date of most recent update
Updated By:          name of developer for most recent update
Called From:         Script, procedure or executable which
                     calls this stored procedure.
Database(s) Used:    list of databases referenced.
```

```
Description:        description of procedure logic, in
                    structured English.
****************************************************/
```

Other Languages

Similar rules should be applied for all languages. A few general ideas follow in the next sections that could be applied to other languages.

Formatting and Structuring Code

- ♦ Variables should all be declared and initialized at the beginning of a script.
- ♦ When declaring variable datatypes, declare system datatypes (string, integer, long) first, followed by object types.
- ♦ Code should be structured so that control of flow within the code is easily readable from the structure.
- ♦ Code is structured by indenting one tab space (defined as 3 spaces) following each **IF**, **DO**, or **FOR**.

    In object-oriented languages, the *object* portion of the function call should be specified before the function name itself, not in the parameter list.

    this.GetText ()

    dw_figs.GetItemNumber ()

    Always add a space before *and* after the opening parenthesis, and after each comma, and after the final parameter listed. Do this even if no parameters are passed to the function. *This is vital if your code is to be readable.*

    this.GetItemNumber (row, column 1)

    Date (Today ())

    this.GetText ()

Naming Conventions

- ♦ By definition, an object name:

    Can have between 1 and 40 characters

    Must start with a letter

    Can be of mixed case

    Can have special embedded characters—$, &, #, –, _

    Cannot include blank spaces
- ♦ When naming variables, either make object and variable names lowercase, with the first letter of each word in uppercase and no underscores between words or all lower case with underscores.

d_TabSheetProperty

w_TaxAndLoanData

ib_number_of_rows

Use either method consistently in all your scripts.

♦ Any SQL commands should be shown in uppercase; however, database objects are usually case sensitive and will usually be in lower case within the SQL commands.

♦ All objects and variables should be named *explicitly*. Do *not* use default names.

♦ *Variable Scope Conventions:* Assigning a prefix for a local variable or function argument is optional. Use a prefix in either case when a datatype prefix is used as shown in Table 4.1.

User-Interface Standards

There are many books on graphical user interface design. We will only hit on a brief outline of why and how to standardize. It is important to remember the basic principles of good interface design:

♦ The user should be in control during the execution of the application.

♦ Users should be able to decide how to proceed and always have the option of changing their minds.

♦ The application should use modal behavior (the user *has* to do a particular action) as little as possible.

♦ Users should be able, at some level, to customize the application to their preferences.

♦ The interface should be consistent within itself, and consistent with other applications in use by the user community. Consistency should be reflected in design, layout, color, and most importantly, in behavior.

♦ Common actions should be reflected in common implementations. Metaphors for data manipulation should be constantly and consistently reused. Allow users to leverage what they learn in using applications with all new applications.

TABLE 4.1 Variable Scope Conventions

Variable Scope	*Convention*	*Example*
Global	g_	g_this_var
Shared	s_	s_that_var
Instance	i_	i_this_here_var
Local	l_	li_row_count
Function arguments	a_	astr_parameter

♦ Users should be able to reflect their activities directly in the software. They should be able to directly view and manipulate their information. The metaphors in the application should present intuitive ways for users to interface with their information.

♦ The interface should be direct in its response to the user. The software should reflect all user actions directly with visible and informational feedback. The application should visually respond to the user and reflect its actions visually.

♦ The interface should allow the users to change their minds and make errors. Primary decisions should allow for cancellation.

♦ The user interface should be pleasing to look at and should have as little clutter as possible. Appropriate aggregations of information should be defined according to the tasks, capabilities, and desires of the user community. (Occasionally, you will build a cluttered-looking screen, because the task at hand and the users demand that a large amount of information is present at one time so that quick decisions can be made. This is a business and utility based decision.)

Designing an Application Interface

To design an application interface you must first understand existing application standards and guidelines for the graphical user interface. For example, there are published guidelines for building Windows 3.1 and Windows 95 applications. In addition, the developer must use and study existing Windows applications.

An application interface is designed for a particular task and a particular set of users. It is necessary to study the users' tasks and work with the users to design a system that will serve them. It is an iterative process.

♦ Understand the overall goals of the system; study any analysis, modeling, and design work that has been done for the system.

♦ Review all existing applications in use by the user community for reusable components and design concepts.

♦ Know your platform.

♦ Classify the users into groups that define required functionality.

♦ Work with user representatives to enumerate the nature, sequence, control required, and importance of each task or task sequence. Understand their requirements for flexibility, availability of information, sequencing, and transaction management.

♦ Build a storyboard of the application area which includes menus, windows with controls on them, navigation metaphors (menus, tabs, toolbars, and so on). Work with the user in iterative design cycles improving the storyboard until the user likes it.

♦ For any critical or problem areas, build a working prototype from the storyboard. Solve difficult problems. Review with the user.

♦ Extend the storyboard/prototype into an application working iteratively with the user providing review and testing. This is a continuous iterative process until the application is complete.

There are many more tasks in building a system; we have isolated just the steps dealing with the user-interface design and implementation. This process can be formalized with complete usability testing.

Reusable Frameworks

An application framework is a set of application objects that work together to implement application-specific and business-specific behavior. In many development environments, there are commercial application frameworks available. It is also standard to build application frameworks within a corporation to gain reusability, control, and standardization of coding practices.

In a graphical environment like Windows, the application objects consist of windows of differing styles, menus, other control objects, or widgets. They have specialization with regard to specific metaphors, graphical representation, and behavior. It is standard to have frameworks to support standard windowing models like single document interface (SDI) and multiple document interface (MDI). In addition, other standard behaviors are supported in controls.

In an object-oriented environment, it is possible to extend these objects and create related classes of objects. Graphical development is ideally suited to object-oriented development and implementation because of the nature of our graphical operating systems. Object-oriented development of graphical frameworks is one of the most productive and powerful types of reuse available in our development architectures. Standard use of frameworks, purchased or developed, is an important part of standardizing the corporate investment in software development. It provides standardization, better quality, and reuse of software investments.

Corporate frameworks would implement behavioral and coding standards like error handling, security, transaction control, data validation, query methods, and so on. In addition, frameworks can implement corporate graphical standards such as color, fonts, layouts, and so on. At the lowest level of inheritance, the objects in the framework can be application- or business-specific. That is, they can be intelligent about reusable corporate entities (or objects) like customers, and embed the methods and attributes of these entities into reusable application objects.

It is important to view the development of a corporate application framework as an investment and allow adequate resources and time to this process. It will pay off, but as in all investment, the payoff happens over time. Development of a framework will actually lengthen the development of a first project. Use of a framework on later projects will save time and money. In addition, it will improve maintenance costs.

5

Application Architecture

Tiered Architecture

Tiered architecture refers to the parsing of application solutions into multiple processes (client, server, middleware, and so on) and the number and design of those processes. Simple client/server implementations use a two-tiered architecture; more complex architectures use additional tiers for varying architectural reasons.

Parsing of application logic and processing is dependent on the use of standard communication *application programming interfaces* (*APIs*) that enable peer-to-peer, client/server, and server-to-server communications.

Two-Tiered Architecture

The classic client/server architecture consists of a server process (most often a relational database), a client process, and the communication between them. This architecture is used to isolate the presentation of information to the client process and the data storage and manipulation to the server process. To properly leverage the client/server architecture, the two processes are deployed on independent and scalable platforms using appropriate hardware and operating systems based on the system requirements.

Many implementations of two-tiered architectures also provide programmable servers. Application logic can be embedded into a logical layer that happens to reside in the server in stored procedures, triggers, and views. This logical layer provides a layer of data independence for the application. The data structures can be modified without major changes to the application due to the programmed layer. This architecture provides for multiple logical layers without the need or advantages of implementing a third physical tier. These solutions are appropriate for many applications.

In a two-tiered system, transaction management is server-based, that is, internal to a single server implementation. It is possible to write heterogeneous transactions, but they must be controlled from a client application with two-phase commit protocols.

You must establish the interfaces between the application's client and server components in a way that minimizes communication between the client and server computers and takes advantage of the hardware resources. Otherwise performance diminishes as time and resources get used by this communication.

The client portion of the application receives data from the server, presents the data to the user, and provides screen interactions for requesting, manipulating, and validating data. The application's server portion:

♦ Processes, stores, and retrieves the physical data
♦ Maps logical data structures to the physical media
♦ Restricts the data to be moved
♦ Ensures that multiple users don't interfere with each other's actions against the data
♦ Maintains various business rules
♦ Executes transaction logic

Multitiered Architectures

Extension of basic client/server architecture to a multitiered environment as shown in Figure 5.1 is commonly done for one or more of the following capabilities:

♦ Queries or transactions in a heterogeneous database environment
♦ Logical isolations of functionality and logic into a middle tier that is not tied to a particular database or development environment vendor and is therefore more reusable and flexible
♦ Modularization of components in generic compiled languages
♦ Deployment of reusable and sharable components
♦ Systems that scale to a very large number of users through the use of routers (TP monitors) to balance the number of processes and enable better use of symmetric multiprocessing

♦ Scalability by creating flexibility in moving resulting functionality from one platform to another in the architecture
♦ Interfaces with object request brokers to enable execution of methods on object servers
♦ Functional advantages such as messaging, data subscription services, event management, and alerts

A more complex usage of client/server architecture will become more pervasive as the tools and technologies improve. This usage will also develop as corporations grow more comfortable with their existing client/server systems and feel capable of entertaining greater complexity.

Open Servers

Many implementations of client/server solutions are *data centric*. That is, they are based on storing and manipulating data. An underutilized component of client/server systems is that of *open services*. The architecture supports the construction of servers with the *Open Data Services* product from Microsoft. This product is a library of functions (APIs) that enable the construction of server processes. The message protocols and basic architecture of a server are built into the API structures. It enables the construction of extensions to the basic SQL Server services and gateways into external data sources.

Servers are constructed in two basic styles:

1. *They can process language events,* which means that they parse and process command strings sent from the client application.
2. *They can process procedure events,* wherein they interpret a remote procedure call (RPC) and execute an appropriate event handler for that procedure.

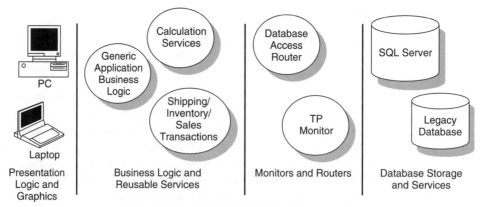

Logically and Physically Distinct Components

FIGURE 5.1 Multitier architecture.

The remote procedure call architecture is easier to construct and is further strengthened by the support of RPCs between server processes. A SQL Server can call the Open Server with an RPC, or it can pass the RPC from a client to another server.

The SQL Server architecture also supports extended stored procedures. It allows you to extend the behavior of a SQL Server without building a separate server application. For example, you can build stored procedures that do mail, fax, or complex mathematical functions—anything you can do in C. The functionality is compiled into a DLL and installed with the standard SQL Server DLL files. The functions are then available to be executed as stored procedures within the server environment, that is, from stored procedures and triggers. In a product inventory application, you could build an extended stored procedure that is fired from a trigger when unit volumes become low. This procedure could fax an order to the appropriate vendor, send e-mail to internal contacts, print the purchase orders, and update the accounting system.

Some of the capabilities available with Open Data Services include:

♦ External gathering of real-time data
♦ External communications
♦ Broadcast messages that result from the logic in a trigger
♦ Gateways into external or legacy data systems
♦ Anything you can build in C

Client/Server Architectural Model

A *client/server architectural model* is a standard for how to build high-quality cooperative processing within your chosen architecture. It is critical that corporations architect a suite of technical solutions for their business processes. It may consist of database servers, GUI development tools, report writers, batch processing tools, real-time processors and monitors, networks, gateways, and communication protocols. Whatever toolset is chosen, the corporation must develop standard solutions using those tools. Standards about how the tools will be used, how communications will proceed, how databases will be designed, and how client applications will behave are the keys to success.

Many corporations and departments worry about standards. Often those standards are about how to name things or how a GUI application should function or look. These are important. But few corporations understand that, more importantly, they need standards on interoperating. That is, how are we going to implement *cooperative processing?* Where will each part of the solution be implemented and why?

What are cooperative processes? When you build a complex system from multiple processes, they must *interoperate* (send messages and pass information). One hopes that the processes work cooperatively. That is, they solve an application problem in the most efficient way possible. They must communicate efficiently and process information in a way that leverages the best features of each of the individual processes. A client/server architectural model defines the way a particular server and development tool should interact to execute a system and formalizes the best design decisions.

The decisions made in this model lay the groundwork for the solid and successful implementation of a system. The issues involved should be addressed before any major development work begins on a strategic system. It requires a thorough understanding of your development platform, your server platform, and the strategic requirements of the application system to be deployed.

Once understood and defined, a programmer's manual can be developed with specific instructions for the implementation of these client/server features. Some of the decisions can be built into reusable tools and objects that represent correct usages. Once a model is deployed all subsequent application development can use it with only minor modifications.

There are key architectural problems that must be addressed by all client/server developers. These are the issues that are standard in a client/server architectural model. The advantage of identifying and classifying these problems enables a corporation to categorize and standardize solutions and be aware of the ramifications of all the choices made.

The cooperative processing issues that should be addressed include:

♦ Connection management
♦ Error handling
♦ Data access
♦ Data validation
♦ Transaction management
♦ Concurrency control
♦ Distributed processing
♦ Security

Connection Management

When a client process needs to communicate with a server process, it is required to establish a connection. A *connection* is a structure established in the client application and at the server process. Communications between these processes use a standard client/server protocol called *Tabular Data Stream* (*TDS*). There are important resource and performance issues with regard to establishing connections, for example, the number of connections the server can support and how fast the application can respond to the user. In addition, there are options to set attributes of a connection that govern its behavior. It is important to design connection behavior and usage to optimize your control over application behavior. This allows you to fine-tune the server load and the application response time to meet your application requirements.

When an application establishes a connection it can set properties of the connection that affect its behavior. Some of these properties are set in the communication protocol API (DB-Library). Some of them are set with Transact-SQL (T-SQL) after the connection is established. In this section we will cover only the properties that are useful in the ongoing execution of a production application. Review product documentation for other aspects that are useful in development and tuning.

Establishing a Connection

As we previously stated, a connection is established between a client and a server when the client issues a request. In the API it is accomplished with the command *dbopen ()*. Before issuing the command, the login structure must be populated with appropriate property values for the connection, including server name, database name, user name, user password, and so on. This may be done directly with the API and a 3GL language or, as with many development environments, this service may be encapsulated into functionality or objects in the development tool. In any case, the native API behavior is under the covers. ODBC connectivity also incorporates this behavior.

The client application creates the connection structure, which is called a *DBPROCESS*, and the programmer populates it. When the client application requests the connection from the server, the server creates a similar structure (server process or spid) at the server, reads the properties sent from the client, validates the user and password, and sets up the state of the connection.

A server can, of course, have many connections with client applications. A client application can have more than one connection to a given server and can hold connections to multiple servers. It is not common to require more than one connection, though occasionally two are useful.

DB-Library Options

You can tune certain attributes of a connection. DB-Library supports the setting of the attributes shown in Table 5.1 before a connection is established. They are useful for system administration from the server (Who is connected?) and configuring aspects of the connection's behavior. *Note: References to DB-Library also apply to Visual Basic DB-Library which is a version of DB-Library for Visual Basic.* These are all useful. You will need to identify which are available to you and which are important to your application.

Connection SET Options

After a connection is established there are options that can be SET to fine-tune the connection's behavior (see Table 5.2). These attributes can be modified at any time. If you are programming in DB-Library you can set some of these attributes with the DB-Library function *dbsetopt ()*. Otherwise, they can be set by submit-

TABLE 5.1 DB-Library Connection Attributes

Attributes	*Action*
DBSETLAPP	Identifies the application name for use in the sysprocesses table. This is useful to track who is using a particular connection.
DBSETLHOST	Identifies the workstation name for use in the sysprocesses table. This helps the system administrator track which workstation is using a particular connection.
DBSETNATLANG	If language support is installed, returns messages in the identified language.
DBSETLPACKET	Sets the tabular data stream packet size for communications between the client and the SQL Server. This is useful for performance optimization. It allows the packets to be larger for more efficiently passing large datasets.
DBSETLSECURE	Establishes that the connection should be established as a secure, or trusted, connection to the server.
dbsetlogintime	Sets the number of seconds that DB-Library will wait for a response from the SQL Server after a login request.
dbsettime	Sets the number of seconds that DB-Library waits for a response to a T-SQL statement.

ting T-SQL statements over the established connection. These options apply only to the connection over which the option setting statements are issued. (Only the most important options are mentioned here; review product documentation for the complete list.) Many of these options should be standardized in the application development process so that connections will behave consistently.

Resource Usage

A connection uses resources at the client and the server. At the server each connection established by a user uses 37K of memory. There is a serverwide configuration value for the number of connections (users) that will be allowed. Additionally, the number of connections possible is governed by the amount of memory that the server is allowed to use. If memory is limited at the server it is important to limit the number of connections that an application holds open. More memory will then be available for caching data pages to improve server performance.

It is common for an application to establish a connection at the opening of an application and keep it open for the duration of the application's execution. This is a good design if the sizing of the server can be large enough to generously accommodate the required number of connections and when the users are using those connections at regular intervals. Some large systems can do better by not holding the connections. This is true when the total number of users is great and the style of usage is occasional. That is, the users will make

TABLE 5.2 Attributes for Fine Tuning a Connection's Behavior

Attributes	*Reaction*
ARITHABORT	Server will cancel a query if an overflow or divide-by-zero error occurs.
ARITHIGNORE	Server will return null if an overflow or divide-by-zero error occurs. If neither **ARITHABORT** or **ARITHIGNORE** is set, the server will return NULL and print a message.
NOCOUNT	Server will not send a message at the end of each statement with the number of rows affected.
DATEFIRST	Sets the first weekday (number 1–7). Standard default is 7 for Saturday.
DATEFORMAT	Sets the order of the day, month, and year for submitting dates.
LANGUAGE	Set the official language for messages and errors. The default is us_english.
ROWCOUNT	Server will return only the number of rows indicated. This feature should be used sparingly, as the server may have to do an inordinate amount of work. For example if you want the first 10 rows of an ordered set of 5,000, it would have to sort the 5,000 rows before it found the first 10. *Do not use this to control program loops.*
TRANSACTION ISOLATION LEVEL	Sets the isolation level for the connection. Options are READ UNCOMMITTED, READ COMMITTED, REPEATABLE READ, and SERIALIZABLE.

a request or send an update and then leave their computers or do extended work on the client machine. This application style is predominant in many service applications (e.g., hospitals). There might be a thousand total users, but only a hundred working users at any given time. Sizing a system for a hundred concurrent users is very different from sizing a system for a thousand users. (In all cases you must allow enough connections to ensure that you will never run out of connections.)

Table 5.3 shows the properties of a connection that are available to manage the development process. They affect the kinds of result information returned by the connection and the stages of work that the server will use to process a statement.

Performance and Response Time

Connections take time to establish. Once established, using the connection is much faster. It is important to understand the nature of the required behavior and response time in the client application. This will help you know whether you can afford the delay caused by repeated connections. If the user application needs to access the server in a continuous fashion the delay will likely be too costly and the application should hold the connection. If the

TABLE 5.3 Connection Properties that Manage the Development Process

Properties	Reaction
NOEXEC	The server will compile but not execute a query. Used with SHOWPLAN to examine the query plan of a statement without executing it.
PARSEONLY	The server will check the syntax of a statement and return error information. The statement is not compiled or executed.
SHOWPLAN	The server will return the query plan that the optimizer generates for the execution of the query.
STATISTICS IO	The server will return information about the work required to execute the query (logical reads, physical reads, pages written).
STATISTICS TIME	The server returns parse, compile, and execution time for the statements submitted.

usage is occasional (every 10 to 15 minutes), it may be possible to release the connection and reestablish it each time, reducing the number of total connections held.

If you are constructing a large system with a large number of users, careful planning with respect to when a connection is established and how long connections are held is an opportunity to more accurately size the system requirements. In systems that need to do this, protocols for using long-running connections and short-running connections should be established. When using SQL Server with an average application load, the most likely preference will be to hold connections.

Error Handling

There are several sources of errors and messages when communicating over a connection with a SQL Server. The server itself can send messages and errors; DB-Library can send error messages as well. It is also possible to build special errors and messages into your server code.

It is necessary to handle these messages and errors in the client application. If you are building a client application using the DB-Library C interface you will build error handling functions yourself. If you are using a client development tool, it may encapsulate some of the error handling or error passing in objects or structures provided by the environment. In all cases, you should isolate error analysis and information in a single place within your application architecture in a reusable function or object. All error processing is reusable. This simplifies error and message management and standardizes the methods used to manage errors.

Once established, the use of these standard mechanisms should be clearly documented and enforced. Error handling mechanisms should be established very early in the development cycle to prevent the implementation of nonstandard methods and to catch developers' errors while they are writing code. SQL Server messages and errors are identified in the table sysmessages. DB-Library errors are identified in the documentation. When programming with DB-Library you will program and install asynchronous error handling routines. If you are building with an application development environment, the error capturing functionality may be provided. In either case, one must architect a set of responses to error information.

SQL Server provides a global variable for tracking error conditions in T-SQL batches, stored procedures, and triggers. It is called *@@ERROR.* (See the *Transact-SQL Reference Manual* for other global variables.) Its value is changed after the execution of every statement. It is set to zero (0) if no error occurs. Otherwise, it is set to the appropriate error number. (See the system table sysmessages.) The global variable @@ERROR can be used to do control of flow logic in T-SQL based on the error return of statements. For example, in transactions you may not want to continue to process a transaction if a statement in the transaction produces an error.

RAISERROR

RAISERROR is a T-SQL statement that places an error message on the standard error structure. It will then get passed directly to the client application. The RAISERROR statement has two primary options: ad hoc messages and user-defined messages. The previous formats of RAISERROR continue to work as before.

An *ad hoc message* includes a message string which can have optionally defined substitution parameters using a C printf()-like syntax. If substitution parameters are used, the arguments for substitution are enumerated after the message, severity, and state. It can be sent with the following command:

```
RAISERROR message_string, severity, state, [,argument [,argument]] [WITH LOG]
```

Severity is a value used to indicate the seriousness of the error. The values are 0 to 25. Values 19 to 25 are reserved for the system administrator and require logging to the server error log. *State* is an integer value about the invocation state of the error. *WITH LOG* indicates whether the error is logged to the SQL Server error log and the NT event log. When RAISERROR is used with a dynamically defined message the error number is always 50000. It is not possible to identify these messages by their error number. Since the message syntax provides for parameters, it enables the construction of very specific error messages. This model is good for constructing very complete messages that can be delivered directly to the user through the application. Because we cannot distinguish the errors by number, it will be more difficult to use it to arbitrate changes in the control of flow in the application.

When RAISERROR is used with an error number (message id), the server will look in the table sysmessages to find the error message that has been pre-defined by the system administrator (see sp_addmessage, sp_dropmessage, sp_altermessage). These messages can be fixed (no variable substitution) or will support parameter substitution. They can also be differentiated by their differing error numbers. This style of error definition should be used when you wish to identify the error specifically in the client application, that is, when the application needs to interpret the error or message to determine control of flow for the application.

The following example illustrates the use of a *user-defined message* to indicate the number of rows modified by an update statement. This is a message that the server component of the application will send to the client component. User-defined error numbers must be over 50000.

```
sp_addmessage error_number, severity, message_string
sp_addmessage 50010, 12, "The update modified %i rows."

RAISERROR (error_number, severity, state, [,argument [,argument]])
RAISERROR (50010, 12, 1, @@rowcount)
```

(@@ROWCOUNT is the number of rows affected by the most recently executed T-SQL statement. There are other possible parameters for RAISERROR. See the *Transact-SQL Reference Manual*.)

It is important not to obscure SQL Server errors and messages. Make sure the information generated by the server arrives in your application.

If you require a complex definition and delineation of user-defined errors and messages, it is possible to dynamically construct messages that incorporate various situational information into the message for parsing in the client application. One might send procedure name, batch identifier, table, action, column, and so on. If you standardize the messages, you can build a single function to parse them in the client application architecture.

Errors and messages are most often generated in triggers and stored procedures. Please review the detailed samples found in Chapter 7.

Error Handling Techniques

There are many useful techniques for managing errors. Review some of these ideas and incorporate the ones that make the most sense for your architecture. Put these behaviors into a standard reusable architecture and all of your applications can have sophisticated error handling behavior.

♦ Establish an application-wide (global) variable that indicates whether the application is in DEBUG mode (development and BETA) or in PRODUC-TION mode. Use this variable to turn on more in-depth error handling or a different style of error handling.

♦ Write all (or certain classes) of errors to a local or centralized *file*. These files can be collected and reviewed by developers.

♦ Write all (or certain classes) of errors to a centralized *table*. This central storage of all errors and messages provides developers and maintenance personnel easy access to monitor the application.

♦ In PRODUCTION mode, provide a user-friendly and minimal message. In DEBUG mode, provide a robust error handling message that will help steer developers to a quick resolution.

♦ When creating your own error messages with RAISERROR, be careful not to obscure the actual server error message which is key to understanding the source of the error.

♦ When sending a RAISERROR message, consider incorporating the name of the stored procedure or a batch identifier in the message to assist in tracking the source of the error. Also include the access type and the name of a table if applicable. Some server errors already include table and column information.

Data Access

Data access refers to bringing data from the database into an application. There are very basic issues that must be understood in this environment. The primary issue concerning data access is to move as little data across the network as possible. It is important to utilize the power of the SQL Server engine to reduce, manage, and structure data as it is retrieved. This reduces the amount of work done by the network and the client. To build scalability into a system, it is very important to be as efficient as possible in using available resources.

The most frequently asked question about data access is: When and how do we move the required information? Data in a client application has a latency period. *Latency* is the time since it was read from the database. This has potential bearing on the current accuracy of the data. We assume that someone else could have modified the data in the database. One has to understand how volatile the data is and how often information should be read into the application. You must read it only often enough to insure that the users have an adequate supply of accurate information to accomplish their tasks.

When moving data into a client application there are at least two primary questions: which technology to use (embedded SQL, DB-Library calls, stored procedures, and so on) and whether to use a set operation or a cursor (row-at-a-time access to the data). Performance, programming costs, and program maintenance costs all come to bear on the decision. In addition, development environments or languages may come with built-in facilities for moving data. You must understand exactly how they work and how to manage them for efficiency.

Stored Procedures

SQL Server Version 6 has a strong architecture based around stored procedures. A *stored procedure* is a program written in T-SQL that is stored in the server. Stored procedures are parsed when they are created, are optimized and compiled the first time they are executed, and remain in memory (cache) for subsequent users. They are the preferred way to manage most of the work done in the server for the following reasons:

♦ Increased performance can result because the parse, compile, and optimization work is done. This is especially important for online transaction processing systems (OLTP) that use small, discrete transactions in high volumes.

♦ Security can be controlled through procedures by granting execute permission on them and revoking any permissions on underlying objects, allowing access only through the stored procedures.

♦ You can isolate the client application from any changes to the underlying database structure by accessing data only through the stored procedures.

♦ Stored procedures provide centralized, reusable software components that can be called from any application. Program the solution once.

Stored Procedure Caveat

Once a stored procedure is executed, it is stored in cache (memory) for subsequent users. Stored procedures executed from cache have been precompiled with an execution plan optimized for the first executor. If the procedure takes parameters that are used in the stored procedure as values in a WHERE clause, it is important to understand the selectivity of the query where they are used. *Selectivity* is the measure of the percentage of the rows to be returned. Selectivity affects the index selection made by the optimizer when analyzing for best performance. You must decide whether the procedure optimization can be appropriately reused or not. The rule of thumb goes like this: *If the volume of data resulting from a query varies from below 5 to 10 percent of the data to above 5 to 10 percent of the data, the stored procedure should be created WITH RECOMPILE.* This will force the server to optimize each submission of the query. You will lose some of the performance advantage of preoptimization, but for large queries or for queries of varying selectivity the savings isn't much. In fact, the wrong query plan for the submitted parameters can give very poor performance results.

The optimizer can often find a useful nonclustered index to help in queries that read less than 5 to 10 percent of the data, but that same nonclustered index will be a serious detriment (more pages to read) for results sets larger than that. In many cases, a table scan is better than nonclustered index if you are reading a lot of the data. (The 5 to 10 percent is purposely vague because it depends on a calculation that relates the size of the data row to the size of the index row and how many index rows fit on a page. If you are varying in the 5 to 10 percent range, you should test how the optimizer does index selection across the entire range. If it is consistent, then you do not need the recompile option. If the optimizer changes its mind somewhere in the range, you do need to create the procedure with the recompile option.)

Embedded SQL and DB-Library Calls

Many development environments allow you to submit embedded SQL to the server from the client application. These can be calls to existing stored procedures, or actually SQL statements created in the client application. To provide logical isolation between the database and the client application, it is often better not to embed data retrieval logic in a client application. But sometimes the tools and the costs of efficiency lead us to do this. For simple statements (SELECT columns FROM table) or when working with tools that automatically generate the SQL for you, this is adequate. Do not embed complex data manipulation that could be reused into the client application. Try to build a stored procedure.

The exception to this is a *dynamically generated statement*. This is a data query or manipulation that cannot be defined at compile time, but is dependent on the state of the application at run time. In these cases it is necessary to develop the statements from the client application, submit all the statements as a single batch (any set of Transact-SQL statements submitted to the server at one time), and allow the server to execute them. To optimally use SQL Server, a development environment must provide an efficient way to submit batches.

The alternative is to submit individual statements one at a time to the server. It is important to weigh the performance degradation imposed by making multiple transmissions across the network. It is critical not to do this inside a transaction because it will decrease concurrency and performance.

Set Operations and Cursors

SQL Server is a relational database and therefore optimizes the use of data sets. Whenever possible, programs should manipulate sets of data. A set may be one row or millions of rows. For performance reasons it is important not to process millions of rows one row at a time. Sometimes it is absolutely necessary, but not as often as we think (see Chapter 8).

SQL Server provides *server-based cursors*. These cursors enable the program to request a set of data and access it one row at a time. Some processes require this. There are two ways to access the cursors: from within a Transact-SQL batch, trigger, or stored procedure; and from a client development language or tool (C, C++, Visual Basic, and so on). In both cases the actual cursor manipulation is done by the server. However, there is a big difference in how the system processes the data.

When you use a cursor in Transact-SQL and do all of the cursor usage from within a single batch or stored procedure, the cursor loops through the data at the server and the data never moves onto the network or into the client application. If you access the cursor from a client application, the server sends a buffer of rows to the client (the buffer size is tunable) and the client application works through the individual rows. Manipulating a cursor from a client is necessarily much slower than manipulating it within the server. *Never move data across the network unless you need to.*

Many client applications use a *browsing metaphor* for searching through rows of data. The user is allowed to select a relatively large data set and browse through it. There are two distinct ways to implement this:

1. You can bring all of the data into the client application at once—a *snapshot.*
2. You can open a cursor and bring more data over as the user scrolls through the information.

The second method may give the user quicker response and may require less memory, but the first method is preferred because it frees up resources at the server and any locks that may be held. Of course, there are limits to how big the snapshot can be. It must fit in memory. In fact, there are very distinct size limits to how much data it is reasonable to bring into a graphical application expecting a user to browse through it in a practical amount of time. The application should be designed to aid the user and require that the size of any snapshot set selected be limited.

Cursors reading data may use a shared lock to manage the pages that they are reading. If *HOLDLOCK* is not used, the pages are freed as they are read, but at least one page is potentially locked while you are still processing a cursor. If this application or any other application tries to modify the locked page, it must wait until the cursor is moved forward. What if the user went to lunch? One could set the isolation level to zero (0)—or use the NO LOCK optimizer hint—to prevent the use of any lock, but it will also ignore other locks and introduce the possibility of inconsistency in the data being read.

As you can see, how to get data into the client application is not a trivial problem. Emphasize the following solutions:

♦ Use stored procedures for complex data manipulations and transactions and whenever else you can justify the extra coding cost.
♦ Use code generating tools and embedded SQL for simple single statements.
♦ Bring sets of data into the client application all at once and then allow browsing.
♦ Program set operations instead of row-by-row operations whenever possible.
♦ Use cursors inside of stored procedures or batches whenever possible.
♦ Send dynamic SQL to the server to be processed in a single batch.

Data Validation

Validating data is a major component of any application. It is critical to assure that each data value meets domain constraints defined by the business activity. These constraints can be *fixed* (e.g., value is always between 2 and 10), *self-referential* (e.g., value *A* must not be greater than value *B*, or new value *A* must not be more than 1.1 times the old value *A*), or *referential* (e.g., value *A* must match a value or constraint coming from another data element or table).

One advantage of SQL Server is its programmability. We can program intelligence and behavior into the server and thereby construct a server that itself controls the quality of the data. When a server is programmed properly it is not possible to get incorrect data into the database. This is a great advantage in this age of open systems when it is possible for end users to get at data with inexpensive over-the-counter tools which know nothing about our data constraints. As long as the server enforces them we can feel comfortable that the users cannot violate the data quality.

In addition, we need to validate data in the client application (field-by-field validation). Why is this? It is important to build client applications that meet high standards for usability, control, and performance. Client-side validation is a key factor in meeting these standards. For a data manipulation application to be usable, it needs to give the user constant feedback about his actions and the quality of the data. It is not sufficient to send the data to the server at the end of an editing sequence and then tell the user that the information he entered 5 to 10 minutes ago was not correct. It wastes time, and it irritates the user. It requires that the transaction be sent across the network multiple times, causing more work for the network, the application, and the server. In addition, the error handling that needs to be constructed in an application will need to be much more robust to deal with failures of complex transactions. Of course, validation can never be 100 percent accurate in the client, since some reference tables may be changing at any time. The goal is to make an error condition from the server a rare instance. This improves usability, control, and performance.

This implies that each field (or in cases of self-reference validations, each set of fields) is validated as the user provides the information. In many development tools such a mechanism is a service of the product. It is necessary to design the most efficient use of the provided mechanisms. Standardized use of validation techniques is another critical design issue that will increase the strength of an application architecture.

SQL Server Validation Techniques

The SQL Server provides several tools for creating validation mechanisms in the server:

♦ Rules
♦ Defaults

♦ User-defined datatypes
♦ Column constraints
♦ Table constraints
♦ Triggers
♦ Stored procedures

Each of these tools is applicable in different situations. *Rules* and *defaults* are relatively fixed and apply to single columns or user-defined datatypes. *User-defined datatypes* encapsulate particular rules and defaults into datatypes that can be reused through a database, enforcing the defaults and rules for every column that uses it. Defaults, rules, and user-defined datatypes are used for atomic value constraints that do not reference other data objects.

Column constraints are an ANSI-compliant mechanism for providing data validation. They have the advantage of not requiring a binding step as do rules and defaults, but they are not reusable. They need to be defined on each column.

Table constraints are also an ANSI-compliant mechanism applied at the table level. They are used for internal reference validations (table.A must be greater than table.B) and for referential integrity based on primary/foreign key relationships.

In general, apply these validation technologies as follows:

♦ For applicationwide and reusable domains, use user-defined datatypes with defaults and rules. (Domains such as phone numbers, zip codes, states, and application-specific domains.)
♦ For column-specific constraints use column constraints. (For example, the age for a kindergarten applicant must be between three and seven.)
♦ For table-specific constraints (intercolumn, referential, primary key, and uniqueness) use the table-level constraints. (For example, the school entrance date must be after the birthdate, or the state must be one of the states in the states table.)
♦ For any validations that cannot be covered with the previous technologies, use triggers. (For example, an order amount cannot exceed the sum of the stock on hand and the stock to be constructed in the next seven days.)
♦ If a trigger can't be used, use a stored procedure.

Use the most reusable and automated process to get the most utility for your effort. Remember that primary and unique constraints construct indexes. Remember as you rearrange indexes for performance that if you have used constraints to build the unique indexes, you will need to drop the constraints and re-create them using the *ALTER TABLE* statement. It will, at first, seem more awkward than standard index manipulation. Remember to specify *CLUSTERED* or *NONCLUSTERED* as is relevant to your tuning process and be aware of the device on which you build the index.

Some of the choices will depend on the tools you are using and what they support. Some database design products generate trigger logic and constraints. It will be advantageous to use the features in the toolset that you have adopted, and to use them consistently.

User-Defined Datatype Caveat

The SQL Server does not support joins between columns defined on user-defined datatypes where the user-defined datatypes have differing names. This is true even if their underlying attributes are identical. It is important to understand your join requirements before defining user-defined datatypes that may be logically the same domain (and might require a join). Note that some different system datatypes can be joined.

Client Validation Techniques

There are many tools available for validating data in the client application. The development environment used to build applications will provide some of them automatically. Use the most reusable and automated tools available.

Many graphic editing controls naturally validate data. They should be automatically populated with valid values, perhaps from the database. When available and natural to the application use:

♦ Check boxes
♦ List boxes
♦ Drop down list boxes (combo boxes)
♦ Radio buttons
♦ Edit controls with constraints

For validations that go beyond what you can accomplish with the graphical controls, use postprocessing when the user leaves the data field, and only in an extreme circumstance go to the server at that moment to see if the data is valid. It is often appropriate to make an extra transmission (round-trip communication) to the server to immediately validate a field, but it has to be measured against system load and performance. You could always wait until the user is ready to write the change to the database and notify him or her then. The total impact of either solution must be weighed against usability, performance, and control over the application.

Transaction Management

The most critical issue in the successful deployment and scalability of a client/server application is the proper implementation of transactions. *Transactions,* or permanent data modifications, are the most concise representation of the business meaning of an application. It is critical to understand the implications of managing data modifications with respect to the business represented and the technology used to implement the business behavior.

A transaction should be purposely defined to contain the smallest unit of work (database modifications) that has meaning to the business. Each single modification statement (INSERT, UPDATE, or DELETE) is, by default, treated as a complete unit of work, sometimes called an *implicit transaction*. When modifications must be grouped together to form an explicit transaction the programmer must explicitly do this with *transaction delineation statements* (BEGIN TRAN and COMMIT/ROLLBACK TRAN).

In the SQL Server a transaction is guaranteed to continue to completion and be permanent, or it will not have happened at all. This is regardless of the amount of work contained in the transaction. The SQL Server manages this through the use of the log and locking mechanisms. Data that is being modified by a transaction is locked from other users. When a process wants to read or write to a page that another process has locked, the process must wait. The waiting process is said to be *blocked*.

It is necessary that a transaction have the shortest duration possible. This is accomplished both by limiting the contents of the transaction to the smallest logical unit of work that has meaning to the business and by ensuring that the transaction executes as quickly as possible. When transactions run over a long period of time, they hold locks over a long period of time and therefore extend the probability of blocking another user. What is a long period of time? It depends. In a high transaction rate OLTP system 200 ms may be too long. In a low transaction rate system, seconds may not matter. In reality, efficiency in transaction management is a key reason why client/server applications fail to scale properly to the required volumes. They generate acceptable transaction rates at low volumes, but are too time consuming for large volumes. The system is slowly crippled by the addition of users. It is difficult to rearchitect a system's transaction management model after the system has been deployed.

To ensure that a transaction runs in the shortest possible time it is necessary to remove certain actions from within the scope of the transaction. In a programmable server like SQL Server the transaction should start and end inside the server. There are many casual styles of transaction implementation that violate this rule.

Application development environments encourage the execution of transaction controls from the client application. They do this by allowing the issuance of transaction control statements in the development environment language. In addition, they often produce multiple data modification statements and send them individually across the network. This involves activity in the client and multiple network transmissions during the scope of the transaction. This makes the transaction many times longer than necessary. The most egregious error is asking the users whether they want to commit the transaction. They could go to lunch. Most of us succeed in avoiding this error.

To properly implement the most efficient transactions with the SQL Server, there are three basic techniques:

1. *Single statement, implicit transactions.* They need no transaction management statements. Since the server handles them implicitly as a transaction, the server will do adequate management unless we want to do a logical check to determine whether or not to roll back the transaction.

2. *Embed the transaction inside a stored procedure.* This stored procedure will be passed all of the data required to manage the transaction. It will validate the data, begin the transaction, execute the data modifications, do logic and error checking, and if all is well, it will commit the transaction. It can alternately roll back the transaction if appropriate.

3. *Construct the complete transaction logic in the client application and send it to the server at one time in a batch.* These dynamic transactions cannot be defined during development. Their scope is determined by the state of the application at runtime (variable tables, variable numbers of rows, and so on). The batch constructed by the application will contain the beginning of the transaction, all of the data modifications, error checking, and the commit or roll back logic.

All of these transaction models exhibit optimal performance because no extraneous work is done within the scope of the transaction. If you have also tuned the database properly to ensure optimal access paths to the data, they will be blazingly quick. Well, optimally quick. This ensures minimal locking and blocking in the production system, enabling the system to support many more users effectively.

Error Checking in a Transaction

It is necessary to check for the error return of each data modification statement used in a transaction. If the error is very severe the server will roll back the transaction. If the server error is less severe (for example, duplicate row, null values, and constraint violations) the server will not automatically roll back the transaction. You must check the global variable @@ERROR and if it is not zero (0), you can roll back the transaction as appropriate. Stored procedures should generally be built with very tight logical constructs so that there is generally not any processing logically following any error except to leave the procedure.

Trigger logic will be executed in the midst of a transaction. Triggers should issue a roll back whenever data fails trigger validation. It should also raise an appropriate error. This will terminate the transaction with appropriate information returning to the client application. The ROLLBACK issued will roll back the transaction to the original start of the transaction whether it is implicit or explicit.

It is important that transaction control be issued as an all or nothing proposition. *Do not* decompose the definition of a transaction in the middle of a trigger. Do not, for example allow three rows of a five-row insert to be inserted and delete the other two. The application must be able to assume that the transaction is being treated as a complete logical unit of work and trust that the server implementation will honor that.

Concurrency Control

Concurrency is the measure of freedom among users in a multiuser system. It is also the ability of the server to efficiently service multiple users. The SQL Server manages concurrent multiple users by issuing locks that prevent interference at the database and ensure data consistency. Applications affect how these locks are deployed and therefore the level of concurrent access available to all users of the system.

Locks are usually managed at the page level (2,048 bytes, and some number of rows.) When multiple users want to read the same page, write the same page, or read and write to the same page, by default the server protects those operations and provides isolation and data consistency. This consistency enforcement does degrade the ability of users to freely get at data. Locking and blocking degrade concurrency and performance. No locking for concurrent users would be faster and provide higher concurrency, but would not provide adequate data consistency. Other issues require software developers to manage the level of concurrency acquired. All management that manipulates the use of locks must be measured against the problems of data consistency, concurrency levels, and performance. All concurrency problems require the same question: to lock or not to lock. It depends. (See Chapter 3 for a complete discussion of locking.)

Preemptive Locking

Occasionally an application requires that a set of values (or a single value) be read before an action, and it is absolutely required that no other process read the data. This is true if you have an application that must generate a primary key for each row that depends on the last previous value. (This is not needed if an IDENTITY column will do. Maybe the key is more complex and requires calculation or generation.) This style of data manipulation should be embedded in a store procedure if possible. The data to be read must be locked as the data is read and the lock must be held until the transaction is complete. No other user must be allowed to read the data while the first user is processing it.

SELECT with *HOLDLOCK* will not suffice, because HOLDLOCK uses a shared read lock. You can use specific locking orders for the server in the SELECT statement that will cause the server to lock the page from users. In the SELECT statement you can indicate the lock to be issued. *UPDLOCK* indicates that an update lock (which is not sharable) is used. *TABLOCKX* indicates an exclusive lock. All locks issued are held until the end of the statement or the transaction if one is in effect.

```
SELECT <columns> FROM <table> (TABLOCKX) WHERE <conditions>
```

Always be careful to minimize the scope of the transaction and the length of time locks are held.

Browsing

It is common for applications to allow users to peruse data in their application and decide at some future point to update the data. Any time data is moved from the database and is not locked, there is the possibility of another user changing the data. The easiest solution is to lock the data. You can do this with a preemptive lock mechanism. This takes little programming. However, it is not a good solution.

Optimistic concurrency control is a method used to manage this problem without locking records for an extended period of time. A collision is caused if one user reads data into an application and another user updates it before the first user does. With optimistic concurrency control you are assuming that any update you do will very likely succeed without a collision. Therefore you do not lock the data. If you proceed with any update and write over another's update, it causes a lost update. This is a standard concurrency problem. The optimistic solution proceeds with the update conditioned by a test to see that the information being updated in the database is the same information that the application read.

There are many different mechanisms used to confirm that the row is the same. *Timestamp* is a feature of SQL Server that marks each row with a unique timestamp. When an application reads data it reads the timestamp and when it issues the UPDATE (or DELETE) it compares the previously read timestamp with the current one. If they are not the same, there has been a collision and the UPDATE will be rolled back. The timestamp solution requires you to carry a timestamp column on each table where you require this control. Other mechanisms can be used as well: comparing all of the columns; comparing the primary key and all of the modified columns; comparing your own dateline column; and so on. Different solutions provide differing levels of concurrency. Timestamps and all columns provide less concurrency because they will flag more collisions; using only the keys and modified columns will increase concurrency because updates of other columns will not cause a collision.

The trickiest part is deciding what to do when there is a collision. A common solution is to abort the transaction, reselect the row getting the new copy, and let the user reedit the data. This is the simplest solution. A more complex solution will require a bigger investment in programming. It will be particularly complex if you submit several rows and some number of them fail. In reality, this should be a rare occurrence and notification of the user that there was a problem may be enough for this rare occurrence.

If update (or delete) collisions are not a rare occurrence (and you have constructed your transactions optimally), you may need to install a logical lock, that is, a column that the client application can use to indicate that records are in use by one user preventing use by another user. A logical lock requires design changes at the server, in the database design, and in the client application.

Repeatable Reads

Sometimes in a transaction you require that the information you work with is stable. That is, no one should be allowed to modify it. *Repeatable reads* refers to this stability. It enables multiple reads of the data to be consistent. (You don't need to actually read the data multiple times.) You need a lock to ensure that other modifiers can't change the data. This is traditionally done with a HOLDLOCK on a SELECT statement. The HOLDLOCK causes the server to maintain all read locks that it obtains as it reads through the data. Other options with SQL Server include *optimizer hints* in the SELECT statement:

```
SELECT columns FROM table (TABLOCK) WHERE conditions
SELECT columns FROM table (TABLOCK HOLDLOCK) WHERE conditions
```

The first option gets a shared table lock on the entire table and holds it until the statement finishes. The second holds the shared table lock until the transaction completes. Remember, these options are locking entire tables from writers. It is necessary to completely understand the requirements, the scope, and the length of time that these locks are being held. If they are being held for any length of time, the statement should be run at a time that will minimize interference with other users.

Distributed Processing

The concept of *distributed processing* is the core of client/server architecture. To construct any given client/server application you will deploy application functionality on at least two processors. These processes must work cooperatively and efficiently. In deciding how to parse an application for client/server deployment there are many considerations.

It is of primary importance to build database independence. The database should be programmed to be self defending. That is, all data consistency and data validation should be embedded in the database definition. Users should be able to use applications (well or poorly constructed) and off-the-shelf tools to access data without fear of damaging the database. This implies that all necessary security, data validation, referential integrity, transaction control, and complex data manipulation be programmed as a part of the production database server. In addition, the server will provide data storage, data access, data administration facilities, and be used for data manipulation (sorting, restriction, and so on). Client software will be responsible for data presentation, data manipulation, driving external processing (e.g., printing), user-interface presentation and interpretation, and screen management.

Some of our processing is cooperatively accomplished at both the client and the server: data validation, connection management, error handling, and security. Other tasks can be accomplished anywhere in the client/server architecture. These include tasks involving data manipulation, calculations, ordering, presentation restrictions, analysis, and so on.

Deciding where to accomplish a given task is not always a simple decision. Many principles need to be considered:

♦ Do the work where the data resides.
♦ Move as little data as possible across the network.
♦ Make as few transmissions (client to server and back) across the network as possible.
♦ Offload work to the least utilized processor.
♦ Use the processor or operating system best suited to the task.
♦ If the function is reusable, run it where it provides best access to all systems.

Many of these principles are at odds with each other. Which are critical to your system? Consider throughput, response time, network congestion, system architecture, and system load. A few sample questions to ask:

♦ Does the task (analysis, calculation, or ordering) seriously impede throughput on the server?
♦ Can I get this information to the user's screen faster if I accomplish this task on the server? At the client?
♦ Can I reduce network degradation by minimizing what is transmitted?
♦ Does this processor or operating system lend itself to this process efficiently?
♦ Where is the system overloaded? Can I make decisions that will help balance the system utilization?

Security

Implementation of security in a client/server system is complex and often neglected. One of the first tasks in the implementation of a system should be the design of the security requirements and systems. Security can be addressed at different levels of complexity.

Primary Database Security

SQL Server enables basic security for database access to commands and database objects (tables, columns, stored procedures, and views). Each application designer must create a map of objects in the database, users accessing the database, and the access relationships between them. With the advent of flexible end user tools for ad hoc database access, it is necessary to properly implement database security that will always be in effect. Except in very small systems, security access should be defined by groups and users are added to groups.

Security for Ad Hoc Tools

If users are going to be using query tools, users should be assigned two logins in the database. Their primary login (which could be mapped to their NT user identification using trusted security connections) should be given the most restrictive access. Any query tool that they use would inherit this level of security. This login should provide limited access (for example, READ ONLY). Another login should be created that can be accessed only through custom-built applications that are designed to modify data. This login can be based on (or calculated from) the primary login and password. This login would not be able to use integrated NT security. When accessing a custom application, users provide their primary login and password (or NT passes it to the server); when the application starts up it generates their secondary password and creates a working connection to the server. Under this secondary login, users will have data modification and extended read capabilities under the auspices of the custom application. Users do not have to know about the secondary login (they should not know it or the password), but the application must be enabled to generate the secondary login and password and connect to the database.

Application Security and Control

It is often necessary to reflect security requirements in an application. The application should reflect security in its presentation and in its behavior. The easiest way to define security for a user is to only present the actions and information that are available to that user. This requires that the application be programmed to be security conscious and able to configure itself based on the user's identification and the user's mapping to groups.

Large application objects (windows, menus, and so on) do not always track one-for-one to database security or database objects. In such a case, define application topics that describe application areas that map to security usages. This will break application security into smaller units than windows or menus. For example, a billing subsystem would require a certain pattern of security for the database and for the application. If you design the security around topics and create a table that maps topics to users, the application can discover what each user is allowed to do and configure itself appropriately.

The application objects, windows and menus, must be constructed to automatically check the security status of the user and configure themselves appropriately. Menus can automatically enable/disable menu options. Windows can enable/disable controls on the window. Windows and menus will alter their appearance and behavior based on the user.

Integrated Security for Application Components

More complex extensions of user- or topic-based security involve constructing objects (discrete application controls) that are security conscious. Your application may require that individual controls (e.g., buttons, list boxes, and so on) alter their appearance or behavior based on the user. Every control on a window might have multiple configurations depending on user security and, by checking the user's security, configure itself appropriately. Such a security implementation prevents an application from duplicating objects that are similar but have differing security status (for example, read-only views vs. modifiable views).

In an object-oriented environment, it is possible to build security consciousness into base system objects that are used throughout a system. Integrated security approaches require the definition of security topics and the mapping of these security topics to users, database objects, and to application components. Reusable base components are programmed to check the security information against attributes that are initialized in the final implementation. To prevent excessive access to the database, maps of the security information can be moved into the application at application open from the database tables as required.

The more extensive your security requirements, the more effort will need to be invested during design and development. Use an architecture that gives you the level of security you require at the minimum of expense. Developing a complete reusable architecture that supports component-level security consciousness will be a major developmental undertaking. If it is designed into a reusable architecture, you only have to do it once.

Replication

Distributed Data Overview

In many situations it is necessary to distribute data across a geographically dispersed client/server environment. Some systems (online transaction processing) require that data be synchronized at all times. Others, such as decision support systems, allow for less frequent synchronization of data. Microsoft SQL Server 6 Replication is a means to copy data from an OLTP system to another system where a lag time between the transactions that create the data and the changes to the copy are acceptable to the subscriber.

Data distribution comes in two flavors:

1. *Two-phased commit* supports distributed transactions. A two-phased commit was available in prior systems with the DB-Library two-phase commit service. With two-phase commit, a transaction is completed on *all* servers or rolled back and not applied to any servers. This data must be 100 percent in sync 100 percent of the time.

   Caution should be used before implementing a two-phased commit replication model. The *tight consistency* requirement will have a negative impact on performance. Update locks will be held much longer and may prevent users from performing tasks. Also, any failure occurring on any server will cause a rollback to occur on all servers.

2. *Replication* supports distributed data. For replication, the lag created by copying the data outside the transaction causes the loose consistency. Replication is a regular part of current systems through the copying of data from one system to another. Microsoft SQL Server 6 has automated that process for us. Replication has a number of benefits, the first of which is improved data availability through autonomous site operations. Performance is also improved by distributing data across multiple servers. This normalizes the central network load and improves network access. Redundancy is another benefit that can be derived from replication.

There is an advantage to physically separating OLTP and DSS systems. Not only will there will be a reduction of network traffic through the decentralization of data, but each database may be tuned for OLTP or DSS characteristics respectively. However, replication is a tool and shouldn't be limited in use to just the segregating of OLTP and DSS data. Replication can be a database tuning aid for moving infrequently referenced data, for creating a redundant data source, or for implementing a distributed data processing architecture.

Organizational models may change. Replication can help facilitate these changes. Replication provides the scalability and flexibility that can support a wide range of organizational models. It is an easy task to reconfigure the distribution of data across system resources.

Overview

The metaphor used for replication is that of a publisher with a publication containing articles. An article is the basic unit of replication. A single table, a group of tables, a vertically partitioned or a horizontally partitioned table may be replicated. Not everything can be published. SQL Server will not publish the internal databases *model, tempdb, msdb,* or any of the *system* tables. In addition, no tables without a primary key can be published, nor can the *identity* property be published. (The column values will always be moved, but the property of generating values will be lost.) Data in *text* and *image* columns is replicated as NULL if you are using transaction-based replication. It is possible to replicate these columns if you are using table refresh replication. Unfortunately, you are then copying all of the text data.

What can be published is classified as either *restricted* or *unrestricted.* An *unrestricted* publication is visible to anyone and is equivalent to the NTFS permission *Everyone,* while a *restricted* publication can only be seen by a server given permission to subscribe. Subscribers are not required to subscribe to the entire publication.

Replication can be started with a *scheduled* database or *scheduled* table synchronization. After that, replication may be continuous or at specific intervals. The SQL Server Log Reader component monitors the log for any transactions which should be replicated. If one is found, it copies the transactions which are to be replicated to a *distribution database.* The replication process stores updates in the distribution database as either SQL commands or stored procedures.

There are three roles in the replication architecture: publisher, subscriber, and distributor. Each of these roles is performed by SQL Server. When SQL Server both publishes and subscribes, it is acting in the capacity of a *distributor.* The distributor will maintain the distribution database and forward the publications to the subscribers. The *publisher* maintains the source database, makes published data from the databases available for replication, and sends copies of all changes to the published data to the distribution server. The *subscription* server maintains a copy of the published data.

Data at the subscription server should be treated as read-only. It is, of course, important that the read-only database option is not set, since replication will be making modifications to the database. Replication expects the subscriber and publisher articles to be synchronized. Since updates are saved at the distributor as SQL statements or stored procedures, the replication update may fail if the subscribed article is changed at the subscriber.

If the data at the subscription server is modified, then it is possible to define an architecture where the changes are replicated back to the original publisher. This approach requires careful planning.

Triggers and constraints are usually only included on the publisher server. However, you may want to include triggers to record certain activities on the subscribers. Since a subscribed article is treated as read-only, there is no need for triggers and constraints at the subscriber to ensure integrity. A publication should include all dependent tables. If an article for publication is a vertically segmented table, then the selected columns should contain any foreign keys.

If the administrator of the publication server also has sa rights on the subscription server, then a *push* subscription can be initiated. And correspondingly, if the administrator of the subscription server has sa rights on the publication server, a *pull* subscription can be initiated.

Models

There are five simple replication models and an infinite variety of ways in which they can be used or combined:

1. Single publisher–multiple subscribers
2. Single publisher using a distribution server
3. Multiple publishers–single subscriber
4. Multiple publishers–multiple subscribers
5. Single publisher–single subscriber (local, self-publishing to a local database)

The *single publisher–multiple subscribers* model is the default model for SQL Server 6 Replication as shown in Figure 5.2.

The single publisher with a distributor can serve two roles: offloading replication to a distribution server or accommodating an inadequate network. A *distribution server* is nothing more than a server that both subscribes to and publishes a publication. This model can be further expanded to include yet other distributor servers (see Figures 5.3 and 5.4). The initial model for distribution over slow networks would be augmented by having a distribution server on each end of the *slow* link that links the publication server to subscribers.

The *multiple publishers–single subscriber* model as shown in Figure 5.5 can be used for centralized data collection from disparate locations. Candidates for this model might be:

◆ Customer orders from sales locations
◆ Warehouse inventory maintenance
◆ Data from autonomous divisions

This architecture does require that the data subscription contain a *location-specific* field. This might be represented as a compound key in the subscriber

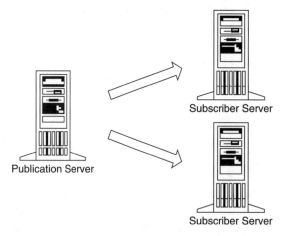

FIGURE 5.2 Single publisher–multiple subscriber model.

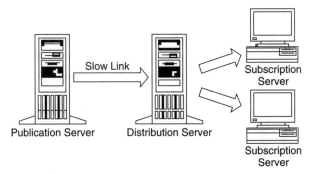

FIGURE 5.3 Single publisher with a distributor and multiple subscribers.

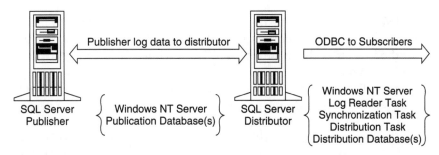

FIGURE 5.4 Single publisher with a distributor and multiple subscribers detail.

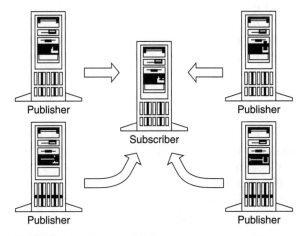

FIGURE 5.5 Multiple publishers–single subscriber (corporate roll-up model).

database. The *multiple publishers–single subscriber* model is an example of an enterprise architecture based upon replication.

The *multiple publishers–multiple subscribers* model can represent an implementation of full distributed data processing (see Figure 5.6). One server could maintain an accounts receivable database and also be the pub-

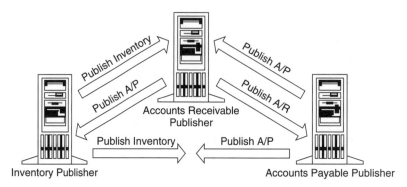

FIGURE 5.6 Multiple publishers–multiple subscribers.

lisher of that data. In turn it could also be a subscriber to inventory data and a subscriber to accounts payable data. The inventory server would maintain the inventory database and publish it while subscribing to other publications, and so on.

The *single publisher/single subscriber* model is a useful tool for OLTP management. Users doing updates can be segregated from users who only read data. The SQL Server in question publishes a database or some portion thereof. (Referential integrity with the necessary foreign keys must be maintained when only a portion of a database is published.) The same SQL Server now subscribes to the publication using a new subscription database. Users who update data connect to the primary database and users who do not update data connect to the subscription database. Before you undertake this endeavor, evaluate your resources carefully. The SQL Server now has three databases: *published, distribution,* and *subscription.*

Planning

As with any endeavor, planning is crucial for success. Is replication really necessary? If it is necessary, is it the best method? But beyond just planning, there are coordination issues which are critical for the success of replication. We'll discuss these after selecting a replication model.

Before picking a replication model, determine the use of replication. Replication may not always be suitable for the required task in the following situations.

♦ Replication is not designed to be a hot backup system and other alternatives should be considered, such as mirroring or RAID-5.
♦ Your choice of replication model may be limited by the type of database. If the database is not yet in production (schema changes are still being made), then the replication model is limited to *snapshot* since schema changes to a publication database are not replicated.

✦ Text or image column data is passed as null and not replicated. Your only choice here is to define a *refresh* cycle using a *snapshot* (see following, Unable to replicate *text* or *image*).

Determine the replication model. The appropriate model is determined by the purpose of the replicated data (see Figure 5.7). Is the requirement for corporate rollup, report generation, decision system support, or master list updating? Maybe the replication application is very specialized. An example might be replicating data through a firewall to a Windows NT server which has a SQL Server subscriber and a Web server. An application program using DB-Library or ODBC on the subscription server (Web server) services the home page by accessing the subscription database and converts the result set to HTML (Hyper-Text Markup Language).

Once a model has been selected, there is another limiting factor. Even though replication is to a subscription database, only one copy of a publication can be replicated to a server. Local copying is required to move the replication data to another database on the same server. This would be handled by a trigger in the first database for each insert, update, or delete which occurs.

With a model selected, you can consider the size of databases and transaction logs. Are the current resources adequate for replication? An additional factor to consider is the maximum retention period of transactions at the distribution server. This period is dependent upon the scheduled transaction dump period of subscribers. When replication is initially set up, the systems creates a *replication_cleanup* task for each publisher/subscriber pairing. A parameter provided to the *replication_cleanup* task is the retention period that transactions will be guaranteed to be retained within the distri-

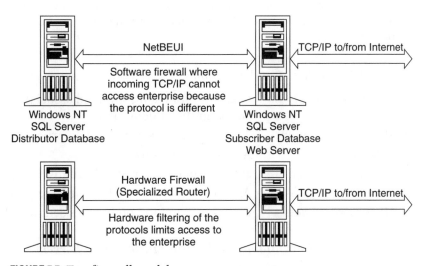

FIGURE 5.7 Two firewall models.

bution database after they have been distributed to a destination database. This parameter is dependent upon the scheduled transaction log dump period of the associated subscription server. If the transaction log dump period is every 6 hours for the subscriber, then the retention period should be set to 12 hours at the distribution server. An easy rule is to have all subscription servers have the same retention period. With a large number of subscriptions and different retention periods, mass storage estimates are little more than a guess.

With replication, the publisher transaction log has a new role, that of an interim holding queue for unpublished transactions. This will require significant additional publisher log space. Does your publisher transaction log have enough space if the distributor server is unavailable for two hours, four hours, or maybe even six hours? As previously discussed, the distributor also needs significant log space based upon the retention period related to the log dump cycle of subscribers. Adequate log space for both the publisher and the distributor cannot be emphasized enough.

Database dumps must be coordinated. Even though the publication database may be dumped at any time, a backup of the distribution database must be made after every transaction log dump of any associated publication server.[1] The design of replication is such that the *recovery point* of the distribution server must *always* be to a point in time later than the last transaction log dump of all related publishers.

Publisher transaction log dumps will truncate the log up to the point of the last transaction successfully published to the distributor and can be made without interference to replication. If the publisher log is truncated and the distributor server is recovered to a prior point in time, then the administrator probably has no choice other than to unsubscribe all subscribers and resynchronize. This is because the truncation of the publisher log may remove a transaction pointed to by the *MSjobs* table in the distribution database.

Distribution Database Tables

MSjob_commands	One entry for each command associated with a transaction in the *MSjobs* table.
MSjob_subscriptions	Associates a subscriber and an article.
MSjobs	Actual transactions.
MSsubscriber_info	Job information for SQL Executive.
MSsubscriber_jobs	Associates each subscriber with a required command.
MSsubscriber_status	Status information on batches sent to subscribers.

Destination Database Table (on Subscription Server)

MSlast_job_info	Has job ID of last job completed successfully.

Publication Database Tables

sysarticles	Row for each of the articles posted by the publication server.
sysobjects	Category field set by replication for each article to be replicated. Set at subscription time and when created.
syspublications	Row for each of the publications posted by the publication server.
syssubscriptions	Associates published article IDs with the IDs of subscription servers.

When the distribution database is created, the SQL Server script *INST-DIST.SQL* is used to create the *MSjob_commands, MSjobs, MSjob_subscriptions, MSsubscriber_info, MSsubscriber_jobs,* and *MSsubscriber_status* tables (see Figure 5.8).

Publication, distribution, and subscription servers must all use the same character set.[2] The documentation states that all servers should use the same sort order. These words are not strong enough and we consider it a documentation error. An example is replication from a case-sensitive server to a case-insensitive server which could lead to dups on an unique index column.

Trusted connections (forced integrated security) are used by the distribution servers to connect to all subscription servers. This requires the Client Configuration Utility on the distribution server to be set to either *Named Pipes* or *Multi-Protocol*. This also requires trust relationships between Windows NT domains who have servers participating in replication.

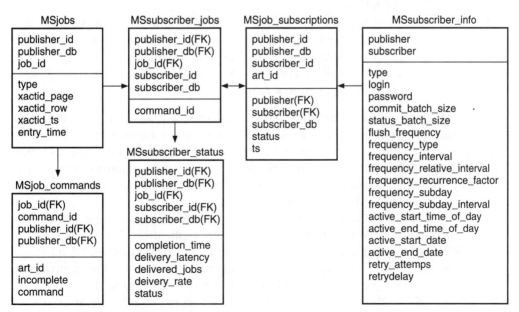

FIGURE 5.8 Distribution database tables.

For all subscribers, the table schema and data of the publication database must be identical to the table schema and data of the subscription database before replication can begin. This is the purpose of synchronization. Analyzing business requirements will establish the appropriate schedule for synchronization. Replication synchronization may be *automatic, manual, no synchronization,* or *snapshot.* Synchronization is only for new subscribers unless there is no replication and the subscriber table is refreshed with a snapshot on a periodic basis. For the situation where no synchronization is done, SQL Server assumes that the schema and data of the subscription database agree.

A synchronization is always a snapshot of the schema and data. It is a mechanism that assures that the published data and relevant schema are equal on both publication and subscription servers. When replication isn't possible (image and text columns), then snapshots can be scheduled on a regular basis. A snapshot replication is nothing more than a periodic synchronization.

Methods of Synchronization

Manual: Done by the administrator in a situation where communications is over an expensive or slow link. A tape can be mailed to the subscription site. A manual synchronization must be acknowledged before replication can proceed.

Automatic: Accomplished by SQL Server.

Snapshot only: Synchronization will be at specific intervals with a snapshot and transactions such as inserts, deletes, and updates are not applied.

No synchronization: Much like manual synchronization, in that SQL Server assumes that the subscription database is synchronized. If no synchronization is done and the schema and data of the subscription database is not an exact match with the publishing database, then replication will fail.

Knowing replication rates and average transaction sizes will help in estimating a server load. The load on SQL Server can be normalized with a separate distribution server and would be independent of any consideration because of a slow subscription link. If the load at the distribution server merits it, establish a multilevel replication architecture with distributors publishing to other levels of distributors.

From SQL Enterprise Manager, use the *Replication Topology Window* from the Server Manager Window to setup replication. You must have sa privileges on both the distribution server and subscription server. With sa privileges, *drag and drop* operations will automatically have the appropriate remote logins created on the different servers. If necessary, the *sp_adduser, sp_addlogin,* and *sp_remotelogin* may be used to configure the servers, however it is much easier to use the graphical interface.

Making It Work

The vital key to making replication work is having adequate disk space for the transaction logs. When you think you have enough space then add some more. The Log Reader client on the distribution server will be reading the publisher transaction log for appropriate transactions to replicate. This process means that the publisher transaction log is now a *temporary holding queue for unpublished transactions*. Note that the transaction log cannot be truncated past the oldest published transaction that has not been transferred to the distribution database. This will be a problem when the distribution server is temporarily unavailable.

The distribution server will need log space. The amount will depend upon the replication transaction rate and the retention period for the distribution transaction log, which is dependent upon subscriber backup cycles. To keep everything manageable, make sure that all subscribers have the same backup cycle period. As we stated earlier, when you think you have enough log space then add some more.

Additional resources are required for replication. While a SQL Server requires a minimum of 16Mb of memory, a distribution server or a combined distribution and publication server requires 32Mb. The distribution database requires a minimum of 30Mb of disk space for the data device and 15Mb for the log device.

Distribution of the data is with ODBC and 32-bit ODBC drivers are required to be installed on all servers that participate in replication. The ODBC drivers were installed by the SQL Server *Setup* program.

Replication uses server connections.

Publication server: Increase the number of user connections by the number of publisher transaction logs which must be accessed. When replication is established, the system automatically creates a *repl_subscriber* login ID for each destination database. This login ID will be aliased to the DBO of the destination database for publisher transaction log access and is used for access to the destination database by the distribution server. These login IDs are not to be used for normal logins.

Distribution server: If the subscription server and the distribution server are different, increase the number of user connections by the number of subscription databases on the publication server. These connections are identical to the *repl_subscriber* usage discussed previously with the *repl_subscriber* login ID set as a user in the *master, distribution,* and *msdb* databases.

Subscription server: Increase the number of user connections by the number of subscription databases. These connections will be used by the distribution server to publish the required article. SQL Server automatically creates a *repl_publisher* login ID. The distribution server will use this login to connect to the subscription server.

Replication requires a trusted connection. The actual replication process must have a Windows NT user account, either *repl_subscriber* or *repl_publisher*, on the respective server. These accounts will have the administrative privilege right *log on as a service* and the account properties set to *user cannot change password* and *password never expires.*

Implementation of replication can be done from the command line with stored procedures or from SQL Enterprise Manager. If replication is to be done from the command line then *User Manager for Domains* must be used to create the *repl_publisher* or *repl_subscriber* accounts. The account should be a member of the Administrators Group with a login ID of *repl_publisher* or *repl_subscriber.* These accounts are different from the normal sa administration account and will be used by the Windows NT SQL Executive service. Once the accounts have been created on the respective servers, consult the Microsoft documentation for constructing of replication scripts.

There may still be another account change necessary. At SQL Server installation time, you were given the choice by the *Setup* program of making the SQL Executive logon account a *LocalSystem* account or an integrated Windows NT domain user account. If the choice was *LocalSystem* account, then an integrated Windows NT account must be created before replication will work. For this account, be sure to specify *password does not expire.* Use *User Manager for Domains* to create this account.

There are 41 stored procedures dedicated to replication. Depending upon the application requirements, the use of scripts using these stored procedures will be efficient; however, replication is certainly easier to implement and maintain with the graphical interface of the Enterprise Manager, and that interface is highly recommended.

When It Doesn't Work

A checklist of items before initiating replication is recommended. Following this checklist may help in identifying common problems.

◆ Is Named Pipes or Multi-Protocol being used? Either of these is required along with a *trusted* connection. If replication is between domains, then domain trusts must be established.

◆ If there was a manual synchronization, has SQL Server been informed that the synchronization is complete?

◆ Have the subscriber databases been created before publishing an article? It is not required but recommended that subscription databases be created first.

◆ Is there adequate log file space? Transactions will not be purged past the oldest transaction not transferred to the distribution database. Extra publisher log space is a necessity. If the distribution server is unavailable, then there will be transactions in the publisher log which cannot be truncated.

- ♦ Verify that the number of user connections is adequate.
- ♦ Verify that the character set and sort order of the publication, distribution, and subscription servers are the same.
- ♦ Has a Windows NT user account been created for the SQL Executive Service? The account should have the following characteristics:
  1. User cannot change password.
  2. Password never expires.
  3. Account is granted the right *log on as a service.*
  4. Account is a member of the Administrators Group.
- ♦ Verify that the directory \SQL60\REPLDATA is available to the publication server.

A Single Subscriber Is Not Receiving Changes

There are a number of conditions which can cause a single subscriber to fail.

- ♦ Is the subscribing database available?
- ♦ Is the subscription server available? Look for a green light in *Service Manager.*
- ♦ Look in the *MSjob_last_info* table of the subscription server subscription database. If there is an entry there, then the system is waiting for an administrative acknowledgement that manual synchronization is complete.
- ♦ Has the *repl_publisher* login ID been removed from the subscription server?

Distribution Server Failure

When the distribution server is recovered after a failure, part of the recovery process is to request transactions from the publication server based upon the oldest *info_id* per job. Distribution of replicated transactions stops until *info_id*s are obtained. If required *info_id*s can't be obtained, then all subscribers need to be resynchronized. At issue here is that *while a distribution server is unavailable, no dump should be made of the publisher transaction log.*[3] If a distribution server is unavailable, the best choice is to expand the publisher transaction log until the distribution server is available.

No Subscribers Receiving Changes

When no subscription servers are receiving changes, the fault is related to either the *Log Reader* task or the *Distribution* task, both of which reside on the distribution server. Changes to replicated tables are stored in the *command* column of the *MSjob_commands* table on the distribution server in the distribution database. If the commands are not in the table, the Log Reader task is at fault, otherwise it is a Distribution task problem. Look at this table using isql/w:

```
SELECT command FROM MSjob_commands
```

If the distribution task is at fault, then do the following[4]:

1. Go to the Task Scheduling Window, Edit Task button and change the *-c* parameter to *c1*. This will cause a commit for every transaction and will fail on the transaction that is causing the problem.

2. After replication has failed, obtain the *job_id* for the transaction as follows:

   ♦ Using the appropriate *publisher_id*, *publisher_db*, *subscriber_id*, *subscriber_db*, select the maximum *job_id* from the *MSsubscriber status* table in the distribution database. This provides our maximum *job_id*.

   ♦ Select the minimum *job_id* from *MSsubscriber_jobs* that is larger than this number using the appropriate *publisher_id*, *publisher_db*, *subscriber_id*, and *subscriber_db*. The result will be the *job_id* of the transaction which is failing.

3. Use ISQL/W to select the command column of the failing transaction.

```
SELECT command FROM MSjob_commands
WHERE publisher_id = 'publisher_id'
AND publisher_db = 'publisher_db'
AND job_id = 'job_id'.
```

At that point there are three choices:

1. Use Transact-SQL to repair the command within the *MSjob_commands* table.

2. Use *sp_MSkill_job* to remove the command from the table and do nothing else.

3. Remove the job with *MSkill_job* and manually recreate the transaction with isql/w.

Publication Database Transaction Log Is Full or Nearly Full

A *log reader task* failure on the distribution server may cause the publication server database transaction log to fill up. Use *sp_repltrans* on the publication server to see if there are any transactions that have not yet been distributed. Use *sp_replcmds* to view transactions that have not been distributed.

Publication Server Failure

A very difficult situation occurs when the publication server fails. It is possible that the transaction log can be recovered; however, this will not always be the case. If the publication database is recovered from an older database copy, then a logical gap now exists between the distribution server and the subscription server. Replication requires that the distribution server can *always* be recovered to a point in time after the latest transaction dump of the subscription database. If this situation occurs, there is no choice but to drop and resubscribe all current subscriptions.

Replication Will Not Start

If the subscriber synchronization was manual, then you have probably forgotten to tell the subscription server that the manual synchronization is complete. To do that:

♦ From the *Server Manager* window, select the subscription server.
♦ Choose *Manage Subscriptions*.
♦ Expand the publication tree by choosing the + box.
♦ Select a publication and article.
♦ Choose *Sync Completed*.

Schema Changes Have Been Made

During the synchronization phase, the table schema was stored in a .SCH file and the table data in a .TMP file in the path \SQL60\REPLDATA of the distribution server for replication. These files are used for subscriber synchronization. Once the subscriber is synchronized, table data changes are replicated and not table schema changes. You must stop replication and force another synchronization cycle to update the table schema at the subscriber.

Subscription Server Failure

Recover the subscription server from a backup tape. After that there may be a choice. If the retention period at the distribution database is adequate, then the distribution database has been storing all transactions and the subscriber will be recovered.

However, if the subscription server cannot be restored to a point of synchronization with the distribution database, then drop and resubscribe to all replication publications.

Unable to Replicate Text or Image

SQL Server does not support transaction-based replication of *text* and *image* columns. Your only choice is to use a table refresh replication of just the *text* or *image* columns on a periodic basis to a log-based destination table. This is equivalent to a periodic snapshot. To maintain proper consistency, a *timestamp* column and primary key columns should be added to the table. The destination table can then be joined to the table containing the other replicated columns.

Unable to Synchronize

In SQL Server replication, the distribution server connects to subscription servers using a *trusted* connection. This is by default and requires that Named Pipes or Multi-Protocol be used as the default network.

If the subscription server and distribution server are in different domains, then a *trusted* connection requires a *trust* relationship between the domains.

Published tables must have a primary key. If a primary key doesn't exist for a table then one must be added.

Tuning Replication

Server Message Blocks (SMBs, see Chapter 9) are used by the Windows NT re- director for Named Pipes communication between Windows NT servers. This interprocess communication is done in either *Core* mode or *Raw* mode.

♦ *Core mode:*   SMB size is 4,356 bytes. Write overhead is 64 bytes and read overhead is 63 bytes. This gives a useful buffer space of 4,292 bytes.
♦ *Raw mode:*   The same overhead as *Core* mode, however the buffer size is 64K.

For Named Pipes, the Windows NT Redirector will use *Raw* mode when:

♦ The application I/O request is larger than 2* the server's read request buffer size.
♦ The application I/O request is larger than 1.5* the server's write request buffer.
♦ Multiple client computer threads are not simultaneously issuing I/O requests to the same server.
♦ Enough memory is available to allow the 64K *Raw* mode buffer.
♦ Communication is not over a slow link.
♦ *Raw* mode is not disabled in the Windows NT registry.

To determine if Windows NT server is unable to use *Raw* mode, use the Windows NT performance monitor to track *Server: Work Item Shortages* and *Server:Blocking Requests Rejected*. By default, Windows NT is only configured with four *Raw* work items to allocate. It may be necessary to increment this value if *Raw* mode requests are failing.

How does all of this relate to replication? The default packet size for the Distribution task, Synchronization task, and Log Reader task is 4,096 bytes which may be set with the *-a* parameter of the respective task command line. If this value is increased, then *Raw* mode will be used if the criterion described above is met. Monitor the events *Server: Work Item Shortages* and *Server: Block-ing Requests* at the subscriber, publisher, and distributor servers. There is a high probability that *MaxWorkItems* and *MaxRawWorkItems* of the *Server Ser-vice* in the Windows NT registry will have to be tuned.

An issue is when the server cannot support SMB *Raw* mode while the client system can. All systems must support SMB mode or none at all since the value in the registry *EnableRaw* is by default true. This field is a parameter of the Server Service and is found in the registry at:

```
HKEY_LOCAL_MACHINE\SYSTEM\CurrentControlSet\Services\LanmanServer\Parameters
```

The safest possible mechanism is to ensure that all systems have adequate memory or disable *RawMode* on all systems.

Messaging

SQL Server has been updated to include the messaging architecture MAPI 1.0. SQL Server mail (SQLMail) can send a message which might be a short text string, query output, or an attached file. Messages can be sent when a SQL Server alert occurs, a SQL Performance Monitor threshold is exceeded, or by a scheduled task to indicate success or failure. The message may be e-mail or e-mail to a pager provider.

But messaging is not just SQLMail. It is the combination of event logging which in turn creates alerts, scheduling task executions, or even e-mail which may be to a user or to a MAPI provider not yet installed—in this case, a pager provider. To see how all this works together, we'll look at three architectures. The first is MAPI; then Windows NT Mail; and finally the SQL Executive architecture where alerts, mail, and task management are integrated seamlessly.

MAPI 1.0

Microsoft MAPI 1.0 is an architecture, not an application programming interface (API). It does, however, have three components which are APIs: Simple MAPI, CMC, and Extended MAPI. The complete architecture consists of the messaging APIs which are used for messaging application interfacing, a separate *service provider* interface, and a *messaging subsystem* which is a component of the operating system (see Figure 5.9). This architecture is considered to be open at the *front end* and open at the *back end*. The front end is open since a common API is involved and the same messaging application can be used with different service providers without recoding the application.

SQLMail uses the MAPI client interface in Windows NT and can use Windows NT Mail or any other MAPI provider to send or receive mail messages. MAPI is designed with a common interface for service providers (see Figure 5.10). FAX is a good candidate as a MAPI provider. Since service providers' interfaces are MAPI compliant, a new provider could be added without changing the messaging application. There would certainly be

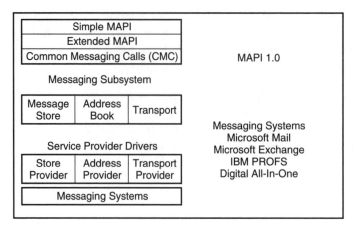

FIGURE 5.9 MAPI architecture.

configuration issues to the application; it is just a matter of another e-mail address.

We can see from Figure 5.11 that all custom applications will have the same service provider interface. In our example, the Visual Basic application captures information from different environments. The resultant mail is passed to service providers which can be the same service providers used by SQLMail. Incoming mail is captured by Microsoft *E-Form*, which interfaces with the user and with the Visual Basic application.

The same situation exists at the back end. Service providers develop their transport by using a common interface (in this case SPI, Service Provider Interface). This gives the messaging developer the ability to develop a messaging application independent of the different transport providers such as MSMail, All-In-One, Fax, or PROFS. In turn, the service provider is responsible for all communication services.

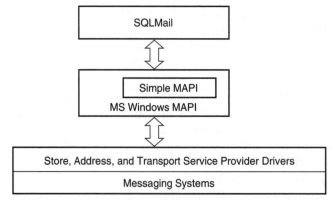

FIGURE 5.10 SQL Server SQLMail and MAPI.

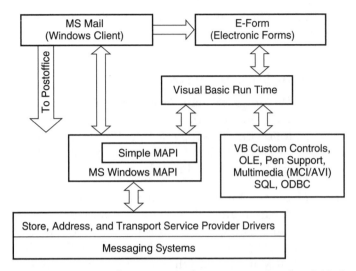

FIGURE 5.11 A complex MAPI application not related to SQL Server to illustrate MAPI usage.

MAPI uses *Transport Neutral Encapsulation Format* (*TNEF*) as a message wrapper. This promotes interoperability between transports without affecting original message properties. In MAPI, attachments may be made to messages and both the message and the attachment may have properties that are not supported by MAPI so TNEF may be used for both.

The messaging subsystem provides *store and forward* capabilities. In the event that a service provider is offline, messages will not be lost. *Auto spooling* is another feature of the messaging subsystem. This functions in the same manner as a print subsystem with messages stored on disk until transport services are available. It is also an ideal accommodation for slow transports since users are not required to wait.

For security, the MAPI messaging subsystem encrypts any information it stores for a service provider. The service provider can either prompt for a user's credentials or remember the credentials from a prior logon, which is called a *unified logon.* Along with optional password protection, the *messaging subsystem* maintains user profiles for identifying service providers of choice.

Simple MAPI and *Common Messaging Calls* (*CMC*) are very close in functionality; however, Simple MAPI is to be used only for existing applications while CMC is to be used for new messaging application development.

Windows NT Mail

SQLMail is a client of Windows NT Mail. It is workgroup oriented with a shared postoffice. The postoffice is a file which defaults to C:\Users\ Default\WGPO. But these defaults need not be used and the postoffice need not be on the server where the mail originated. See Figure 5.12 for the Windows NT Mail architecture.

Creating the Windows NT Postoffice

SQLMail requires Windows NT mail. As we previously stated, Windows NT is workgroup based and uses a workgroup postoffice. If a postoffice does not exist, then use the following steps to create the Windows NT Mail postoffice. If a Windows NT mail account already exists which can be used by SQLMail, then the following section may be skipped.

- Select *Mail* from the *Main* group. Don't be surprised if you are on a Windows NT workstation and this is your own mail account. SQLMail runs *piggyback* on an existing Windows NT mail account. If it is your own account then select *Mail*, *PostOfficeManager* from the toolbar to create an account for SQLMail and skip the next step. This same procedure can be used to create a workgroup postoffice on Windows NT server.
- From the dialog box, select *Create Postoffice*.
- Create the account. Be sure that a nonnull password is used. The initial release of **SQL Server 6.0 SQLMail** will fail with a null password, even though one is acceptable to Windows NT.
- Test it by sending mail to yourself.

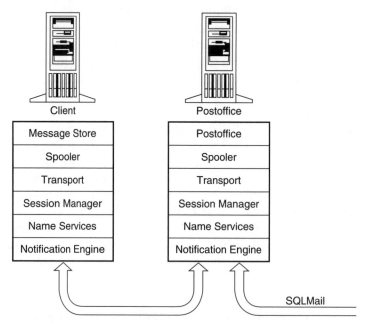

FIGURE 5.12 Windows NT Mail architecture using MAPI.

♦ Since Windows NT Mail is workgroup oriented, the WGPO directory must be shared. Use *File Manager* for this. If the file system is NTFS, then all users must have *change* permission to the WGPO directory. If the postoffice is in the same domain as SQL Server, then the permissions are given to *Everyone*, otherwise the permissions are given to *Guest*.

When Windows NT Mail Doesn't Work

Recreating the Postoffice

When Windows NT Mail doesn't work, an alternative is to delete the WGPO and create a new postoffice. Microsoft publishes information on recreating the workgroup postoffice by editing only registry keys, which is discussed in the following section. However we have found that it has been necessary to also delete the old WGPO before you can successfully create a new WGPO. This procedure is probably useful only when the initial system mail installation fails. Consider doing this when the workgroup postoffice path looks like:

```
D:\Users\Default\WGPO\WGPO.
```

Deleting the postoffice is done with the following steps:

♦ Ascertain that there are no current users of the workgroup postoffice.
♦ Use *Isql/w* and issue *xp_stopmail* to stop SQLMail.
♦ Delete the workgroup postoffice. Typically this will be D:\Users\Default\ WGPO. If WGPO is not deleted, then when a new postoffice is created, it will have the path D:\Users\Default\WGPO\WGPO, which isn't correct.
♦ Run REGEDT32 from the *File* menu of *File Manager* and delete *Microsoft Mail* from the following key. Note that there may not be a *Microsoft Mail* key if Mail was never started automatically by SQL Server *Setup*.

```
HKEY_USERS\
      Default\
        Software\
          Microsoft\
            Mail\
              Microsoft Mail
```

After key deletion, the registry entry should look like this:

```
HKEY_USERS\
      Default\
        Software\
          Microsoft\
            Mail
```

♦ Also delete Microsoft Mail from the following keys:

```
HKEY_USERS\
   S-1-5-...\
      Software\
          Microsoft\
             Mail\
                Microsoft Mail
HKEY_CURRENT_USER\
   Default\
      Software\
         Microsoft\
            Mail\
               Microsoft Mail
```

♦ Follow the initial postoffice creation procedure.

Reinitializing the Postoffice

Select and delete *Serverpath* and *Login* from the following registry key. This procedure assumes that there are no current mail users, and SQLMail has been stopped. If SQLMail has not been stopped, then from *isql/w*, issue *xp_stopmail*.

```
HKEY_USERS\
   Default\
      Software\
         Microsoft\
            Mail\
               Microsoft Mail
```

HKEY_USERS contains all actively loaded user profiles. HKEY_CUR-RENT_USER is the database which describes the current user. Also edit or add *ServerPath,* and *Login* in HKEY_CURRENT_USER.

Moving the Postoffice

To move the postoffice, perform the following tasks:

♦ Ensure that mail in not in use by other users.
♦ Stop mail from *isql/w* with *xp_stopmail*.
♦ Move the WGPO and all subdirectories to the new location. Verify that user permissions are maintained and that the directory is shared.
♦ In the registry edit *ServerPath* to the new path in the following keys:

```
HKEY_USERS\
   Default\
      Software\
         Microsoft\
            Mail\
               Microsoft Mail
```

```
HKEY_USERS\
   S-1-5-...\
      Software\
         Microsoft\
            Mail\
               Microsoft Mail
HKEY_CURRENT_USER\
   Default\
      Software\
         Microsoft\
            Mail\
               Microsoft Mail
```

SQLMail Password Has Been Forgotten or Changed

SQLMail runs on an existing Windows NT Mail account and the password is that of the Windows NT Mail account. If you ever change the password of the Windows NT Mail account, then this registry value must be updated. The password can be found in the registry at:

```
HKEY_LOCAL_MACHINE\
   SOFTWARE\
      Microsoft\
         MSSQLServer\
            MSSQLServer\
               MailPassword
```

If the new password is known, then change the registry to reflect the new value. If you've just forgotten it, then your problem is solved.

SQL Mail

Architectural Considerations

It is possible with Windows NT and SQL Server to define a remote mail server and a remote alert server. Which alerts are forwarded to the alternate server depends upon the severity code option parameter entered when the *Alert Engine* of Enterprise Manager is configured. If, for example, a severity code level of 19 is entered and a different server name is given, then all fatal errors will be forwarded to the alternate server event log which diminishes network bandwidth.

Should the Windows NT postoffice reside on SQL Server? If it doesn't, then further diminishing of bandwidth will occur. Another consideration is a remote mail server combined with an alternate alert server. The alternate alert server can handle all alerts, some of the alerts (severity 19 or higher for example), or just the fail-safe alerts which occur and are not handled normally.

Creating the SQLMail Account

SQLMail is a client of Windows NT mail and runs piggyback on an existing Windows NT Mail account. Consequently the login and password entered in the *Mail Login* dialog box of SQL *Setup* is that of an existing Windows NT mail account. As discussed previously, a separate Windows NT account should be created for SQLMail; however, it isn't necessary.

SQLMail requires that the **MSSQLServer** service use a *LocalSystem* account and not a user account. This means that there may be some security access problems since a *LocalSystem* account has no associated user information. In particular, Novell NetWare Servers and LAN Manager user-level security will not let a *LocalSystem* account access their resources. If access to a network share for backup is required, see the Microsoft documentation (Chapter 5 of the *Microsoft SQL Server Administrator's Companion*), for creating a *NullSessionShare* in the registry.

```
\\HKEY_LOCAL_MACHINE
          \System
          \CurrentControlSet
                 \Services
                     \LanmanServer
                     \Parameters
NullSessionShares: REG_MULTI_SZ:CONCFG
```

SQLMail also requires that the **MSSQLServer** service account have the option *Allow Service to Interact With Desktop*. To verify this option and the account type, from *Control Panel* in *Main* go to *Services* and select and then double-click *MSSQLServer*. Select *Allow Service to Interact With Desktop* if necessary and verify that *System Account* is selected.

After the Windows NT mail postoffice has been created, do the following to create SQLMail:

♦ In SQL Server Setup, select SQL Server *Set Server Options*.

 ♦ Select *Auto Start Mail Client*.
 ♦ Select *Mail Login* (the SQLMail dialog box will appear).
 ♦ Enter the *Mail Login Name*.
 ♦ Enter the password.
 ♦ Confirm the password.
 ♦ Check *Copy SQLMail configuration from current user account*.
 ♦ Press *Continue*.
 ♦ Press *Change Options*.
 ♦ Press *Exit to Windows NT*.

The SQL Server SQLMail account password and user_ID can now be found in the registry at:

```
HKEY_LOCAL_MACHINE\
  SOFTWARE\
    Microsoft\
      MSSQLServer\
        MSSQLServer
```

When SQLMail Doesn't Work

The following are issues when SQLMail does not function:

♦ The Windows NT Postoffice account password may have been changed. Edit *MailPassword* in the registry key if necessary:

```
HKEY_LOCAL_MACHINE\
  SOFTWARE\
    Microsoft\
      MSSQLServer\
        MSSQLServer
```

♦ The MSSQLServer service must have a LocalSystem account, not a user account. To verify the account type, from *Control Panel* in *Main* go to *Services* and select and then double-click *MSSQLServer*. Verify that *System Account* is selected. Select *System Account* if necessary.

♦ The option *Allow Service to Interact With Desktop* must be set. To verify this option, from *Control Panel* in *Main* go to *Services* and select and double-click *MSSQLServer*. Select *Allow Service to Interact With Desktop* if necessary.

♦ Mail has not started. Use *isql/w* and issue *sp_startmail*, or use SQL Server *Setup*, select *Set Server Option*, and then select *Auto Start Mail Client*. If the *Setup* option is used, SQL Server must be stopped and restarted for SQLMail to start.

Interfacing SQLMail

SQLMail is implemented as a set of *extended stored procedures* defined with the dynamic library module SQLMAP60.DLL, along with one stored procedure and are listed in Table 5.4. For programming examples of using MAPI, please refer to the stored procedure *sp_processmail*. The next section describes how to obtain a copy of *sp_processmail*.

The Postmaster

Every postoffice needs a postmaster and SQLMail is no exception. SQLMail can be considered query based. When a user sends mail to another user using *xp_sendmail*, it is sent directly to the user mail inbox. However, mail which is sent to the SQL Server mail account is forwarded automatically to SQL Server for processing. For this reason, SQLMail needs a postmaster and *sp_process-mail* is our postmaster. It is a system stored procedure which must be sched-

TABLE 5.4 Extended Stored Procedures for SQL Mail

Extended Stored Procedure	Description
xp_deletemail	Deletes a specified message.
xp_findnextmsg	Finds the next message in the mail box.
xp_readmail	Reads a message and/or an attachment from the mail box.
xp_sendmail	Sends a message and/or a query result set and/or an attachment to specified recipients. The *xp_sendmail* has fourteen different parameters, some of which are illustrated here:

```
xp_sendmail 'user1', @query='sp_configure'
xp_sendmail @recipients='user1; user2',
@message='The master database is full.'
```

xp_startmail	Starts a SQL Server Mail client session.

```
xp_startmail ['user'][,'password']
```

xp_stopmail	Stops a SQL Server Mail client session.
sp_processmail	Processes mail in the InBox of SQL Server. Finds, reads, responds to, and delegates mail messages. Can return results of a query to a message sender. Can be called by SQL Executive as a scheduled task.

uled on a regular basis by the Enterprise Manager. *sp_processmail* reads the SQLMail inbox and forwards the completed queries to the destination recipients. Mail which is sent to another user functions much like commercial enterprises like UPS and FEDEX in that the mail bypasses the postmaster and is delivered directly to the user.

The *sp_processmail* is a relatively short system procedure stored in the system table *syscomments*. Retrieving the procedure can be done with:

```
SELECT syscomments.text FROM sysobjects, syscomments
WHERE sysobjects.name = 'sp_processmail'
AND syscomments.id = sysobjects.id
```

The *sp_processmail* can be tailored for individual needs. It automatically deletes mail which has been read and a possible change is to not delete a particular class of mail. Other customizations are possible. Normal operation of *sp_processmail* is to send the result set as an attachment. A possible customization is to place the result set in the body of the message by setting the parameter *@attach_results* to *false*.

You'll probably want to organize your mail. This can be done by defining a protocol relating to the *@subject* and *@use* parameters. Possible examples of such a protocol used for these parameters by *xp_sendmail* and *sp_processmail* might be:

```
@subject = 'SQL:distribution', @use = 'distribution'
@subject = 'SQL:pubs', @use = 'pubs'
```

Using SQLMail

Actually, the SQLMail users' diagram found in Figure 5.13 is not quite true. Tasks, triggers, and stored procedures can send e-mail; however, alerts do not send e-mail but only cause the SQL Executive to send e-mail. But before we can proceed we must define an alert. An *alert* is caused by an event. An *event* is declared (or created) from an entry in the Windows NT application log when the following occur:

◆ Severity 19 or higher *sysmessages* errors
◆ Error messages with severity codes of 110, 120, or 130
◆ Any RAISERROR WITH LOG statement
◆ An event logged by *xp_logevent*
◆ Any sysmessages message modified with *sp_altermessage_with_log*

When an alert is processed there is the option of running a task. If the alert in question is not a one-time alert, then *running a task when the alert occurs* is a requirement. If this is not done then there will be a significant negative impact on performance, and a possible *broadcast-storm* if the mail server or alert server is remote.

SQL Server Performance Monitor cannot actually create a log entry in the Windows NT application log or send e-mail; however, its actions cause those events. When a performance monitor alert occurs, the task *sqlalrtr.exe* with parameters is run which places an entry in the log file. So for the performance monitor there are actually two alerts, the *performance monitor alert* which executes a task at a threshold, and which in turn writes the application log and creates an event for a *SQL Executive alert* (see Figure 5.14).

Alerts are managed in the SQL Enterprise manager. E-mail will be sent for alerts and task completion status. A success or failure task completion e-mail message will be sent, or optionally no message. An additional option is

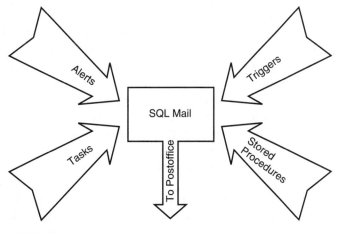

FIGURE 5.13 SQLMail users.

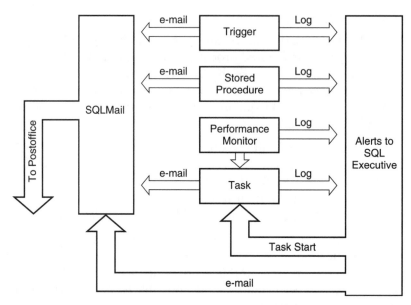

FIGURE 5.14 Integrating e-mail, task management, and alerts.

to log the success/failure status in the Windows NT application log. These options are set by the *Task Options* of **SQL Enterprise** manager.

Automated Backup Using Alerts, E-Mail, and Tasks

A transaction log threshold alert is a good example of using alerts to manage the SQL Server. E-mail can be sent indicating a critical transaction log level. The SQL Server alert mechanism can start a task that schedules a backup of the log at the same time e-mail is sent. E-mail can then be sent at different points during the backup procedure to indicate progress. The final e-mail message will be a success message that the backup is complete. Of course, the first e-mail message should be to a pager so that the administrator knows that a contingency exists and to start e-mail monitoring to gauge the progress. A nice touch is to implement a program with a red icon for an unanswered alert, changing the color to orange for contingency operation in process, yellow for incomplete recovery but contingency situation no longer exists, and green for no alerts. The program will poll the e-mail InBox for known messages and status determination. Failure to receive a message at a particular point will cause the icon to flash, indicating a failure during contingency recovery.

Illustrated is a model of an automated dump. It is a straightforward matter when used within the context of the **SQL Executive**. The tasks to define an automated dump of a database log named **ABC** are as follows:

♦ Define error messages as follows:

Error code	*Message*
75001	ABC log exceeds 80%
75002	ABC log dump started
75003	ABC log dump complete

♦ Create an alert for message 75001 using the SQL Executive to start the backup task and to send e-mail to the operator, Howard, and to start a TSQL task.

The task:

```
EXEC sp_altermessage 75001, WITH_LOG, FALSE
EXEC xp_sendmail 'Howard', @message = 'Dump of ABC log starting'
EXEC xp_logevent 75002, 'Dump of ABC log starting'
DUMP TRANSACTION ABC to ABC_Dump1 WITH INIT
EXEC xp_sendmail 'Howard', @message = 'Dump of ABC log complete'
EXEC xp_logevent 75003, 'Dump of ABC log complete'
EXEC sp_altermessage 75001, WITH_LOG, TRUE
```

To start the process, set a performance monitor alert on the ABC log file using a task name something like:

```
D:\SQL60\BINN\SQLALRTR -E 75001 -D ABC
```

A protocol is required to build and use your stored procedure. Follow the general order of the following steps before using the procedure.

♦ Create and test your stored procedure.
♦ Create an operator in SQL Server Manager. Operators must be defined before alerts are defined. Test sending mail to the operator by using the *test sending* mail command button when creating the operator.
♦ Define the messages.
♦ Define your alerts using the message numbers. Ensure that continuous alerts has *delay between responses* set to a reasonable value. It will be in seconds. For now, do not define a task for the alert. In general you should never define a continuous alert without a task. Doing so may saturate the system with alerts, but since we're creating the alert there is no problem. Answer yes to the *invoking alert* dialog box when exiting from the Enterprise Manager alert management dialog.
♦ You have an alert and an operator. Go to isql/w and issue the command:

```
xp_cmdshell "D:\SQL60\BINN\SQLALRTR -E 75001 -D ABC"
```

♦ This command is forcing the alert you created. You should find mail in the operator inbox. When you do, embellish this step by going back to **SQL Server Enterprise manager** and adding the name of your backup stored procedure as the task for your alert. You might want to test this procedure on a small database or you can substitute a dummy task since you know your backup task already works.

♦ From isql/w reissue the xp_cmdshell command to force another alert. This time your backup will occur, so be prepared for it.

♦ Your last step is to start the performance monitor and use the text from xp_cmdshell above as the command line for a performance monitor alert task. To do this:

1. Start SQL Server performance monitor.
2. Choose the View menu and select Alert.
3. Choose the Edit menu and Add to Alert.
4. In the dialog box set *Object:* SQLServer-Log, *Counter:* Log Space Used %, *Instance:* ABC, select *Alert If Over,* enter the actual percentage. Since we are still testing enter a small value. This will ensure that we get an alert.
5. Since we're testing, select *first time*. The last task is to enter the xp_cmdshell text we used before without the quotes.
6. Test it. After successful testing go back to **SQL Server** performance monitor and change *first time* to *every time* and raise the percentage to a reasonable threshold level. If you used a place holder task for the alert in Enterprise Manager, replace it with your backup stored procedure.

For performance monitor alerts to occur, both the **SQL Performance Monitor** and **SQL Execution** must be running. An important issue is to disable further alerts while the dump is in process. What can't be used to disable the alert is *sp_updatealert.* It only disables the alert for this server, and the alert is handed to the fail-safe server. What we have done is alter the message so no logging occurs.

This small program can certainly be embellished with such features as automatic creation of **SQL** dump devices and possibly a monitor task which sends e-mail on a periodic basis, or sends e-mail when the task fails to complete in a specific time. One doesn't want to arrive for work at 7 A.M. and find that the backups have failed. It is nice to know about the problem, no matter when it occurs.

Notes

1. Please see *Microsoft SQL Server Administrator's Companion* (Microsoft Corporation, © 1995), pp. 504–505.
2. *Microsoft SQL Server Administrator's Companion* (p. 438) states that servers participating in replication *should* use the same character set and that the same sort order *is not required.* Other Microsoft documentation states that all servers participating in replication *must* use the same character set and sort sequence. We prefer the latter.
3. This is a very difficult issue. A possible solution is to unsubscribe all subscribers to the database and then resynchronize after the distribution server is available. See the *Microsoft SQL Server Administrator's Companion,* pp. 504–505.
4. *Microsoft SQL Server Administrator's Companion,* pp. 510–512.

6

Database Design

Overview

A database is usually one piece of a much larger application. This chapter assumes you have done the large-scale planning discussed in Chapter 4 and are ready to start putting together a specific database.

In databases, as in most applications, design is where everything starts. The choices you make when you design a database influence all aspects of your work, from data integrity to performance. But don't think you can do it once; database development is an iterative process. Be ready to test and change your design as you go along.

One common error is to work through a design and then present it triumphantly to the users. They won't be happy, and it'll take a long time to get everything straightened out. Prevent this problem by surveying your users early and often. Get feedback from them at each stage of development, and check your work with your peers, too.

A good database design includes:

♦ *Data definition.* Identify the business objects and how they relate to each other.

♦ *Business functions.* The database is a model of the business. It needs to support and enforce business conventions and recognize legitimate and illegitimate transactions.

♦ *Performance.* Review needed reports and think through how they will work with your design. Twelve-way joins for a common query don't make much sense, but this might be acceptable for something that doesn't come up frequently.

In order for you and others on your staff to support the design, strive for:

♦ *Flexibility.* Everything changes. Keep notes and diagrams on your design. Anticipate changes and consider how they will work with your design.

♦ *Readability.* Make sure others can understand your design. Use meaningful names with consistent use of case and number (singular/plural).

This chapter has four main sections:

1. *Identifying Needs:* Getting precise requirements for the application.
2. *Creating the Logical Design:* Showing all the things in the database and how they relate to each other.
3. *Creating the Physical Design:* Translating the logical design into a physical design by creating and implementing SQL commands, resulting in a prototype.
4. *Tuning the Database Design:* Testing the database against your requirements; refining table design, indexes, and physical placement of data to improve performance.

In real life, each of these steps is iterative and blurs into the others. If you understand your application and data well, you may be able to make some of the tuning decisions (such as denormalization and space assignment) during the logical design or physical design stages.

Identifying Needs

When designing a database, start by listing requirements. Get functional requirements in *quantifiable* terms. Press for specifics! You won't get all the information you want the first time round, but you'll get some, and ideas on how to change your questions for the next pass. A starting checklist includes these things:

♦ A description of the business, with detailed information (flowcharts to show how tasks relate to each other, lists of forms and reports, timing goals, notes on what works and what does not) on how data is currently handled.

- Performance and availability requirements for each functional area.
- Number and kind of users. What do they need from the application? How sophisticated are they? How stable are their requirements? Are there need conflicts between groups? Are some user groups dominant?
- Amount of data and projected growth.
- Security needs.
- Business rules (pay bills within 30 days, keep no inventory longer than six months, track shipments out of state for tax purposes) for each functional area.
- Reports or required output for each functional area.
- Internationalization requirements.

You also need to consider:

- The general nature of the application. Is it mostly online inserting, updating, and deleting; primarily reporting; or a combination? Is it a new system or a conversion?
- Hardware for both client and server sides, network setup, and whether it is local or distributed.
- Interaction with other software, home grown and off the shelf.
- Applicable standards (ISO 9000, internal or external systems, and methodologies).
- Time and staff available.
- Projected life of this application.

Creating the Logical Design

Once you've collected all the information you can get, start plotting the logical design. This involves creating an entity-relationship (E-R) model to show the things in the database and how they relate to each other. After you've got them all recorded, you *normalize* the things and their relationships (apply a set of rules to reduce data redundancy and protect data integrity). A good E-R diagram shows the kind of data in a database and how it relates. Anyone who understands databases and knows something about the business should be able to write intelligent queries from an E-R diagram. This is a good place to go back to your users. They'll probably be able to see errors you don't.

When you have a solid E-R diagram, examine the business rules you have coaxed from your users and consider how they will affect both the database design and the application design. Can a department exist with no employees? Can an employee exist who is in no department? Is it possible to change primary key values (e.g., an employee number or social security number)? Can your company sell more widgets than it has on hand? Are any of these principles likely to change? This information is critical to the application's behavior, and determines how your things interrelate. Put together charts showing how the business rules apply to the database and let the users review them.

Finally, establish expectations (and requirements) for the performance of the application's various pieces as part of the logical database and application design. You must understand these expectations early because they will impact your design. Among other performance statistics, it is critical to have at least:

- The volume of information and its expected rate of growth
- The initial and projected number of total users and concurrent users (those actively using the application at any one time)
- The number and nature of interesting transactions and reports, including target response times, data volume, and approach, if the manipulations are complex

At this point, make preliminary assessments of the performance goals. Are they reasonable and achievable? If not, why not? Performance limitations will become clearer as you create the physical design and run benchmarks, but you need to look for them during the logical design stage, too.

Entities, Attributes, and Relationships—Step 1

In designing a logical database and application, first determine what *entities* are important to the application. An *entity* is something you can uniquely identify. Examples are employees, departments, customers, or individual purchases.

The entities have *attributes* (also called properties). These might include the birth date of an employee, the name of a department, the address of a customer, and the date of a purchase.

Relationships are associations among the entities—an employee is in a department, a customer makes a purchase, an employee handles a certain kind of purchase.

During the logical database design, you identify the entities, attributes, and relationships in the application. The entities will eventually translate to tables, the attributes to columns, and joins (or, occasionally, special tables called *relation tables*) represent the relationships. Most database designers deliberately use the terms *entity* and *attribute* during the early logical design stage and switch to *table* and *column* as they get closer to the actual structure. Table 6.1 shows how the terms line up.

TABLE 6.1 Relational Terminology

Database	*Relational Theory*	*Traditional*
Table	Entity	File
Row	Tuple	Record
Column	Attribute	Field

By the time you are ready to implement your design:

◆ Each table will have a set number of columns; it will be square or rectangular, rather than irregular.
◆ Each column will have a name and a datatype.
◆ Each row will have a column or group of columns that uniquely identify it.

The Process

You set up entities, attributes, and relationships by going through a process such as the following:

◆ Identify each independent entity (thing) and give it a name.
◆ List the attributes (characteristics or properties) of each entity.
◆ Select or create one attribute as the *primary identifier*. If a single attribute won't work, use a group of attributes. The relational model requires a primary identifier because relational data is not stored in any particular order. To retrieve a specific row, you must be able to describe it uniquely.
◆ Classify the relationships between entities as one-to-many (departments have many employees but employees have only one department) or many-to-many (orders may include many products and products can appear on any number of orders). If the relationship is one-to-one, consider merging the two entities.
◆ Change each many-to-many relationship into a connecting (*associative* or *relation*) table.
◆ Make sure each one-to-many relationship includes ways to connect the entities (shared attributes you can use for joins). Typically, the primary identifier in one entity (customer identification number in a customer entity) connects with a secondary identifier in another (customer identification number in an order entity where the order number is the primary identifier). These pairs are often called *primary* and *secondary keys* or *primary* and *foreign keys*.
◆ Examine the entities, attributes, and relationships again and test them against normalization rules.

One way to get a list of entities is to work from existing paper systems, such as order forms, weekly reports, and invoice lists. You can start by listing all attributes and then grouping them into entities; or work from the other end, starting with entities and figuring out their attributes. Either way, you'll move things around more than once before you have a working system.

Entity-Relationship Diagrams

Diagram entities as named boxes, with attributes as enclosed lists and primary identifiers marked in some way (in Figure 6.1 they are underlined). Lines show the relationships between entities. Verbs describe the relationships: a customer *issues* an order. An order *contains* products.

As you analyze the relationships between entities, you often spot problems. An order, for example, can contain more than one product, and a product can appear in more than one order. The order and product entities shown in Figure 6.1 have a many-to-many relationship. This calls for a new (associating or relating) entity and some rearranging of attributes. If you leave things as they are, it will be very difficult to design a table with a square or rectangular shape. How many product# columns will you have in the order table? What if a customer orders more products than you have allowed for? The idea is to break the many-to-many ($n : n$) relationship down to two relationships. It usually turns into a one-to-many ($1 : n$) and many-to-one ($n : 1$) relationship.

The primary identifier in an association entity often includes more than one attribute to ensure uniqueness as shown in Figure 6.2.

Normalization

The purpose of normalization is to cut down on data duplication and protect data integrity. This means small tables with narrow rows, fewer null values, and less data redundancy. Normalized tables are easy to maintain and update as your design needs change.

Normalized tables also have advantages in terms of physical design:

♦ Accessing data and creating indexes is faster, since you have more rows per page and fewer logical and physical I/Os.
♦ With more small tables, you have more indexing opportunities. (Each table can have only one clustered index, and it is generally your best index.) The indexes may be easier to transverse, since they are narrower and shorter.
♦ More tables means more opportunities for precise data placement.

Most books describe first through fifth normal forms (and Boyce/Codd normal form, between the third and fourth forms) but database designers generally concentrate on the first three. Each normal form is a test you apply to

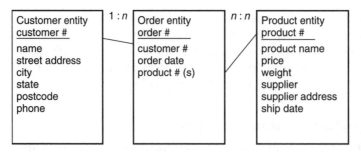

FIGURE 6.1 Entity-relationship design.

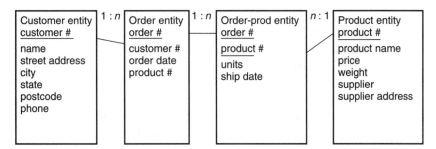

FIGURE 6.2 Refined E-R design.

your design. Depending on your application, you may decide to ignore some of the changes normalization suggests. Since denormalization implies prior normalization, the usual method is to normalize the database during the design stage and denormalize during the prototype phase as performance requirements indicate.

The *first normal form* (sometimes written as *1NF*) requires every column to be atomic—it can hold only one value. A customer *name* attribute, for example, decomposes into first name, last name, and middle initial; a *phone* attribute into area code and phone number. In the same way, repeating groups or attributes are forbidden. An order entity with *product1, product2, productn* doesn't pass 1NF. An E-R diagram will often help you spot these problems before you normalize. First normal form is important because the relational model does not allow a table to have varying numbers of columns or columns of uncertain size. Even ignoring theory, there are practical reasons for 1NF:

♦ If you have multiple columns of the same type (product1, product2, . . . product15), the table is difficult to query (how do I find all the rows with product *abc* in some product column?). This kind of table structure is also awkward to print or display on the screen—or even just to understand.

♦ If you have multiple pieces of information in a single column, data retrieval becomes dauntingly complex. Imagine the SQL needed to find product *abc* in a column that may contain up to 15 products! Sizing the column is also problematic.

The *second normal form* (2NF) applies to entities with compound primary identifiers and requires you to make sure that attributes apply to the whole primary identifier, or *key*. If the primary identifier is a single attribute, the table complies with 2NF by default.

In the example sketched previously, *units* in the order-product entity passes the test—it applies to a particular product in a particular order, and not to the product or the order alone. *Ship date* may actually apply to the order as a whole, depending on the business rules. (If the company ships each line item as it is ready, ship date belongs in the order-product entity, but if the company ships only after the whole order is prepared, the ship date is an attribute of the order.) This is why database design is tough.

After you check your design against 2NF, move attributes that don't relate to the whole key to a different entity or reconsider the compound identifier. If all attributes relate to only one of the elements in the primary identifier, you may need to change the primary identifier or create an additional entity with that column as the primary key. The second normal form eliminates redundancy, and verifies that each compound primary identifier really is the unique identifier for the entity.

The third normal form considers the tie between the primary identifier and each attribute. The supplier address in the product entity applies to the supplier attribute and not to the product number primary identifier. Remove it and create a new entity to hold supplier information.

Once you've been through the normalization process, review your requirements and make sure you can create the required reports from the structure you've created. Are there paths between related pieces of data? Is all the data you need available through the entities and attributes?

Business Functions and Rules—Step 2

The next step in logical database and application design requires the application designer (you) to apply the business functions and rules your users have provided. In SQL Server, the tools you use are datatypes (including user-defined datatypes), constraints, unique indexes, defaults, rules, stored procedures, and triggers.

- Columns that must be unique may need a unique index.
- Columns used in more than one table are candidates for user-defined datatypes.
- Columns in which you want SQL Server to enter a particular value are possible sites for defaults.
- Columns with simple limits on values may take a rule.
- Consider constraints or triggers for columns with value range determined by cross-column comparisons.
- Handle more complicated business rules with stored procedures and triggers.

During the design stage, create a chart for each table showing the requirements you know of in terms of these tools. At this point, you can start thinking of your normalized entities as tables, and the attributes as columns. When you move to prototyping, use the chart to create SQL statements. (The section on building the application gives information on how to choose the appropriate SQL commands, since SQL Server provides more than one way to implement defaults, rules, and unique indexes. At this point, work on the conceptual level.)

Datatypes define the type of data you can store in a column, and SQL Server provides a wide range of possibilities. For each column, consider:

◆ Function (the kind of data stored)
◆ Range (how large or small the data can be)
◆ Storage size (how much space it takes up)

For example, a social security number can be a character datatype or a numeric datatype. The first takes nine bytes of storage. Defining it as an integer reduces the number to four bytes. Since there is no need for alphabetic or special characters in a social security number, the integer may be a better choice.

Nulls add another wrinkle to datatypes. You can use nulls as place holders for:

◆ Missing information (customer declines to state age)
◆ Incomplete data (middle name is illegible)
◆ Inapplicable answers (no *spouse's name* for a single person)

Specify not null for primary keys and *must enter* columns; null for columns where information is not required or is likely to be unavailable. For example, you always want an order date associated with each order, so you would create that column as not null. On the other hand, you wouldn't necessarily know the ship date when you entered the order, so that column could allow nulls.

User-defined datatypes are based on system datatypes. They are one way of enforcing datatype compatibility, by specifying all aspects of a datatype including null status and type, length, precision, and scale. You can use the same user-defined datatype for numerous columns.

A *unique index* is the only way to ensure uniqueness of one or more columns across a table. Not all tables need an index for performance reasons. If you know a column must be unique (such as the primary identifier) sketch in a unique index. You can decide later if it should be clustered or nonclustered.

Defaults insert values (such as today's date) when no other value is supplied. Defaults must be the same datatype as the column. A default character string ("no value") will not work for a numerical column. Some developers use explicit defaults to avoid null values.

Rules validate values. There are three types of rules:

1. A set of values using the set operator IN
2. A range of values with BETWEEN or comparison operators
3. A pattern match with LIKE

Rules specified in the create table statement (table-level check constraints) can compare values in two columns in the same table. For example, you might want to use a check constraint rule to make sure a ship date is never earlier than its order date.

Stored procedures are named objects in the database consisting of one or more SQL statements. They can contain procedural logic, accept input parameters and generate output parameters, and run faster than individual statements. They also prevent the user from getting bogged down in complex syntax. SQL Server system procedures offer many examples of what stored procedures can do.

Triggers enforce referential integrity or other business rules. You can have up to three triggers on each table (INSERT, update, and delete) and the triggers can refer to other tables, call stored procedures, and execute other triggers. SQL Server fires a trigger when the specified data modification action takes place. Construct triggers to enforce business rules. For example, what happens when a customer becomes inactive? Do you keep the information on the customer as long as there is related information (a disputed sale)? Do you remove the customer information and archive it in an *inactive* table? Do you delete customer information and flag matching values in other tables (add an inactive customer column to the order table)? What the trigger does depends on how the business handles these cases.

Once you have sketched these elements for each table, revise your schema as needed. Table 6.2 shows an example for one table.

Performance Requirements—Step 3

For the performance assessment, review user requirements. What are the major queries and reports? Are many joins required to get the results you need? Pin down how often reports will be run, and find out if they need to happen during prime time or can be run when there is less pressure on the system.

Decision support systems (DSS) and online transaction processing systems (OLTP) address two different environments. You can clearly characterize

TABLE 6.2 Table Definition Example

Column	Datatype	User Datatype	Null Status	Default	One-Column Rule	Other Considerations
product#	numeric	numtype	not null		btw 0000000 & 9999999	Must be unique
name	varchar(20)	nametype	not null			
type	varchar		not null	appl	appl, game, edu, hardware, supply, book	
notes	varchar(200)		null			
price	smallmoney		not null			
weight	decimal		not null			
supplier#	numeric	numtype	not null		btw 0000000 & 9999999	Must exist in supplier entity

some applications as one or the other. Others will have aspects of both, which presents difficult problems in physical design.

At this point, you can look at major activities and try to categorize them. Generally speaking, a decision support system is heavy on queries and reports but light on updates. Transactions tend to be complex and result in long locks. Speed is not usually critical—many of the reports can be run in nonpeak time. Pages are moved in and out of cache as queries run, but there are relatively few disk writes.

An OLTP system shows some opposite characteristics. The emphasis is on data modification, often with many concurrent users. Lock contention can be high, especially if there is competition with DSS activities. Referential integrity checks call for many joins. Disk writes are frequent.

Table 6.3 compares the two kinds of systems. The tuning section gives information on how to deal with the differing requirements.

Building the Application

Physical database design, like logical database design, usually requires several passes.

- ◆ Translate the logical database design (entities and relationships and business rules) into a set of tables, defaults, rules, triggers, and indexes.
- ◆ Consider physical placement issues, including database size and location, log size and location, and use of segments for individual tables. Make the best decisions you can and plan to make adjustments during the tuning phase.
- ◆ Develop a prototype.
- ◆ Run required queries and reports against the prototype and evaluate speed, accuracy, and reliability.

TABLE 6.3 OLTP/DSS Comparison

Topic/Action	*DSS*	*OLTP*
Transactions	Long-running transactions	Many short transactions
Locking	Long locks	Short locks
Reports	Many	Few
Data modifications	Few	Many
Joins for referential checks	Few	Many
Speed	Not critical	High
User connections	Not critical	Many concurrent
Disk input/output		Significant
Cache use	Significant	

◆ Change the physical design and prototype as needed. Preliminary proto-types may use only token amounts of data, but for real results you need a load close to what you expect in actual deployment.
◆ Continue to test and change the prototype until overall goals are met.
◆ Put the application under full load and move into the tuning phase to work on specific problems.

In many cases the progress from logical to physical design is fairly direct. The SQL commands let you do the following:

◆ Create tables
◆ Create indexes
◆ Set up integrity controls
◆ Review existing physical resources (disk space)
◆ Place objects on segments for maximum accessibility

During this translation from logical to physical design, remember that individual tables exist in the context of the structure of the entire application. Collect information on issues and make educated choices, remembering that standardizing components in isolation won't work. When you move into the tuning phase, you'll be looking at specific queries and reports.

Creating Tables

Table creation, at its simplest, includes naming a table and its columns. For each column, you specify:

◆ Name
◆ Datatype (including size or precision and scale for some datatypes)
◆ Null status

Stripped-down create table syntax looks like this:

```
CREATE TABLE table_name
(
        column_name         datatype      [NULL | NOT NULL]
        [, column_name      datatype      [NULL | NOT NULL]]...
)
```

Full syntax involves many more options:

```
CREATE TABLE [database.[owner].]table_name
(
        {col_name datatype [NULL | NOT NULL | IDENTITY]
                [constraint [constraint [...constraint]]]|[[,]constraint]}
                [[,] {next_col_name | next_constraint}...]
)
[ON segment_name]
```

It includes these elements:

◆ Name, datatype, and (optional) null and identity information for each column. The identity property generates and holds sequential numbers, and is available to columns based on nonnull exact numeric and decimal (but 0 scale) datatypes.
◆ One DEFAULT constraint per column.
◆ One CHECK constraint (column-level rule) per column.
◆ Any number of table-level check constraints per table.
◆ One PRIMARY KEY constraint (unique index on a column that does not permit nulls) per table.
◆ Up to 249 UNIQUE constraints (unique indexes on columns that permits nulls) per table.
◆ Up to 31 FOREIGN KEY constraints per table (each of which can reference at most 16 columns).

You can create unique indexes, defaults, rules, and referential integrity checks in the CREATE TABLE statement or separately. Table 6.4 shows how the commands relate.

There are some advantages in defining constraints in the CREATE TABLE statement:

◆ Locating all the code in one place may make it convenient to maintain and easy for others to find and read.
◆ Creating defaults and rules as separate objects is a SQL Server extension and may not be as portable as using the CREATE TABLE syntax.
◆ Implementing references is easy and direct.
◆ The table-level check constraint provides features not available in rules, and is less complex than a trigger

TABLE 6.4 Table Definition Components

Category	*In CREATE TABLE Statement*	*In Other SQL Statement*
Unique index	Unique constraint	Create unique index (on null column)
	Primary key constraint	Create unique index (on non-null column)
Referential integrity	References constraint	Create trigger
One-table cross-column comparison	Check constraint (table level)	Create trigger
Column value limit	Check constraint (column level)	Create rule & sp_bindrule
Column default	Default	Create default & sp_bindefault

Using separate SQL statement also has benefits:

♦ You can create libraries of defaults and rules to use with multiple columns and tables and prevent errors by changing defaults and rules in one place rather than in many.
♦ You can change defaults, rules, indexes, stored procedures, and triggers without touching the table structure.
♦ Triggers and stored procedures are more flexible and powerful than constraints: They can cascade changes, reference multiple tables and objects, use complex logic, and roll back illegal transactions.
♦ The syntax for the separate commands is less complex and easily tested in isolation.

In this section, we'll handle the elements conceptually, give some examples so you can compare different methods, and allow you to decide how to write the code.

Column Names

Set up some conventions for table and column names. Make the names meaningful and be consistent in case, number, use of abbreviations, special characters, and so on. Don't call one table *authors* and another *titleauthor*, or one column *au_fname* and another *auth_lname*.

Null status is actually not required (the not null default goes into effect if you do not specify a status) but your intention is easier to understand if you explicitly include null status. Since it is possible to change the null status default with sp_dboption or the SET statement, you'll avoid confusion by spelling it out.

Datatypes

SQL Server determines the size of a column by the datatype and whether or not you allow NULLs in the table definition (see Table 6.5).

The first principle in datatype choice is to pick the "natural" datatype. Unless there are specific performance or space issues, assign a phone number a character datatype rather than a numeric datatype, because you're more likely to use it with character functions (substring) than with mathematical operations (addition) or functions (sqrt). Other guidelines include:

♦ Use the smallest datatype possible (smallint rather than int)—small datatypes take up less space.
♦ Use numerics rather than strings—numerics compare faster.
♦ Use fixed-length character and binary datatypes rather than their variable-length relatives—fixed-length datatypes require less overhead. However, if the fixed-length field adds appreciably to the size of most rows, the variable-length datatype is going to be better.

TABLE 6.5 Datatype Sizes

Category	Datatype	Size
Character	char(n)	n
	varchar	Data size
	text(n)	0 or multiple of 2K
Binary	binary(n)	n
	varbinary(n)	Data size
	image	0 or multiple of 2K
Exact Numeric: Integers	int	4
	smallint	2
	tinyint	1
Exact Numeric: Decimals	numeric, decimal	2–17, depending on precision and scale
Approximate Numeric	double precision	8
	float (precision)	4 or 8, depending on precision
	real	4
Money	money	8
	smallmoney	4
Datetime	datetime	8
	smalldatetime	4
Bit	bit	1
	text/image	>=16 +2K (minimum)
Timestamp	timestamp	8

♦ Choose compatible datatypes for join partners—if SQL Server has to convert datatypes on one side in a join, it can't use an index on that join.

All columns that allow null values are handled as variable-length columns.

♦ For character and binary columns, SQL Server translates them internally into varchar and varbinary columns. Joining a char not null column to a char null column requires a char-varchar conversion.

♦ For other datatypes, null does not present these problems. However, there is increased overhead in data storage. SQL Server documentation gives information on how to calculate these values.

User-defined datatypes allow you to create datatypes based on system datatypes and null status and apply them to any number of columns. Create the datatypes before you create tables that will use them. Here are examples for name columns (authors, employees, customers, and managers):

```
EXEC sp_addtype 'nametype', 'varchar(20)', 'NOT NULL'
go
EXEC sp_addtype 'initialtype', 'char(1)', 'NULL'
go
```

In a create table statement, they'd look like this:

```
CREATE TABLE employees
(
fname nametype,
lname nametype,
initial initialtype,
...
)
go
```

You can note null status, but be careful—you can override the user data-type null status by spelling out a conflicting one in the create table statement.

```
CREATE TABLE employees
(
fname nametype NULL,
lname nametype NOT NULL,
initial initialtype NULL,
...
)
go
```

If you create defaults and rules as separate objects, you can bind them to user-defined datatypes, so that the default for order dates and ship dates is today's date.

Null Status

As you create tables, explicitly specify null or not null status for each column, both to clarify your own thinking and make your work easily understood. If you don't specify null status, SQL Server uses the default not null. However, since the default is settable, the meaning of a create table script that does not specify null status can change dramatically and mysteriously.

In the logical design stages, you made preliminary decisions about which columns should be null. At this point, you may want to reconsider your decisions in light of physical implications. Since character and binary columns that allow nulls are treated as varchar and varbinary, define them that way explicitly and check join partners for such columns. Wherever possible, join columns should have the same datatype, including null status. Otherwise, SQL Server will perform conversions.

User-defined datatypes can help you enforce datatype consistency.

Defaults and Default Constraints

You can create a default (today's date) for order dates with the create default-sp_bindefault combination or the create table statement. Either way, you begin by defining any user datatypes you will need in the table definition:

```
EXEC sp_addtype 'datetype', 'smalldatetime', 'NOT NULL'
go
```

For the first solution, the table definition is simple:

```
CREATE TABLE orders
(
order# numeric(6,0) IDENTITY,
customer# ssntype NOT NULL,
orderdate datetype NOT NULL
)
go
```

To put a default into effect, you create it and then bind it to a specific column or (as here) to a user-defined datatype:

```
CREATE DEFAULT datedefault AS getdate()
go
EXEC sp_bindefault 'datedefault', 'datetype'
go
```

To do the same with a constraint, include it in the create table statement:

```
CREATE TABLE orders
(
order#       numeric(6,0)                      IDENTITY,
customer#    ssntype                           NOT NULL,
orderdate    datetype     DEFAULT getdate()    NOT NULL
)
go
```

Rules and Check Constraints

Rule creation follows a similar process. These statements create a rule that limits acceptable input for a column and binds the rule to a particular column:

```
CREATE TABLE products
(
product#     numeric(7,0)        IDENTITY,
name         varchar(20)         NOT NULL,
type         varchar(8)          NULL,
description  varchar(50)         NULL,
weight       decimal(6,2)        NOT NULL,
price        smallmoney          NOT NULL,
supplier#    suppltype           NULL
)
go

CREATE RULE typerule
As @type IN ('appl', 'book', 'edu', 'game', 'hardware', 'supply')
go

EXEC sp_bindrule 'typerule', 'products.type'
go
```

To include the rule in the create table statement as a check constraint, try this:

```
CREATE TABLE products
(
product#      numeric(7,0)          IDENTITY,
name          varchar(20)           NOT NULL,
type          varchar(8)            NULL
      CONSTRAINT typeck CHECK (type IN ('appl', 'book', 'edu', 'game',
      'hardware', 'supply')),
description   varchar(50)           NULL,
weight        decimal(6,2)          NOT NULL,
price         smallmoney            NOT NULL,
supplier#     suppltype             NULL
)
go
```

Naming a constraint (here *typeck*) is not required. However, it makes your work easier if you need to change a constraint. You could write the constraint code as:

```
CREATE TABLE products
(
product#      numeric(7,0)          IDENTITY,
name          varchar(20)           NOT NULL,
type          varchar(8)            NULL
      CHECK (type IN ('appl', 'book', 'edu',
      'game', 'hardware', 'supply')),
description varchar(50)             NULL,
weight        decimal(6,2)          NOT NULL,
price         smallmoney            NOT NULL,
supplier#     suppltype             NULL
)
go
```

Table-level check constraints can compare two columns in the same table. A rule cannot handle this situation. To make sure that the shipdate is never earlier than the orderdate, create the orders table with a check constraint like this:

```
CREATE TABLE orders
(
order#        numeric(6,0)                        IDENTITY,
customer#     ssntype                             NOT NULL,
orderdate     datetype       DEFAULT getdate()    NOT NULL,
shipdate      datetype                            NOT NULL,
CONSTRAINT datecnstr CHECK (shipdate >= orderdate)
)
go
```

Integrity Constraints

Reference constraints, foreign key constraints, triggers, and stored procedures are mechanisms to protect data integrity. Reference and foreign key constraints, like other constraints, are specified in the create table statement. Triggers and stored procedures are created with Transact-SQL create trigger and create procedure statements. Trigger and stored procedure code can use Transact-SQL procedural extensions that allow logic such as if-then, while, return, and goto label. Since you can create code in modules, you can use the same pieces over and over again with chained calls. Integrity constraints in the create table statement are less flexibile and powerful.

Foreign Key and Reference Constraints

Reference constraints ensure that a column value exists in another table. For example, the order number in the orderlines table must match a unique order number in the orders table. In this example, the uniqueness of the order number in the orders table is guaranteed by declaring it a primary key (more about this in the index section). The orderlines CREATE TABLE statement includes a references clause.

```
CREATE TABLE orders
(
order#       numeric(6,0)                        IDENTITY
     CONSTRAINT pko# PRIMARY KEY,
customer#    ssntype                     NOT NULL,
orderdate    datetype     DEFAULT getdate()  NOT NULL,
shipdate     datetype                    NOT NULL,
CONSTRAINT datecnstr CHECK (shipdate >= orderdate)
)
go


CREATE TABLE orderlines
(
order#       numeric(6,0)       NOT NULL
     REFERENCES orders(order#),
product#     numeric(7,0)       NOT NULL,
unit         smallint           NOT NULL
)
go
```

For references to multicolumn keys, use the table-level references syntax. The multicolumn keys must have unique indexes.

```
CREATE TABLE hiorderlines
(
order#       numeric(6,0)       NOT NULL,
product#     numeric(7,0)       NOT NULL,
```

```
unit            smallint            NOT NULL,
        CONSTRAINT hiolfk FOREIGN KEY(order#, product#)
            REFERENCES orderlines(order#, product#)
)
go
```

Stored procedures allow you to control user actions and improve performance. Generally speaking, you deny the user access to underlying tables and force queries and updates through stored procedures. The stored procedure has its own permission system, separate from underlying tables. Since stored procedures are parsed and resolved on creation, they run faster than individual statements. They also reduce network traffic.

Users must execute stored procedures to perform the tasks the stored procedures handle, but triggers fire automatically. They are activated by INSERT, DELETE, or UPDATE actions on a table and exist outside the permission structure. No one, not even the SA, can stop a trigger from firing except by removing it. A trigger is the final defense of data integrity.

Both triggers and stored procedures offer performance advantages:

♦ They reduce network traffic. The actual code is stored on SQL Server; the client passes only the command.
♦ They run faster than independent statements because they are parsed on creation and compiled on first execution.

Stored Procedures

System procedures are examples of how you can use stored procedures. Stored procedures allow you to:

♦ Create reusable reports (sp_depends, sp_helptext)
♦ Steer users through multistep operations (sp_configure, sp_dboption)
♦ Enforce referential integrity (sp_adduser)
♦ Prevent direct changes to critical tables (sp_addtype, sp_bindrule)

A simple CREATE PROCEDURE statement looks like this:

```
CREATE PROCEDURE tally
AS
        SELECT orderdate, count(order#)
        FROM orders
        GROUP BY orderdate
go
```

You run a procedure with the execute statement:

```
EXECUTE tally
EXEC tally
```

If it's the first statement in a batch, you can just give the procedure name.

```
tally
```

Stored procedures run quickly because they are *precompiled*. For procedures that have occasional changes in parameter value, you can use *execute with recompile*. It generates a new plan for you. However, the next user may get your new plan or the old one. If you know that the stored procedure parameter values are going to vary so widely that no query plan is optimal, CREATE the procedure WITH RECOMPILE so it will get a new plan every time. In this case, the plan is not stored in cache (see Figure 6.3).

Triggers

Each table can have up to three triggers—one each on insert, update, and delete. Base triggers on your business rules. How do you handle changes to primary keys, such as product number? What do you do about modifications to foreign keys? Actions include, but are not limited to those shown in Table 6.6. You can handle some, but not all, of these situations with constraints in the create table statement.

Triggers can be used to:

◆ Check data validity (a customer number in a new order matches one in the customer table).
◆ Cascade a change through the database (discontinue one product and substitute another for it in all orders starting today).
◆ Cancel or roll back illegal changes (don't delete a customer who has outstanding orders).

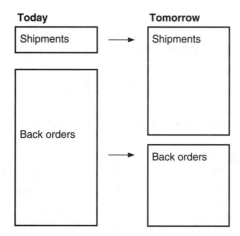

FIGURE 6.3 Different values require different plans.

TABLE 6.6 Trigger Actions

Action	Primary key	Foreign key
Insert	Make sure it is unique (in most cases you'd use a unique index for this).	Validate it against primary key.
Delete	Keep it as long as there is related information *or* Delete it and archive related information *or* Delete it and all related information (cascade delete) *or* Delete it and flag matching values in other tables.	No integrity implications.
Update	Change all the matching values in other tables *or* Forbid changes to primary keys *or* Change and archive old values.	Validate new value against primary key.

- ◆ Enforce complex rules (sales are not allowed on holidays unless the customer is an employee and the product is on the holiday special list).
- ◆ Perform calculations or make comparisons and take steps based on the results (keep totals up to date; give a discount to customers with orders over some amount).

Triggers typically roll back a transaction if it is not appropriate. A simple trigger, forbidding all deletes to the customer table, looks like this:

```
CREATE TRIGGER deltrig
ON customer
FOR delete
AS
BEGIN
     PRINT "You cannot delete rows from this table."
     ROLLBACK TRANSACTION
END
go
```

You could accomplish the same end by denying all users delete permission on the table.

Triggers use the conceptual *inserted* and *deleted* tables to perform comparisons and make decisions. The rows in the inserted and deleted tables have the same structure as the rows in the target table. Updates with triggers are handled as deletes followed by inserts, so rows are stored in both tables. (When no trigger is involved, an update is sometimes done in place (see Chapter 2). For insert, the row is added to both the target table and the *inserted* table. For deletes, the row is removed from the target table and stored in the *deleted* table. For updates, the row is changed in the target table. The original version of the row is held in *deleted* and the new version in *inserted* (see Table 6.7).

Here's a trigger that cascades a delete from the master table (orders) to the detail table (orderlines) using the deleted table. Integrity constraints in the create table command cannot handle this kind of action.

```
CREATE TRIGGER orddeltrg
ON orders
FOR DELETE
AS
DELETE orderlines
FROM orderlines ol, deleted d
WHERE ol.order# =d.order#
go
```

Triggers can also move data from one table to another. This example handles deletes from the products table. It rolls back the delete if there are outstanding orders for the product and archives the rows in another table if there are no orders.

```
CREATE TRIGGER proddeltrg
ON products
FOR DELETE
AS
IF @@rowcount =0
      RETURN
ELSE
IF EXISTS
      (SELECT * FROM deleted d, orderlines ol
      WHERE d.product#=ol.product#
      and shipdate is null)
      BEGIN
            RAISERROR ("There are outstanding orders. Delete rolled
            back", 16, -1)
            rollback transaction
      END
ELSE
      INSERT INTO oldproduct
      SELECT * FROM deleted
go
```

TABLE 6.7 Inserted and Deleted Tables

Action	*Target Table*	inserted *Table*	deleted *Table*
Insert	New row added	New row added	
Delete	Row removed		Predelete row added
Update	Row changed	Postupdate row added	Preupdate row added

When you design triggers, look at the database or application as a whole. You'll probably see some overlapping needs where you can use the same code. You'll also get ideas of how action on one integrity constraint might affect others. Table 6.8 shows how you might analyze your needs for one table.

Since triggers are critical to data integrity, it's important to test them very thoroughly before putting them in place. For more examples of triggers see Chapter 7.

Creating Indexes

Unindexed data is stored as *heaps,* and accessed by *table scans.* Indexes help locate data for retrievals. They are also useful for data modification commands in that they find the row you want to change. But indexes also need maintenance. As you add, delete, and update rows, the index pages may change, depending on the kind of indexes you have and how full the pages are. Index upkeep can slow performance.

You can create indexes as part of a create table statement or separately, with create index statements.

Types of Indexes

There are two types of indexes, *Clustered* and *Nonclustered.* Either can be created as unique. Clustered and nonclustered indexes are both *b-tree structures,* but there are important differences between them.

The bottom level of a clustered index is the actual data. Rows are stored in index order. This means you can have only one clustered index per table, because rows can have only one physical order. A clustered index does not add significantly to the size of the table. A 10-byte index on a 100-byte table adds 1 to 2 percent to the table size (see Figure 6.4).

Nonclustered indexes, on the other hand, point to the data; the physical order of the data has no particular relationship to a nonclustered index. You can have as many as 249 nonclustered indexes per table. A nonclustered index tends to be about one level deeper than a clustered index and adds a significant amount of space. A 10-byte nonclustered index on a table with 100-byte rows adds about 20 percent (see Figure 6.5).

TABLE 6.8 Trigger Design Example

Table	Change	Trigger Action
orders	insert row	Check customer# against customers table
		Generate new order#
	delete row	Cascade delete to orderlines table
	update order#	Forbid: force delete + insert

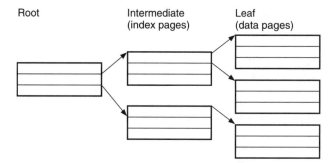

FIGURE 6.4 Clustered index.

Because of their structures, clustered and nonclustered indexes have different interactions with queries and data modification statements, as shown in Table 6.9. Properly designed indexes greatly aid data retrievals. Clustered indexes determine the physical order of data, so when rows are added or deleted the clustered index changes too, and these modifications can be expensive. Nonclustered index changes prompted by data modifications are usually less radical. In designing your indexes, you have to weigh the frequency and importance of queries against inserts, updates, and deletes.

What Should You Index?

Indexes are the single best tool for performance. To determine which indexes to create, you need to understand the logical design, know which queries and data modification statements users will run, and have some idea of how often they will run them.

In some instances, often in decision support environments, you don't know what the queries or the mix of queries are. You can still make some sensible decisions in this case. Start by considering indexes on primary keys and foreign keys. If there are too many (say, more than about three per table) back off on some that are not likely to be used. You will refine these choices as you test and tune.

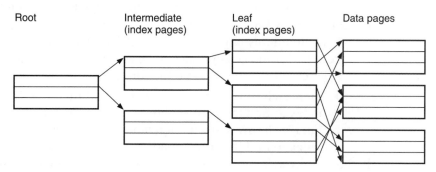

FIGURE 6.5 Nonclustered index.

TABLE 6.9 Nonclustered versus Clustered Indexes

Statement	Nonclustered	Clustered
SELECT	Speeds search Makes no changes to index or data pages	Speeds search Makes no changes to index or data pages
INSERT	No help in search, insert goes to last page if there is no clustered index Adds new pointer on index page Adds pointers in other nonclusteredindexes pointing to new row	Speeds search Reorganizes data and possibly index pages to make room for new row Updates associated nonclustered indexes If page splits, adds new page and changes nonclustered indexes affected by the split
DELETE	Speeds search Removes pointer from index page Removes pointers for other nonclustered indexes pointing to deleted row	Speeds search Reorganizes data and possibly index pages to remove deleted row Updates associated nonclustered indexes If row is last on page, page is deallocated
UPDATE	Speeds search Reorganizes index pages if row is deleted from one page and inserted in another	Speeds search Requires index changes for split or removed pages

Strive for a level of acceptable overall database performance before you solve individual problems. Here are some more specific guidelines.

Index all primary keys. Typically, many transactions reference primary keys. If you have a primary key that is seldom used in a query (you have a surrogate key) and its uniqueness is guaranteed by some external mechanism, consider removing the index on it. But remember: The only way to guarantee uniqueness is with a unique index.

Index all foreign keys—except for foreign keys to lookup tables. Foreign keys commonly appear in WHERE clauses in queries. If all foreign keys and primary keys have indexes, the query optimizer can consider executing the join in either direction, that is:

1. Find each row in the primary table and then use the foreign key index to find the corresponding rows in the foreign table.
2. Find each row in the foreign table and then use the primary table index to find the corresponding rows in the primary table.

If there are too many indexes on a given table, consider not putting indexes on foreign keys to lookup tables. There is a good chance that the query plan will find the selected rows in the principal tables and then locate the matching rows in the lookup tables.

Index both sides of common joins.   For common joins, consider creating an index on the appropriate columns of both tables. In a given query, the optimizer will use the index on one table or the other. Having both lets the query optimizer choose the most efficient access order for the specific query. However, make sure you don't end up with too many indexes.

Index columns often used in range queries, sorts, and grouping.

Index primary keys for uniqueness.   A primary key implies that all rows must have a unique value in the primary key column or columns. With SQL Server, you can ensure this by creating a unique index on the primary key columns. A unique index is no more costly than a nonunique index.

Index for uniqueness whenever index columns are unique.   There is no penalty for using uniqueness in indexes. If the columns of an index must be unique, explicitly make the index unique. It'll ensure uniqueness and help the optimizer. For example, if a column or group of columns is labeled as unique and a query calls for an equality match with a column in another table, at most one row in this table will match. This knowledge is particularly useful when the optimizer evaluates the order to process a join.

Index columns that cover common queries.   If the information is in a nonclustered index and you don't need to read the data pages, access can be very fast.

Table 6.10 identifies some of the index requirements for the products table.

TABLE 6.10   Refined Table Example with Index Requirements

Column	Datatype	User Datatype	Null Status	Other	Index
product#	numeric	numtype	not null	Must be unique	unique, primary key
name	varchar(20)	nametype	not null		sorts? single row matches
type	varchar		not null		few types
notes	varchar(200)		null		
price	smallmoney		not null		matches, range searches?
weight	decimal		not null		
supplier#	numeric	numtype	not null	Must exist in supplier entity	foreign key, limited number of rows in supplier table

As you identify possible indexes, review the following rules:

Don't have more than three to five indexes on a table.   If you have more than this many indexes on a table, the disadvantages of indexes start outweighing the advantages:

- ◆ The overhead of updating the indexes becomes large.
- ◆ The chances that a given index will be used is diminished.
- ◆ Symmetric multiprocessor versions of SQL Server (starting with Release 4.0) provide increased throughput which exacerbates lock contention problems when updating rows in tables with multiple indexes.

Don't create compound indexes (indexes on two or more columns) with columns in any old order.   Make sure the first column of the index has high selectivity (does not have a large percentage of duplicates). Since SQL Server only keeps index statistics on the first column of an index, the query optimizer gets more information if that first column is highly selective. This is especially true of a nonclustered index.

Don't index tables with fewer than about five pages.   A table this size will usually remain in cache and will require fewer than five reads to find the matching rows, so the query optimizer may not use the index. Of course, you may still want to index for uniqueness.

Don't create indexes that won't be used (except for ensuring uniqueness).   Indexes require time and space. SQL Server must maintain every index each time you add rows to the table, and each interesting nonclustered index may add 10 percent or more to the table's size.

Clustered or Nonclustered?

Now that you have an idea of what columns to index, decide if the indexes should be clustered or nonclustered.

Clustered

A clustered index is your single best index, and you only have one per table. All tables except very small ones should have a clustered index! Almost any query that references the column with a clustered index will find it useful.

In addition, clustered indexes lead to more compact space use. A table with no clustered index is stored as a heap, or chain of pages, with all new rows added to the last page (or to a new page after the last page). As rows are deleted they are removed from their locations, and you end up with a table that looks like Swiss cheese. Adding a clustered index will reorganize the table, remove the holes, and result in fewer pages. You'll do best by putting the clustered index on a column or set of columns that is updated relatively randomly. If you pick a column like order_date, where you mostly add rows for the current date and delete some older rows, you'll develop a *hotspot* (a location that many users access) and grow Swiss cheese again.

Use a clustered index when you often:

♦ Use the column in queries or joins and performance is important.

♦ Use the column in range queries (*date>= 1/1/90 and date <= 1/1/91*). Clustered indexes are much faster than nonclustered indexes in range queries.

♦ Use the column in order-by queries. Here again, clustered indexes are much better than nonclustered ones.

♦ Use the column in GROUP BY queries.

♦ Request a single row (i.e., equality match on all columns of a unique index). A clustered index is slightly faster than a nonclustered index.

♦ Need to distribute data randomly.

Primary keys on most tables need indexes, but clustered indexes may not be the best choice. Weigh the frequency of queries and joins involving the primary key against those selecting a range of values or an ordered set, where nonclustered indexes are not very useful. Consider a table (such as authors) with authors' names and social security numbers. The social security number is the primary key, but you will seldom look for social security numbers between 111111111 and 111223333 or list them in ascending order. However, these range and sort queries will probably be common on the name column.

When accessing a single row, a nonclustered index is just one read worse than a clustered index. Many accesses against a primary key are in fact single row accesses (searching for a particular social security number, for example). Use the powerful clustered index where it does the most good, and put a unique nonclustered index on the primary key.

Avoid creating clustered indexes on a serial field, date field, or other field that has activity clustered around certain pages of the table when there is heavy insert activity. If you have a clustered index on one of these fields or no clustered indexes, all inserts and many updates will try to access the same page. This will cause lock contention problems. It may help to create a clustered index on something else (a user-id field or a region code) that will help to spread the access across the table. On the other hand, if the column is mostly used in range or sort queries, a clustered index can be very useful.

In choosing the clustered index for a table, pick the column (or group of columns) that has the physical ordering most often used.

Nonclustered

You can have up to 249 nonclustered indexes, but beware of too many! Indexes take up room, take time to maintain, and slow down update performance. Use a nonclustered index in the following situations.

♦ *A single row is requested (equality match on all columns of a unique index).* The clustered index is only a little faster than the nonclustered in this case. If you've used the clustered index elsewhere, a nonclustered index is useful for this kind of query.

♦ *Index covering can be used.* If all the columns of a table required to satisfy a query are in a nonclustered index, then the index *covers* the query. The query may be satisfied by reading only the index pages. If there is a composite nonclustered index on product name and id and supplier # in the products table, both these queries are covered:

```
SELECT supplier#
FROM products
WHERE name = "gizmo" and product# = 9977236
go

SELECT name, product#
FROM products
WHERE supplier# = 78
go
```

The first query is more efficient because the leading index item is in the WHERE clause, but the second also benefits. A covering nonclustered index also will work with aggregate queries and order by queries.

Index coverage may help you even if the first column of the nonclustered index doesn't show up in the WHERE clause. Consider:

```
SELECT count(name)
FROM products
go
```

SQL Server can do this by counting the number of leaf index entries in the name, product#, supplier# nonclustered index which have a nonnull name. SELECT count(*) FROM products will also do this. To cover common queries, consider adding columns to an index, but be careful that the index doesn't get too wide.

♦ *A table needs more than one index.* Since you're allowed only one clustered index, use it where it will do the most good, and put nonclustered indexes on other columns you often access. This may include the primary key.

♦ *Uniqueness must be ensured but performance is not critical, or the clustered index has been used elsewhere.* Use a unique nonclustered index.

Don't use a nonclustered index if more than about five percent of the rows have to be read. SQL Server will generally do a table scan rather than use a nonclustered index to satisfy the query.

Planning Indexes

Review your index notes. Look at the queries and reports in your requirements document and make decisions about the kind of indexes you need for each table.

If you do a lot of sorts and range retrievals based on price, you might end up choosing the three indexes shown in Table 6.11.

Syntax

You can create indexes in the CREATE TABLE or CREATE INDEX statement. The CREATE TABLE statement does not allow nonunique indexes, but otherwise the methods have the same capabilities. Here's how you would build a unique nonclustered index on the product number with a CREATE TABLE statement:

```
CREATE TABLE products
(
product#      numeric(7,0)      IDENTITY,
name          varchar(20)       NOT NULL,
type          varchar(8)        NULL
        CHECK (type IN ('appl', 'book', 'edu',
          'game', 'hardware', 'supply')),
description  varchar(50)       NULL,
weight       decimal(6,2)      NOT NULL,
price        smallmoney        NOT NULL,
supplier#    suppltype         NULL,
CONSTRAINT prodix UNIQUE NONCLUSTERED (product#)
)
go
```

TABLE 6.11   Refined Table Example with Indexes Defined

Column	Datatype	User Datatype	Null Status	Other	Index	Index Notes
product#	numeric	numtype	not null	Must be unique	unique nonclustered	unique, primary key
name	varchar(20)	nametype	not null		nonclustered	sorts? single row matches
type	varchar		not null			few types
notes	varchar(200)		null			
price	smallmoney		not null		clustered	matches, range searches?
weight	decimal		not null			
supplier#	numeric	numtype	not null	Must exist in supplier entity		foreign key, limited number of rows in supplier table

You can remove unique and primary key constraints with the ALTER TABLE statement only. To add indexes on existing columns, use the CREATE INDEX statement.

The CREATE INDEX statements for handling the indexes separately are:

```
CREATE UNIQUE NONCLUSTERED INDEX prodix
ON products (product#)
go

CREATE CLUSTERED INDEX priceix
ON products (price)
go
```

You can remove these indexes with the DROP INDEX statement.

Good Index Practices

Choosing and creating indexes is just the first step.

♦ As you select indexes, record your rationale. This will save you time later when you need to revisit the indexes.
♦ Plan to test indexes. The only practical way to find out if an index is actually used is to SET SHOWPLAN ON and look at the query plans for those using the indexed columns.

Planning Capacity

Once you have a preliminary physical design for your application, consider how much space it will require. You can project sizes for:

♦ Tables
♦ Indexes
♦ Databases
♦ Transaction logs

When you create the database, you specify the database size and log size (if you put it on a separate device, as you should) in the CREATE DATABASE statement. It's important to have some idea of how large you want the database to be before you execute the command. It's relatively easy to make the database and log larger (with the alter database statement) but more complicated to make it smaller.

To create a 100Mb bigbiz database with a 20Mb log on a separate database device, the command looks like this:

```
CREATE DATABASE bigbiz
ON datadev=100
LOG ON logdev=20
go
```

Estimating Table and Index Size

In order to determine the space required for tables, you have to know the size of a row and the number of rows you expect.

To calculate the size of a fixed-length row:

◆ Figure the size of each column (see the section on datatypes)
◆ Total the column sizes
◆ Add four bytes for each row

Next, determine how many of these rows will fit on a page. A page is 2,048 bytes, but 32 bytes are used for header information and are unavailable for user data. That leaves 2,016 bytes. If a row is 100 bytes long, you have room for 20 rows on each page (no fractions—a row never spans pages). If you expect two million 100-byte rows, they will require at least 100,000 pages.

For indexes, do a similar calculation. Determine the size of an index entry, and estimate the number of entries per page. Then move on to the next index level and do the same. See your *Microsoft SQL Server Administrator's Companion* manuals for more information.

Since a database is more than the sum of its tables, add more space for:

◆ Stored procedures, defaults, rules, and triggers you plan to create (include a factor for object text and procedure plan space in system tables)
◆ Expanding system tables (additional logins and user accounts, more rows in sysobjects, and so on)

Sizing the Transaction Log

You specify the size of the transaction log in the CREATE DATABASE statement LOG ON option or (when allocating additional space for the database) in the ALTER DATABASE statement LOG ON option.

Determining the transaction log's size depends on a number of things, and there are no crisp guidelines on how big it should be. A good first guess is 10 to 25 percent of the size of the database.

If the transaction log is not large enough, you will get an error message when the server attempts to do the next logged activity. If this happens on a regular basis, you should increase the size of the transaction log. Several factors impact the log size:

◆ A transaction that makes many changes. Until SQL Server completes the transaction, all its transaction log entries must remain in the transaction log even if the database owner does a DUMP TRANSACTION or has the TRUNC. LOG ON CHKPT. option turned on.
◆ A transaction that runs for a long time. Until SQL Server completes the transaction, all transaction log entries subsequent to its beginning (even transaction log entries for other transactions) must remain in the trans-

action log even if the database owner does a DUMP TRANSACTION or has the TRUNC. LOG ON CHKPT. option turned on.

♦ Multiple transactions.

Put the log on a separate database device to prevent competition with other objects and allow use of the Enterprise Manager and Performance Monitor to trigger dumps. A separate physical disk is a better choice yet—it improves performance and allows full recovery if there is a failure on the database disk.

Tuning the Application

The tuning phase is for zeroing in on particular problems. Once you've got the database working and have met or approached your overall goals, look for specific areas where you're not getting the performance you need. Changes can include the following:

♦ Modify the logical and physical design.
♦ Examine your indexes.
♦ Change the data storage and distribution.

Where you start depends on your application and specific problems. Sound database design and appropriate indexes give the best performance. Objects placement can also have a considerable effect.

Modifying Design: DSS versus OLTP

Decision support systems (DSS) and on-line transaction processing systems (OLTP) have different requirements for table structure, indexes, and physical storage. You may need to modify your database design to get the performance you need.

Decision support systems often support long-running queries that analyze some portion of the database and produce reports and summary information. This means a large number of analysis queries or reports and relatively few data modification commands. DSS applications move many pages through the data cache, which can reduce performance of OLTP transactions running on the same SQL Server.

When tuning for DSSs, it makes sense to:

♦ Add extra indexes to speed SELECT statements (but usually keep the total per table below five).
♦ Selectively denormalize tables (reduce the number of tables and increase the number of columns in each table) so that you can access commonly retrieved information without excessive joins. Use this technique with caution and only as a solution to a specific problem! Remember that nor-

malization produces narrow rows and increases your opportunities for indexes. Careless denormalization can lead to slower performance and data integrity problems.

An OLTP system characteristically has many small transactions, mostly involving changes to the data. Because of this, it requires sophisticated data integrity protections, generally resulting in a large number of joins, as foreign keys are checked against primary keys. Each transaction typically must be very fast (subsecond response time). Many users need to make changes simultaneously, so there are multiple online connections and significant disk input/output.

For OLTP applications:

♦ Target indexes precisely for the actions you want to perform (but not too many—each additional index increases the amount of work for data modification transactions)
♦ Adjust the table design so each transaction affects only a small number of tables. The application code needs to minimize how much each transaction does and how long the transaction takes.

Never Tune "In General"

Applications are seldom 100 percent DSS or OLTP. You consider the whole application when tuning, but make changes in particular areas. Each time you tune one activity to improve its performance, you slow something else down. If you do not understand the side effects of your actions, you can make things worse. Test after each change, and assess its effect on the activity in question and the application as a whole. Keep notes on your actions and their results. If overall performance suddenly degrades, you want to know why.

Denormalization

Denormalization implies normalization, so unless you know your application extremely well, normalize first and denormalize only with cause—and then conservatively. Create and prototype the entire application (or complete segments of it) before you measure performance of particular parts. Identify critical transactions and determine the following:

♦ Required response time
♦ Frequency of execution
♦ Number of users
♦ Size of data set and physical distribution
♦ Particular periods of use
♦ Participating tables, columns, and associated integrity constraints

When denormalization is effective, it allows you to speed retrievals by cutting down on the number of some or all of the following relevant items:

- Tables
- Rows
- Joins
- Indexes
- On-the-fly computations

But beware! Even as denormalization makes retrievals faster, it may slow data modifications. It's likely to introduce data integrity issues and complicate application maintenance. You'll want to review these areas as your application grows and changes.

Normalization techniques include the following:

- Splitting tables
- Merging tables
- Copying columns from one table into another (data duplication)
- Adding columns for reverse indexing
- Creating derived columns for calculated data
- Using summary columns (existence counts, aggregates)
- Adding interrow derived data columns
- Creating new tables to shortcut paths among indirect relationships

Splitting Tables

Figure 6.6 shows the two kinds of table splits: horizontal and vertical (supertype-subtype splits are a special type of vertical split). Both can improve performance under certain circumstances, and both make your application more complex. In either case, you trade one large table for two or more smaller ones.

For horizontal splits you accomplish this by either of two methods:

- Segment the table so that one table contains the most commonly accessed rows and the other contains the rest of the rows.

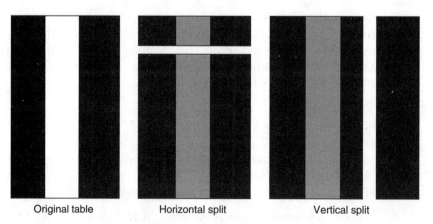

Original table   Horizontal split   Vertical split

FIGURE 6.6 Horizontal and vertical splitting.

♦ Copy some parts of the table so that one table contains the most commonly accessed rows and the second contains *all* the rows.

For vertical splits, the technique is applied to columns instead of to rows. You can either:

♦ Divide the table so that one table contains the most commonly accessed columns and the other contains the rest of the columns.
♦ Copy some parts of the table so that one table contains the most commonly accessed columns and the second contains *all* the columns.

Use table splitting with care. Make sure you understand why you are doing it and what you want to gain.
Use horizontal table splitting in the following situations:

♦ Reducing a large table will reduce the number of index pages read.
♦ You can make a distinction in the kind of data, such as national and international accounts.
♦ You need to distribute the data physically.

Horizontal splitting can improve the statistics information in an index by dividing the table based on the values in an indexed attribute.

You might want to put authors who haven't written a book in the last five years in a separate table, since there will be few queries about them. Indexes on author names and id numbers will be more useful, and access to current authors will be faster. You'll still be able to get hold of information about inactive authors by querying the oldauthors table.

Administrators often use horizontal splitting to archive historical data when it is seldom queried. Maintaining two separate tables can be a headache, and data that should be in one can show up in another unless there are clear business rules (no new edition in the last three years; no new title in the last five) that dictate which table a row belongs in. If one of the segments contains a small proportion of the rows, and these rows are the active ones, horizontal splitting is a huge win. You may even find that the relevant rows stay in cache.

Vertical

Use vertical splitting in the following situations:

♦ Common transactions frequently access a particular subset of table columns.
♦ The table has a very broad row, making it difficult to fit on data pages.
♦ A large number of optional fields exist in many rows.

Placing frequently used columns in a separate table can make access much faster. For example, if most queries about books include title, price, and sales, move those columns into a separate table (add title_id) for joins). Keep the less-used information (type, publisher, advance, notes, and so on) in a background table. Finding critical information will be much faster, particularly because one of the background columns is notes, a varchar(250) column. The data pages for the new titles table are much narrower, so you will get many more rows per page.

Notice that two tables (titles and titles_bkgr) now have the same primary key (title_id). You'll have to introduce new integrity constraints to make sure that every row in one table has a matching row in the other and that foreign keys are valid against both tables.

The subtype-supertype problem is a special case of vertical table splitting.

Sometimes an individual thing has characteristics different from other things in a table. Consider city employees. Some are firefighters, and these firefighters have attributes (badge numbers) you want to maintain—but other employees don't have badges. In this case, *employee* is a supertype, and *firefighter* is a subtype. You might represent this two ways:

♦ Make one table for the supertype and all its subtypes (all employees). The firefighter-specific badge_no is NULL for any employee who is not a firefighter.

```
CREATE TABLE employee (
        lname          char(15) NOT NULL,
        fname          char(15) NOT NULL,
        emp_id         char(5) NOT NULL,
        badge_no       char(5) NULL)

go
```

♦ Make two tables: one for the supertype (employees) and one for the special features of the subtype (firefighter_badges). The nulls for badge_no are avoided but you need an extra join to get information about firefighters. You'll also need to put logic in queries to check whether or not employees are firefighters.

```
CREATE TABLE employee (
        lname          char(15) NOT NULL,
        fname          char(15) NOT NULL,
        emp_id         char(5) NOT NULL)

go
CREATE TABLE firefighter_badges (
        emp_id         char(5) NOT NULL,
        badge_no       char(5) NOT NULL)

go
```

If you have many subtypes (firefighters with badges, police with guns, social workers with specialties, and so on) what do you do?

◆ Make one table for each subtype (*n* tables: firefighters, police, social workers . . .) and eliminate the supertype:

```
CREATE TABLE police (
       lname          char(15) NOT NULL,
       fname          char(15) NOT NULL,
       emp_id         char(5) NOT NULL
       gun_id         int not null)
go
CREATE TABLE firefighters(
       lname          char(15) NOT NULL,
       fname          char(15) NOT NULL,
       emp_id         char(5) NOT NULL,
       badge_no       char(5) NOT NULL)
go
```

◆ Make one table for each subtype and one for the supertype (*n* + 1 tables).

The number of attributes in the supertypes and subtypes, the distribution of rows between the subtypes, and access to the tables influence your choice of strategy. You need to balance the danger of duplicate columns against improved performance.

The supertype-only solution, at best, has a few rows with nulls in one column. At worst, it results in long rows with many null columns, leading to large data and index pages. You may end up with many indexes (badge_no, gun_no, specialty) on the table. Both of these conditions can lead to poor performance.

The subtype-only solution works well when most of the attributes are subtype characteristics. You can keep the rows narrow and create good indexes. However, to get information on all employees, you'll need to look at many separate tables. It may be difficult to maintain consistent supertype characteristics.

The subtype-supertype combination is worth considering when attributes are divided evenly between subtype and supertype characteristics. Getting full information on employees will require joining the supertype and subtype and subtype tables (see Table 6.12).

It is possible to implement hybrid solutions; that is, you may put a number of subtypes into separate tables and combine others in a single table.

Merging Tables

When problem queries usually call for data from two tables, it may make sense to merge them into one. For example, if the most common report on book titles is on financial data—advances and royalties—you could collapse the titles and roysched tables into one table. The obvious problem here is the possibility of a very wide row. You may be able to accomplish your aims by duplicating one or two columns instead of merging tables.

TABLE 6.12 Subtypes and Supertypes

	Supertype Table Only	*Subtype Tables Only (One for Each)*	*Supertype Table and Subtype Tables*
Number of tables	1 table	n tables	$n + 1$ tables
Number of attributes	If most attributes belong to the supertype, keep one supertype table.	If few attributes belong to the supertype and many to the subtypes, create subtype tables only.	If attributes are divided roughly equally between the supertype and the subtypes, create a supertype table and supporting subtype tables.
Distribution of Rows		If rows are unevenly distributed with many NULLs, use subtype tables or the supertype-subtype combination.	
Access to tables	If access to the data is commonly from a mixture of subtypes, keep the data together.	If access to subtype data is independent, use separate subtype tables.	If access to subtype data is independent or from more than one subtype, use the combination.

Adding Columns for Duplicated Data

Joins can slow performance, particularly in commonly run reports. You can reduce the number of joins by duplicating join attributes. (But test to make sure it is really more efficient to run queries against a lot of duplicated data than to do the joins.) Consider adding columns when the duplicated columns will benefit common transactions and:

♦ The joins require access to many rows and the table with the join column has a very broad row or is clustered on an unrelated attribute.
♦ The data is duplicated from the master to the detail tables.
♦ The duplicated attribute's table is rarely updated but is accessed often.

Consider three tables representing divisions, departments, and employees. Employees are in one department, and departments are in one division.

```
CREATE TABLE div(
name        char(15),
div_num     char(5))

go

CREATE TABLE dept(
div_num     char(5),
dept_name   char(15),
dept_num    char(5))

go
```

```
CREATE TABLE emp(
dept_num       char(5),
emp_name       char(15),
emp_num        char(5))

go
```

You need a three-way join to find everyone in the Western division. If you copy one column from the div table (div_name) into the emp table, you can get the information you need by querying just the emp table.

```
CREATE TABLE emp(
dept_num       char(5),
emp_name       char(15),
emp_num        char(5)

div_name       char(15))

go
```

There are some problems with this technique.

♦ You now have the div_name in two tables, and you need to create ways to make sure the data remains consistent.
♦ Having the same data in two places requires more storage space.

Adding Columns for Calculated Data

When queries require calculations, you can save time by adding a column to store results. If year-to-date sales and book prices are stored in the titles table and many queries perform math to figure total sales (price * ytd_sales), you may want to add a column to hold this data so that retrievals are easier. This is particularly useful in the following situations:

♦ Calculations are complex.
♦ Calculations involve many rows.
♦ Results are ordered by the calculated result.
♦ You use the expression to identify which rows to select and might want to index it.
♦ Inserts and updates are less important than queries.
♦ The row size does not increase significantly.

Adding Columns for Aggregate Values

Many transactions call for *existence checks* to validate master rows associated with detail rows. For example, to determine whether a given publisher has published books you might do a count:

```
SELECT count(*)
FROM titles
WHERE pub_id= '1234'
```

If this kind of transaction is common, you can improve performance by establishing a count column in the master table (publishers in this case), although the technique is even more useful if the detail table is not a direct child of the master table. Use triggers to update the count in the master table whenever you INSERT or DELETE a detail row, and whenever you UPDATE its foreign key. Consider using counts when:

♦ The transactions only request existence checking.
♦ The master table is related to many detail tables and they all require checking for associated rows.
♦ The existence checks cover many entities or must read many tables.
♦ The overhead of maintaining the counts is low; that is, the data does not often change.

You can use the same method for other aggregates (SUM, AVG, MAX, or MIN). This method has the limitations associated with any calculated column:

♦ You need a mechanism to update the aggregate column each time its data changes (usually implemented in triggers).
♦ Data modification performance is slowed.

Adding Columns for Interrow Derived Data

Some transactions often use data derived from the comparison of two or more rows of the same table. These comparisons show up as self-joins or aggregates in SQL. You can create an interrow column to hold that information directly. Consider a startup company, where employees often change departments. The employee table holds the employee's number, department, and the date the employee joined the department:

```
CREATE TABLE empl
   (id char(9),
    dept char(3),
    joindate datetime)

go
```

To find current departments for all employees, you need to search all the rows on the employee and find the one with the latest join date, like this:

```
SELECT id, dept
FROM empl e
WHERE joindate =
      (SELECT max(joindate) FROM empl WHERE id = e.id)
go
```

On the other hand, you can add an *active* column where *Y* indicates the current department. When the employee leaves a department and you enter a new row, a trigger can change the active status of the earlier row (based on joindate) to *N* and assign *Y* to the new one.

```
CREATE TABLE empl
  (id char(9),
   dept char(3),
   joindate datetime
   active char(1))

go
```

With the new table definition, the query to find the employee's current department is less complex:

```
SELECT id, dept
FROM empl
WHERE active = 'Y'
go
```

Interrow derived data rows can reduce performance for INSERTs, UPDATEs, and DELETEs, since you have to calculate the new value for each data modification.

Creating Tables to Speed Indirect Relationship Queries

Sometimes you can identify a common query which requires a large number of tables in a join and reduces performance. Frequent culprits are queries on indirectly related tables and the associative tables that connect them.

For example, in the pubs database there are six tables that report on authors, titles, and sales of books: titles, titleauthor, authors, sales, salesdetails, and stores. If you want to determine which authors have had their books sold by a given store, you need a six-way join. To improve the performance of this query, you might create a table (author_stores) with two columns, author_id and store_id. When a store sells a book, you add a row to that table for each author of the book. In this way, SQL Server can display the names of authors and stores with just a three-way join (authors, author_stores, and stores).

Indirect relationship tables usually have many rows with complex, many-to-many relationships, and they are hard to maintain. A single sale already calls for inserts to sales and salesdetails. With the new table, it also requires look-ups against titleauthor (to find the author_id for the title) and inserts into the author_sales table. However, for particular queries, adding a table for an important indirect relationship may significantly improve performance.

Tuning Indexes

For slow performance on particular queries or updates, one of the most useful things you can do is review them carefully in light of how the query optimizer handles them. Good indexes can be ignored by queries that don't take advantage of how the optimizer works.

Some additional areas to check when you review indexes include the following:

- ◆ Hotspots
- ◆ Index widths
- ◆ Query Coverage
- ◆ FILLFACTOR

You should also become familiar with the UPDATE STATISTICS command.

Are There Hotspots?

Avoid creating clustered indexes on a serial field, date field, or other field that has activity clustered around certain pages of the table. If you have a clustered index on one of these fields or no clustered indexes, all inserts and (perhaps) many updates will try to access the same page. This will cause lock contention problems. It may help to create a clustered index on something else (e.g., a user-id field, or a region code—something that will help to spread the access across the table).

Are Indexes Too Wide?

The narrower the index, the more index entries will fit on an index page. This may also reduce the number of levels in the index. Avoid indexes on many columns.

Should the Nonclustered Index Be on a Separate Segment?

There is some value to placing a commonly used nonclustered index on a separate segment from the data. This may help to spread the disk accesses across multiple devices. If you have disk striping this is not important. Remember: A clustered index and its data are always on the same segment.

Is the Query Covered?

If all the columns of a table required to satisfy a query are in a nonclustered index, then the index covers the query. The query may be satisfied by reading only the index pages. The optimizer will consider this in evaluating the cost of the index. Consider adding additional columns to an index so that it can cover common queries. Be careful that the index doesn't get too wide.

Is There Enough Free Space?

For tables that are seldom updated, keep the free space to a minimum for fast-running queries.

The FILLFACTOR parameter in the CREATE TABLE, ALTER TABLE, and CREATE INDEX commands lets you specify how full initial index pages (for clustered and nonclustered indexes) and data pages (for columns with clustered indexes only) should be. The default fillfactor of 0 creates indexes that are full at the leaf level and have room for about two rows in the intermediate pages. This is a reasonable compromise between too full and too empty, since it reduces the space required while leaving some room for the next inserts. SQL Server does not maintain the fillfactor after index creation. With random UPDATE and DELETE, expect the pages to become about 75 percent full. Legal values range from 1 to 100.

FILLFACTOR is a short-term solution, useful when you expect a flurry of inserts or updates after you create an index and you want to do the following tasks:

- ♦ Reduce lock contention (in effect, simulating row level locking).
- ♦ Prevent page splits as data is added to full pages.
- ♦ Spread initial rows across multiple pages.

If you need to reestablish the FILLFACTOR, drop and recreate the index, specifying fillfactor. For more information see the section on DBCC SHOW-CONTIG in Chapter 10.

Placing Objects

When you create a database, you automatically get three segments.

- ♦ The system segment holds all system tables (sysobjects, sysusers, and so on).
- ♦ The default segment contains all user tables.
- ♦ The logsegment is for the database log (syslogs table).

You can create additional segments and put objects on those segments. But be careful! A complicated segment structure can make space management very difficult. Generally speaking, make sure the logsegment is on a separate device from the data. This will give improved performance because reads and writes to the log and data do not compete. At the same time, it makes for better recoverability.

You can also place heavily used tables on separate segments in order to allow reads and writes to multiple tables at the same time. Splitting a table and its nonclustered (not clustered!) index has the same effect. However, dividing activity evenly between two disks seems to give about a 20 percent improvement, instead of the 50 percent improvement you might expect.

C H A P T E R

7

Coding Techniques

There are a large number of special SQL language features in the SQL Server. One of the difficulties in developing applications with SQL Server is figuring out how to put the various features together. This chapter presents an overview of various SQL Server features and gives examples of how to code those features.

We start with a discussion of simple SQL techniques. We provide simple examples of familiar statements like SELECT, INSERT, UPDATE, and DELETE statements as well as introduce some of the new features in SQL Server Version 6 such as CASE, cursors, and dynamic execute.

Next, we cover a number of neat SQL tricks. These are more sophisticated techniques that can be useful to solve specific problems.

The third and fourth sections provide examples for using stored procedures and triggers. Each of these sections starts with the basic syntax of procedures or triggers and then gives examples for solving specific problems.

The final section in this chapter provides an explanation of how you can add your own messages to the sysmessages table and reference those messages in a RAISERROR statement.

Simple SQL Techniques

This section contains some examples of SQL statements. We start with absolutely trivial examples and work our way up to more complicated examples. All of the examples in this section can be used in the sample database—pubs—shipped with SQL Server.

Simple SELECT

The simplest form of a SELECT statement includes:

- A *SELECT list*—identifies which columns to return.
- A *FROM clause*—identifies which table to access.
- A *WHERE clause*—identifies which rows are desired.

A simple SELECT statement looks like this:

```
SELECT title FROM titles WHERE title_id = 'BU1032'
```

This query selects the title column from the titles table for all rows. In this case, at the most one row, because there is a unique index on the title_id column that has a title_id of BU1032.

Correlated SELECT

SQL Server allows you to specify a SELECT statement in almost any place that you can put an expression in another SELECT statement. In the following example, the third column specified is actually another SELECT statement. But notice in the embedded SELECT statement, there is a reference to the table in the containing SELECT statement.

List the title, type, and price of each book and, for each book, list the average price of books of that type.

```
SELECT title, type, price,
       (SELECT avg(price) FROM titles t2 WHERE t2.type = t1.type)
FROM titles t1
```

For each row in the titles table (t1), this query calculates the average price for books of this type. Note that it might be more efficient in this case to create a temporary table with the type and average price for that type of book as follows (for more examples of GROUP BY, see the section on GROUP BY later in this section):

```
SELECT type, average_price=avg(price) INTO #titles FROM titles GROUP BY type
go
SELECT t1.title, t1.type,  t1.price, t2.average_price
```

```
FROM titles t1, #titles t2
WHERE t1.type = t2.type
go
```

This approach calculates the types and average price once and then joins the result to the titles table.

Nested SELECT

A *nested select* is a SELECT statement in which another SELECT statement appears. The following is a simple example of this construct.

List the publisher names of all publishers who publish books of type psychology.

```
SELECT pub_name FROM publishers WHERE pub_id IN
        (SELECT pub_id FROM titles WHERE type = 'psychology')
go
```

Select the list of publisher ids for all books of type psychology. For each publisher id, select the name of the publisher. Note that the SQL Server recognizes that this example can be processed as a join.

INSERT . . . VALUES

The simplest form of an INSERT statement inserts a single row into a table. The values for the columns are specified. It is also possible to include a list of which columns you want to insert (and the order that the columns will appear in the VALUES clause). The values in this case must be constants or variables.

Insert a new publisher, with pub_id equal to 9910, pub_name of SQL Publishing, city of Healdsburg, state of CA, and country of USA.

```
INSERT INTO publishers
        VALUES ('9910', 'SQL Publishing', 'Healdsburg', 'CA', 'USA')
go
```

INSERT . . . SELECT

It is also possible to insert zero, one, or many rows into a table with an INSERT statement using a SELECT clause. The SELECT clause is evaluated; returns zero, one, or many rows; and all of these rows are inserted into the table specified in the INSERT statement.

```
USE pubs
go
CREATE TABLE ca_publishers (pub_id char(4),pub_name varchar(40),city
varchar(20),state char(2), country varchar(30))
```

```
INSERT INTO ca_publishers SELECT * FROM publishers WHERE state = 'CA'
go
```

The previous statement inserts into the ca_publishers table all of the rows in the publishers table where the state is equal to CA. If there are no matching rows, then no rows are inserted. If one row has a state equal to CA, then that one row is inserted into ca_publishers. If many rows have a state of CA, they are all inserted into the ca_publishers table.

Simple DELETE

The DELETE statement deletes zero, one, or many rows from a table. It deletes all rows that match the WHERE clause. The following statement deletes all rows from the publishers table where the pub_id is 1756. This may be one row or zero rows (it cannot be many rows in this case because there is a unique index on the publishers table pub_id).

```
DELETE publishers WHERE pub_id = '1756'
go
```

Note that in the pubs database, this DELETE statement will fail with the following message:

```
Msg 547, Level 16, State 2
DELETE statement conflicted with COLUMN REFERENCE constraint
'FK_employee_pub_id_2FAF1EF9'. The conflict occurred in database 'pubs',
table 'employee', column 'pub_id'
```

There is a foreign key constraint on the employee table. Since there is a row in the employee table with a pub_id of 1756, the corresponding row of the publishers table cannot be deleted.

Referencing Another Table with DELETE

It is possible to reference additional tables in the DELETE statement. These other tables would then be referenced in the WHERE clause to identify which rows are to be deleted from the original table.

This example deletes all publishers who publish psychology books.

If there are no rows in the publishers' table that publish books with a type of psychology, then no publishers will be deleted.

```
DELETE publishers
FROM publishers, titles
WHERE publishers.pub_id = titles.pub_id
AND titles.type = 'psychology'
go
```

Note that this probably does much more than you might have had in mind. It deletes any publisher of psychology books even though the publisher may also publish other books. Also note that this statement does not affect the titles table. Rows are only deleted from the publishers table as a result of this statement. Of course, in the pubs database there is a reference constraint on the titles table. This DELETE statement will fail with the following message:

```
Msg 547, Level 16, State 2
DELETE statement conflicted with COLUMN REFERENCE constraint
'FK_titles_pub_id_0E4E2B2E'. The conflict occurred in database 'pubs',
table 'titles', column 'pub_id'
```

This and the previous example point out the advantage of using declarative referential integrity (in these two cases, constraints). The referential integrity constraints enforce business rules that you have defined. In this case, you cannot have titles published by a publisher who does not exist.

Simple UPDATE

An UPDATE statement modifies zero, one, or many rows, setting the columns specified in the SET clause. All rows that match the WHERE clause are modified. The following UPDATE statement changes the publisher of title BU1032 to the publisher 0736.

```
UPDATE titles SET pub_id = '0736' WHERE title_id = 'BU1032'
go
```

If there is no row with a title_id equal to BU1032, then no rows are affected. There can be at most one row matching this title_id since there is a unique index on the title_id column of the titles table.

Referencing Another Table with UPDATE

In an UPDATE statement, you can specify additional tables in the FROM clause in order to identify which rows of the table you want to update. The following UPDATE statement updates all rows in the titles table published by pub_id 1389 to specify that they are now published by New Moon Books. The publishers table is included in the FROM list and a clause is added to the WHERE clause to specify that that the new pub_id should be the pub_id of the row in the publishers table with a pub_name equal to New Moon Books.

```
UPDATE titles
SET titles.pub_id = publishers.pub_id
FROM titles, publishers
```

```
WHERE publishers.pub_name = 'New Moon Books' /* Which row to read */
AND titles.pub_id = '1389' /* Which row to update */
go
```

Checking for Duplicates

After using bulk copy to load many rows into the titles table, you may want to find which books have the same title.

```
SELECT DISTINCT t1.title_id
FROM titles t1, titles t2
WHERE t1.title = t2.title
  AND t1.title_id != t2.title_id
```

The AND clause makes sure that we don't include all title_ids (since all titles are equal to themselves). We only include those cases where two titles are the same and the corresponding title_ids are different.

CASE

An important new feature in SQL Server Version 6 is the CASE expression.

Use of Case Expression in the SELECT List

The following example demonstrates the use of a CASE expression in the select list. It selects all of the rows from the sysobjects table, and translates the type column (which holds a one or two character identification of the type of object) into a string that identifies the object type. Note that the CASE expression has an expression immediately following the keyword "CASE", and the value of that expression is compared to the value in each WHEN clause. The values for the type column are described in the *Microsoft Transact-SQL Reference* under "sysobjects".

```
SELECT Owner=user_name(uid),Name=name,
       Type=CASE type
               WHEN 'C'  THEN 'Check Constraint'
               WHEN 'D'  THEN 'Default'
               WHEN 'F'  THEN 'Foreign Key'
               WHEN 'K'  THEN 'Primary Key or Unique'
               WHEN 'P'  THEN 'Stored Procedure'
               WHEN 'R'  THEN 'Rule'
               WHEN 'RF' THEN 'Replication Procedure'
               WHEN 'S'  THEN 'System Table'
               WHEN 'TR' THEN 'Trigger'
               WHEN 'U'  THEN 'User Table'
               WHEN 'V'  THEN 'View'
               WHEN 'X'  THEN 'Extended Stored Procedure'
```

```
              ELSE            'Unknown'
         END
FROM sysobjects
ORDER BY type, user_name(uid), name
```

Here are the partial results of this **SELECT** when run in the pubs database:

Owner	Name	Type
dbo	CK_authors_au_id_02DC7882	Check Constraint
dbo	CK_authors_zip_04C4C0F4	Check Constraint
dbo	CK_jobs_max_lvl_2719D8F8	Check Constraint
dbo	CK_jobs_min_lvl_2625B4BF	Check Constraint
dbo	CK_products_type_717CE256	Check Constraint
dbo	CK_publisher_pub_i_089551D8	Check Constraint
dbo	CK_emp_id	Check Constraint
dbo	datecnstr	Check Constraint
dbo	DF_authors_phone_03D09CBB	Default
dbo	DF_employee_hire_d_30A34332	Default
dbo	DF_employee_job_id_2BDE8E15	Default
dbo	DF_employee_job_lv_2DC6D687	Default
dbo	DF_employee_pub_id_2EBAFAC0	Default
dbo	DF_jobs_job_desc_25319086	Default
dbo	DF_orders_orderdat_01B34A1F	Default
dbo	DF_publisher_count_09897611	Default
dbo	DF_titles_pubdate_0F424F67	Default
dbo	DF_titles_type_0D5A06F5	Default
dbo	FK_discounts_stor_2160FFA2	Foreign Key
dbo	FK_employee_job_id_2CD2B24E	Foreign Key
dbo	FK_employee_pub_id_2FAF1EF9	Foreign Key

CASE with Subqueries

The following example uses a **CASE** expression where the expressions include subqueries. This query will list all user tables in the database (rows in the sysobjects table with type = "U"), and for each table will display "Too Many Indexes" if the table has more than three indexes, "No Indexes" if the table has no indexes, and "Fine" if the table has between one and three indexes. Notice in this case that each WHEN clause contains a boolean expression. We use column headers (*owner=* and *index_status=*) to make the meanings of the result columns more clear.

```
SELECT owner=user_name(uid),name,
       index_status=
       CASE (SELECT count(*)
             FROM sysindexes i
             WHERE i.id=o.id AND i.indid !=0)
             WHEN 0 THEN 'No Indexes'
             WHEN 1 THEN 'Fine'
```

```
            WHEN 2 THEN 'Fine'
            WHEN 3 THEN 'Fine'
            ELSE 'Too Many Indexes'
      END
FROM sysobjects o
WHERE type='U'
ORDER BY name
```

This is the partial result of running the query against the pubs database:

```
owner                          name                           index_status
------------------------------ ------------------------------ -------------
dbo                            authors                        Fine
dbo                            ca_publishers                  No Indexes
dbo                            discounts                      No Indexes
dbo                            employee                       Fine
dbo                            jim                            No Indexes
dbo                            jim2                           No Indexes
dbo                            jim3                           Fine
```

Using CASE to Calculate Multiple Aggregates in a Single Pass

The next example uses multiple CASE expressions to calculate several counts. It reports the number of books of type "psychology", "mod_cook", and "trad_cook". For each type, the CASE expression returns 1 if the book is of that type and 0 if it is not. These numbers are then summed across the entire table. The query plan and statistics IO output for this query show that that SQL Server is able to create this result set in a single pass through the table.

```
SELECT
      Psychology=
            sum(CASE WHEN type = 'psychology' THEN 1 ELSE 0 END),
      Modern_Cooking=
            sum(CASE WHEN type = 'mod_cook' THEN 1 ELSE 0 END),
      Traditional_Cooking=
            sum(CASE WHEN type = 'trad_cook' THEN 1 ELSE 0 END)
FROM titles
```

The following are the results of this query:

```
Psychology Modern_Cooking Traditional_Cooking
----------- -------------- --------------------
5           2              3
```

GROUP BY

The GROUP BY clause in a SELECT statement allows you to develop summary information and group the results by one or more of the columns in the result set. A GROUP BY clause is usually used with an aggregate (SUM, COUNT, and so on), and the aggregate is then calculated for various values. For example, the following query (without a GROUP BY) calculates the average price of all of the books:

```
SELECT avg(price) FROM titles

---------------------------
14.42
```

The following query (with a GROUP BY) calculates the average price for each type of book:

```
SELECT type, avg(price) FROM titles GROUP BY type
type
------------ ---------------------------
UNDECIDED    (null)
business     11.64
mod_cook     11.49
popular_comp 21.48
psychology   13.50
trad_cook    15.96
```

GROUP BY can also be used in a query that involves a join. The following example lists each author id, last name, and first name, with a count of how many books that author has written:

```
SELECT a.au_id, a.au_lname, a.au_fname, count(*)
FROM authors a, titleauthor ta
WHERE a.au_id = ta.au_id
GROUP BY a.au_id, a.au_lname, a.au_fname
```

Note that the ANSI standard requires that all of the columns in the select list must either appear as an argument to an aggregate function or must appear in the GROUP BY clause. Previous releases of SQL Server allowed the following statement:

```
SELECT a.au_id, a.au_lname, a.au_fname, count(*)
FROM authors a, titleauthor ta
WHERE a.au_id = ta.au_id
GROUP BY a.au_id
```

With SQL Server Version 6, this statement yields the following two error messages:

```
Msg 8120, Level 16, State 1
Column 'a.au_lname' is invalid in the select list because it is not contained
in either an aggregate function or the GROUP BY clause.
Msg 8120, Level 16, State 1
```

```
Column 'a.au_fname' is invalid in the select list because it is not contained
in either an aggregate function or the GROUP BY clause.
```

If you have existing applications that rely on this statement working, you can use the trace flag 204. Submit the following statement in your application before the statement with a GROUP BY (it must be in a batch separate from the GROUP BY, as the trace flag does not take effect until the end of the batch):

```
DBCC TRACEON(204)
```

This statement preserves the previous behavior of GROUP BY. For more information about GROUP BY extensions and trace flag 204, see the section on Dangerous GROUP BY.

Group By . . . Having

In a SELECT statement with a GROUP BY clause, the HAVING clause determines which groups should be returned. Logically, the SQL Server evaluates all rows of the table, develops the appropriate aggregates, and then uses the HAVING clause to determine which rows should be returned to the user. In the following example, the SQL Server determines how many books were written by each author. It then uses the HAVING clause to determine which rows should be returned. Only those authors who have written more than one book (where count(*) > 1) will be returned.

```
SELECT a.au_id, a.au_lname, a.au_fname, count(*)
FROM authors a, titleauthor ta
WHERE a.au_id = ta.au_id
GROUP BY a.au_id, a.au_lname, a.au_fname
HAVING count(*) > 1

au_id          au_lname                              au_fname
-------------- ------------------------------------- -------------------- ----
--
213-46-8915 Green                                    Marjorie             2
267-41-2394 O'Leary                                  Michael              2
486-29-1786 Locksley                                 Charlene             2
724-80-9391 MacFeather                               Stearns              2
899-46-2035 Ringer                                   Anne                 2
998-72-3567 Ringer                                   Albert               2
```

Execution of GROUP BY

The following describes the logical order of activities done by the SQL Server when processing a SELECT statement with a GROUP BY clause (the second and third bullet can, in fact, be combined).

- ♦ Build a work table with the columns in the GROUP BY lists plus one additional column for each aggregate to be calculated. This table has a unique clustered index with the option ignore_dup_key turned on.
- ♦ Load the groups into this work table, taking advantage of the ignore_dup_key option to discard any duplicates.
- ♦ Calculate the aggregates for each of the groups.
- ♦ If the trace flag 204 is turned on, get the values for any column in the SELECT list that is neither grouped nor aggregated, by joining to the original table on the grouping columns.

Dangerous GROUP BY

Previous releases of SQL Server allowed you to include columns in the SELECT list that were not in the GROUP BY clause and that were not aggregated. The SQL Server still allows this if you turn on trace flag 204 as described earlier in this chapter.

We recommend that you not take advantage of this trace flag. You may be tempted to use it if you have existing programs that run successfully on older versions of SQL Server. Many people who have taken advantage of this extension have received wrong answers. Sometimes they notice that they get the wrong answer, and sometimes they don't.

Consider the example of GROUP BY shown previously:

```
SELECT a.au_id, a.au_lname, a.au_fname, count(*)
FROM authors a, titleauthor ta
WHERE a.au_id = ta.au_id
GROUP BY a.au_id
```

It makes sense to us to exclude the au_lname and au_fname from the GROUP BY, since the au_id is the primary key of the authors table and grouping by that should be sufficient. This will give the correct answer if trace flag 204 is turned on (it will give two error messages if it is not). Nineteen rows are returned.

Next, let's modify this example slightly by changing which table we select au_id from in the SELECT list:

```
SELECT ta.au_id, a.au_lname, a.au_fname, count(*)
FROM authors a, titleauthor ta
WHERE a.au_id = ta.au_id
GROUP BY a.au_id
```

We expect to get the same result, since our only change is which table we take the au_id from, and right in the WHERE clause we say that a.au_id = ta.au_id. Unfortunately, our result includes 475 rows. The reason is captured in the fourth bullet of the Execution of GROUP BY section in this chapter:

Get the values for any column in the select list that is neither grouped nor aggregated, by joining to the original table on the grouping columns.

The SQL Server joins on the grouping columns to get the value of ta.au_id. Unfortunately, none of the grouping columns are in the titleauthor table. The result set includes the 19 rows we expected, but each one is joined to every row in the titleauthor table. There are 25 rows in the titleauthor table, so we get $25 \times 19 = 475$ rows in the result set.

Here is another example. Note again that this example requires using trace flag 204:

```
SELECT title_id, avg(qty)
FROM sales
WHERE title_id = 'PS2091'

title_id
-------- -----------
BU1032    27
PS2091    27
PC8888    27
PS2091    27
PS2091    27
TC3218    27
TC4203    27
TC7777    27
PS2091    27
MC3021    27
PS1372    27
PS2106    27
PS3333    27
PS7777    27
BU7832    27
MC2222    27
BU2075    27
MC3021    27
BU1032    27
BU1111    27
PC1035    27
```

The second column is the correct average for title_id PS2091. Unfortunately, after generating the average the SQL Server had to join back to the sales table to get the title_id column, and it again generated one result row for every row in the sales table (notice that PS2091 shows up multiple times, since there are multiple rows for PS2091 in the sales table).

Sometimes the extension yields reasonable results, but it often yields strange results. Even though you think your existing applications are okay, we recommend that you avoid turning on trace flag 204. On previous releases, we described this feature as a black hole. You can now avoid the black hole by forgetting that you ever heard of trace flag 204.

Cursors

Support for cursors is introduced in this release of SQL Server. Cursors allow you to step through the rows of a query and take some additional action with each row. They are an important new feature in the SQL Server, but it is important to only use them when they are needed. In particular, you can often replace a cursor with set-level processing. See Chapter 8 for a discussion of the importance of relational thinking.

Sometimes a cursor will be exactly the right solution to a problem. It will allow you to use Transact-SQL to solve a problem, executing the entire solution on the server. That is one of the advantages of using cursors—the individual rows do not have to be returned across the network.

Cursor Processing

There are five primary steps in using a cursor:

1. Declare the cursor.
2. Open the cursor.
3. Fetch the next (or first) row.
4. Close the cursor.
5. Deallocate the cursor.

We will look at each of these steps. We will also describe the syntax and discuss how to use it.

Declare the Cursor

The DECLARE cursor statement defines the SELECT statement that will be associated with the cursor. It also identifies whether a copy should be made of the result set when the cursor is opened, whether updates are allowed to the selected rows, and what type of locking should be done. An example of a DECLARE statement looks like this:

```
DECLARE getdbs CURSOR FOR SELECT name FROM master..sysdatabases FOR READ ONLY
```

This declares a cursor for the SELECT statement *SELECT name FROM master..sysdatabases*. This cursor will be read-only so only shared locks will be held.

The SELECT statement is not executed at this point.

Open the Cursor

The OPEN statement opens the cursor. The SELECT statement is executed, and the results are ready to be accessed. The following example opens the cursor getdbs:

```
OPEN getdbs
```

Fetch the Next (or First) Row

The FETCH statement allows you to select the NEXT row in the result set and place the column values into variables. There are options to select the first row, last row, previous row, or a specific row from the result set. The following statement selects the next row into the variable @a:

```
FETCH NEXT FROM getdbs INTO @a
```

After executing this statement, always check the value of the global variable @@fetch_status. This variable will have one of the following values:

- ♦ 0   Row is successfully accessed.
- ♦ −1   Requested row is not in the result set (for example, you have fetched beyond the last row).
- ♦ −2   Requested row is no longer in the result set (for example, you fetch previous and the row has been deleted by another user).

Close the Cursor

The CLOSE statement closes the cursor. After the execution of the CLOSE statement, you can open it again with the OPEN statement. The following statement closes the cursor getdbs:

```
CLOSE getdbs
```

Deallocate the Cursor

The DEALLOCATE statement deallocates the cursor. After the execution of the DEALLOCATE statement, you can declare the cursor again with a DECLARE cursor statement. The following statement deallocates the cursor getdbs:

```
DEALLOCATE getdbs
```

Cursor Example

The following example demonstrates the use of cursors to facilitate system administration. The cursor is used to step through all of the database names listed in the sysdatabases table. For each database, the WHILE loop executes three DBCC commands: CHECKDB, CHECKALLOC, and CHECKCATALOG. Note that you may see spurious error messages (such as 2504) if these databases are not all in single-user mode.

```
DECLARE getdbs CURSOR FOR SELECT name
FROM master..sysdatabases FOR READ ONLY
DECLARE @a varchar(30)
OPEN getdbs
FETCH NEXT FROM getdbs INTO @a
```

```
WHILE @@fetch_status <> -1
BEGIN
      DBCC CHECKDB (@a)
      DBCC CHECKALLOC (@a)
      DBCC CHECKCATALOG (@a)
      FETCH NEXT FROM getdbs INTO @a
END
CLOSE getdbs
DEALLOCATE getdbs
```

Dynamic EXECUTE in a Stored Procedure

SQL Server now includes the ability to execute a string. The following procedure demonstrates one of the uses of the dynamic EXECUTE statement. This procedure reports the number of rows in a table. The owner and table name are passed as parameters. The dynamic EXECUTE statement executes a string that is created within the stored procedure.

```
CREATE PROCEDURE getsize (@owner varchar(30), @name varchar(30))
AS
      EXECUTE ('SELECT count(*) FROM '+@owner+'.'+@name)
go
EXEC getsize 'dbo', 'authors'
-----------
23
```

Dynamic EXECUTE with Cursor

The next example demonstrates the value of the EXECUTE statement in executing a SQL statement that has been dynamically created. In this case, a cursor is used to get the owner name and table name for all of the user tables in the database. The EXECUTE statement then executes the string "UPDATE STATISTICS owner.tablename" for each table in the database. The EXECUTE statement also prints a message indicating which table has just been processed. SQL Server does not support printing character expressions directly in the PRINT statement, but the EXECUTE statement can be used to print the dynamically created string.

```
DECLARE listusertables CURSOR
      FOR SELECT user_name(uid),name FROM sysobjects
      WHERE type = 'U' FOR READ ONLY
DECLARE @owner varchar(30), @name varchar(30)
OPEN listusertables
FETCH NEXT FROM listusertables INTO @owner, @name
WHILE @@fetch_status <> -1
BEGIN
      EXECUTE ('UPDATE STATISTICS '+ @owner + '.' + @name )
```

```
        EXECUTE ('PRINT "Updated Statistics for '+@owner+'.'+@name +'"')
        FETCH NEXT FROM listusertables INTO @owner, @name
END
CLOSE listusertables
DEALLOCATE listusertables
```

The first few lines of results from executing these two batches appear like this:

```
Updated Statistics for dbo.authors
Updated Statistics for dbo.publishers
Updated Statistics for dbo.titles
Updated Statistics for dbo.titleauthor
Updated Statistics for dbo.stores
```

Neat SQL Tricks

We spend much of our time developing relational database applications, reviewing applications for others, or consulting on application development. One of the things that we've noticed is that using SQL as a development language requires a different set of tricks than other forms of application development. This section includes a set of techniques that we have found useful in developing relational database applications.

Difference Operations and Outer Joins

Applications often have to identify all the rows in one table that don't have a match in another table. This is often called a *subtraction* or *difference operation*. Consider the following two tables:

```
a
    id
    1
    2
    3
    4
b
    id
    3
    4
    5
```

Then a-b (The ids in a that don't have a match in b) would be:

```
    id
    1
    2
```

And b-a (The ids in b that don't have a match in a) would be:

```
id
5
```

The common (and perhaps most obvious) way to phrase a-b is:

```
SELECT a.id FROM a WHERE NOT EXISTS
    (SELECT b.id FROM b WHERE a.id = b.id)
```

An alternative is to do this using an outer join and a temporary table. In an outer join, the table whose column appears in the WHERE clause on the side of the * is called the preserved table. That is, all rows that have a match in the nonpreserved table appear in the result. In addition, one row appears in the result set for each row of the preserved table that does not have a match.

```
SELECT a.id aid, b.id bid INTO #dif FROM a,b WHERE a.id *= b.id[1]
```

```
#dif
    aid bid
    1    NULL
    2    NULL
    3    3
    4    4
```

Then, to identify those that are in a but not in b:

```
SELECT aid FROM #dif WHERE bid IS NULL
```

```
    aid
    1
    2
```

The second approach using an outer join was faster on previous releases, but the WHERE NOT EXISTS approach appears to be faster for this example on SQL Server Version 6. Outer joins are nonetheless a useful technique in certain instances. Consider adding them to your toolbox.

Cross Tabulations

A cross tabulation allows you to summarize data in a two-dimensional grid. Cross tabulations are commonly required for viewing data summaries (see Table 7.1).

This is an order table, with one row for each order, including the order number, the customer name, the product name and the quantity for the sale. Analyze the data and prepare a summary with each customer listed in one row. The columns should be the quantity of each product purchased. Table 7.2 shows the desired appearance.

TABLE 7.1 An Order Table

Order id	Customer Name	Product Name	Quantity for the Sale
1	Russell	Plants	6
2	Hillary	Books	12
3	George	Stars	55
4	George	Stars	3
5	Russell	Plants	5
6	Russell	Plants	89

TABLE 7.2 Summary of the Order Table Showing Quantity Columns for Each Product

Customer	Stars	Books	Plants
George	105	33	66
Hillary	33	24	NULL
Russell	638	36	77447

Preparing this output using SQL is not trivial. We show three different ways to develop this output. All three approaches make one critical simplifying assumption: We assume that we know ahead of time how many columns we want and how the columns are identified (in this case, stars, books and plants). The problem is much more difficult if you don't know this ahead of time.

1. *Use a sequence of outer joins.* Each one develops another column of the result.

```
SELECT DISTINCT results_customer=customer
INTO temp
FROM table

SELECT      results_customer,
            stars = sum(quantity)
INTO        temp_one
FROM        temp,table
WHERE       results_customer*=customer
AND         product = 'stars'
GROUP BY    customer

SELECT          results_customer, stars, books = sum(quantity)
INTO        temp_two
FROM        temp_one, table
WHERE       results_customer *= customer
AND         product = 'books'
GROUP BY    results_customer, stars
...
```

The first SELECT creates a temporary table temp[2] which contains a list of the customers. This is done to ensure that every customer appears in the result. The second SELECT creates a table temp_one which contains one row for each distinct customer, with one column identifying the customer and a second column giving the quantity of stars bought. A customer who did not buy any stars will appear with a stars quantity of NULL.[3] The third SELECT creates another temporary table temp_two. This table contains the two columns created in temp_one and contains a third column including the quantity of "books".

Outer joins are used to ensure that all customers will be listed in the final set. Without outer joins, we would only see rows for those customers who bought all of the products.

2. *Perform a self join of the table.* To set this up, we first create a temporary table with a list of all customers, products, and sums. Then this table is joined to itself once for each of the product columns.

```
SELECT DISTINCT customer
INTO       cust
FROM       table

SELECT     customer, product, qty = sum(quantity)
INTO       aggs
FROM       table
GROUP BY   customer, product

SELECT cust.customer, stars =s.qty, books = b.qty, etc.....
FROM cust,
      aggs s,
      aggs b,
      etc......
WHERE cust.customer *= s.customer
AND    cust.customer *= b.customer
AND    etc.....
AND    s.product = 'stars'
AND    b.product = 'books'
AND    etc......
```

Programmers usually have an easier time visualizing the first scheme. It is also more easily extensible to large numbers of columns. The second solution usually performs much better. Don't try to collapse the aggregation [the sum() and the GROUP BY] into a single step with the self-join. It doesn't work that way.

3. *Take advantage of the CASE construct, and evaluate all of the sums simultaneously.* This approach again requires that you know how many products there are when you write the statement:

```
SELECT customer,
      stars = sum(quantity*
```

```
          (CASE WHEN product = 'stars' THEN 1 ELSE 0 END)),
     books = sum(quantity*
          (CASE WHEN product = 'books' THEN 1 ELSE 0 END))
FROM salestable
GROUP BY customer
```

This statement uses the notion of a characteristic function. The first CASE expression returns 1 when the product is "stars" and 0 otherwise. The second CASE expression returns 1 when the product is "books" and 0 otherwise. In each case this value is multiplied by the quantity for the row. If the row is for the specified product ("stars" or "books"), the quantity is added to the sum. If the row is not for the specified product, a 0 is added to the sum. This technique allows multiple sums to be calculated in a single pass through the data.

Creating Serial Numbers in an Existing Table

There is often a need to insert a sequence number into an existing table or to generate a unique number to identify individual rows. A number of different approaches can be used. In this section we demonstrate a way to insert a unique sequence number into a column in an existing table, as well as show how to use cursors, and the identify property to facilitate creating serial numbers.

Crude Serial Number Creation

The following statement updates the table setting a column called seq_num_field to a unique integer:

```
UPDATE table_name
SET t1.seq_num_field =
(SELECT count (*) FROM table_name t2
WHERE t1.primary_key >= t2.primary_key)
FROM table_name t1
```

This example assumes that there is an existing column (primary_key) which uniquely identifies each row. This column must not be null. The correlated UPDATE statement sets the seq_num_field for each row to be the number of rows that have a primary_key value less than this column's key value.

This scheme will not work if the existing primary key has more than one column.

This will execute quite slowly for a large table. For each row, it makes another pass through the table checking to see how many rows have a primary_key value less than this row. We have found this useful in a number of instances where the existing primary_key was a long variable-length character string, and we wanted to create a serial number.

Using Cursors to Create Serial Numbers

With Version 6, we can do something similar using cursors. The approach is to read each row of the table, and update the "sequence" column to the next integer value. Prior to Version 6, a similar approach could be taken using DB-Library programming.

The following example is written as a stored procedure, but it could have been done as a batch instead.

```
CREATE PROCEDURE update_keys AS
DECLARE @primary_key char(1), @seq int
DECLARE @count int
SELECT @count=0

DECLARE addseq CURSOR FOR
    SELECT primary_key, seq_num_field FROM table_name
    FOR UPDATE OF seq_num_field
OPEN addseq
FETCH addseq INTO @primary_key, @seq

WHILE (@@fetch_status=0)
BEGIN
    SELECT @count=@count+1
    UPDATE table_name
      SET seq_num_field=@count
      WHERE CURRENT OF addseq
    FETCH addseq INTO @primary_key, @seq
END
CLOSE addseq
DEALLOCATE addseq
```

Note that there must be a unique index on the table in order to have an updateable cursor. The table required for this procedure could be defined as follows:

```
CREATE TABLE table_name (seq_num_field int,
    primary_key char(1))
go
CREATE UNIQUE CLUSTERED INDEX abc ON table_name(primary_key)
```

First the procedure declares the cursor. Note that it uses the FOR UPDATE OF clause. This indicates that the procedure expects to update the table, setting the specified column. If that row is updated, the SQL Server will hold an exclusive lock on that page.

The procedure then SELECTs each row, updating the sequence number to the next integer value. It continues until the global variable @@fetch_status is not 0, indicating that there are no more rows in the result set.

Creating Serial Numbers Using the Identity Property

Numeric or decimal columns can be given the IDENTITY property starting with SQL Server Version 6.0. This specifies that every time a new row is inserted into the table the specified column will be given a unique value (unique across that table). The following example inserts rows into table x by selecting all of the rows of table y. Since table x has a column with the identity property, each row of table x will have a unique value in that identity column.

```
CREATE TABLE y (primary_key int)
CREATE TABLE x (primary_key int, sequence numeric(6,0) IDENTITY)
INSERT INTO x (primary_key)
     SELECT primary_key FROM y
```

Each table may have at most one identity column. This column must be of type tinyint, smallint, int, or numeric or decimal, with a scale of 0. After the INSERT statement, the global variable @@identity contains the identity value just inserted. It is possible for the table owner, the database owner, or the system administrator to explicitly insert values into this column.

Managing Serial Numbers

If you don't want to use the IDENTITY property to maintain unique serial numbers in a table, you can create a surrogate key field using a column of type int and control the inserts into the table to increment the serial column values. This serial field column in a table guarantees that each row in a table will be different.

One approach follows. This particular approach is safe; that is, you will never get two rows with the same value of id. As long as you have a unique clustered index on the id column of x, access using INSERT, UPDATE, DELETE, or SELECT will be efficient. However, it may lead to performance problems in the application. Assuming there is a clustered index on id, any INSERT statement inserts all new rows at the end of the table. This last page may become a hotspot in your application.

```
INSERT INTO x (id, status)
SELECT max(id)+1, 0
FROM x
```

One of the problems with this approach is that you don't know what value was assigned for id. But consider the following approach:

```
SELECT @var  ax(id) FROM x
INSERT INTO x (id, status) VALUES (@var,0)
```

It is possible that some other process will add a new row to the table between the execution of the SELECT and the INSERT statements. You can improve on this approach by doing the SELECT and INSERT in a transaction:

```
BEGIN TRAN
SELECT @var=max(id) FROM x HOLDLOCK
INSERT INTO x (id, status) VALUES (@var,0)
COMMIT TRAN
```

Now the operation is safe (no user can insert a new row after you have done your SELECT—assuming that there is a unique inde on the id column) but you can now deadlock if another user executes this same transaction while you are executing it. If you both do the SELECT and then attempt the INSERT, the result is a deadlock since you each hold a lock that conflicts with a request of the other user.

The following refinement is safe, and will avoid deadlocks. Create a second table containing a single row, single column, holding the largest id value. When you need a new value, execute the following transaction. At the end of the transaction, @varnam contains the next available id number.

```
BEGIN TRAN
     UPDATE table SET id = id+1
     SELECT @varnam=id FROM table
COMMIT TRAN
INSERT INTO x (id, status) @varnam, 0
```

This approach still has one problem. It is possible that after executing the transaction (updating the table holding the highest value used) the application will fail before it has successfully inserted the new row into table x. This will result in some id numbers not being used. For most applications, this is acceptable.

Code Generation Techniques

Several years ago, we were using another relational database product and had a significant revelation. We realized that the SQL language can help us generate code. We can create a series of tables with information about our application, and then use SQL statements to write SQL code that we can submit to the database engine, or even C code. These techniques are great practice for your SQL skills and are often very productive ways to get a job done.

Generation Techniques—SQL to Create SQL

The first technique uses SQL to generate SQL statements. The SQL Server provides a very powerful database engine and you can harness its power. This is particularly useful for system administrators writing queries against the SQL Server system tables. It can also be extended beyond that use.

```
SELECT 'UPDATE STATISTICS' + name
FROM sysobjects WHERE type = 'U'
```

This generates the following results:

```
UPDATE STATISTICS authors
UPDATE STATISTICS titles
...
```

This gives you a script to update statistics on all the user tables in your database.

Here is a refinement to the previous technique. The following SELECT writes a script to do an UPDATE STATISTICS on those tables that don't have any index statistics (indicated by the distribution column in sysindexes being 0 for at least one of the indexes on the table).

```
SELECT DISTINCT 'UPDATE STATISTICS ' + o.name
FROM sysobjects o, sysindexes i
WHERE o.id = i.id
AND i.indid BETWEEN 1 AND 250
AND i.distribution = 0
AND o.type = "U"
```

With a little thought you could write procedures to generate code for the following:

- ♦ A trigger for INSERT that validates presence of foreign keys in other tables.
- ♦ A stored procedure that takes all the columns for a table as parameters and does an INSERT into the table. You might use SQL to generate this starting point, and then modify each one to add the specific validations required for that table.

You may find that you can get close with just the SQL code but need to use C or a GUI scripting language to complete the activity.

Generation Techniques—SQL to Create C

We inherited a large application that did statistical analysis of large volumes of insurance claim data. The application was given a table with a large number of columns and calculated various ratios. In this example, we sum three columns and divide by the sum of two others:

```
(c1+c2+c3)/(c4+c7)
```

We were asked to make some modifications to the code. We were able (with quite a bit of effort) to model the problem into a set of relations. The relations captured the sums to be formed into numerators and denominators and ratios of those numerators and denominators. We worked with the customer to adjust parts of the definition of the problem so that our model would apply.

Initially, we did the code directly using SQL from the tables. SQL was too slow for the volume of calculations on each row so we used SQL to generate C code to do the calculations.

The tables looked roughly like Tables 7.3 and 7.4.

The first table indicates that the sum c1_2_3sComps is the sum of buckets g_p2330, g_p2331, and g_p2332. This is then used as the dividend in a ratio where the divisor is c2_amalgams.

Sample generated code looks something like the following:

```
c1_2_3sComps        =
(g_p2330    ) +
(g_p2331    ) +
(g_p2332    ) +
(g_p2333    ) +
0 ;
c1sAmal_Perm        =
(g_p2140    ) +
0 ;
c1sAmal_Pri         =
(g_p2110    ) +
0 ;
```

The rest of the C program reads a row, does the calculation, and then accumulates results or does inserts into the SQL Server.

TABLE 7.3 Sample Data from the Aggregate Table

aggregate_name	bucket_name
c1_2_3sComps	g_p2330
c1_2_3sComps	g_p2331
c1_2_3sComps	g_p2332

TABLE 7.4 Sample Data from the Ratio Table

dividend_agg	divisor_agg	factor
c1_2_3sComps	c2_amalgams	1
c2_amalgams	c2_4xrays	1.19
c2_amalgams	total_procedures	1

There are a number of advantages to this scheme:

1. We used the relational model—which allowed us to understand the problem better.
2. The customer can change the formulas being used and automatically recreate the code. Although not a daily occurrence, the customer does find that about once a year there is reason to make some modifications.
3. We were able to get optimal performance while still controlling the process. This particular activity needed to be coded in C. We were able to do it without *writing* hundreds of lines of C code. Instead, we *generated* hundreds of lines of C code.

Handling a Hierarchy (Bill of Materials)

A database will commonly require you to use the *bill of materials technique* for a parts explosion problem, where parts may be made of other parts.

The following example builds a bill of materials based on the table PCGdp that is built by a database analysis tool in order to display a call tree. This technique is commonly required for a parts explosion problem.

The table PCGdp has the following description:

```
CREATE TABLE PCGdp
    (
    fromdb                  varchar(30)             NOT NULL,
    fromown                 varchar(30)             NOT NULL,
    fromobject              varchar(30)             NOT NULL,
    toserver                varchar(30)             NULL,
    todb                    varchar(30)             NULL,
    toown                   varchar(30)             NULL,
    toobject                varchar(30)             NOT NULL,
    )
```

This table maintains a list of which procedures reference which object within the SQL Server. If procedure A called procedure B (using EXEC), there would be a row in PCGdp something like:

```
DBNAME, dbo, A, SERVERNAME, DBNAME, dbo, B
```

Using this table, the following procedure (*display_tree*) will produce a call tree showing all the objects that A references directly as well as indirectly: If A calls B and C, and both B and C call D, the output will look as follows:

```
A
        B
                D
        C
                D
```

The procedure makes the temporary table *#stack* to develop intermediate results and remember your place. The procedure makes the temporary table *#lines* to build up the results, including spacing.

```
CREATE PROCEDURE display_tree (@cursrvr varchar(30),@curdb varchar(30),
     @curown varchar(30),@curobj varchar(30)) AS
DECLARE @level int, @line1 varchar(80),@line2 varchar(80)
/* The table #stack will contain all of the objects referenced by @curobj */
/*   srvr - srvr name
     db - database name
     own - owner
     obj - object name
     level - reference level. If A is the parameter, its rows in #stack
will
     have a 'level' of 1. Any object that A calls, will have a level of 2
*/
CREATE TABLE #stack (srvr varchar(30),db varchar(30),
     own varchar(30),obj varchar(30), level_num int)
/* The table #lines contains the lines that will be output - with spaces
inserted at the beginning of each line to create the indenting in the
output. */
CREATE TABLE #lines (srvr_db varchar(61),own_obj varchar(61))
/* Insert the parameters as the first row in #stack */
INSERT INTO #stack VALUES (@cursrvr,@curdb,@curown,@curobj,1)
SELECT @level = 1
/* @level starts at 1, and proceeds up and down, as rows are
processed. If there are any calls at the current level, those are processed -
and any calls at that level are processed. Given the example above, the rows
encountered would be A, C, D, B, D. This is a depth first search - and
inserts
the rows in the correct order into #lines */
WHILE @level>0 AND @level < 8
BEGIN
/* If there are any more rows at this level, process the next one */
     IF EXISTS (SELECT * FROM #stack WHERE level_num = @level)
     BEGIN
/* Set the variables as the values from #stack (note this will get the last
row in #stack with this level number */
          SELECT @cursrvr=srvr,@curdb=db,@curown=own,
               @curobj=obj FROM #stack WHERE level_num = @level
/* Insert this row into #lines */
          SELECT @line1=SPACE(2*(@level-1)) + @curown + '.' + @curobj
          SELECT @line2=SPACE(2*(@level)) + 'ON' + @cursrvr + '.' + @curdb
          INSERT INTO #lines VALUES(@line1,@line2)
/* Remove the row from #stack - since it has now been processed */
          DELETE FROM #stack WHERE level_num=@level AND srvr=@cursrvr
               AND db=@curdb AND own=@curown AND obj=@curobj
/* Insert into #stack any row from PCGdp that represents a call from this
current row*/
          INSERT #stack
               SELECT toserver,todb,toown,toobject,@level+1
               FROM PCGdp
```

```
                    WHERE fromdb=@curdb AND fromown=@curown
                       AND fromobject=@curobj
/* If any rows were found, increment level, and process those rows */
                   IF @@ROWCOUNT>0
                   BEGIN
                         SELECT @level=@level+1
                   END
            END
/* We are done processing at the current level, go back up one level */
            ELSE
            BEGIN
                   SELECT @level=@level-1
            END
END
/* Display the results */
SELECT * FROM #lines
/* Drop the temporary tables */
DROP TABLE #lines
DROP TABLE #stack
RETURN
```

Stored Procedures

Stored procedures provide a number of advantages over using a series of Transact-SQL Statements:

- ♦ They provide improved performance because the server only parses them when created, and once optimized the query plan stays in cache (until forced out because it is least recently used). Having the query plan stay in cache is typically only a significant advantage if the stored procedure completes in under one or two seconds. Otherwise, the relative gain is small.
- ♦ They provide improved performance because of reduced network traffic.
- ♦ They allow you to create reusable code that resides on the server, making it easy to find and reuse.
- ♦ They provide an extra level of security and control. You can GRANT access to the procedure and deny (REVOKE) direct access to the tables or views.

Stored Procedure Syntax

The Stored Procedure Syntax is depicted in the following sample:

```
CREATE PROCEDURE
  [owner.]procedure_name[;number]
  [[(]@parameter_name datatype [=
  default] [OUTPUT]]
  [,@parameter_name datatype
  [=default][OUTPUT]]...[)]]
```

```
[WITH RECOMPILE]
AS sql_statements
```

Output Parameters

Output parameters allow you to return values to a calling procedure from a stored procedure. The calling procedure can then reference the returned values. As an example, see the following pair of procedures:

```
CREATE PROCEDURE callee (@parm int OUTPUT) AS
        SELECT @parm = 7
        RETURN
go
CREATE PROCEDURE caller AS
        DECLARE @var int
        EXEC callee @var OUTPUT
        SELECT @var
go
EXEC caller


-----------
          7
go
```

Giving Help for Stored Procedures

By using a default value for parameters, you can provide users with help on how to use a stored procedure. Test the parameter value inside the procedure. If it is still the default, the procedure can display a help message. Create this logic as follows:

```
CREATE PROCEDURE test (@a int = NULL) AS
        IF @a IS NULL
        BEGIN
                PRINT 'To run this procedure enter EXEC test value'
                PRINT 'where the value is an integer between 1 and 10'
                RETURN
        END
        /* The real part of the procedure... */
        RETURN
```

Using Temporary Tables in Stored Procedures

If you create a temporary table in a stored procedure and then try to reference it, the query optimizer component of the SQL Server will not have good information about the size of the table and distribution of data when it compiles the stored procedure.

In the following example, the query optimizer will not consider using the index on the table #temp to process the select statement:

```
CREATE PROCEDURE summarize_prices AS
SELECT type,avg_price=avg(price)
     INTO #temp
     FROM titles
     GROUP BY type
CREATE UNIQUE CLUSTERED INDEX #tt ON #temp(type)
SELECT titles.title_id, titles.type, titles.price/#temp.avg_price
FROM #temp, titles
WHERE #temp.type = titles.type
```

In order to allow the query optimizer to consider using this index, you have to create the table and index in one stored procedure and then execute a second stored procedure that will do the select with the join. Doing the following will allow the query optimizer to consider using the index. Note that the order of creation is important. First create the temporary table, then the inner procedure which references the temporary table. We have to create the temporary table first or the **CREATE PROCEDURE** statement will fail. We then drop the temporary table (it was needed only to allow the create procedure to succeed). Finally, we create the outer procedure. We had to create the inner procedure first, or we would have gotten an error message when we created the outer procedure.

Create the summarize_prices_inner using the **WITH RECOMPILE** option to ensure that it will be recompiled each time the procedure is run. This will ensure that the execution plan for this procedure created by the query optimizer takes into account the current number of rows and distribution of values in the table #temp1 every time the procedure is executed.

```
CREATE TABLE #temp1 (type char(12) not null,avg_price money null)
go
CREATE PROCEDURE summarize_prices_inner WITH RECOMPILE AS
SELECT titles.title_id, titles.type, titles.price/#temp1.avg_price
FROM #temp1, titles
WHERE #temp1.type = titles.type
go
DROP TABLE #temp1
go
CREATE PROCEDURE summarize_prices_outer AS
SELECT type,avg_price=avg(price)
     INTO #temp1
     FROM titles
     GROUP BY type
CREATE UNIQUE CLUSTERED INDEX #tt1 ON #temp1(type)
EXEC summarize_prices_inner
go
```

Stored Procedure Transaction Error Handling

The following example shows how to manage transaction logic and error handling in a stored procedure. This stored procedure modifies the primary key of the tasks table and then cascades that change to two other tables. If there is an error in modifying any of the three tables, the transaction is rolled back and an appropriate error message is returned with RAISERROR.

```
CREATE PROC rename_task (
@oldtaskid id10type,
@newtaskid id10type)
AS
DECLARE @numrows int,
        @rowsave int,
        @message varchar(50),
        @error   smallint
BEGIN TRAN
UPDATE tasks
SET    task_id = @newtaskid
WHERE  task_id = @oldtaskid
SELECT @numrows = @@rowcount,
       @message = convert (varchar(50), @numrows),
       @error   = @@error
IF @error = 0
   BEGIN
      IF @numrows = 1
         BEGIN
            UPDATE consult_task
            SET    task_id = @newtaskid
            WHERE  task_id = @oldtaskid
            SELECT @numrows = @@rowcount + 1,
                   @message = convert (varchar(50), (@@rowcount+1)),
                   @error   = @@error
            IF @error = 0
               BEGIN
                  SELECT @rowsave = @numrows
                  UPDATE working
                  SET task_id = @newtaskid
                  WHERE task_id = @oldtaskid
                  SELECT @numrows = @@rowcount + @rowsave,
                         @message = convert(varchar(50),(@@rowcount+@rowsave)),
                         @error = @@error
                  IF @error = 0
                     BEGIN
                     RAISERROR (@message,16,1)
                     COMMIT TRAN
                     END
            ELSE
                     BEGIN
                     RAISERROR ('Update of work table failed.',16,1)
                     ROLLBACK TRAN
                     END
               END
            ELSE
               BEGIN
```

```
                        RAISERROR ('Update of consult_task table failed.',16,1)
                        ROLLBACK TRAN
                        END
              END
          ELSE
              BEGIN
                  IF @numrows = 0
                      BEGIN
                          RAISERROR ('No rows in task table to update.',16,1)
                      ROLLBACK TRAN
                          END
                      ELSE
                          BEGIN
                              RAISERROR ('More than one row in task table to rename.',16,1)
                              ROLLBACK TRAN
                          END
              END
          END
      ELSE
          BEGIN
          RAISERROR ('Update of tasks table failed.',16,1)
          ROLLBACK TRAN
          END
```

Triggers

Triggers are special stored procedures that are associated with a table for one or more of the following actions: INSERT, UPDATE, or DELETE. When the specified action occurs, the trigger is automatically invoked.

Some application designers use triggers to implement part of the application. We try to make a (somewhat fuzzy) distinction between application logic (which goes in the client side of the application or in stored procedures) and database design (which we implement in triggers).

Examples of code that we view as database design and place in triggers follow:

- ◆ Referential integrity (although some of this can now be done using declarative referential integrity)
- ◆ Business rules internal to a table that can't be done in rules. This includes things such as that the termination date must be after the start date. It is possible to do this using constraints, and we prefer the use of constraints over the use of triggers when possible.
- ◆ Cascading changes required by certain types of denormalization. For example, you have an invoice header table and an invoice detail table. The invoice detail table has one row for each invoice item. In the invoice master table you have decided to maintain a total invoice value column, which is the sum of the value of the items for this invoice. You can create a trigger for INSERT, UPDATE, and DELETE on the detail table that adjusts the

total in the invoice header table every time there is a modification to the detail table.

In addition, we might use code in a trigger to watch for certain conditions in the table and call stored procedures either within the server or (using DLLs or Open Data Services) outside the server. An example would be a trigger for INSERT or UPDATE for an inventory table that monitors stock on hand and places orders as the stock reaches some threshold.

Trigger Syntax

```
CREATE TRIGGER [owner.]trigger_name
  ON [owner.]table_name
  FOR {INSERT , UPDATE , DELETE}
  AS sql_statements
```

Or, using the IF UPDATE clause:

```
CREATE TRIGGER [owner.]trigger_name
  ON [owner.]table_name
  FOR {INSERT , UPDATE}
  AS
    [IF UPDATE (column_name)
      [{AND | OR}
      UPDATE (column_name)]...]...
    SQL_statements}
```

A single trigger may be for one action, two actions, or all three actions (INSERT, UPDATE, and DELETE). In a trigger for UPDATE or DELETE, you can use the *IF UPDATE(column_name)* test. This will be true if the column appeared in the SET clause of an UPDATE statement, or if the column appears in the column list or for an INSERT statement.

The IF UPDATE(column_name) test can be useful in a trigger if you only want to execute certain code when a given column is affected.

Trigger Guidelines

Triggers are invoked once by the server for each INSERT, UPDATE, or DELETE statement for the table. If there are multiple rows affected by the statement, the trigger is invoked once only for all of the rows.

When the trigger is invoked, two special tables are created called *inserted* and *deleted*. These tables are created when any trigger is invoked. They have exactly the same columns, column names, and datatypes as the table the trigger is associated with.

When a trigger is invoked, the changes required by the statement that cause the trigger to be invoked (an INSERT, UPDATE, or DELETE statement) have already occurred. In a trigger for INSERT, the rows are already in the associated table. In a trigger for DELETE, the rows have already been deleted from the table. In a trigger for UPDATE, the rows have already been modified. None of these changes are yet visible to other users. The pages that contain these rows or the entire table are locked.

If the statement that caused the trigger to be invoked was an INSERT, the inserted table has all of the rows that were just inserted into the table, and the deleted table has no rows. If the statement that caused the trigger to be invoked was a DELETE, the rows that were deleted appear in the deleted table, and the inserted table has no rows. If the statement that caused the trigger to be invoked was an UPDATE, the affected rows are all in the deleted table, with the values that they had at the beginning of the statement, and the inserted table contains the rows, with the new values based on the execution of the UPDATE statement.

These two tables, inserted and deleted, can be used in SQL statements in the trigger to make appropriate changes to other tables or to determine whether business rules have been violated.

The trigger is invoked regardless of how many rows were affected by the INSERT, UPDATE, or DELETE statement. In particular, even if no rows were affected (for example, executing a DELETE statement where no rows match the WHERE clause) the trigger is still invoked.

At the beginning of a trigger, the value of the global variable @@rowcount is the number of rows affected by the statement that caused the trigger to be invoked. The value of @@rowcount is changed by the next INSERT, UPDATE, DELETE, or SELECT statement that is executed. Therefore, the first thing to do in most triggers is to assign the value of @@rowcount to a local variable.

Whenever you review a trigger it is a good idea to make sure that it handles three different cases depending on how many rows were affected by the statement that caused the trigger to be invoked: zero rows, one row, or many rows. It is a common mistake to assume that a trigger will only be invoked with a single row in inserted or deleted. Even though that may be true for the moment in your application, you should always create triggers that cope with all three cases.

The case of 0 rows affected is usually not a significant problem. However, on complicated triggers, we usually check for the zero-row case at the beginning, and return (exit the trigger) if zero rows are affected.

Verifying the Presence of Foreign Keys

The following trigger for INSERT on sales verifies that every row inserted into the sales table has a matching row in the titles table. Notice that the first thing it does is to capture the value of @@rowcount into a local variable (@rows). If there is any row in inserted that doesn't have a match in titles, then the transaction is rolled back and an error code is returned to the application (using the RAISERROR statement).

This same functionality can be done using the new declarative referential integrity available in SQL Server Version 6.

```
CREATE TRIGGER salesins
ON sales FOR INSERT
AS DECLARE @rows int
SELECT @rows = @@rowcount
IF @rows != (SELECT count(*)
    FROM inserted, titles
    WHERE inserted.title_id = titles.title_id)
BEGIN
    RAISERROR ('Invalid title identifier.',16,1)
    ROLLBACK TRANSACTION
END
```

Cascading Delete Trigger

The example shown in this section does a cascading delete: When one or more rows are deleted from the titles table, all rows for that title are deleted from the sales table.

This trigger does an "IF EXISTS" test to see if there are any rows in the sales table that match the rows in the deleted table. It only does the delete from the sales table if there are matching rows. The trigger could just execute the DELETE statement without doing the test. The advantage of this style of coding is that in the case where there are no matches, a DELETE statement has not been executed; therefore, no exclusive locks are held on the sales table, and the delete trigger on the sales table does is not invoked. There is some extra reading required with this approach however, since the SELECT statement must be executed (at least until one matching row is found) and then the DELETE statement requires reading the same rows again.

```
CREATE TRIGGER titlesdel
ON titles FOR DELETE AS
IF EXISTS (SELECT *
FROM sales, deleted
WHERE sales.title_id = deleted.title_id)
    BEGIN
        DELETE sales
        FROM sales, deleted
        WHERE sales.title_id = deleted.title_id
    END
```

Imposing a Business Rule on UPDATE

The following trigger compares the old and new price in the titles table on update of the titles table. It compares the two prices and disallows the change if the increase is greater than 10 percent.

The test to see if the title_id changed is common in some tables. Note that the **IF EXISTS** test is joining inserted and deleted on title_id. If the user has changed a title_id, this join will not find matching rows. Many database designs disallow changing the primary key value, though this is not always acceptable. We have assumed this requirement in this trigger. There is a subsequent example that shows how you can use a trigger to cascade a change to a primary key.

The **IF EXISTS** test is comparing the old and new values of the price column, checking to see if there are any rows which exceed a price increase of 10 percent. The **IF EXISTS** test will work regardless of the number of rows in inserted and deleted.

```
CREATE TRIGGER titlesupd
ON titles FOR UPDATE AS
IF UPDATE(title_id)
     BEGIN
          RAISERROR ('Can't change title_id',16,1)
          ROLLBACK TRANSACTION
     END
IF EXISTS (SELECT * FROM inserted, deleted WHERE inserted.title_id =
deleted.title_id AND inserted.price/deleted.price > 1.1)
     BEGIN
     RAISERROR ('Bad Increase.',16,1)
     ROLLBACK TRANSACTION
     END
```

Changing the Primary Key Trigger

The following trigger allows changes to a primary key in the titles table. It ensures that at most one row is being changed. (This is required to make the changes in the tables where this column appears as a foreign key.) The change is propagated to the foreign key tables.

Note that the requirement of only one row being affected occurs because we have no way to match the rows in inserted and deleted if there are more than one. The UPDATE statement involves three tables (inserted, deleted, and titleauthor), but there is only one join clause (where ta.title_id=d.title_id). This is only reasonable when inserted and deleted each contain only one row.

Note also the test for @row equal to 0. If no rows are affected by the UPDATE statement that caused this trigger to be invoked, there is no need to do any work. The test is not necessary since the update to the titleauthor table would work correctly for no rows in the inserted and deleted tables. However, it often makes it easier to write triggers if you deal with each of the interesting cases one at a time. Here we first deal with no rows affected (doing nothing), many rows affected (denying the change by rolling back the transaction), and finally the case where exactly one row was affected and we want to cascade the change to the titleauthor table.

```
CREATE TRIGGER updtitles
ON titles FOR UPDATE AS
DECLARE @rows int
SELECT @rows = @@rowcount
if(@rows = 0)
        RETURN
  IF UPDATE(title_id)
      BEGIN
      if(@rows != 1)
            BEGIN

            ROLLBACK TRAN
            RETURN
            END
      UPDATE titleauthor
      SET ta.title_id = i.title_id
      FROM titleauthor ta, inserted i, deleted d
      WHERE ta.title_id = d.title_id
      UPDATE sales
      SET s.title_id = i.title_id
      FROM sales s, inserted i, deleted d
      WHERE s.title_id = d.title_id
      END
```

RAISERROR

There are two styles of **RAISERROR** that can be used in your stored procedures, triggers, or batches. The style that we have used in examples in this chapter have all been of the form:

```
RAISERROR ('string or variable',severity,state)
```

This is the easiest way to insert ad hoc messages into your code. Unfortunately, this form of **RAISERROR** always results in an error value of 50000 (the error number is stored in the global variable @@error after the error occurs). With the second form of **RAISERROR**, you can cause a specified error number to be stored in @@error. This second form uses messages saved in the sysmessages table.

RAISERROR with the sysmessages Table

You can use the sp_addmessage stored procedure to save error messages in the sysmessages table. The stored procedure requires three parameters (there are optional additional parameters that allow you to specify different languages, whether this message should be written to the NT event log when it occurs, and whether this new message should replace an existing message). The first parameter is a unique message id for this message. The second is a severity number between 1 and 25. The third parameter is the text of the message.

The message text may include C style substitution.

```
EXEC sp_addmessage msg_id, severity, 'text of message'
```

After adding this message to the sysmessages table, you can use a RAISERROR statement in a trigger, stored procedure, or batch. In the RAISERROR statement, you specify the msg_id of the message you want to issue, the severity and state, and optionally, substitution arguments.

```
RAISERROR (msg_id , severity, state [, argument1 [, argument2]] )
```

This form of RAISERROR is very useful for errors that are identified in triggers. After the error has been raised, the trigger can issue a ROLLBACK to roll back the transaction. The application can then check the value of @@error to determine which error had occurred.

The following is a sample sp_addmessage call:

```
EXEC sp_addmessage 50002,16,'No matching row in the %s table'
```

The following RAISERROR will present the message, and set the value of @@error to 50002.

```
RAISERROR (50002,16,1,'tasks')
```

This is the message that is displayed:

```
Msg 50002, Level 16, State 1
No matching row in the tasks table
```

Notes

1. The SELECT list in a SELECT statement may contain two forms of column aliasing. These column aliases change the heading that will appear in the results and change the name that will be used for the column if you are using a SELECT INTO statement. The two forms of column aliasing are:

```
SELECT alias = expression
SELECT expression alias
```

For example: "SELECT cost=quantity*price FROM tablename" or "SELECT quantity*price cost FROM tablename".

These two SELECT statements are equivalent. For both, the column heading in the result will be "cost". We have used both styles of column aliasing in the book.

2. We have chosen to not create these as real temporary tables (where the first column is #). We have left these as we might when debugging the queries. When this is used in a production application, the tables would all be defined as temporary tables—with the possible exception of the last one. You may want to leave that as a permanent table since you have invested a fair amount of effort in this process—and the result table may be useful for more than the immediate usage.

3. The ISNULL function could be used to convert this to a zero if that is preferred:

```
books=isnull (sum(quantity),0)
```

8

Technical Discourses

This chapter holds discussions of two very primary issues: *transaction management* and *relational processing techniques*. While seemingly very basic, they are both critical to successful development and poorly understood by the general developer community. When we go into the field and examine software solutions that are not succeeding, it is surprising how many of them can be traced back to a primary misunderstanding of these core principles. They are referenced elsewhere as applicable, but this presentation is meant to isolate the key issues in a very basic manner.

Transaction Design Discussion

A Logical Unit of Work

Recently, at a seminar filled with expert client/server developers, we heard someone define *a logical unit of work*. This person stated that a logical unit of work is whatever you do between two commits. This seemed a pretty cavalier definition of a topic which is, for many of us, a key to proper implementation of client/server technology.

There is a tendency to define application architecture according to the capabilities and defaults of the tools in use. Transaction management models tend to be designed after the simplest model used by the tools vendor. In general, we should come up with a more tightly defined, theoretical definition of transaction management issues so we can have a picture of what an ideal implementation would be. Then, let's devise solutions that come as close as possible to that definition.

So, what is a logical unit of work? In actuality, at runtime, it *is* whatever we do between two commits (or, with SQL Server, what we do between BEGIN TRAN and COMMIT TRAN). But what *should* we do between those two commits? SQL Server, because of its inherently powerful transaction control model, gives us a way to tightly control the content and extent of transactions. This model suggests formal and more effective solutions for modeling transactions.

One should define a logical unit of work from the business perspective because we are building *business* solutions. Generally, a transaction concerns itself with modifications made to data—that is, INSERTs, UPDATEs, and DELETEs. If we define a transaction based on the business, a transaction is a single piece of work (combination of data modifications) that has meaning unto itself and leaves the data in a correct and meaningful state. For example, inserting a new employee record into the system is a transaction. It is meaningful to add this single piece of information to our data. The addition of two employee records is not a transaction, because at the end of one of the additions, the database is still correct and meaningful. Both modifications are not *required* for the business meaning to be fulfilled.

If you have a business activity that requires two or more data modification statements—for example, a debit and a matching credit—two data manipulations are required to build what the business views as a transaction. Without either one, the database would not be correct or in a meaningful state. From the business viewpoint, we can define a transaction to be *the smallest logical unit of work that has meaning for the business.* (Not the simplest implementation of groups of data manipulations that a development tool supports.) Understanding and applying these basic points enables us to model better applications and to use better judgment when choosing how to manage transactions with high-level tools that have their own default behaviors.

Implementation Issues

Beyond the discussion of logical meaning, transaction design has major implementation implications: control, concurrency, locking, and performance. Why is it critical that a transaction implementation be the *smallest* unit of work?

Relational database engines use a form of exclusive locking to control access to records of data that are modified. The SQL Server uses the page as the smallest granularity of the locking mechanism. Each lock represents at least one page locked in the database. A page is 2,048 bytes and will usually hold multiple rows of data (see Chapter 3). Let's look at these two key points:

1. If a page is locked exclusively, no other processes can write to that page or read that page. Other processes that want an exclusively locked page will simply wait until the lock is released. (There are a few exceptions, like deadlock, but that is another story.)

2. All exclusive locks on pages are held until a transaction completes. That is, until a COMMIT TRANSACTION or ROLLBACK TRANSACTION is executed. So it behooves us to create transactions that are as small as is meaningful and that are executed in the shortest time possible.

Here is a simple example. We have a transaction that has to update two records in two different tables. It encloses the two modification statements with BEGIN TRAN and COMMIT TRAN.

```
BEGIN TRANSACTION
      The transaction begins.
UPDATE/INSERT/DELETE
      Lock the first page.
UPDATE/INSERT/DELETE
      Lock the second page.
COMMIT
      Locks are release.
```

At the moment we start to issue the COMMIT TRAN we hold exclusive locks on two pages. If any other users want the pages, they have to wait for us to release the locks. If the transaction is controlled inside a stored procedure or a single, self-contained batch, the transaction will execute very quickly. Assuming good indexing, it will be as fast as possible.

On the other hand, the transaction could be controlled and executed from the client application. This usage is promoted by many development environments and generic solutions. Let's look at the worst case.

```
      Send BEGIN TRAN across the network to the server.
BEGIN TRANSACTION
      The transaction begins.
      OK comes back.
      Send modification statement across the network.
UPDATE/INSERT/DELETE
      Lock the first page.
      OK comes back.
      Send modification statement across the network.
UPDATE/INSERT/DELETE
      Lock the second page.
      OK comes back.
      Send the COMMIT TRAN across the network.
COMMIT TRANSACTION
      Locks are released.
      OK comes back.
```

We have added the time it takes for eight trips across the network to the time originally involved in executing the transaction. Of course, the amount of time is related to the specific system. In the optimal case we have probably increased the time of the transaction by a factor of 10, possibly much more.

Processes that are waiting for locked pages are blocked. They are waiting. The odds that you will interfere with one or more users increases with the extended duration of the transaction. In the worst case, multiple updaters are locking pages, being blocked by each other, and all waiting for a series of blocks to be released. The worse case can completely lock down the tables involved and prevent other users from proceeding. (Sometimes the blocking can lead to a much more dramatic slowdown—taking the factor of 10 and making it a factor of 100 in throughput. . . .)

In reality, few of us code the worst case. But frequently developers write transactions that involve network transmissions. In very low volume transaction environments (or with noncore business transactions), you may get away with it. If you have a high-volume transaction environment and are trying to get maximum performance out of your client/server application, you *must* take care not to do this.

Summary of Key Points

Transactions are attempts to change the database from one valid business state to a new one. Good transaction implementations have two important criteria:

1. They represent the smallest possible business logical unit of work.
2. Their execution duration is the shortest possible.

Both criteria are directed at improving performance. They improve performance at the client application with improved response time. More importantly, they improve concurrency and therefore overall performance and throughput on the server. This is because we have minimized the duration of the locks required to support the transaction.

Transaction Solutions

How do we implement these transactions with SQL Server? Basically there are three ways to issue the transaction:

1. Call a stored procedure in which you have embedded the transaction.
2. Build and execute a batch in which you have embedded the transaction.
3. Send the pieces of the transaction to the server in several transmissions, committing the transaction in the last transmission.

The last case was covered previously. It incurs too much overhead from multiple transmissions. It increases the duration of the locks held and of the transaction. *It is not the right way to do it.* Use it only in situations where performance and concurrency are not important and the expense and complication of development is important.

Executing a stored procedure is the next most obvious solution. The client application calls the stored procedure passing the required values for the transaction. In the stored procedure you validate the values, issue a BEGIN TRAN, and begin the data modifications. You include error checking for possible server errors for each of the modification statements, some logical analysis, and a COMMIT TRAN or ROLLBACK TRAN. The transaction is executed in its entirety at the server. There are no network transmissions during the execution of the transaction. Review the index design to provide optimal access times. This provides ideal transaction performance: the shortest possible duration.

A stored procedure is good for transactions that are known at compile time. That is, we know which tables are to be updated and we know how many rows are to be updated. While this is true much of the time, we have application problems which require us to determine the nature and content of the transaction at runtime. This is called a *dynamic transaction.*

Dynamic transactions occur in more complex situations where we have a business logical unit of work that is determined by the nature of the interaction of the user with the application. An order header with detail lines is an example. We may determine that the smallest transaction must include the order header and all of the detail lines. In this case, we cannot determine ahead of time how many detail lines there will be. Therefore, we cannot build a stored procedure. The client application must examine the environment (how many rows entered or updated) to determine the exact number and content of the modification statements to be issued.

Building a batch of Transact-SQL (T-SQL) is the next choice. Dynamic execution of SQL with EXECUTE is one version of this. The client application will build a batch. *Batch* is a formal concept when using the SQL Server. It is a single transmission to the database containing T-SQL. The content of the batch is determined by the application. Any tool that you use to build client applications should give you robust support for building T-SQL batches with any contents you like. This is key to gaining the flexibility you need to support all application situations.

To support our order header–detail transaction, the application identifies the order header row and the number and content of the modified detail lines. It builds a batch (usually a string variable) that contains the BEGIN TRAN, the required modification statements, any error handling required, any logic required, and ROLLBACK TRAN and COMMIT TRAN as necessary.

The client application sends this batch as a single transmission to the server. The server checks the syntax, parses, optimizes, and compiles the batch. Then it executes it. The execution of this batch gives us the same excellent transaction performance parameters as the stored procedure. It has to compile and optimize it, but we can't precompile something that hasn't been defined.

Stored procedures and single batches are the best ways to contain transactions. Any deviation from this model runs the risk of degrading performance. Of course, you can deviate from these choices, but it is helpful to understand the risks and performance degradations you will incur. Sometimes the risk is minimal and worth it. It depends on your application environment, the system load, the transaction rate, and your client development tool. The goal is to get optimal performance and concurrency from applications by doing the best job of engineering solutions that work efficiently with the SQL Server.

Relational Thinking, Relational Processing

Programming a relational database is a science. Isn't it? Or is it really more of an art? Few of us who use relational databases to solve business problems are truly versed in the mathematics of the relational model, which *is* scientific. If we were, we might be able to more accurately predict the optimal way to process any given business problem. Instead we study the tables, we look at the desired results, and with our experience we come up with a process that produces the correct results.

But some ways of writing a solution are better than others with respect to the reusability of the solution pattern, developer time, maintenance time, flexibility, and—last but not least—performance. How do we choose *how* to design a solution?

Designing *relational* instead of *procedural* solutions is one critical step in better utilizing the technology at hand. Relational databases are designed to manage *sets* of data. They are not optimal for managing lots of individual *rows* of data (the area where procedural processing excels). Can we take any, or perhaps every, problem and design a solution that uses data sets instead of data rows?

Certain solutions are fairly obvious to all of us. Everyone would write UPDATE ALL THE ROWS THAT . . . instead of using a cursor and looping—For Each Row: UPDATE. But what happens when the process gets very complicated? What solutions come to mind for the programmer? Many of the developers that we have dealt with move to a procedural solution when the going gets very tough. Why? Because it is the technique with which they have the most experience and training. Some of this experience and training comes from our prerelational days; many computer science graduates leave college with little or no relational training. We all need mentoring and study to develop the skills necessary to solve complex problems in a relational way.

Relational versus Procedural

Procedural processing looks vaguely like the following.

For each row:

♦ Based on logic and the data in the row apply Operation 1, and/or
♦ Based on logic and the data in the row apply Operation 2, and/or
♦ Based on logic and the data in the row apply Operation 3, and/or (and so on)

That is, find each row and loop through the possible operations on that row.

A relational view of the same problem would like more like this:

♦ Apply Operation A to all of the qualifying rows, then
♦ Apply Operation B to all of the qualifying rows, then
♦ Apply Operation C to all of the qualifying rows, then (and so on)

That is, instead of looping through the rows and applying operations, *step through the operations and apply to all the rows that qualify for that operation.* Operations 1 to 3 are not necessarily the same as Operations A to C. It is often necessary to recast the operation into relational terms.

Often the operation has to be decomposed when being applied to the whole set. For example, what was considered Operation A may require an Operation A.1 for NULL values and an Operation A.2 for non-NULL values. (Occasionally these different operations can be written to utilize one table scan, that is, be done at the same time.) The two set operations will still likely outperform the row operation, especially for large datasets. You may be required to create temporary datasets to control a midpoint in the processing. The ability to store interim datasets (the results of partial steps toward a solution) may improve your ability to design a relational solution.

Why would a relational solution be better? Well, for a very small data set, equal programming skills, and equal resulting code clarity, the procedural and relational solutions might be comparable. But if you have a medium to large dataset, or if the row looping operations are nested, the processing time of the relational method can be much faster (orders of magnitude). If we have learned to conceptualize set operations, the processing logic may also be clearer to other programmers.

Of course, there are some limits to replacing all procedural processing with relational processing. If the number of operations generated by decomposition begins to approach the number of rows, we might be losing ground toward our goal of improving performance and clarity. Some problems really *are* procedural. It happens. Remember that a relational database is optimized for set operations. Let it do its job.

An Example

Let's explore a problem whose shape and nature is very common because it is constructed on a three-tiered, master-detail relationship. This relationship is a natural structure in the entity/relationship model, and therefore common in our relational databases.

We have a manufacturing operation that creates products. We'll call the individual items *pieces*. These pieces are grouped after manufacturing into *pallets* and a group of pallets is tracked by the system in an object called a *batch* (see Figure 8.1). A batch relates to many pallets and a pallet relates to many pieces. We have a process that looks at all of the batches for a month and processes records for each batch, for each pallet, and for each piece. In this discussion, it is not really important what we do to them. (This could just as easily be an accounting or a personnel problem—anything.)

The Procedural Solution

This problem looks procedural to many, many programmers. Often because the people who actually work with the batches, pallets, and pieces have explained it that way. That's how they think of the processing sequence. The procedural solution outline looks like this:

- ♦ Get the list of batches
- ♦ For each batch
  - ♦ Process the batch record
  - ♦ Get the list of pallets
  - ♦ For each pallet
    - ♦ Process the pallet record
    - ♦ Get the list of pieces
    - ♦ For each piece
      - ♦ Process the piece record

This approach requires three cursors working against the data structures. We are essentially writing row-at-a-time processing. Is this bad? Well, it certainly

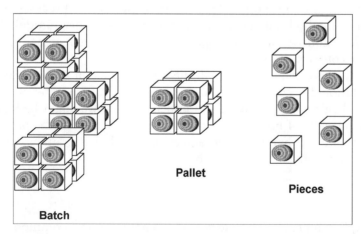

FIGURE 8.1 A batch is composed of many pallets; a pallet is composed of many pieces.

works and can give the correct answer. If the data sets are small, the performance may be acceptable. In this particular case, the programmer was originally told to process about 30 batches at a time. The performance wasn't great, but it was acceptable given the constraints, and the programmer developed a very clear understanding of the process. Incidentally, we discovered that, infrequently, the accountants reprocessed 1,000 batches at a time. Suddenly, the solution was totally unacceptable. It couldn't finish in a reasonable period of time (say, over the weekend). Actual mileage always varies. The point is that there is a significant growth in the time period as the number of batches grows. It may even be a geometric growth depending on the techniques available for getting the matching pallets and pieces.

The Relational Solution

The good news is that developing the procedural solution through design, research, and testing phases smoked out the process and we now have a very good idea what the process is supposed to do. (This is not to imply that you should write the procedural solution as an exercise, but we're trying to look on the bright side. The rewrite is not too time consuming.)

Now, when you've been looking at a problem from a procedural view, the next step—looking at it from a relational view—is sometimes tough. Let's walk through it.

Our simple starting relational version looks like this:

♦ Process all the batches.
♦ Process all the pallets; join to batches as required.
♦ Process all the pieces; join to pallets and batches as required.

This may be too simple. Conditional logic may be required to separate some distinct sets of batches, pallets, and pieces. So we decompose the operations as required.

♦ Process all the batches where X (where X is qualifying information embedded in joins and in conditional qualifications).
♦ Process all the batches where Y.
♦ Process all the pallets where Z and so on.

The processes will be different for each of the conditions to process the data correctly. Too much decomposition is bad, but it would have to be excessive. (To resolve borderline problems you have to thoroughly study access paths, optimization techniques, caching efficiency, and logical I/O required to properly optimize.) When decomposing the operations produces a high number of suboperations, the logic may become difficult to read and you may do too many scans through the data. You may *have* a procedural problem. But remember, there are many, many fewer procedural problems than we think.

It is also possible to gain performance by partially shifting to a more relational solution. For example, process the highest level with a cursor and move the other processes to set operations. Sometimes a particular level in the master/detail relationship will require a cursor. Even so, the rest can be optimized by moving to a relational solution.

Scalability

The most important quality that you can gain with this rewrite is improved performance. Many things contribute to the performance improvements:

- ◆ The individual count of SQL statements executed grows linearly when you issue multiple cursors against the inner loops of the processing as the number of batches grows. With the relational solution the number of individual SQL statements executed does not change.
- ◆ Transact-SQL is an interpreted language and processing conditional logic and cursors in an interpreted language affects code execution time.
- ◆ In pre-cursor implementations of our Transact-SQL programs, some of the gyrations used by programmers to isolate a single row (for example, "set row count 1" and "select data where the key value is the minimum value greater than the previous value") are inefficient.
- ◆ The server has more optimization leverage in large operations than with many small operations. That is, the server's ability to optimize access to a large single dataset is better (due to index structures, buffering, and so on) than getting the large dataset a row at a time.

In most cases, the procedural solution will hit a wall with performance as the datasets processed get larger. This will often catch a development team that tests against unrealistically small test datasets. The relational solution might outperform the procedural solution for small volumes, but the difference will grow as volumes increase. Actual volumes and time are relative and what works is always a factor of the demands for your specific problem.

While the principles here are very important and applicable in most situations, there are examples where cursor processing can be faster than what seems like set processing (but isn't really). An example is a nested query that ends up selecting a value for each row (correlated queries) where the nested query is doing a large and repetitive analysis. You need to understand the performance aspects of any given solution to apply performance-improving metrics to it.

Mentoring and Rules of Thumb

Our example is a relatively easy one, but very applicable to many application problems. This technique can also be applied to complex and exotic problems. The following problems are complex and can be solved either procedurally or relationally. The relational solution is much faster.

◆ Calculate all of the hours between two datetimes minus the hours on any given holiday or weekend for hundreds of thousands of rows where the datetime values themselves might be on a holiday or weekend.
◆ For a column with three values *A, B, C,* and a key that has multiple rows (duplicate key values, not the primary key): For each key value find the count of keys that have one or more *A* values; the count of keys that have one or more *B* values but no *A* values; and the count of keys that have one or more *C* values but no *A* or *B* values—all distinct sets.

Even as we describe them, they look like set operations. But they didn't look that way at first because procedural thinking is natural for us. Thinking relationally is harder and less natural, and we must learn to do it.

How do we learn to solve problems relationally? The same way you get to Carnegie Hall: Practice, practice, practice! The best way is to find, hire, or train a Mentor (create a titled position). This experienced program designer can work with others to extend their understanding of efficient design techniques. It is important to train developers in the more sophisticated relational operations: group by, use of temp tables, outer joins, and correlated queries. After that, concepts of mathematical transformations and characteristic functions provide a continuing learning path. A good mastery of these techniques puts the proper tools into the hands of the developer.

It's a good idea to define a set of guidelines for T-SQL usage. Certain usage configurations flag possible problems for a programmer's manager to see when reviewing early design plans. Assign a senior technical review person (mentor) to review the solution. In pre-cursor days, the big flag was SET ROW COUNT. It should not be allowed in any T-SQL program without a sign-off from a senior technical person. It is often an indication that the programmer cannot think of any relational solutions which may exist. SET ROW COUNT is sometimes useful, and the senior technical reviewer will recognize and authorize proper usage.

Other language elements also require technical review. The most important of these is the use of cursors—particularly nested cursors. Have them reviewed. Technical review is required anyway, and the technical reviewer can explore problems with the developer and provide education along the way. Very difficult problems almost always benefit from multiple minds working on the solution. The final solution may have the best from both developers and be far better than any one programmer's design.

New ways of thinking promote new ways of solving problems. Moving to more relational solutions buys us measurable improvements in our applications. For those of us who like technical challenges and learning, there is still much to learn about the optimal use of the SQL language. It continues to challenge us in interesting ways. For those of us interested in cost efficiency and performance, we must remember that a continuing investment in education and mentoring improves the overall efficiency of an organization and the success of its applications.

9

Infrastructure

It must be understood that Windows NT is actually a distributed operating system. Although Windows NT is an implementing vehicle for client/server systems, Windows NT itself is implemented with the client/server paradigm. Internally within Windows NT, protected subsystems use the client/server paradigm to communicate with the Windows NT kernel. Moving upward in the Windows NT architecture, Windows NT itself is the server and the individual application servers such as SQL Server, SNA Server, and System Management Server function only as clients of Windows NT, even though they act in the server capacity for client users. Numerous servers other than SQL Server are mentioned or discussed in this book. Some of these are the Windows Internet Naming Service (WINS), alert servers, mail servers, backup domain controllers, browsers, and replication (publication, subscription, and distribution). There are others, but the point is that Windows NT is not monolithic. If SQL Server is installed on a machine with other servers, obviously there will be competition for machine resources and network bandwidth.

It is important to know how all these servers and services interact. For example, later on in this chapter we go through the details of how Windows NT resolves NetBIOS and TCP/IP names. The exact mechanism is important, since knowing how the mechanisms work can aid the system administrator in configuring the network, or diagnosing problems. SQL Server probably needs network bandwidth more than any other server, and an understanding of where that bandwidth is spent is necessary to reclaim it.

Features such as Domain Host Control Protocol (DHCP) significantly reduce configuration errors and the probability of misdirected data or broadcast storms. Some sections in this chapter have an *issues* subsection on trade-offs and implementation considerations to enhance SQL Server performance.

Network Models

Complex systems cannot be built without defining models or abstractions. There are many models in the networking world; some are vendor originated and others are derived from communal efforts.

OSI Model

The *Open System Interconnect* (*OSI*) Reference Model document, started in 1980 and delivered in 1984, is published by the International Standards Organization (ISO). This model forms the basis for nearly all networking models. The OSI Model can be used directly, used for a basis of comparison, or modified. It is composed of seven layers, each of which independently performs its own unique function before communicating with the subsequent layer.

Application layer	A window for application processes to access the network.
Presentation layer	Network translator. Encryption and compression are done here. Redirectors operate at this level. See the next section for a complete explanation of redirector functions.
Session layer	Node name recognition, security, task synchronization with checkpoints in the data stream are accomplished at this layer.
Transport layer	Data is delivered error free, in sequence without losses.
Network layer	Message addressing, translating logical address to physical.
Data link layer	Places data frames from the Network Layer onto the physical medium.
Physical layer	Medium—twisted pair Ethernet cable, radio waves, and so on.

When all layers of the OSI Model are considered, there is not one single protocol driver. Each layer performs its own task, adds its own information to the resultant message, and passes the message down to the next level. It is a collection of *protocol drivers* which constitutes a system. Figure 9.1 illustrates what happens to data as it passes downward through the seven levels to the network.

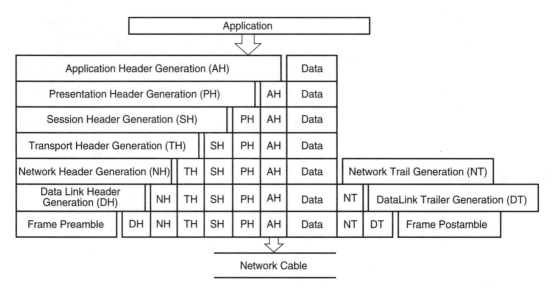

FIGURE 9.1 OSI Layers and message generation.

IEEE Models

The IEEE 802 project divided the OSI model into the logical link control (LLC) and media access control (MAC) layers at the data link level. The media access control consists of standards defined in IEEE Project 802 documents 802.3, 802.4, and 802.5, which represent Ethernet (CSMA/CD), token bus, and token ring, respectively (see Figure 9.2).

IEEE Project 802 Standards Documents

- ◆ 802.1 OSI Model and Network Management
- ◆ 802.2 Logical Link Control
- ◆ 802.3 CSMA/CD (Ethernet)
- ◆ 802.4 Token Bus
- ◆ 802.5 Token Ring

Interface Models—NDIS and TDI

With the diversity of network interface cards, actually getting a system to communicate was almost an art. To resolve interfacing problems, in 1989 Microsoft and 3Com developed a standard for communication between the MAC Layer and the higher protocol drivers in the OSI model. This standard is known today as the *Network Device Interface Specification* (*NDIS*). Another interface was defined above the protocols, at the top of the OSI transport layer. Protocol drivers are now sandwiched between the transport driver interface (TDI) and NDIS (see Figure 9.3). An example of the standard in use today is the

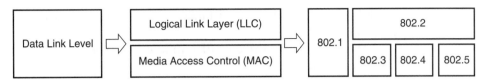

FIGURE 9.2 Redefinition of OSI Data Link Layer by Project 802.

NWLink protocol, which is an NDIS-compliant version of the Internetwork Packet Exchange (IPX/SPX) compatible protocol. TDI is now a standard interface for protocols and NDIS is a standard interface for adapter card drivers. This advance in network modeling paved the way for the protocol stacks used today in Windows NT and Windows 95, which can not only use more than one protocol at a time but can use more than one protocol on the same network adapter card. This capability is available on enterprise systems such as Open VMS but is not normally available to clients of Windows NT. This interface standard for protocols simplifies the binding process, which translates to fewer management issues. *Wrapper* functions used to surround network adapter card drivers complete the model.

Microsoft enhancements to the OSI model consist of two interface standards. The first interface standard is TDI. It is at the transport level which assures that all protocols will use a common interface. The other addition is at the MAC level (IEEE Project 802 split the data link level into LLC and MAC levels, as mentioned earlier), which provides a common interface for network adapter card drivers.

Microsoft then added a server-side redirector which provides the interface between the I/O manager and the appropriate transport driver interface (TDI), the common interface to the protocol drivers. An example of a client-side redirector is VREDIR.386, the Windows for Workgroups Network Redi-

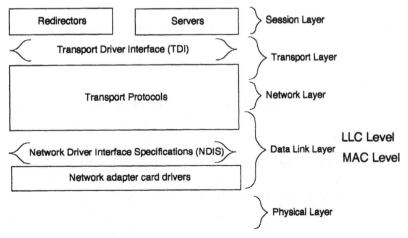

FIGURE 9.3 TDI and NDIS, Microsoft additions to the modified OSI model.

rector which supports Named Pipes over NWLink and is found on the Windows NT 3.5 CDROM.

The client-side redirector of Windows for Workgroups performs the following processes:

♦ Domain logons
♦ Logon scripts
♦ Messaging
♦ Named Pipes
♦ Remote procedure calls (RPC)

Routing Models—MUP and MRP

But we're not quite through with our abstractions. This time our model has higher functionality and is expanded. In the previous TDI-NDIS model, the *Servers* box was used to denote a generic network file system definition. We'll use the user application model shown in Figure 9.4 to expand that definition with a choice of two APIs for interfacing, I/O API or WNet API.

NCP, SMB, NFS, and VINES are indeed file systems, but not in the common sense. They are *network file systems*. As can be seen from the model, more than one file system may be active simultaneously in Windows NT. (At a lower level of functionality, we could say that more than one protocol is active simultaneously.) The default Windows NT requestor can simultaneously access other workstations and other network file systems, each using a different protocol. The Multiple UNC Provider (MUP), a program which resolves server *share-points*, distinguishes between the different file systems. UNC is the Universal Naming Convention for names such as *Server**share_point*. (Sorry for the confusion here since we have an acronym embedded within an acronym.)

The other application model uses WNet API for access to third-party network file systems through the Multiple Provider Router (MRP). In this model, third-party vendors may supply a vendor-specific interface for accessing the network (see Figure 9.5).

Issues

We have discussed historical issues here, but are they relevant to SQL Server? The answer is yes. We'll discuss what protocols to use later, but consider the following for now:

♦ All network interface cards (NICs) should be NDIS compliant. A NIC may work if it is not NDIS compliant; however, the performance may be an issue. Version 2.0.1 of NDIS allows a single machine to have as many as four network adapter cards installed. Each adapter card can support a maximum of four protocols with a limit of eight total protocols for the

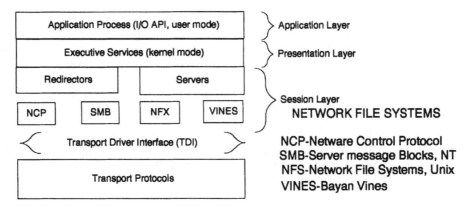

FIGURE 9.4 User access to Multiple UNC Provider.

machine. There is no adapter card or protocol limit with NDIS version 3.0. Windows NT 3.5x supports device drivers and protocols written to NDIS 3.0.

- ◆ If possible, all NICs should be 32-bit. 8-bit, 16-bit, and 32-bit NICs are available. If the bus for the machine is 32-bit, then the NIC should be 32-bit. An 8-bit NIC will have four times the internal software overhead.
- ◆ Why did we mention Universal Name Convention (UNC) provider? Because name resolution, whether at the NetBIOS or TCP/IP level, requires network bandwidth. In a following section we'll discuss *name resolution,* which can result in a loss of network bandwidth when not properly done.
- ◆ Since the server may be in a heterogeneous environment, there may be multiple protocols. One Windows NT tuning trick is to reorder the protocols on the protocol stack from the Windows NT *Control Panel* and place the most active protocol at the top of the stack. A better choice is to configure SQL Server for only one protocol. In *Direct-Hosting,* discussed later, bypassing a layer of the OSI model results in a 20 percent performance improvement. This, of course, assumes that SQL Server is dedicated to one machine, and a remote bridge is used for protocol conversion. If most of the network traffic is NetBEUI, then why should those clients suffer overhead costs of possibly less frequently used protocols such as TCP/IP? The *Multi-Protocol* feature of SQL Server offers the additional functionality of listening on multiple protocols simultaneously, but it is at the cost of network bandwidth.

    If the network appears to be randomly unreliable, investigate the protocol stacks. The most active protocol should always be at the top of the stack. What is more important is that the protocol stack order be maintained for *all* systems. Tuning the protocol stack on one system may effectively detune another system.

◆ If multiple protocols are required, consider using more than one NIC. This creates subnets by default and is useful for network load balancing.

◆ There may be more than one frame type (see earlier, IEEE models 802.2 vs. 802.3). There is also a NetWare issue. NetWare 3.x uses the IEEE 802.3 Ethernet frame type while NetWare 4.x uses the 802.2 Ethernet frame type. Windows NT will support 2 frame types bound to a NIC (binding associates a protocol with a NIC).

◆ Direct Hosting can realize a 20 percent performance improvement for the NWLink IPX protocol. This is obtained by bypassing the NetBIOS layer of the protocol stack. The following are considerations for direct hosting:

1. Windows for Workgroups 3.11 machines will direct host with each other by default.
2. Windows for Workgroups 3.11 will direct host with Windows NT 3.5x only if the client initiates the session. This is because the implementation of direct hosting bypasses the NetBIOS layer and the Windows NT Redirector and interfaces directly to the Windows NT Server. If Windows NT initiates the link, it is at the behest of the redirector, and consequently it will use NetBIOS (see Figures 9.6 and 9.7).
3. Windows NT Server 3.5x and Windows NT Workstation cannot direct host each other.
4. The Windows for Workgroups *System.ini* cannot have the statement *DirectHost=NO*.
5. The Windows for Workgroup machine must be bound to the NWLink IPX/SPX protocol and not the NWLink NetBIOS protocol.

Recalling our networking model, we quickly realize that the ability to have multiple protocols and multiple frame types is a significant performance issue. Microsoft states that a 20 percent increase in performance occurs when using *Direct Hosting* which bypasses a layer of the OSI Model.

Application Process (Wnet API)		
Multi Provider Router (MPR)		
LANManWorkstation	Provider DLL	LANManServer
User Mode		
Kernel Mode		
Windows NT Redirector	Other Redirector	Windows NT Server

FIGURE 9.5 Third-party access to Multiple Provider Router.

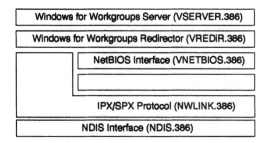

FIGURE 9.6 Client WFWG Direct Hosting bypassing NetBIOS.

Windows NT Server	Windows NT Redirector

TDI

NWNBLINK.SYS	NWLNKSPX.SYS

NWLNKIPX.SYS

NDIS

FIGURE 9.7 Windows NT Direct Hosting bypassing NetBIOS.

Network Protocols

Windows NT 3.5x supports the TCP/IP, NWLink, NetBEUI, and DLC protocols. Within these protocols are various IPC mechanisms that enable Windows NT to communicate with Digital (DECNet), MAC, Novell, Unix, and OS/2 clients. Windows NT is a relatively new product but appears to be much more mature considering the number of supported protocols. SQL Server can use NetBEUI, NWLink, or TCP/IP. DLC is used for network printers and is not used by SQL Server.

DLC	Data link control protocol
NetBEUI	NetBIOS Extended User Interface protocol
NWLink	Novell IPX/SPX compatible protocol
TCP/IP	Terminal Control protocol/Internet protocol (Internet)

Data Link Control (DLC)

DLC is a protocol for communicating with IBM computers. It is also used to communicate with printers such as the Hewlett-Packard IIISi that use a network adapter card to connect to the network directly. Windows NT DLC works with either token ring or Ethernet MAC drivers and can transmit and receive Digital/Intel/Xerox (DIX) format frames when bound to an Ethernet MAC.

NetBEUI Frame (NBF)

Some definitions are in order before starting any discussion of NBF:

NetBEUI   NetBIOS Extended User Interface, a transport layer protocol base, which originally included the NetBIOS interface.

NetBIOS   A programming interface. Although included with the original NetBEUI, the interface is now used for protocols other than Net-BEUI by higher-level programs such as print and file services.

NBF   NetBEUI Framing, an enhanced version of NetBEUI.

NBT   NetBIOS on TCP/IP (see TCP/IP).

NBF is the native Windows NT protocol and as such enables interprocess communication with NetBIOS, Named Pipes, Mailslot, NetDDE, RPC over Net-BIOS, and RPC over Named Pipes using NBF. NBF does not support sockets or RPC over Sockets programming.

NetBEUI has two limitations:

1. It cannot be routed since a network address isn't included with the computer name.
2. NetBEUI is limited to a maximum of 254 sessions. The workstation and server services overcome this problem by writing directly to the terminal driver interface (TDI), which is 32-bit. However a general solution to this problem is provided by the definition of NET-BIOS.SYS. This is a matrix of TDI handles organized by local session number (LSN, 1 to 254). Each process can have up to 254 sessions per local area network adapter (LANA) number, not just a total of 254 sessions. Each binding path is represented by a LANA number.

NetBEUI and NBF provide for both *connectionless* and *connection-oriented* traffic. Connectionless traffic may be *reliable* or *unreliable*. *Unreliable connectionless messaging* is used for NetBEUI or NBF. No guarantee of delivery is made and the sender is not notified that the message has been sent. If the sender *is* notified that the message has been sent and not when it has been delivered, then it is called *reliable connectionless messaging*. If the sender *isn't* notified when the message is sent, then it is unreliable connectionless. In either case, delivery is not guaranteed. This mechanism is similar to the user datagram protocol (UDP) of TCP/IP. *Connection-oriented* messages will always have an acknowledgment and delivery is guaranteed.

NBF has been enhanced with the adaptive sliding window protocol (ASWP). A sender is able to dynamically tune the number of LLC frames (see OSI previously) sent using ASWP. If the network is lightly loaded and if too few frames are sent, then bandwidth is unused.

If the network is heavily loaded and too many frames are sent before an acknowledgment, it can only exacerbate an already bad situation. To explain, assume that the window size is 10 frames. This means that 10 frames will be transmitted before an acknowledgment is given. If the network is heavily loaded, the frames which are not received in time are considered to be *lost* frames. Retransmission is not just a single frame, but the number of frames determined by the window size will only make a congested network worse. Limiting the window size will throttle the traffic and reduce congestion.

Tuning

NetBEUI is the native protocol of Windows NT 3.5x and previous Windows ancestors. Since Microsoft controls the architecture, continual refinement has added numerous features including self-tuning. However, problems can develop. We'll look at registry entries which can be set; however, nothing should be done without first analyzing output from the Windows NT Performance Monitor and understanding the documentation in the Windows NT Resource Kit. These parameters are usually set when:

♦ The network is slow.
♦ The network is fast (fiber optic, FDDI). Time parameters default to Ethernet speed of 10Mb/s while FDDI is 100Mb/s.
♦ The machines on the network are slow.
♦ Initial default configuration values are too low and the actual usage is much higher than the initial configuration. Changes in this class of parameter are always made at the expense of memory and should be considered carefully. If one is changed, then others may need to be changed. For example, if the number of buffers is increased, then the number of packets must be increased.
♦ The network is unreliable.
♦ A parameter has *No Limit*, and it is desired to place a limit on that resource.

Before making any parameter adjustments, use the performance monitor to analyze what appears to be a problem. We say "what appears to be," because you may be looking at a symptom and not the actual problem. Try to analyze the apparent problem from different perspectives. If you reach the same conclusion when analyzing from different perspectives, then you've probably identified the problem. Quite often parameters are interrelated, and changing one may require a change in another parameter. If possible, change only one parameter at a time. Observe the network under normal load conditions before deciding that the change is acceptable.

Another issue is that network timing parameters are typically set for Ethernet which is 10Mb/s. If you are using fiber optic (FDDI) which is 100Mb/s, then changes are certainly merited.

Use caution before changing any registry values. Take proper precautions such as backing up the system. If there is any doubt as to your capability to edit the registry, then don't do it. An improperly edited registry can result in failure of the operating system. The registry editor, **Regedt32**, may be run from the *Run* window of the *File* menu within the *File Manager*. The registry parameters may be found at:

HKEY_LOCAL_MACHINE\SYSTEM\CurrentControlSet\Services\NBF\Parameters

AddNameQueryRetries	Retry count. Adjust this only if NBF is registering addresses on a network that drops many packets. The default is 5.
AddNameQueryTimeout	Timeout interval. Adjust this only if NBF is registering addresses on a slow network or on a network with slow computers. The default is 5000000 (500 ms, in 100-ns units).
GeneralRetries	Retry count. Adjust this only if NBF is registering addresses on a network that drops many packets. The default is 5.
DefaultT1Timeout	Acknowledge wait interval. Adjust this only for slow networks or slow computers. The default is 6000000 (600 ms in 100-ns units).
DefaultT2Timeout	Companion to T1. Typically half or less of T1. The default is 1500000 (150 ms in 100-ns units).
DefaultTiTimeout	Inactivity timer. Adjust only on a network which is slow or uses slow computers or the network is unreliable. The default is 300000000 (30 s in 100-ms units).
GeneralTimeout	Specifies the time between successive STATUS_QUERY and FIND_NAME requests. The default is 500000 (500 ms in 100-ns units).
InitAddresses	Specifies the number of initial addresses to allocate within memory. Addresses correspond to NetBIOS names. Default is 0, no limit.
InitAddressFiles	An address file is a client using TDI. Default is 0, no limit.
InitConnections	The number of initial NetBIOS connections. Defaults to 1.
InitLinks	Number of initial LLC (IEEE Project 802 changes to the OSI model) links. Defaults to 2.
InitReceiveBuffers	Specifies the initial number of receive buffers to allocate for NDIS communication. Defaults to 5.

InitReceivePackets	Specifies the initial number of receive packets to allocate for NDIS communication. Defaults to 10.
InitRequests	Initial NBF requests. Used for in-progress connect requests, remote adapter status, find name status, and so on. Defaults to 5.
InitSendPackets	Initial number of send packets. Default is 30.
InitUIFrames	Initial number of UI frames to allocate. Used for connectionless services such as datagrams. Default is 5.
LLCMaxWindowSize	Specifies the number of LLC frames that can be sent before polling and waiting for a response. Reduce this value if the network is unreliable. Default is 10.
LLCRetries	The number of retries NBF will poll a remote workstation after a T1 timeout. Default is 8.
MaxAddresses	The maximum number of addresses that NBF will allocate. Each address is associated with a unique NetBIOS name. Default is 0, no limit.
MaxAddressFiles	Each address corresponds to a client opening an address. Default is 0, no limit.
MaxConnections	Maximum number of connections. This value is not related to SQL Server connection count, but to the number of NetBIOS connections. Default is 0, no limit.
Maximum-IncomingFrames	Sometimes used to control incoming NBF frames before sending an acknowledgment. Set when Microsoft LAN Manager has a low value for maxout at the client. Corresponds roughly to **maxin** of Microsoft LAN Manager. Default is 2.
MaxLinks	Number of remote adapter links. Default is 0, no limit.
MaxRequests	Maximum number of NBF operations. Default is 0, no limit.
NameQueryRetries	NAME_QUERY retry count. Default is 3. Adjust for networks which drop packets.
NameQueryTimeout	Adjust for slow machines or a slow network. Default is 5000000 (500 ms in 100-ns units).

QueryWithout-SourceRouting	Token ring only. Tells NBF to send half the queries without routing information. Default is 0, false.
UseDixOverEthernet	DIX is the original ethernet. NBF cannot talk to the standard IEEE 802.3. Default is 0, false.
WanNameQueryRetries	When used with RAS, the number of times a NAME_QUERY will be retried. Default is 5.

Issues

So far, we have identified several issues for NBF:

♦ Since NBF is not routable, a practical network is probably 100 or fewer nodes. The stated Microsoft guideline for usage as a departmental network is 20 to 200 nodes. For very large networks, use TCP/IP.

♦ When configuring NBF, all machines should have approximately the same computer speed. This also means that all network adapter cards should be equivalent.

♦ All clients should have the same level of software and identical configuration parameters when possible. An example of this is the registry parameter **MaximumIncomingFrames** which corresponds roughly to the LAN Manager parameter **maxin**. Values in the registry are really for *one* implementation of NBF. It won't do any good to have two network interface cards, one with the slow machines and the other with the fast machines, since there is only one set of configuration parameters in the registry.

♦ If direct hosting is attempted and fails (machine hangs), then an older implementation of WFW may be in use. This happens when older implementations of Windows for Workgroups do not provide adequate named pipe support when running direct-hosted IPX. If Named Pipes is not needed by the client, then in the registry for the Server Service at the server, set the registry entry **EnableWFW311DirectIpx** to false. It can be found in the registry at:

```
HKEY_LOCAL_MACHINE\SYSTEM\CurrentControlSet\Services\
        LanmanServer\Parameters
```

Since this is being done at the server, direct hosting will be disabled for the entire LAN.

♦ NBF may be the fastest Windows NT protocol since the default buffer size is 4096, while other protocols use smaller buffer sizes. (Note: SPX-II can use blocks up to 4096.) A special factor to consider is the switch to *Raw Mode* which is done automatically using 64K Server Message Blocks (see Interprocess Communication, Named Pipes, below).

♦ NBF uses a sliding window, which means that each message is not given acknowledgment (ACK) on an individual basis but only after a number of messages have been received. The size of this receive window is based upon the value of **MaximumIncomingFrames** in the registry. The adaptive sliding window protocol (ASWP) tries to determine the best window size for current network conditions and will change this value dynamically.

Resolving Problems

When the NBF protocol is in use by SQL Server, the SQL Server utilities **readpipe** and **makepipe** can be used to test the integrity of named pipe services, the *interprocess communication* mechanism for NBF.

makepipe [/**h**] [/**w**] [**p** *pipename*] where

/**h**	Displays usage.
/**w**	The wait time in seconds between read and write. The default is 0.
/**p**	The pipe name. The default name is **abc**.

readpipe /**S***servername*/**D***string* [/**n**] [/**q**] [/**w**] [/**t**] [/**p** *pipename*] [/**h**]

/**S***servername*	The name of the server where you just ran **makepipe**.
/**D***string*	A test character string.
/**n**	Number of iterations.
/**q**	Without this option, **readpipe** reads the pipe and waits.
/**w**	Wait time to pause during polling. The default time is 0.
/**t**	This overrides polling and asks for Transact SQL named pipes.
/**p***pipename*	Pipe name.
/**h**	Display activity.

To use these utilities, run **makepipe** from one machine as a command line operation, then go to another machine and try to communicate using **readpipe**.

NWLink

NWLink is the Microsoft implementation of both the internetwork packet exchange (IPX) network layer and sequenced packet exchange (SPX) transport protocols. NWNBLink is the NetBIOS implementation within NWLink.

In Windows NT 3.5x, Microsoft provides *direct hosting* which completely bypasses the NetBIOS interface, allowing direct access to the IPX binding. This significantly improves network performance; however, it can only be initiated by a Windows NT client such as Windows for Workgroups 3.11. Since the Windows NT Redirector does not support direct hosting, a Windows NT computer cannot initiate a direct hosting session. A protected mode redirector, VREDIR386, is supplied with Windows NT on a CD-ROM for use with Windows for Workgroups direct hosting. IPX enables direct hosting by supporting Socket IDs for use by applications. Novell has a NetBIOS implementation within the IPX protocol. The Microsoft implementation of this protocol (NBIPX) can be bypassed when both a Socket ID and the IPX protocol is available. These sockets are implemented at the Windows NT Server Service level, enabling a bypass of the Windows NT Redirector. This is equivalent to bypassing the transport layer in the OSI Model and connecting directly to the session layer.

NWLink can be used with many different frame types on a network. Ethernet, token ring, FDDI, and ArcNet topologies are supported. Some caution should be used however. On Ethernet networks, the standard framing format for Netware 2.2 and Netware 3.1 is 802.3. Starting with Netware 4.0, the default frame format is 802.2. On Windows NT, both frame types of NWLink can be bound to the same network interface card. Even though Windows NT can bind NWLink to more than one network interface card, Windows NT is not capable of acting as an IPX router.

NWLnkSPX Tuning

In general Microsoft implementations of Novell IPX/SPX protocols are not tunable, since they must agree with the Novell host strategy. Configuration parameters may be set; however, very little else can be done. Because of this, even though IPX/SPX is routable, every packet requires an acknowledgment. On a very large WAN, this becomes a problem. If the implementation is SPX II, however, then windowing (sending acknowledgments only after a fixed number of packets have been sent) and the ability to set a maximum frame size are supported in the Microsoft NWLink implementation. Global SPX parameters in the registry that may be of interest are listed below. The registry editor, ***Regedt32***, may be run from the *Run* window of the *File* menu within the *File Manager*. These parameters may be found in the registry at:

```
HKEY_LOCAL_MACHINE\SYSTEM\CurrentControlSet\Services\NWLnkSPX\Parameters
```

ConnectionCount	Probe count for remote connection attempts. This is a protocol connection count and is not related to the SQL Server connection count. Related parameter is **ConnectionTimeout**. Default is 10.
ConnectionTimeout	Elapsed time between probe attempts. Related parameter is **ConnectionCount**. Default is 2 (1 s in 0.5-s units).

InitPackets	Initial packet allocation count. Default is 5.
InitialRetransmissionTime	Specified wait time for a probe. Default is 1 in 0.5-s units.
KeepAliveCount	Number of probe attempts before declaring a timeout. Related parameter is **KeepAliveTimeout**. Default is 8.
KeepAliveTimeout	Specified wait time before sending a probe. Related parameter is **KeepAliveCount**. Default is 12, 6 s in 0.5-s units.
MaxPackets	Maximum number of packets that SPX will allocate. Default is 30.
MaxPacketSize	Maximum packet size which may be used when negotiating packet size. The correct size will be used by SPX-II if it is less than **MaxPacketSize**. Default is 4096.
RetransmissionCount	Number of probes to send while waiting for acknowledgment of data. Default is 8.
SpxSocketEnd	End of range to autoassign sockets. Default is 0x7fff.
SpxSocketStart	Range start for autoassigned sockets. Default is 0x4000.
SpxSocketUniqueness	Number of sockets to reserve when autoassigning. Default is 8.
WindowSize	Specifies the window size for SPX packets. Default is 4.

NWNBLink Tuning for Novell NetBIOS, Microsoft Extensions

Microsoft supports the Novell implementation of NetBIOS with the NWNB-Link protocol. When NWNBLink is connected to a Novell server, then communication must adhere to the Novell NetBIOS protocol implementation. However, when using NWNBLink to communication with another Windows NT machine, Microsoft has enhanced the protocol so that under certain conditions (both machines sending data) a separate acknowledgment isn't required for the data. This is done by *piggybacking* the acknowledgment of each packet received with another outgoing data packet. NWNBLink can determine whether or not the other machine uses a Novell NetBIOS implementation. If it doesn't and the other machine is a Windows NT machine, these features will be used automatically. The improvement comes about not by reducing the amount of transmitted information, but because the *acknowledge wait* period is removed from the communication cycle. The following registry values are unique to the Microsoft extensions of the Novell NetBIOS (NWNB-

Link) and are not applicable to NetWare systems. Registry editing precautions should be followed as previously discussed. The values may be found in the registry at:

```
HKEY_LOCAL_MACHINE\SYSTEM\CurrentControlSet\Services\NWNBLink\Parameters
```

AckDelayTime	Delayed acknowledgment timer value. Default is 250 ms.
AckWindow	Specifies the number of frames to receive before sending an acknowledgment to the sender. If both sender and receiver are on a fast link, then **AckWindow** may be turned off. If 0 then no acknowledgment to sender. If sender is on a fast link and receiver is on a slow link, then the sender may keep sending frames continually by forcing acknowledgments. Default is 2. **AckWindowThreshold** is a related field. Default is 2.
AckWindow-Threshold	Threshold value for the round-trip time. If 0 then NWNBLink relies on **AckWindow**. Used by NWNBLink as a basis for determining if it is necessary to send automatic acknowledgments. Default is 500 ms.
EnablePiggy-BackAck	When set to 1, there is no back traffic. When sender and receiver are not participating in a two-way conversation, then set **EnablePiggyBackAck** to 0. There is no acknowledgment with this approach and the message is equivalent to the user datagram protocol of TCP/IP (see following, UDP). An example is the continual updating of a stock quotation which doesn't require an acknowledgment.
Extensions	If set, then use the Microsoft extensions as defined here. The default is 1, true.
RcvWindowMax	The maximum number of frames that can be received at one time. Default is 4.

NWNBLink Tuning for Novell NetBIOS

These parameters are for the Microsoft implementation of Novell NetBIOS and do not contain special extensions by Microsoft. The parameters are located in the registry in the same section as discussed previously.

```
HKEY_LOCAL_MACHINE\SYSTEM\CurrentControlSet\Services\NWNBLink\Parameters
```

BroadcastCount	Number of times to send a broadcast. Defaults to 3. No entry is equivalent to the default.

BroadcastTimeout	Time interval in 0.5 s between sending find-name requests. Defaults to 1, 0.5 s in 0.5-s units.
ConnectionCount	Number of times to send a connection probe. If **Internet** is set to 1, then the value is doubled. Related parameter is **ConnectionTimeout**. Default is 5. No entry is equivalent to the default.
ConnectionTimeout	The time in 0.5 s between sending probes when initiating a session. Default is 2, 1 s in 0.5-s units. No entry is equivalent to the default.
InitialRetransmission-Time	Time in ms for the retransmission time. Default is 500. No entry is equivalent to the default.
Internet	Specifies changing the packet for class 0x04 to 0x14(Novell WAN broadcast). Default is 1, true. No entry is equivalent to default.
KeepAliveCount	Number of times to send a session-alive frame before timing out with no response. Related parameter is **KeepAliveTimeout**. Default is 8. No entry is equivalent to the default value.
KeepAliveTimeout	The time in 0.5 s between session-alive frames. Related parameter is **KeepAliveCount**. Default is 60, s. No entry is equivalent to the default value.
RetransmitMax	Maximum retransmission count before assuming that the link is defective. Default is 8. No entry is equivalent to the default value.

NWLinkIPX Tuning

Novell internetwork packet exchange (IPX) is routable and functions at the OSI network level while Novell sequenced packet exchange (SPX) functions at the OSI transport layer and is not routable. Tuning parameters for IPX may be found in the registry at:

```
HKEY_LOCAL_MACHINE\SYSTEM\CurrentControlSet\Services\NWLinkIPX\Parameters
```

ConnectionCount	Number of times that a probe is sent when SPX is trying to connect to a remote node. Default is 10. Related parameter is **ConnectionTimeout**.
ConnectionTimeout	The time in 0.5 s between connection probes when SPX is trying to connect. Default is 2, 1 s.

DedicatedRouter When set to 1 (true), this computer is a dedicated router and will not have services running on it. Default is 0, false.

DisableDialin-Netbios When set to 1 (true), IPX should prevent NetBIOS type 20 packets from going out over dial-in WAN lines. Only set false when a NetBIOS application must connect to a remote computer over a dial-in WAN line. Default is 1, true.

DisableDialoutSap When set to 1 (true), SAP announcements are not sent over the WAN. Reduces router-to-router SAP traffic and allows the *Gateway Service for Netware* or the *Client Service for Netware* to correctly discover servers on the WAN. Default is 0, false.

EthernetPad-ToEven When set to 1 (true), Ethernet cards should set frames to an even number of bytes to accommodate ODI drivers which are not character-oriented. Default is 1, true.

InitDatagrams Number of datagrams initially allocated by IPX. Related to **MaxDatagrams**. Default is 10.

KeepAliveCount Number of times a keep-alive probe is sent before timing out with no response. Related parameter is **KeepAliveTimeout**. Default is 8.

KeepAliveTimeout Time between probes sent by SPX to verify the link is still active. Related parameter is **KeepAliveCount**. Default is 12, 6 s specified in 0.5-s increments.

MaxDatagrams Maximum number of datagrams that IPX will allocate. Related parameter is **InitDatagrams**. Default is 50.

RipAgeTime IPX maintains a Routing Internet Protocol (RIP) cache. This time is the interval before IPX requests a RIP update. When a RIP announcement is received, the time is reset. Default is 5 min, specified in min.

RipCount The number of times the RIP protocol layer will attempt to find a route on the network before giving up. Related parameter is **RipTimeout**. Default is 5.

RipTableSize Number of buckets in the RIP has table. To expand this, it should be a prime number. Default is 7.

RipTimeout	Time between RIP packet requests when trying to find a route on the network. Related parameter is **RipCount**. Default is 1 in 0.5-s (0.5 s).
RipUsageTime	Minutes to wait before an entry in the RIP cache will be deleted. Timer is reset when a packet is sent to the remote computer. Default is 15 in min.
SingleNetwork-Active	When set to 1 (true) either the LAN or the WAN may be active, but not both. Used as an aid for *Gateway Service for Netware* or *Client Service for Netware* to correctly locate Netware servers on the WAN when dialed in. Default is 0, false.
SocketStart	Start of IPX autoassigned sockets. Related parameters are **SocketEnd** and **SocketUniqueness**. Default is 0x4000.
SocketEnd	End of address range when IPX is autoassigning sockets. Related parameters are **SocketStart** and **SocketUniqueness**. Default is 0x8000.
SocketUniqueness	Specifies the number of sockets reserved when autoassigning sockets. Default is 8, which means autoassign will start at 0x4008. Related parameters are **SocketStart** and **SocketEnd**.
SourceRouteUsage-Time	Number of minutes an unused entry can remain in the token ring source routing cache before it is flushed. Default is 10.
VirtualNetwork-Number	Virtual network number for this computer. Default is 0. Range is 0 to 4294967295.
WindowSize	SPX uses this value in the allocation field of the SPX packet to tell the remote how many frames are available for receiving data. Default is 4.

TCP/IP

For operation in a heterogeneous environment, Microsoft has provided Windows NT 3.x with a rather complete implementation of the transmission control protocol/Internet protocol (TCP/IP). This obviates the need for scaffolding products such as SQL Bridge (see following). Some features such as domain host control protocol (DHCP) and Windows Internet naming service (WINS) actually go beyond nominal TCP/IP implementations. DHCP dramatically simplifies TCP/IP configuration management issues and relieves the user of configuration responsibilities. WINS, while a Microsoft-specific implementation, is implemented very efficiently. With WINS, Microsoft has given TCP/IP a higher level of functionality with the implementation of NetBIOS naming conventions.

Users specify resources using UNC naming conventions, and WINS automatically resolves the IP address for ARP to use in resolving the MAC address.

MICROSOFT SQL BRIDGE (DISCONTINUED)

The additional functionality of Windows NT 3.5x supplanted Microsoft SQL Bridge in March 1995. The current capability of Windows NT 3.5x is such that Microsoft no longer considers the SQL Bridge necessary. As an example, SQL Server can now communicate with DECNet via Sockets. The sole purpose of SQL Bridge was to convert Named Pipes to TCP/IP Sockets for outgoing traffic and from TCP/IP Sockets to Named Pipes for incoming traffic; however, Named Pipes is now available in TCP/IP via NBT, NetBIOS for TCP/IP. Windows for Workgroups TCP/IP-32 3.11 and Windows NT 3.5x TCP/IP use the same code base and consequently have the same features, functions, and performance.

The Microsoft Windows NT 3.x TCP/IP implementation functions with the following environments:

◆ Internet
◆ Windows for Workgroups
◆ Windows NT (including RAS)
◆ LAN Manager for UNIX Host
◆ LAN Manager
◆ Pathworks for Open VMS (DECNet)
◆ IBM mainframes
◆ TCP/IP hosts
◆ NFS hosts

Architecture

Recall that the OSI network model consists of seven layers. TCP/IP remaps those seven layers to a four-layer conceptual model as shown in Figure 9.8.

The model in Figure 9.8 shows that what is known as TCP/IP actually consists of five protocols:

1. TCP
2. UDP
3. ICMP
4. IP
5. ARP

TCP/IP has wide interoperability in a WAN, but does not have a reputation for being fast. This is due in part to the large size of the protocol stack, which contains five complete protocols.

TCP

TCP is a connection-oriented protocol with data transmitted in segments. Data is transmitted as a stream, that is, with no defined boundaries. A *session* must be established before a connection-oriented protocol can be used. Ses-

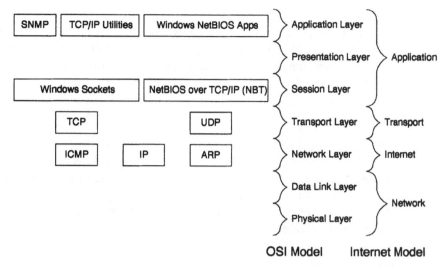

FIGURE 9.8 Relating the OSI model to the Internet model.

sions communicate between port numbers, with some ports reserved for dedicated use.

TCP is a reliable protocol, and unlike a broadcast or a datagram, a reliable protocol requires an acknowledgment (ACK). Reliability is obtained by identifying each segment. If an ACK is not returned, the sender retransmits the data. If the data is received damaged, it is discarded since the sender will automatically retransmit. Segments will be reassembled correctly at the destination. Packets containing a message segment have a *time to live* which is decremented each time the packet passes through a router. Unlike the captain from the Wagner opera *The Flying Dutchman*, packets will die after a specific period of time.

UDP

User datagram protocol (UDP) is a connectionless protocol and does not require a session. Unlike TCP, messages in UDP are not sent as a data stream. The reliability is the responsibility of the application and no acknowledgments are required. The arrival of datagrams and the correct sequencing of packets is not guaranteed. It is not a broadcast message since the destination port and IP address of the recipient are required. It's like mail. We send you a letter and expect that you'll get it, though there is really no guarantee that you will. *Unreliable connectionless messaging* is when the sender is not notified that the datagram has been sent. *Reliable connectionless messaging* is when the sender is notified that the datagram has been sent. In either case, the user is not notified of receiver receipt of message. UDP ports are distinct and separate from TCP ports even though some of them use the same port number.

ICMP

All TCP/IP implementations have the Internet Control Message Protocol (ICMP), which provides all error and message reporting. To ensure delivery, ICMP messages are contained within IP datagrams. Common ICMP messages are echo request, echo reply, redirect, source quench, and destination unreachable.

IP

Internet protocol (IP) is used by both TCP and UDP. It is a connectionless protocol responsible for routing and addressing packets between hosts. This means that a session need not be established before exchanging data. An acknowledgment is not required, and is the responsibility of the upper layer, TCP. With a connectionless protocol, packets might be lost, delivered out of sequence, duplicated, or lost.

ARP

The address resolution protocol (ARP) obtains hardware addresses using a broadcast. The hardware addresses are mapped to corresponding IP address and saved in cache.

SNMP

The Simple Network Management Protocol (SNMP) is used within Windows NT 3.x for the reporting of management and status information. Although originally developed as a tool for use in monitoring bridges and routers, SNMP has been expanded to include reporting for the following:

- Windows NT systems
- LAN Manager servers
- Gateways or routers
- Mainframes or minicomputers
- Terminal servers
- Wiring hubs

SNMP in Windows NT is implemented as an agent. SNMP agents perform **get**, **get-next**, and **set** operations requested by the SNMP management system. **Trap** is the only operation initiated by SNMP agent software. The **trap** operation alerts SNMP management systems to such things as disk failures, password violations, or quota failures. The exact information returned can be determined by examining the *management information block* (*MIB*).

The management system and the SNMP agent in Windows NT understand the concept of a MIB. MIBs are structures used to communicate status or configuration parameters back to the SNMP management system. Monitoring of networks is done by the SNMP protocol using MIBs for data collection.

Internet MIB II	Superset of Internet MIB I. One hundred seventy-one items are defined for fault or configuration analysis.
LAN Manager MIB II	Ninety items defined for statistical, share, logon, and user information. MIBs are read-only.
DHCP MIB	Fourteen items defined for monitoring the domain host control protocol (DHCP).
WINS MIB	Seventy items defined for monitoring the Windows Internet naming service (WINS).

Domain Host Control Protocol (DHCP)

Before Windows NT 3.x, management of TCP/IP networks was not easy. Maintenance of IP addresses was done manually and errors occurred quite often. If an IP address was entered incorrectly, there was a chance that a *broadcast storm*[1] would occur, possibly disabling the host or even the network. DHCP solves this problem by maintaining a pool of IP addresses, with possible subnets, which are leased to clients. With DHCP, the user plays no part in configuring TCP/IP addresses.

DHCP is defined as an extension of the Internet BOOTP protocol defined in Internet Request For Comment (RFC) 1542. All DHCP communication is implemented using the Internet user datagram protocol (UDP) and by default uses the BOOTP server and client ports. For DHCP to work, all routers must support RFC 1542 and act as *BOOTP relay agents*. If RFC 1542 is not available, then each subnet must have its own DHCP server.

DHCP leases IP addresses to requestors. Addresses are leased for a specific period of time and must be renewed. Each server maintains a pool of addresses that can be issued.

The DHCP server cannot be a DHCP client, and must have an IP address configured manually. When the DHCP server is defined, it is a good idea to also make it the WINS server (see Name Resolution).

DHCP may be configured from *Main:Control Panel:Networks*. The WINS server and all TCP/IP utilities will also be found there. Plan to overlap IP addresses when configuring multiple DHCP servers. Twenty-five percent of the IP address pool on a DHCP server should be common to a pool of IP addresses on another server. For example, if there are two DHCP servers, place on the first server 75 percent of the IP addresses the first server is primarily responsible for and 25 percent of the addresses from the second server. If DHCP server two were then to go offline, an emergency pool of IP addresses equal to 25 percent of DHCP server two original allocation is available on DHCP server one to prior clients of server two. Reverse the percentages for the other DHCP server.

When the Windows NT 3.5x DHCP server is defined, the following may be DHCP clients:

- ♦ Windows NT 3.5x workstation
- ♦ Windows NT 3.5x Server (when the server is not the DHCP server)
- ♦ Windows for Workgroups 3.11 with TCP/IP-32
- ♦ LAN Manager 2.2c (OS/2 LAN Manager 2.2c is not supported)
- ♦ Microsoft Network Client 3.0 for DOS with real mode TCP/IP

To understand subnetting, we must look at an IP address. An internet address is 32 bits divided into 8-bit octets and displayed in dotted-decimal notation. From these octets the following address classes are defined.

	Hex Prefix	Netword ID	Host ID	Networks	Network ID Range	Hosts
Class A	0	7 bits	24 bits	126	1–126	16,777,214
Class B	10	14 bits	16 bits	16,384	128–191	65,534
Class C	110	21 bits	8 bits	2,097,152	192–223	254
Class D	1110	<multicasting hosts, broadcast address>				
Class E	1111	<experimental>				

These translate to valid address ranges of:

Address Class	Beginning Range	Ending Range
Class A	001.x.y.z	126.x.y.z
Class B	128.0.y.z	191.255.y.z
Class C	192.0.0.z	223.255.255.z

For any given IP address, there is an associated subnet mask. The default subnet mask for a Class B address (in dotted decimal notation) is 255.255.0.0. If we wish to redefine the standard Class B IP address with sixteen subnets, the new subnet mask would be 255.255.240.0, and represented in binary:

Class B default subnet mask	11111111	11111111	00000000	00000000
Class B subnet mask with 16 subnets	11111111	11111111	11110000	00000000

DHCP solves subnetting issues. IP address ranges are entered at the DHCP server along with an exclusion list for reserved IP addresses (optional routing IP addresses may also be defined). These IP address ranges, *scopes,* may have subnets. All subnet mask calculation will be performed automatically by the DHCP server when an IP address is leased to a client. With DHCP, a user is no longer involved in TCP/IP address configuration.

Host and NetBIOS Name Resolution

There are two classes of name resolution. TCP/IP naming conventions in Windows NT involve IP addresses and NetBIOS names, while naming conventions in the UNIX environment involve IP addresses, host names, and domain names. Host name resolution is done with the Unix domain naming service (DNS) for fully qualified domain names (FQDN). The other name resolution service is WINS, a Microsoft-specific implementation for NetBIOS names.

There are different resources to perform either of these functions, and some of them overlap in functionality. We'll look at the resources available before discussing how they are used in resolving names. These resources include files, services, and broadcast messages. The LMHOSTS and HOSTS files may be found in the directory **c:\<winnt>\System32\drivers\etc.**

HOSTS file	A file of Internet FQDN names used by Microsoft TCP/IP utilities. Entries are in the form: 131.107.16.1 Training.Microsoft.Com. Associates an IP address with a fully qualified domain name.
LMHOSTS file	A file of NetBIOS names formatted in the form: 131.107. 16.1 *domain-controller* #PRE#DOM:*domain_name*. Associates an IP address with a Windows NT domain controller in a Windows NT domain.
DNS service	Domain name service. A feature of the UNIX environment. Resolves FQDN names to IP addresses. Windows NT does not provide a DNS service, which is a feature of Unix environments.
WINS service	Windows Internet naming service, an enhanced NetBIOS name server (NBNS). WINS reduces network traffic by eliminating the B-node broadcast for name resolution. A WINS client registers when it starts, and name resolution is only a single message directed to the WINS server. When a WINS client attempts to register a name, a challenge is issued for duplicate names, since NetBIOS names may not be unique in different domains. WINS has two advantages: It is no longer necessary to maintain a LMHOSTS file at each client computer and a user is no longer involved with TCP/IP address configuration.
	LAN Manager 2.2c for MS-DOS and Microsoft Network Client 3.0 may be WINS clients, but do not register NetBIOS names.
B-node broadcast	Uses a combination of UDP datagrams (both broadcast and directed) and TCP to communicate. NetBIOS names are resolved using a local broadcast.
P-node broadcast	Uses only directed datagrams to communicate. UDP broadcasts are not made. Instead the NetBIOS naming service (NBNS) and NetBIOS datagram delivery service (NBDD) are used together to provide name lookup.
M-node broadcast	A combination of B-node and P-node. Tries to resolve name with B-node and if that fails attempts NBNS and NBDD of P-node.

H-node broadcast   Uses P-node by default. If that fails, attempts to resolve the NetBIOS name with B-node.

Host Name Resolution

All of the preceding items are features of Windows NT except DNS, the Unix domain name service. Discussed in the following are the steps for name resolution. If name resolution is not configured properly, excessive network bandwidth may be consumed in resolving names.

Host name resolution is necessary to convert the host name to an IP address. The address resolution protocol (ARP) can then convert the IP address to a network MAC address. A host name is an alias used to reference a TCP/IP host. Host names are not used in Windows NT commands except in TCP/IP utilities such as PING or FTP. A host name is resolved with the following steps:

Step 1.   The system PINGs the host computer for *hostname*. If the local host name is the required hostname, name resolution is complete.

Step 2.   If resolution is not complete, the system parses the HOSTS file. If the *hostname* exists, resolution is complete.

Step 3.   Sends a message to the registered DNS. If it doesn't respond, retries up to 6 times at intervals.

Step 4.   If DNS fails to resolve the host name, the source host checks the local NetBIOS name cache before making three attempts to contact the configured WINS servers.

Step 5.   If WINS fails to resolve the host name, WINS sends three B-node broadcast messages on the local network.

Step 6.   If no response is made to the broadcasts, the LMHOSTS file is parsed.

Step 7.   When all previous steps fail, the only alternative is to configure the IP address manually.

NetBIOS Name Resolution

The WINS server is the primary tool used for netBIOS name resolution. WINS servers can be configured to use the LMHOSTS file directly. This may be desirable for non-WINS clients who cannot register with the WINS server. Another alternative is to place a proxy agent on subnets which have non-WINS clients. The proxy agent must be a WINS client and will forward to the WINS server a name-resolution broadcast of a non-WINS client. A proxy agent isn't required if the routers have *BOOTP Relay Agent* (Request for Comment 1542) enabled. However, the best choice is not to enable BOOTP Relay Agent, since this inhibits B-node broadcasts from propagating throughout the domain. There can only be one WINS proxy agent on a subnet that has non-WINS clients. If there are no non-WINS clients on a subnet, there can be a maximum of two proxy agents per subnet.

NetBIOS name replication occurs between WINS servers with the concept of *push* and *pull*. *Push* servers notify *pull* servers, and the pull servers then proceed to request the new information. Replication is done between pairs of WINS servers and changes eventually migrate to all WINS servers. From the *Replication Partners* choose either push or pull to configure a server as a push or pull partner. To replicate in both directions, each server must be configured as both a push and pull server.

NetBios name resolution occurs when a user requests access to a network resource. For example, when a user enters a command of the form: **net use** x:*computer**share**file*.

The actual steps to resolve a NetBIOS name are shown following. It should be obvious that a WINS server must be configured, or B-node broadcasts will occur to the detriment of network bandwidth.

Step 1.　Check the NetBIOS name cache.

Step 2.　If not resolved, send a name query request to the configured WINS server.

Step 3.　If still not resolved, try the secondary WINS server.

Step 4.　If still not resolved, implement B-node name broadcasts.

Step 5.　If B-node resolution fails, parse the LMHOSTS file. When the IP address is identified as a remote host, the source host checks for a route table. If none is available, ARP is used (either cache or broadcast) to obtain the address of the configured default gateway. However, parsing the LMHOSTS file isn't necessary if the router is configured to forward B-node broadcasts.

Tuning for Performance

There are numerous TCP/IP configuration parameters, so we only mention those whose values are performance based. As discussed previously, please follow proper precautions before editing the registry. All values can be found in the registry at:

```
HKEY_LOCAL_MACHINE\SYSTEM\CurrentControlSet\Services\Tcpip\Parameters
```

ArpCacheLife　　ARP is the address resolution protocol. This value is the lifetime of a cache entry. Default is 600 s, 10 min.

ArpCacheSize　　ARP cache size. Default value is 62. When new names are added, they replace the oldest names. If the requested name is not in the ARP cache, then the *host name* resolution is started. This can involve broadcasts to a registered domain name

	server or B-node broadcasts. This should be increased for a large network.
DefaultTTL	The default *time to live* of a packet. It is decremented by one for each router through which the packet passes. The default value is 32 s. Normally this value is adequate. Be careful if this value is adjusted. For example, if you have five routers through which a packet may pass and **DefaultTTL** is set to six, then packets will die because their **DefaultTTL** expires as the network slows down. This will exacerbate an already bad situation on a loaded network since the system will force the retransmission of packets and further slow it down.
EnableDead-GWDetect	Backup gateways may be defined in the Advanced portion of the TCP/IP configuration dialog in the Control Panel. Setting this value directs TCP to perform *Dead Gateway Detection* if a gateway fails to respond. TCP will ask IP to change to a backup gateway. Default is 1, true.
EnablePMT-UBHDetect	A black hole is a router which does not return ICMP destination unreachable messages. Setting this value to true will detect those black holes. Note that in setting this value to true, the maximum number of retransmissions will be increased. Default is 0, false.
ForwardBuffer-Memory	Memory IP allocates for packets. Default is 74240, enough for fifty 1480 byte packets. When this buffer space is full, the router begins discarding packets at random. If IP routing is not enabled, then no buffers are allocated.
NumForward-Packets	Number of packets to reserve for IP routing. Related parameter is **ForwardBufferMemory**. Default is 50. No allocation is done if IP routing is not enabled.
TcpSendDownMax	Specifies the maximum number of bytes queued by TCP/IP. Default is 16384.
TcpWindowSize	The maximum TCP receive window available. The number of bytes that a sender may transmit without receiving an acknowledgment. Computed as the minimum of 0xffff or four times the maximum TCP datasize on the network or 8192 rounded up to an even multiple of the network TCP data size.

Tuning for NetBIOS Activity

These parameters are specific to NetBIOS over TCP/IP. As discussed previously, take extreme precautions before editing the registry. TCP/IP NetBIOS parameters may be found in the registry at:

```
HKEY_LOCAL_MACHINE\SYSTEM\CurrentConstrolSet\Services\NetBt\Parameters
```

BcastName-QueryCount	Number of times NBT will broadcast a name query without receiving a response. Related parameter is **BcastQueryTimeout**. Default is 3.
BcastQuery-Timeout	Time interval between successive broadcast name queries. Related query is **BcastName-QueryCount**. Default is 750 ms, in ms.
CacheTimeout	The time interval that names are cached in the remote name table. Default is 0x927c0 ms (10 min).
NameSrv-QueryCount	The number of times NBT will query a WINS server before timing out. Related parameter is **NameSrvQueryTimeout**. Default is 3.
NameSrvQuery-Timeout	Time interval between successive name queries. Related field is **NameSrvQueryCount**. Default value is 750 in ms.
NodeType	1 = Bnode, 2 = Pnode, 4 = Mnode, 8 = Hnode. Used for WINS server name resolution broadcasts.
Size/Small/Medium/Large	Name table size to store local and remote names. 1 = small, 2 = medium (128), 3 = large (256). Default is 1 (small). Set to 3 (large) when acting as a proxy nameserver.

Diagnostic Utilities

Since TCP/IP is a WAN networking system using five protocols, error diagnosis is a major problem. Microsoft implementations of the standard Unix TCP/IP diagnostic utilities are included with the Windows NT TCP/IP installation. All of these utilities function at the command-line level of Windows NT.

Utility	*Function*
PING	Verifies configurations and tests connectivity.
FINGER	Retrieves system information from a remote computer which supports the TCP/IP FINGER service.
ARP	Displays and manages a cache of locally resolved IP addresses to MAC addresses.

IPCONFIG	Displays the current TCP/IP configuration for both the WINS server and DHCP.
LPQ	Gets print queue status for a host running the LPD service.
NBSTAT	Displays NetBIOS names resolved to IP addresses.
ROUTE	Manages the local routing table. The local routing table can be viewed or edited.
HOSTNAME	Returns the local host name for authentication by RCP, RSH, or REXEC.
TRACERT	Displays the packet path to the destination.

Diagnosing Connection Problems

Proper session communication verification requires a number of steps. These steps can be thought of logically as starting at the lowest possible level of the OSI network model and working our way up, testing each layer for functionality. We start first with PING in a sequence of four steps:

PING 127.0.0.1	Verifies that TCP/IP is installed correctly. 127.0.0.1 is a reserved IP address.
PING <ip address>	PING to your own IP address; that is, the IP address of the server or workstation currently in use.
PING <default gateway>	Actually tests the network. You may PING any local IP address, however.
PING <remote node>	The remote node IP address should be through the default gateway IP address that was successfully PINGed previously. Of course, failure at any one of these points will help to localize the problem.

The next step is to verify session communication. If the Windows NT-based system is an Internet Specification, Request for Comment (RFC) compliant NetBIOS-based host, then use a **net use x:\\destination_host** or a **net view** command, either of which should function. If this step is unsuccessful then use the following procedure:

- ♦ Verify that the target host is NetBIOS-based.
- ♦ Confirm that the scope ID (IP address range) on the target host matches that of the source host.
- ♦ Verify that the correct NetBIOS name was used.
- ♦ If the target host is remote, check the LMHOSTS file for the correct entry.

If the Windows NT-based computer is not an RFC compliant, NetBIOS-based host, create a session with **ftp** *destination_host* or **telnet** *destination_host*. If this fails, then use the following procedure:

- ◆ Verify that the target host is configured with the Telnet daemon or the FTP daemon.
- ◆ Confirm that you have correct permissions on the host.
- ◆ Check the HOSTS file for a valid entry if you are connecting using a host name.

Choosing a Protocol

If your requirements can be quantified, choosing a protocol should be easy. We mentioned DLC previously; however, it is a network printer protocol and is not useful to SQL Server.

TCP/IP TCP/IP is the protocol of choice for interoperability in a WAN environment. It is not always as fast as other protocols, but it is reliable and is required for large networks.

NWLink Required for interfacing with Novell NetWare. Older versions of IPX/SPX require each packet to be acknowledged. This limits network size even though the protocol is routable. The newest version of SPX-II has a window which enhances performance.

What if there are no requirements to support NetWare? The NetBIOS version of NWLink, NWNBLink has implemented piggyback acknowledgments between Windows NT systems. It is possible for the sender to send data continually under certain conditions. Do not limit consideration of NWLink or NWNBLink protocols to environments with NetWare.

NBF NetBEUI Frame. The protocol is not routable, but it has the most flexibility for tuning and performance enhancements. We might even call those *negative performance* enhancements, since there are many tuning parameters for slow networks, slow computers, and unreliable networks. It is the native Microsoft protocol, and if enough memory is available at the source and destination when using the server message blocks of Named Pipes, then *RAW* mode transfers can be up to 64K. Consider NBF for small networks. Microsoft states that NBF is designed for 20 to 200 stations.

Interprocess Communication

Figure 9.9 depicts how *interprocess communication* fits into the overall schema of SQL Server communications.

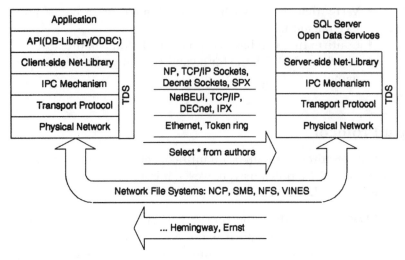

FIGURE 9.9 SQL Server and different interprocess communication mechanisms.

Server Message Blocks

Some mention should be made of server message blocks (SMBs), which are important for both NetBIOS and Named Pipes. SMB is an X/Open and OSF/DCE standard. Microsoft worked very closely with the X/Open committee to ensure that SMB became a standard. LAN Manager 2.x and Windows NT computers interoperate because they use SMBs. Interprocess communication mechanisms which use SMB are automatically tunable by the operating system. SMB interoperability is provided for the following systems:

MS OS/2 LAN Manager	DEC PATHWORKS
Microsoft Windows for Workgroups	Microsoft LAN Manager for UNIX
IBM LAN Server	3COM 3+Open
MS-DOS LAN Manager	MS-Net

While not an interprocess communication mechanism, SMBs play an important part in interprocess communication. Like the transport protocols TCP/IP, IPX/SPX, and NetBEUI, SMB is actually a network file system protocol. For a description of tuning SMBs, see Chapter 6, Replication.

Named Pipes

Named Pipes is the default interprocess communication mechanism for Windows NT and uses SMBs. Named Pipes (NPFS, Named Pipe file system) and Mail Slots (MSFS, Mail Slot file system) are implemented as file systems even though they are both interprocess communication mechanisms. The most important feature of these file systems is that security is provided though the *impersonation* mechanism (see following, File Systems, Security, for a detailed discussion). No other Microsoft Windows interprocess communication mechanism supports security.

Named Pipes allows two processes to communicate with memory buffers used as a communication mechanism. A pipe may be *one-way,* in which case it is an *anonymous* pipe, which is equivalent to a mail slot where messages flow in only one direction. A *two-way pipe* allows both processes to read and write so that information flows both ways at once. Pipes may exist in multiple instances and may operate with different modes at each end of the pipe. Pipes may be byte or message oriented, overlapped or blocking.

SQL Server communicates with Named Pipes (over either NetBEUI or TCP/IP) with Window NT, MS-DOS, Win95, Windows for Workgroups, and OS/2 clients. It can also simultaneously support TCP/IP Sockets for communication with Macintosh, UNIX, or VMS clients and SPX Sockets for Novell Netware. To communicate properly using Named Pipes, all machines on your network must be using the same implementation. Named Pipes provides the full interoperability of SMB, (see previously, Server Message Blocks).

NetBIOS

NetBIOS has evolved from the original session/layer interface of a ROM chip. Today, NetBIOS is an interprocess communication mechanism which can be used with any NetBEUI (NBF) compliant protocol. Once the session is established by the NetBIOS interface, messages can be exchanged as NetBIOS messages or as SMB messages. Since NetBIOS is the native session/layer interface, it has the widest range of interoperability. Some of the NetBIOS implementations are:

NBF	NetBEUI Frame
NBT	NetBEUI for TCP/IP
NBIPX	NetBEUI for Novell IPX

Remote Procedure Calls

Remote Procedure Calls (*RPC*) is a message passing facility that allows an application to call services available on various machines in a network without regard to their location. RPC simplifies the development of distributed applications. The RPC built into Windows NT is compatible with the Open Software Foundation's Distributed Computing Environment (OSF/DCE) RPC. RPC can be used to build distributed applications that include not just other Windows NT systems, but any system that supports DCE compatible RPCs—including systems from DEC, HP, and other vendors.

The RPC mechanism is network-independent and is unique in that it uses the other IPC mechanisms to establish communication between the client and the server. RPC can use Named Pipes, NetBIOS, or TCP/IP Sockets to communicate with remote systems. If the client and the server are on the same machine it can use the Local Procedure Call (LPC) system to transfer information between processes and subsystems. This makes RPC the most flexible and portable of the IPC choices available.

Windows Sockets

Windows Sockets is an API based on the Berkeley UNIX (BSD) 4.3 release. BSD sockets were originally designed as a local interprocess communication mechanism (IPC), but cooperating vendors have evolved the sockets concept into a standard for the TCP/IP community.

A *socket* defines a bidirectional endpoint for communication between processes. There is a data representation difference between Internet and Intel however, with the sockets standard being the *big-endian* model for on-the-wire representation. *Big-endian* and *little-endian* represent different byte ordering at the hardware word level. The hexadecimal value 1234 is represented in the Intel architecture as 3412, hence the name *little-endian* since the first byte on the left is the least significant. If SQL Server runs on an Intel-based architecture, then all bytes must be reordered before transmission when using TCP/IP. With the current speed of computers approaching 150 MHz, the extra overhead is probably not as significant an issue as it used to be.

Windows Sockets offers the same functionality as the TCP and UDP protocols in that service may be connectionless or connection-oriented. A connection-oriented service will use a data stream and provide a reliable connection, while the datagrams will be the feature of a connectionless service. In a connectionless service, delivery is not guaranteed and messages may arrive out of order or not at all.

Unlike Named Pipes or Mail Slots, Windows Sockets cannot have security. This makes sense since Mail Slots and Named Pipes are implemented as file systems which have access control lists (ACLs) and access control entries (ACEs) for file security, while Windows Sockets is a connection mechanism and not a file system.

Network Support with RAS

Remote Access Server (*RAS*) was originally shipped with Microsoft LAN Manager 2.1 in 1991. RAS has since been upgraded to Version 1.1a and currently provides a full and seamless access to an enterprise network for computers running Windows NT, Window for Workgroups 3.11, and MS-DOS Version 3.1 or later. RAS Version 1.1 is available for OS/2 Version 3.1. This allows you to work on the network while connected with nondedicated telephone lines.

Significant architectural changes have been made to the Windows NT RAS server. In Windows NT 3.1, RAS functioned as a NetBIOS gateway. In Windows 3.5x, RAS is a software-based multiprotocol router. It is not a remote control program. The function and architecture of RAS and remote control programs are different. RAS is dedicated to communications and does not run applications. The RAS client normally runs applications from the remote workstation, while the remote control system runs applications from the host-side CPU. For client/server applications, RAS has an advantage in that network traffic is significantly reduced with message compression. For scalability, a RAS server can be upgraded with additional ports without upgrading the server CPU. If a significant number of ports are added, additional memory and disks may be needed. For remote control applications, an additional or upgraded CPU must be purchased for each additional port.

RAS as a SLIP Client

Serial Line Internet Protocol (SLIP) for TCP/IP is available as a Windows NT 3.5x client to support older Unix implementations. Machines running Windows 3.5x may connect to Unix machines running a SLIP server. SLIP does have limitations and is not a secure connection mechanism.

- SLIP does not support encrypted authentication.
- SLIP does not provide automatic negotiation of network configuration.
- SLIP does not provide a mechanism to control the connection.
- SLIP does not have a frame checksum and will be unable to detect errors on a noisy line.
- SLIP only supports TCP/IP.
- SLIP does not provide user authentication. The Remote Access Phone Book bypasses user authentication.

RAS as a Software Router

RAS supports Windows Sockets, NetBIOS, Mail Slots, Named Pipes, Remote Procedure Calls (RPC), Windows NT Network (Win32) API, LAN Manager API, and the RAS API. Access to RAS may be with ISDN, PSTN (Public Switched Telephone Network), or X.25. The RAS server supports the Internet Point-to-Point Protocol (PPP) as a wrapper for NetBEUI, IPX, or TCP/IP.

Any combination of IPX, TCP/IP, or NetBEUI may be loaded by a remote client using PPP. This feature is supported in both Windows 95 and Windows NT 3.5x. When configuring the RAS server, the system administrator has the ability to limit access only to the server or to the LAN for the client using any one of the NetBEUI, IPX, or TCP/IP protocols. This control of access to the LAN is logically equivalent to a programmed router. More precisely, it is a software-based multiprotocol router. In Figure 9.10, the RAS server functions as a router

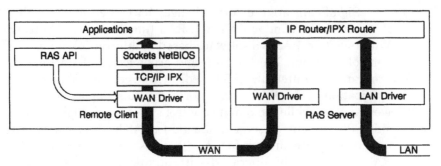

FIGURE 9.10 PPP architecture of RAS.

for IP and IPX. This assumes that the incoming protocol is either IP or IPX. *It is very important to note that the RAS computer cannot have any other services running when configured as a router.*

Windows NT does not process the Routing Internet Protocol (RIP) requests that maintain a TCP/IP router table. Consequently Windows NT is only suitable as a router in small, single-subnet networks. Any requirements beyond this require the use of a commercial router.

RAS as a NetBIOS Gateway

Even though RAS is a software-based multiprotocol router, it also functions as a NetBIOS gateway as shown in Figure 9.11.

A user remotely accessing the system with NetBEUI can only access resources on the network that support, for example, a printer or a server which only use the TCP/IP protocol. The same analogy is true for the IPX protocol. In summary, a NetBEUI user has access to any resource in the enterprise which supports the TCP/IP, IPX/SPX, or NetBEUI protocols.

The RAS server has a stated limit of 256 simultaneous connections. Microsoft has only tested 256 simultaneous connections. Many more connections when using the TCP/IP protocol may be possible. However, NetBEUI is

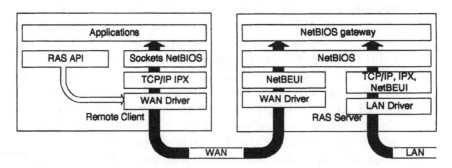

FIGURE 9.11 NetBIOS gateway architecture.

limited to a maximum of 250 simultaneous connections since this is the size of the NetBIOS name table.

RAS Security

Security is an issue when considering remote access. Windows NT is a secure system and is rated at the C2 level by the U.S. Department of Defense. This means that access to system resources can be discretely controlled and all access to the system can be audited and recorded.

♦ All authentication and logon information is encrypted when using the PPP protocol.
♦ Callback security is available. After the initial connection is established, the line is dropped, and the client is dialed back.
♦ Since RAS participates in the Windows *trusted domain* architecture, all auditing features of Windows NT are available. System administrators are able to give/revoke remote access permissions on a user-by-user basis. This means that remote access callback must be explicitly granted.
♦ When configuring RAS, it is possible to limit access to all resources that the RAS host computer can see, or only to the server.
♦ A RAS user must be or have a Windows NT account and have RAS dial-in permission.

Encryption Schemes

CHAP	*RSA Message Digest 5 (MD5)—Challenge Handshake Authentication Protocol (RAS Client Only).* A nonreversible encryption algorithm invented by RSA Inc.
MS-CHAP	*RSA Message Digest 4 (MD4).* A Microsoft version of RSA MD4. The most secure encryption algorithm that Windows NT 3.5x supports and that uses the RC4 algorithm.
DES	*Data Encryption Standard.* Sponsored by the National Bureau of Standards.
PAP	*Password Authentication Protocol.* Supported by PPP for plain text password authentication.
SPAP	*SHIRVA Password Authentication Protocol (RAS Server Only).* SPAP is a version of PAP implemented by SHIRVA in its remote client software.

Determination of Encryption Scheme

Method Used	**Type of RAS Connection**
MS-CHAP	Windows NT 3.5x RAS client connecting to a Windows NT 3.5x RAS server

MS-CHAP	Windows NT 3.5x RAS client connecting to a Windows NT 3.1 RAS server
CHAP, SPAP, or PAP	Third-party RAS client connecting to a Windows NT 3.5x RAS server
CHAP, SPAP, or Clear-text	Windows NT 3.5x RAS client connecting to a third-party RAS PPP server
Clear-text	Windows NT 3.5x RAS client connecting to a third-party RAS SLIP server
DES	MS RAS client 1.1A connecting to a Windows NT RAS server (3.1 or 3.5x)

The security level is controlled by the RAS server. The system administrator has the ability to set logon/authentication security in four modes:

- ◆ Accept any authentication including clear text.
- ◆ Accept clear text terminal login only.
- ◆ Accept only encrypted authentication.
- ◆ Accept only Microsoft encrypted authentication.

If Microsoft encryption is to be used then MS-CHAP will be used. This implies that the client is a Microsoft machine. Data encryption is also available.

RAS and the Internet

As shown in Figure 9.12, there is considerable flexibility in configuring Windows NT to access the Internet. When configured as an Internet service provider, the user dials in for a connection as a client running Windows NT 3.5x or Windows 95. Since RAS is also a PPP Internet server, any other Internet PPP client can also access the RAS server. From there the user has whatever privileges have been accorded to the client by Windows NT to access remote or local resources. If the user has access only to local resources at the RAS server, SQL Server can be used to replicate data tables over to the RAS server for access by the RAS client.

A SQL Server application can use SQL replication to supply a SQL subscriber client on the Windows NT RAS Server (see Figure 9.13). Data is retrieved from the replicated database by conventional means with either ODBC or DB-Library. It can then be used by browser support programs to create Hypertext Markup Language (HTML) for web-page servicing.[2] For example, this can be done with Netscape, which can interface with Visual Basic.[3] The internet need not be the actual Internet, but can be an internal enterprise *Intranet* used to disseminate corporate information within the enterprise. At this time, Windows NT Web Servers are available from the following vendors:

| Folio Info Server | Folio Corporation   (801) 229-6650 |
| Net Publisher | Ameritech Library Services (708) 866-1100 |

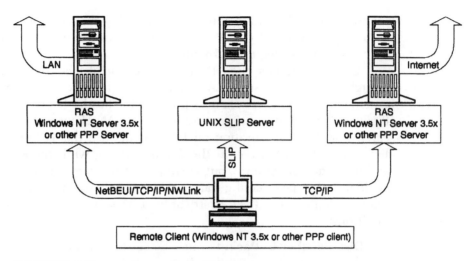

FIGURE 9.12 RAS as an Internet provider.

Netscape Commerce Server	Netscape Communications Corporation (415) 528-2555
Netscape Communications Server	
Purveyor	Process Software Corporation (800) 722-7770
WebSite	O'Reilly & Associates (707) 829-0515

Microsoft SQL Server may be placed on the World Wide Web (WWW). Using ODBC, SQL Server data can be accessed and converted to HTML and used by a home page.

In Figure 9.13, protocol isolation is used as a firewall rather than a commercial router. Incoming traffic from the internet uses TCP/IP and replication messaging is either NetBEUI or IPX. The RAS server is configured with routing disabled. This isolates incoming traffic to the RAS server. As discussed previously, RAS configuration tools provide the system administrator the choice of giving incoming RAS traffic access only to local resources or to network

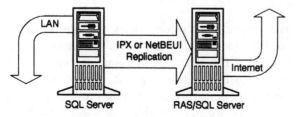

FIGURE 9.13 SQL Server supporting a RAS server.

resources. Other factors to consider are limiting the availability of the trivial file transport protocol (TFTP) and privileges on the guest account to RAS clients, which does require authentication.

Although not illustrated, the RAS server can also be configured as a pass-through router from a small LAN to the internet. Some registry changes must be made to do this. These changes preserve the header IP address so that each IP packet is marked as originating from the LAN client rather than the RAS server. For this configuration all LAN clients use the TCP/IP protocol and clients have the RAS server as the *default gateway,* while the RAS server does not have a default gateway but is simply on the same subnet as the service provider. This type of configuration will typically use a class C address. This configuration requires the Registry at the RAS server to have set the following conditions:

DisableOtherSrcPackets must be set to 1 to preserve LAN clients' IP address in the Registry key:

```
\HKEY_LOCAL_MACHINE\System\CurrentControlSet\Services\RasArp\Parameters
```

If your subnet is in the same network class as your service provider, which is likely, **PriorityBasedOnSubNetwork** must be set to 1 for the following Registry key in order to route packets from the LAN to the Internet:

```
\HKEY_LOCAL_MACHINE\System\CurrentControlSet\Services\RasMan\PPP\IPCP
```

File Systems

Windows NT supports three file systems:

FAT   *File Allocation Table.*   A legacy file system originally developed for MS-DOS

HPFS   *High Performance File System.*   A file system developed for OS/2.

NTFS   *New Technology File System.*   The native Windows NT file system.

Escalating user requirements for additional file security have helped evolve the design of file systems. The ODS-2 file system of OpenVMS uses a *careful write* mechanism while other file systems, such as the OS/2 HPFS and the Windows NT NTFS systems, use a *lazy write.* In the *careful write,* the operating system performs I/O operations in a manner and order so that the errors and ensuing error recovery are manageable, for a worst case, no matter what happens.

The OS/2 HPFS file system and the Windows NT File System (NTFS) do have two features in common. They both use a B-tree for quick file access and each employs the *lazy write* file system. But this is where the similarity ends. The most important difference is one of architecture. In Windows NT, the Cache Manager manages disk caching and lazy writes so these features are available to all file systems. In OS/2, disk caching and lazy writes are only done by HPFS.

The NTFS file recovery strategy guarantees that the volume structure will not be corrupted and that all files will be accessible after system failure. Extensive recovery procedures are used to recover file system data. Even though NTFS does not guarantee protection of user data when a system crash occurs, applications can use *cache write-through* and *cache flushing* to assure that the data is written.

A lazy write file system will reduce the overall number of writes to the disk. However, since the disk I/O operations are not serialized, the disk is at risk of being in an inconsistent state. If HPFS fails while in an inconsistent state, then the volume must be reconstructed with the **chkdsk** utility. Since the state of the disk isn't known, **chkdsk** must be run at each boot, which can be a problem with a large disk. Even with running **chkdsk**, the disk cannot always be recovered to the user's satisfaction.

Windows NT[4] employs the lazy write technology used in HPFS; however, it also uses technology common to SQL Server users in creating a log file. Changes are written to the log file using the *lazy commit* feature of the Cache Manager. The transaction is not written to the log file directly, but cached and later written to the system log file as a background process. When recovering from a system failure, NTFS reads through the log file and redoes each committed transaction. It also undoes (rolls back) any transactions that were not committed at the time of failure. Whenever Windows NT is booted, it checks the disks for a *dirty* volume. If the volume is dirty, then the program **chkdsk/f** is used for recovery. But not all I/O operations in Windows NT use the lazy write technology. Cache flushing and cache write-through are efficient and available. For example, SQL Server maintains its own recovery system with the cache write-through feature of NTFS.

FAT

FAT is a very simple file system, and has low overhead because it is simple. However, there are limitations.

◆ File names are limited to 8.3, that is, an eight-character file name and a three-character extension.
◆ FAT File size is limited to 2^{32} bytes while NTFS is limited to 2^{64} bytes
◆ Few attribute bits are available in the directory entry.
◆ Even though a duplicate FAT table is maintained, it is often not in sync.

- ♦ Performance on large disks is less than desired because of the linear searches of the FAT table.
- ♦ Deleted files are easy to recover if they have not been overwritten, since only one byte is changed in the FAT table.
- ♦ Although fast because of its simplicity, FAT is not robust.
- ♦ On large disks cluster size is very large, resulting in very inefficient disk utilization. FAT is not scaleable since a 16K cluster will be used on a 640Mb disk, regardless of the file size. (Actually a cluster size of 10K is all that is required to cover a 640Mb disk; however, since the cluster size must be a power of two, it is rounded up to 16K.)

HPFS

HPFS was designed to be fast, and it is, but it isn't scalable. File sizes are limited to 2^{32} bytes, but the most limiting factor is the 512-byte sector size. Access to the disk is always on a sector basis since cluster (integral number of sectors) access is not supported. The disk layout is different and quite interesting, since it employs a concept of *bands* which contain bit maps every 16Mb. This reduces disk head movement and enhances system performance.

HPFS has many features not available in FAT. Security is available to users of HPFS only when HPFS is used by the OS/2 operating system. HPFS security structures are not recognized by Windows NT. Extended attributes are available. HPFS will replace faulty sectors and warn the system administrator when there are too many *hot-fixes*. Even though the system is very fast, it is not scalable because of the small sector size.

NTFS

NTFS can mimic POSIX with case sensitivity, permits Unicode names, permits aliasing of file names with hard links, supports long file names, has a maximum file size of 2^{64} bytes, and allows multiple time stamps. Windows NT supports cluster (integral number of sectors) sizes of 512, 1,024, 2,048, and 4,096 bytes. The appropriate size is determined automatically by Windows NT based upon the physical size of the disk. NTFS also supports multiple data streams, an important feature for OLE compound files. When looking at the basic layout, the NTFS file system has no resemblance to classical file systems, since small files are embedded within the directory itself, thereby reducing disk accesses.

All pertinent file information is stored within the file record including name, attributes, security descriptors, and attribute flags. If the file is too large to be stored in the directory, the attributes will contain pointers to other disk sectors using a logical cluster number (LCN) which is relative to the volume. The LCN will represent a *run*, a contiguous allocation of sectors for either file data or *extended attributes* which are too large for the master file table (MFT). Clusters within a file are relative from zero and are identified by a virtual cluster number (VCN).

Note that in both the FAT and HPFS file systems, a directory scan and one or more disk accesses must be made before a file can be opened. With NTFS, access to a file is much quicker; it could be in the directory itself. This design feature, along with caching and lazy writes, accounts for the enhanced performance of NTFS. Note that we use the word *directory* very loosely here since the NTFS directory may contain files, rather than just providing a pointer to a file as in other file systems.

NTFS maintains two boot records for additional reliability. The first is at the beginning of the volume and the second is at the logical middle of the volume. Both FAT and HPFS are vulnerable to system accessibility failure since they only have one copy of the boot record.

However, NTFS does have some caveats. The first is that *hot-sparing* of sectors is only done for SCSI disk drives and not IDE, MFM, or ESDI disk drives. *Hot-sparing* is the remapping of a faulty sector to a known good sector. If the operation is a write, then there is no problem; another sector is used without risk of data loss. If the system is not operating in *fault-tolerant mode* with redundant copies (mirroring or striping with parity), and the operation is a read, then whatever data can be recovered from the defective sector is moved to the new sector. Data might be lost. If the system is fault tolerant, the redundant copy of the data will be used in the remapped new sector.

The other caveat is that in spite of all the recovery mechanisms within Windows NT, a failure may actually occur. If the system fails when writing to the log file, or when creating the mirror copy of the Master File Table (MFT) record, there is no guarantee that everything can be recovered successfully.[5]

Security

File security is only available with NTFS under Windows NT. MS-DOS does not have file security and the file security structure of HPFS is not recognized by Windows NT. File security cannot be understood without first understanding the security architecture of Windows NT. Security within Windows NT is implemented as a client/server model as shown in Figure 9.14.

Logon processes	Accept logon requests from users.
Local Security Authority	LSA is used by the logon process to ensure that a user has access to the system.
Security Account Manager	SAM contains the user accounts database and is used by LSA.
Security Reference Monitor	Ensures that a user has permission to access an object.

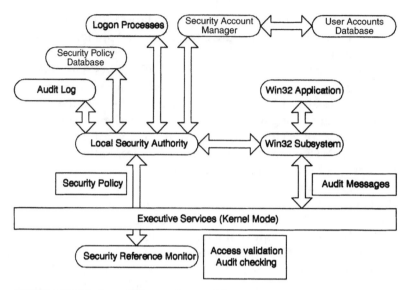

FIGURE 9.14 Windows NT security model.

Security Access Token	If a logon is successful, the Security Access Token (SAT) will contain the user's security ID and the security IDs of EVERYONE (see Groups) and other groups. It also contains any assigned user rights and is stored in the user process.
Object	Anything in Windows NT. Some examples are: directory, symbolic link, printer, thread, process, file, file system, port, device, event, semaphore, section, segment, and mutex.

Each object within Windows NT contains an Access Control List (ACL). Within the ACL are two types of entries, *discretionary access denied,* and *discretionary access permitted.* The object owner controls the Access Control Entries (ACEs) in the ACL which allow or deny permissions. ACEs within an ACL must be ordered with the discretionary access denied entries preceding the discretionary access permitted entries. When the Security Reference Monitor (SRM) checks an object AL for user permission, further examination of the AL is terminated if the user is denied access, even though a subsequent ACE would allow access. SRM can combine access privileges. If a user requests Read Access and Write Access and belongs to two different groups, one of which has Read Access and the other Write Access to the same file, then access will be granted.

User access to objects is very complex since there are many different classes of access tokens. Within the Windows NT system, user access rights are a mapping between *specific access types, standard types,* and *generic types.* User access rights to a file are Read, Delete, Write, Change Permission, Execute, Take Ownership, and No Access; however, this is really a simplification. Access rights to an object such as a file are much more complex, since access involves token mappings.

Specific File Access Types

ReadData	WriteEA (Extended Attributes)
WriteData	Execute
AppendData	ReadAttribute
ReadEA (Extended Attribute)	WriteAttributes

Standard Types (for All Objects)

SYNCHRONIZE	Synchronizes access to an object
WRITE_OWNER	Assigned to write owner
WRITE_DAC	Used to grant or deny access to the Discretionary ACL
READ_CONTROL	User to grant or deny access to the security descriptor and owner
DELETE	Used to grant or deny delete access

Following are the access mappings for user Read Access and Write Access. They illustrate the point that there are many more issues than simply reading a file. Even though you may be able to read a file, you may not always be able to read the attributes, or the extended attributes for that matter.

Generic Type	Mapped from Specific and Standard Types
FILE_GENERIC_READ	STANDARD_RIGHTS_READ
	FILE_READ_DATA
	FILE_READ_ATTRIBUTES
	FILE_READ_EA
	SYNCHRONIZE
FILE_GENERIC_WRITE	STANDARD_RIGHTS_WRITE
	FILE_WRITE_DATA
	FILE_WRITE_ATTRIBUTES
	FILE_WRITE_EA
	FILE_APPEND_DATA
	SYNCHRONIZE

The client/server security model is implemented with a technique called *impersonation*. Impersonation occurs when a process, acting on behalf of a user process in security context, attempts to access a resource. To understand this technique, the following definitions are made:

Subject	The combination of the user's access token plus the program acting on the user's behalf. The access token is found in the user process and contains the user's security ID (SID), the SID of all the groups the user is a member of, and the user assigned rights.
Security context	Security context occurs when a process or a program is acting on a user's behalf.
Simple subject	Normally impersonation is done by a protected server; however, a *simple subject* is a process that is assigned a security context when the corresponding user logs on.
Server subject	A process which is or functions like a protected mode server such as the Win32 subsystem, and which may have many subjects.

Every process has a Security Access Token (SAT), even the Security Reference Monitor (SRM) in the previous diagram. Kernel mode services of the Windows NT Executive have much higher access privileges than users and when performing a task for a client, they use the security token of the user, hence the term *impersonation*. What is important to remember is that everything in Windows NT is an object and has an access token. The scenario is something like this:

Hello, Executive Service? Please print this file for me, and if SRM asks, here is my SAT to show that I can do this.

Fault Tolerance

Within Windows NT, fault tolerance is more than just a *recoverable* file system. It is also the inclusion of such features as uninterruptible power supply (UPS), disk mirroring (RAID 1), disk striping with parity (RAID 5), and a tape backup system. But these RAID implementations are all software, and even though they work, they may incur unacceptable overhead. Another alternative is redundant arrays of inexpensive disks (RAID) supported at the hardware level.

RAID has six levels, three of which are supported by Windows NT.

RAID Level	*Description*	*Windows NT Supported*
Level 0	Disk striping	Yes
Level 1	Disk mirroring	Yes
Level 2	Disk striping with error correction code (ECC)	
Level 3	Disk striping with ECC stored as parity	

| Level 4 | Disk large blocks; parity stored on one drive | |
| Level 5 | Disk striping with parity distributed across multiple drives | Yes |

RAID 0   *Striping.*   A Windows NT stripe set may have 2 to 32 disks. Data is broken up into bands. With only two disks in a stripe set, half of the data would be on one disk and half on the other disk. With separate disk I/O channels and the data written simultaneously to both disks, performance is enhanced. If a disk in a stripe set fails, then all disks must be restored. The boot or system partitions cannot be striped.

RAID 1   *Mirroring.*   Windows NT can mirror any disk partition. In fact, it can mirror either the boot or system partitions. A mirrored partition may be FAT, HPFS, or NTFS. The mirrored disk need not have the same configuration, and can actually be larger; however, the extra space will be wasted. *Duplexing* is simply mirroring with a separate controller for each disk channel. RAID 1 ensures against loss of data from a single device failure.

RAID 5   *Striping with Parity.*   A Windows NT stripe set with parity may be 3 to 32 disks. The number of useful disks will always be one less than the number of disks in a stripe set with parity. After a failed disk has been replaced, the disk can be rebuilt by choosing the *Regenerate* command from the *Fault Tolerance Menu* of *Disk Administrator.* Regeneration can only be done with RAID 5, since RAID 1 does not have parity.

As hidden capabilities of Windows NT unfold, we see that whenever possible features are implemented as subsystems.[6] An example discussed previously is the Windows NT Cache Manager. Rather than implementing a specific capability for NTFS, the features are generalized for use by all file systems. *ft*Disk is the fault tolerant disk driver responsible for managing both disk mirroring and striping and it too has been generalized to work with FAT, HPFS, and NTFS. An example is that Windows NT may have striping and mirroring at the partition level, while SQL Server can use striping for backup/restore of database devices, which need not be a complete disk partition. The same is true for mirroring within SQL Server. SQL Server devices may be mirrored to a different SQL Server device, independent of Windows NT mirroring. Use of the DUMP command to create a striped disk backup set is illustrated in the following:

```
DUMP DATABASE <database_name> TO DISK = <dump_device1>, DISK =
    <dump_device2>, DISK= <dump_device3> WITH STATS
```

The nice thing about the SQL Server DUMP DATABASE command is that the devices are created (if they don't exist) when the dump occurs. It also possible to specify a mixed striped dump set by intermixing device names such as DISK, TAPE, FLOPPY, and PIPE, although PIPE typically wouldn't be used.

File System Issues

RAID 5

If you're considering a RAID implementation, its use is probably within the context of an enterprise system. Software RAID has severe limitations which include software overhead plus the inherent limitations of attempting to do RAID on a desktop machine rather than an enterprise machine such as the Digital Equipment Alpha.

Before implementing RAID 5 on a desktop system, analyze your hardware carefully. In a single-controller environment two or three disks are probably the limit, since you may start to realize controller loading problems. And even if you do add additional disk controllers, the main memory becomes the limiting factor—not because of speed, but because it isn't multiported. There are no multiports[7] for memory because the Intel architecture is based upon a bus and at various times in prior incarnations of the x86 architectures programmed I/O (PIO) was faster than direct memory access (DMA). This certainly surprised us, because on all the prior computers we have dealt with, DMA was the most optimal I/O operation. The bandwidth issue is complicated even further when discussing *cycle-stealing* (CPU cycles are stolen for I/O) versus *interleaving* where I/O access to memory occurs during a subcycle of the major CPU cycle.

There are multiported disks but new 1.2 gig SCSI disks which sell for less than $500 do not have multiporting. The Intel architecture was really designed for desktop data entry and does not have the internal infrastructure to support enterprise level functions from a single machine, although distributed use of these machines in a client/server environment appears to work very well. We continue to tell ourselves that the Intel architecture is limited[8] when compared with enterprise level systems and we use the term *elongated calculator* as a reminder not to overcommit systems designed with the Intel architecture. This is by no means a negative term, since they do have fantastic cycle rates compared to legacy equipment. The term reminds us that these cycle speeds, although very high, do not compensate for a smaller 32-bit bus and therefore do not always translate to increased I/O bandwidth.

Desktop architectures are a mixed bag right now. In the recent past, Vesa Local Bus (VLB) systems looked like they would determine the future direction of the I/O bus for desktop systems. However, that architecture is unbuffered and is actually a direct connection to the CPU. This is the reason that mother boards never have more than three VLB slots. VLB systems have been described as "slowing the CPU down to the speed of the disk." In the Peripheral Component Interconnect (PCI) world of Intel, the buffered bus interface, it's a different story.[9] Although the bus is buffered, the basic problem involves PCI's premature release, probably because Intel thought it would lose market share. If a PCI system is six months old, it is out of date. There are numerous revision levels and there isn't any stability with an estimated 70 to 80 percent of existing boards violating specifications. But since the specifications are vague, the problems will not be resolved soon.

What does all of this translate to? If you are interested in RAID 5, consider something like the Digital Equipment Alpha which is a 64-bit implementation. It's not just RAID 5 but the supporting infrastructure that must be considered. Personally, we simply wouldn't consider any RAID implementation unless it was a DEC Alpha. The real world is currently moving to a 128-bit architecture. The 32-bit architecture, while more than adequate for the desktop, falls far short for enterprise applications.

Selecting a File System

There really isn't a choice since file systems are evolutionary. FAT is first and certainly fast, but as discussed previously, it isn't scalable (cluster sizes become unwieldy with large partitions), it cannot handle long file names, and it is not robust.

HPFS is the next evolutionary step with a design tailored for speed, the ability to handle long file names, and security for OS/2 only. However, the 512-byte sector size is a limiting factor. A B-tree is used for fast access to data and a lazy-write feature is implemented which defers immediate writing. The lazy-write tends to normalize I/O and improves performance. However, the transfers are not serialized and the consistency of the structure is questionable after recovery.

NTFS evolves beyond HPFS and supports long file names and security within the Windows NT environment. It also adds special features such as multipath I/O to support OLE, and embeds small files into the directory to minimize the number of disk accesses for small files. It uses the B-tree and lazy-write technology of HPFS, but addresses the inconsistent recovery state by adding a log file. Cache write-through is used for all structural changes so that access to all files is guaranteed upon recovery. The log file uses the lazy-write and incomplete transactions will be rolled backed and completed transactions will be redone at recovery time. Microsoft guarantees recovery of the structures; however, complete recovery of all user data is not guaranteed. Caching is used by default within NTFS; however, NTFS clients can use cache write-through as SQL Server has done to implement the SQL Server data security model, which avoids use of the lazy-commit log. Performance issues are addressed with B-tree access, caching, imbedding of small files directly into the directory, 4096-byte logical blocks, and the lazy-writes.

As a rule of thumb for sizing systems, FAT can be used up to about 200Mb, HPFS up to about 500Mb, and anything beyond that should be NTFS.

In summary, enterprise problems require enterprise solutions. Hardware today is not expensive. SQL Server is typically used in an enterprise environment and the hardware of choice is the Digital Alpha with hardware RAID. The File system of choice is NTFS because of its performance enhancements, scalability (cluster sizes up to 4,096 bytes), security features, and recoverability.

Managing Users

In the Windows vernacular, a *Domain* is an abstract definition of a collection of workstations and/or servers. Within a domain, there are three types of servers:

1. *Primary Domain Controller(PDC).* The first Windows NT Server configured is always the PDC for the domain.
2. *Backup Domain Controller(BDC).* A Windows NT server which is installed after the PDC. There can only be one PDC in a domain, and the remaining Windows NT servers are candidates to be a BDC.
3. *Server.* Any other Windows NT server which is installed after the PDC and which is not a BDC. SQL Server and SNA Server are examples of this class of server.

There are a number of other server functions such as Windows Internet Naming Service (WINS), Domain Host Control Protocol (DHCP), System Management Server (SMS), and Browsers or Master Browsers. But our interest here is not in the definition of the Windows NT infrastructure necessary to support an enterprise, but only with account domains (trusted domains) and resource domains (trusting). We'll come back to domains after we discuss another abstraction, *groups.*

One of the biggest shortcomings of the DEC OpenVMS operating system is the ability to manage user privileges when there are many users. Individual privileges are given to individual users, which becomes a logistical nightmare for even a moderately sized network. Windows NT solves this problem by assigning rights and privileges to groups and not to users and then placing users within an appropriate group. There are three types of groups: *Special, Local,* and *Global.*

Special Groups

Special groups are really only built-in groups with predefined user rights and do not contain user or group accounts.

Network   This group includes any user, current or future, who connects to a shared resource on the network.

Interactive	Anyone who logs on locally is automatically included in this group. The user joins the *network group* after accessing a share on the network.
Everyone	It is a simple management task to give everyone permission to a resource, and then deny that resource to a selected few.
Creator-owner	This is only assigned at the directory or installed-printer level within Windows NT.

Local Groups

The question to ask is: Is this computer a member of a domain? If the computer isn't a member of a domain, then local groups can only contain local accounts. However, if the computer does belong to a domain, then local groups can contain:

Local accounts	These are accounts from untrusted domains, either untrusted Windows NT systems or LAN Manager, IBM LAN Server, or NetWare systems. These are *not* logon but network access accounts. When groups are created for managing untrusted (local) accounts, some consideration should be given to avoid commingling trusted and untrusted accounts. The MSSQLServer Service is an example of a local account. It must be configured as a local account for SQLMail and not as a user account which users log onto.
Domain accounts	Domain accounts should be placed in global groups since dealing with singular accounts is micromanaging.
Domain global groups	The most effective way to manage a domain. Permissions are given as a group.
Trusted domain accounts	A mechanism to give a single domain account access to a resource in a trusting (resource) domain.
Global groups from a trusted domain	The proper way to manage a resource domain. Global accounts are contained in the global group, and the global group is a member of a local group in the resource domain.

Global groups cannot be granted permissions. Permissions and rights can be given only to local groups. Local groups cannot contain other local groups; however, local groups can be given user rights, permissions on NTFS files and directories, and permissions on share names.

When creating an account on the primary domain controller (PDC), that account is automatically a global account unless it is an account from an untrusted domain, in which case it is a local account. Local accounts are *not* logon accounts, but accounts from untrusted domains or from systems other than Windows NT (LAN Manager 2.x, Novell Netware, or IBM LAN Server). These accounts are created only for access to resources on the local domain and can be placed in either local or global groups at the PDC. The local groups will be replicated from the PDC to all backup domain controllers (BDCs) of the domain by the *netlogon Service*. With this mechanism, an account from an untrusted domain has access only to the resources of the domain that exist either on the PDC or on any of the BDCs. Some caution should be used, however, since it is probably not wise to commingle accounts from trusted and untrusted domains. Local accounts cannot be used in trusting domains. This means that local accounts are only useful in local groups.

Normal or global domain accounts can be placed in global groups and used in trusting (resource) domains. When a normal (global) account is created, the user automatically becomes a member of the domain users group.

A Windows NT workstation joins a domain by selecting *network* from *control panel*. When a workstation joins a domain, the following occurs at the workstation:

♦ The Domain Admins Group is added to the workstation Administrator Local Group.
♦ The Domain Users Group is added to the workstation Users Local Group.
♦ The Domain Guests Group is added to the workstation Guests Local Group.

As can be readily seen, if permissions on a resource are granted to the workstation Users Local Group, then when the workstation joins the domain, all members of the domain automatically have access to that resource simply by being members of the Domain Users Group.

Built-in groups are divided into two categories, administrator and operator type. These groups exist on both the workstation and the server and cannot be deleted. The system administrator can create new local groups; however, there cannot be a naming conflict with other local or global groups.

Built-in Local Operator Groups

Backup operator	Workstation and domain controller
Replicator operator	Workstation and domain controller
Server operator	Domain controller
Printer operator	Domain controller
Account operator	Domain controller

Built-in Local Groups

Users	Domain controller and workstation
Guests	Domain controller and workstation
Administrators	Domain controller and workstation
Power Users	Server (not PDC) or workstation

Global Groups

We have already discussed global groups to some degree. Essentially, global groups exist only in a domain. Global groups have no built-in rights and obtain their rights from the local group which contains them. Global groups cannot contain other local or global groups; however, local groups can contain global groups. Permissions can be assigned only to local groups. A trusting (resource) domain can assign permissions to a local group which has a global group from a trusted domain as a member. When viewing groups from other domains, the name will be prefixed for ease of identification. As stated previously, domain local groups only occur on the servers within the domain. Global groups can be used on servers in the domain by placing them in local groups. For workstations within the domain, global groups from the trusted domain must be placed in local groups of the workstation. Administrators can create new global groups as desired. Built-in global groups are a special category of global groups which cannot be deleted.

Built-in Global Groups

Domain administrators

Domain users

Domain guests

User Manager for Domains

Now that we understand the concept of groups within Windows NT, we must use these concepts when SQL Server uses *integrated* or *mixed security*. These require that Windows NT logon accounts be created first for each user. These will be normal logon accounts and will automatically be members of *Domain Users*. User accounts can be created with *User Manager for Domains* from the *Administrator Tools* group.

Creating user accounts does take some foresight. After the domain architecture is established but before any accounts have been created, a decision must be made as to which accounts will have either a user (USR) profile or a mandatory (MAN) profile. In lieu of either of these, the system will use a default profile. The important issue here is to first establish an *Admins Profile Edit* account so that the normal administration account does not become confused as to wallpaper, startup groups, or other profile parameters. Create all profiles for new accounts before creating the new accounts. Create a mandatory profile for those users who run only a specific application. Those users are controlled by deleting icons from the program group. The *File Manager* group icon will be among those icons deleted so users cannot manually run a program. The only application that will run will be the application specified in the *startup* group. Other user account maintenance includes: setting or changing user name, full name, description, and passwords. It includes resettable flags for the following conditions:

- ♦ User must change password at next logon
- ♦ User cannot change password
- ♦ Password never expires
- ♦ Account disabled
- ♦ Account locked out

The *account locked out* flag is set automatically when there are too many invalid login attempts. This flag cannot be set, it can only be cleared.

Group membership can be established as well as the hours of logon and the account expiration date. The administrator has the choice of giving the user the ability to log on from any terminal, or from a list of up to eight terminals. Profiles can be defaulted or a profile path can be set. The home directory can be set along with a logon script and a share that may be connected to. If a logon script is used, it should be set in the REPL$ path for replication to servers within the domain. If a logon script is used, the user *netlogon* share must point to the replication directory which is:

```
\\<winnt_root>\SYSTEM32\REPL\IMPORTS\SCRIPTS
```

and the user must have at least RX permissions on this path. The connection is established by using the drive letter set in the LASTDRIVE statement in CONFIG.SYS. Replication of user logon scripts is managed from *Administrator Tools, Server Manager, Computer, Properties* of Windows NT Server.

After the user accounts have been created, you'll need to create two local groups for SQL Server. The first group we'll call *SQLUsers* and the second *SQLAdmins*. You may place domain user accounts, global groups, or domain groups into either of these groups. For example, if everyone in the domain can use SQL Server, place the global group *Domain Users* into the local group *SQLUsers*. We do this because only local groups can be assigned privileges and rights. For the group *SQLAdmins*, place only those global accounts which will have administration privileges on SQL Server. Of course, if SQL Server supports more than one user database, you will correspondingly have more local groups. Once the local groups have been created and populated, use SQL Security Manager to assign permissions.

User Manager for Domains is also used for local and global group maintenance. Administrator-created groups may be deleted and group membership can be managed with the deletion or addition of members.

Managing Windows NT

Domains

Once domains are set up, the *netlogon Service* provides logon authentication and pass-through authentication for Windows NT users. Windows for Workgroups Redirector VREDIR.386 performs an equivalent service. Each user has only one logon account with this service.

Replication of logon scripts and mandatory profiles is done to servers in a domain. This allows a server other than the PDC to authenticate a user logon when the logon is not local. Of course, local logons use the local profile rather than the server based profile.

There are two types of domains, *resource domains* and *trusted domains*. A trusted domain is just another name for an account domain. Resource domains are never trusted domains, but are trusting domains. However it is possible for an account domain to trust another account domain. Creating trusts is an administration function where passwords are exchanged between administrators. The administrator in the account domain enters a domain name in the *permitted to trust this domain*, while the administrator of the other domain enters the trusted domain name in *trusted* domains. Trusts in *User Manager for Domains* were discussed previously. Trusts are not transitive. If Domain_A trusts Domain_B, and Domain_B trusts Domain_C, then Domain_A does not trust Domain_C. However, it is possible for Domain_C to trust Domain_A only if a separate trust relationship is created between Domain_C and Domain_A.

There are four domain models. In each of these models, resources are always in a trusting domain. Resource domains never trust other resource domains.

1. *Domain model.*
2. *Master-domain model.* One or more domains trust one domain (see Figure 9.15). In this model, all accounts are placed in the trusted domain and all the resources are located in the trusting domains. The size of the enterprise really dictates how many domains are needed. In fact, if very few accounts are needed, then everything may be placed in a workgroup. Of course, there is much more administrative work to managing users on an individual basis. So the very small organization will be a workgroup while the master-domain model with an account domain and multiple resource domains can support up to 15,000 users. Degrees between domains depend upon the particular infrastructure of the enterprise.

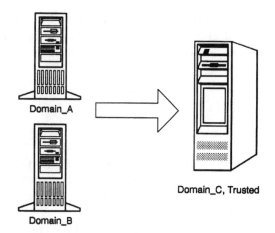

Domain_A

Domain_B

Domain_C, Trusted

FIGURE 9.15 Master domain model—two resource domains trusting an account domain.

> **3.** *Multiple master-domain model.* We see that additional management is required (see Figure 9.16). If the multiple trusted domains are local, then it is probably a poor enterprise model. However, this model might be appropriate when each trusted domain is located in a different state or city.
>
> **4.** *Complete-trust model.* All domains trust each other. It requires a significant administrative effort to implement one. The unofficial word from Microsoft is that complete trust models are not appropriate in Cairo, a distant future release of Windows NT. Therefore, we won't illustrate this model.

Server Manager

The Windows NT Server *Server Manager* is used to manage domains. There are two server managers. Windows NT workstations have a server manager in the

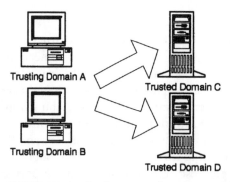

Trusting Domain A

Trusting Domain B

Trusted Domain C

Trusted Domain D

FIGURE 9.16 Multiple master domain model—two trusted account domains for each trusting domain.

control panel and Windows NT Server has a server manager in the *control panel* and in the *Administrative Tools* program group. We discuss the server manager from *Administrative Tools* of Windows NT Server.

The server manager from the Windows NT *Administrator Tools* group is your window to the work currently being performed by SQL Server. From the server manager, the administrator can view connected users and resources, shared resources in use, open files, file locks, and named pipes in use. If necessary, the administrator can terminate access to all of these resources but only after sending a message to users warning them that resources are about to be terminated.

A domain has only one primary domain controller (PDC). With the Server manager, an administrator can promote a backup domain controller (BDC) to PDC. Of course, the administrator should *Synchronize Domain* before this is done so that all account databases are synchronized. *Promoting to PDC* is a task that is done when maintenance work must be done to the PDC. There will be no interruption of work for users; in fact, they won't even know that it is occurring.

Administrative alerts may be setup in the Server Manager. When administrative alerts occur, messages can be sent to either a *computer* or to a *username*. Workstations, servers, or BDCs may be added or removed from a domain. Windows NT services may be started and stopped from the Server Manager. These include all services necessary for normal Windows NT operation such as the *Alerter Service,* the *Server Service,* the *Messenger Service,* and the *Replicator Service.*

Elsewhere in this book we have discussed SQL Server replication. Earlier in this chapter, we discussed replication between WINS servers. We also discussed replication by the *netlogon* service which updates user accounts on BDCs. The replication discussed here is the same replication discussed earlier for logon scripts and user profiles. This is not SQL Server replication, but the replication of logon scripts or profiles, or any other directory which is placed in the REPL$ path. Replication is required for the Systems Management Server (SMS), discussed in the following. However, getting replication to work requires a number of steps for the export server, which are shown here. Similar steps are required for the import computer.

♦ Create an account for the Directory Replicator Service to use.
♦ Set all logon hours are allowed.
♦ Make the account a member of the domain's backup operators, domain users, and replicator groups.
♦ Set Password never expires in the account.
♦ Add to the domain's Replicator group the right to *logon as a service.*
♦ In Server manager, configure Directory Replicator to start automatically and logon under the directory replicator account.
♦ Set the replication paths properly referencing: \\<winnt_root>\system32\repl\. . . . If the export directory is on an NTFS partition, then the

replicator group on the export server should be granted full access to the export directory tree.

System Management Server

The Gartner Group concluded in a study involving two thousand PCs, "Getting the Code to the Node," that the cost of software support, distribution, and installation is over four times the cost of the actual software acquisition price. The Microsoft Systems Management Server attempts to address those costs by providing tools to perform the following tasks:

♦ Collect and maintain an inventory of software and hardware.
♦ Manage the unattended distribution and installation of software.
♦ Manage network applications, and where possible share applications. Share applications from a distribution server.
♦ Troubleshoot software or hardware problems for DOS or Windows Clients.

Systems Management Server (SMS) supports operating systems using Windows NT, LAN Manager 2.2, IBM LAN Server 3.x, Novell NetWare 3.x and Novell NetWare 4.x (in 3.x compatibility mode). For clients, SMS supports Windows NT 3.x, Windows 3.x, Windows 95, Windows for Workgroups 3.x, OS/2 1.3 and 2.x, Apple Macintosh (System 7), and MS-DOS 5x or later.

Communication is by LAN, RAS, or SNA. For each of these communication modes SMS provides a *sender* service. For future releases of SMS, DEC is working to integrate SMS with the DEC Polycenter management system, and IBM is working to integrate SMS into the NetView 6000 management system. At a future date, Microsoft plans to provide an event generator for SMS so the SNMP traps can be used to report management information in a management information block (MIB) (see SNMP).

There are different roles for computers in a SMS architecture. Before we illustrate an SMS architecture (see Figure 9.17) let's discuss the SMS concept of a site and list the possible computer roles. The SMS environment consists of sites, domains, servers, and clients. Each site may have more than one domain. One site from the collection of sites is designated the *Central site*. All other sites are *primary* or *secondary* sites. Sites are organized in a hierarchical manner. A *secondary site* does not have an SQL database, and the inventory information is stored on a *primary* site which is the parent of the secondary site.

Central Site	*Primary Site*	*Secondary Site*
Site Server	Site Server	Site Server
SQL Server database	SQL Server database	
Domains	Domains	Domains
Logon Server	Logon Server	Logon Server
Distribution Server	Distribution Server	Distribution

Helper Server   Helper Server   Helper Server
Clients   Clients   Clients

Collection and Maintenance of a Hardware and Software Inventory

The *SMS Site Server* name is really an alias for a primary domain controller (PDC) while the *SMS Logon Server* name is an alias for a Windows NT, LAN Manager, LAN Server domain controller, or a Novell NetWare server. This is necessary, since control of the client systems is maintained with use of logon scripts replicated from the REPL$ script path of the PDC to logon servers. System Management Server Logon Script (SMSLS) will be embedded within the logon script. SMSLS is used for the collection of hardware and software configuration information. There are many different files for the different types of clients. The script files are shown following. The software inventory collection scripts are installed by the following files:

SMSLS.BAT	Windows NT, MS-DOS, Windows 3.x, Windows 95
SMSLS.CMD	OS/2 LAN Manager and LAN Server clients
SMSLS.SCR	NetWare system logon script for NetWare clients

Software Distribution

Software is distributed as a *job*. The job consists of a SMS *sender* shipping a *package* with *instructions* to a distribution server. A job may the installation of software such as Microsoft Access at a client site or the shipping of data files

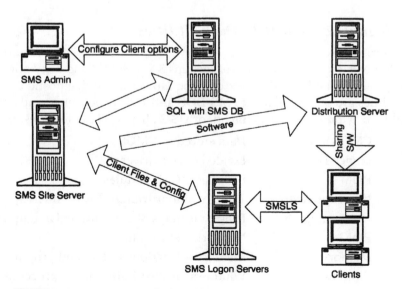

FIGURE 9.17 Basic SMS architecture.

to a remote site. The distribution server is then responsible for the storage of the software for future use. The instructions are delivered to the logon server and may include configuration changes at the client as well as the installation of icons.

A *package* is either software or data. If it is software that is not sharable, it will be sent directly to the client site. The included *instructions* will give the disposition. If the software is to be shared, then it will be sent to the client's local distribution server. A package is compressed before shipping and decompressed by the SMS *Despooler* at the distribution server. Since the application is shared, the software is not actually loaded into the client computer but is loaded from the distribution server when needed at execution time. Software metering is not done. Shared applications are only supported by the Windows 3.x and the Windows NT 3.x operating systems.

SMS, through the distribution server, supports the distribution of commercial or custom applications, data files, or any other task related programs that may be run on a client and which are not shared. This support is for MS-DOS 5 and later, Windows 3.x, Windows NT 3.x, and Macintosh System 7 systems. Data files can be copied to the client computer. This mechanism is quite similar to shared software distribution in that the instructions are exported to the logon server and the package is exported to the distribution server. All of this is implemented at the client with the Package Command Manager (PCM) component of the Systems Management Server. PCM gives the user the choice of which packages to install. The user selects an application to install from the PCM and the PCM connects to the distribution server and installs the application. For Windows NT based systems, PCM supports unattended package installation.

Diagnostics and Help Desk Utilities

Microsoft Systems Management server supports as clients Windows NT 3.x, Windows 3.x, Windows for Workgroups 3.x, OS/2 1.3 and 2.x, Apple Macintosh (System 7), and MS-DOS 5.x or later. However the diagnostic and help desk utilities are only available to MS-DOS and Windows clients, and are not available to Windows NT, Macintosh, or OS/2 clients. These features include:

CMOS info	Data stored in CMOS
Device Drivers	Loaded device drivers
ROM	Installed ROM modules
Interrupt Vectors	Table of all hardware/software interrupts
UMB mapping	Programs maps of conventional and upper memory
PING	Network test results
Memory	Memory allocation, system and program modules
Windows	Windows task list information, procedures
Resources	GDI and global heap

Remote Control	Control of client keyboard and mouse
Restart	Restart remote client
File transfer	Transfer files between server and client
Remote execute	Starts an application remotely

All information can be viewed in real time. Programs currently loaded in memory are displayed as well as system usage of resources such as the GDI and global stacks. Using the *Remote Control* utility, an administrator views the client's screen and can take control of its keyboard and mouse.

Notes

1. A broadcast storm is any situation when more than 10 percent of the total messaging traffic is broadcast messages for lost connections, host or NetBIOS name resolution, or other support functions. Data transfer between server and client is not a broadcast, but a connection-oriented reliable connection with acknowledgments. When the broadcast level is greater than 20 percent of the total messages, the network may be close to being unusable.
2. Microsoft has provided a *Wide Area Information Server* for use on the WWW in the Windows NT 3.5 Resource Kit. For installing WAIS and other tools such as an internet *Gopher* and *Domain Name Service,* please consult the Windows NT 3.5 Resource Kit, Vol. 2, Chap. 21.
3. "Automate Web Data Retrieval," *Visual Basic Programmer's Journal,* Nov. 1995.
4. On Windows NT, both FAT and HPFS are implemented as lazy write file systems. (Helen Custer, *Windows NT File System,* p. 35.)
5. Helen Custer, *Inside the Windows NT File System,* p. 58.
6. Helen Custer, "The Layered Driver Model," *Inside the Windows NT File System,* Chap. 2.
7. Multiple buses are a useful analogy for a multiported memory.
8. Microsoft announced that SQL Server 6 using Compaq ProLiant 4500 5/133 with Windows NT 3.51 server achieved a TPC-C benchmark transaction rate of 2454.97 transactions/min at a price performance level of $241.64. (*Dow Jones News,* Oct. 16, 1995.)
9. Bob Chronister, "What's Wrong with PCI," *Windows NT Magazine,* Sept. 1995, p. 88.

C H A P T E R

10

Operations

This chapter is where it all happens. We install SQL Server and manage it. Not all issues are covered, but we discuss those issues which we consider important. We also warn you of the ramifications of different issues. There are four major sections to this chapter:

1. *Installation.* We identify the relevant issues for installing SQL Server. Review this section before you attempt to install SQL Server. We also list a number of tasks that must be accomplished before installing SQL Server.
2. *Server Management.* In this section we cover device management: *sp_configure* usage, security, error recovery issues, and problem resolution. Special attention is given to recovering user and system databases from configuration errors.
3. *Database Management.* This section addresses data loading and offloading, managing users with management guidelines, *sp_dboption* usage, and DBCC usage.
4. *Backup and Recovery.* We discuss when to use the various DUMP DATABASE and DUMP TRANSACTION options. We provide solutions for various situations that you will encounter.

Installation

This section is not a substitute for the *Microsoft SQL Server Administrator's Companion* but a review of important installation issues that will help you step through a preliminary installation.

Successful endeavors always require planning. We all know someone who has made an installation without reading the release notes. Quite often, information is found there that is not in the formal documentation.

The topics in this section are arranged in alphabetical order and not in the order of importance or interest. Review each topic before installing SQL Server.

Accounts

SQL Executive

You should create a *SQLAdmins* group and place a user account for use by the SQL Executive in that group using the Windows NT *User Manager for Domains*. This account must also belong to the Windows NT Administrators local group and must be granted the rights *Log on as a Service, Password Never Expires*, and *Allowing All Logon Hours* for connectivity tasks with other servers in the domain. At setup, the default account presented for SQL Executive use is the local Windows NT administrator account. If you enter the password for that account, it is now the SQL Executive account.

During the installation, the SQL Executive account defaults to the Windows NT administrator account. You can accept this by entering the password and verifying it or replace it with the account you have just created.

SQL Mail

After SQL Server is installed, you may use SQL Server Setup to define a mail account for SQL Server. You do this by selecting *Set Server* options, followed by selecting *Mail Login* from SQL Server Setup. There is no default account presented in the dialog box and the administrator must enter a normal user account[1] which may be the Workgroup Postoffice (WGPO) for Windows NT. This is because SQL Mail runs *piggyback* on an existing Windows NT account and the first account to start Workgroup Mail becomes the Workgroup Postoffice.

There is another very important issue. For SQLMail to function, the SQL Server MSSQLServer Service must have the *Allow Service to Interact with the Desktop* right. When SQL Server is installed, the account for the MSSQLServer Service defaults to a LocalSystem account which is required for SQLMail to operate. Don't change this to a normal Windows NT account.

Character Sets

When you install SQL Server you must choose a *character set*. This decision is difficult to change later. If you decide to change the character set, then you must rebuild your databases and reload your data. Three main character sets are offered: ISO 8859-1 (default), Code Page 850, and Code Page 437. It is also possible to install a custom character set.

Unless you have some compelling reason to choose a different character set, we recommend ISO 8859-1, which is the default character set for SQL Server. If you are using a Sybase SQL Server running on a different platform, this character set is more likely to be compatible with that server. These same choices are available on other platforms as well—so it is possible to have a compatible installation with any of these character sets.

If most of your applications are based on the English alphabet, common symbols, and numerals, the choice of character set is not critical because these characters appear in the same location in each of the character sets. To find out what character set is in use for an existing server, look at the error log for that server. One of the last things written to the error log when the server is booted is the character set and sort order in use.

The following is a sample from the error log:

```
95/11/20 09:37:53.42 spid1    on top of default character set:
95/11/20 09:37:53.42 spid1          'iso_1' (ID = 1)
```

ISO 8859-1

ISO 8859-1 is the current default for SQL Server. This character set is also known as *Latin 1, ANSI,* and *ISO-1* (in the error log sample the sort order is identified as 'iso_1').

Code Page 850

Code Page 850 was the default on some earlier releases of SQL Server such as 4.2x. If you are upgrading an earlier release of SQL Server, or want to run this server on a network that includes other servers with this character set installed, you may want to choose this code page. This is a multilingual character set and is most likely to provide support for applications that use languages of Europe and North and South America.

Code Page 437

Code Page 437 is commonly used on workstations. It includes many graphics characters. If you want to store special characters for graphics in your database, this is a good choice. However, Code Page 850 and ISO 8859-1 provide more characters if you use languages other than U.S. English.

Additional Character Sets

Although your documentation only lists the character sets ISO 8859-1, Code Page 850, and Code Page 437, it does state that the delivered product will have additional character sets. These character sets are enumerated in Table 10.1.

CHKUPG

You'll want to run *CHKUPG* before doing an upgrade of a 4.2x installation. CHKUPG checks the database status, checks that all necessary comments exist in the *syscomments* table, and checks for keyword conflicts.

Environment

Networking[2]

If SQL Server is not available to the complete enterprise, consider placing the server on a subnet with access available through a commercial router. Network bandwidth will then be limited only by SQL Server messaging and the traffic of the supporting network infrastructure. It is important to standardize on one network protocol if at all possible. Extra protocols in the protocol stack of Windows NT will add extra overhead to communications.

Single Processor

If possible, put the SQL Server on a machine that only runs SQL Server. This should be a machine that functions only as a Windows NT Server. There are three installation options for Windows NT Server, the SQL Server host:

1. Primary domain controller (PDC, the first Windows NT server installed in this domain)
2. Backup domain controller (BDC)
3. Windows NT Server

Always pick the last choice for the machine hosting SQL Server. As discussed in Chapter 9, Windows NT is a distributed operating system and SQL Server

TABLE 10.1 Additional Character Sets

Code Page	Character Sets
1250	Central European
1251	Cyrillic
1253	Greek
1254	Turkish
1255	Hebrew
1256	Arabic
1257	Baltic

should be placed on a dedicated machine to isolate it from other Windows NT infrastructure. SQL Server is resource intensive and this isolation will make it easier to tune.

Domains

The Windows NT logical structure is a domain that is a collection of machines. *Trusts* exist between domains and users are always placed in account domains. Resources are always placed in resource domains and resource domains trust account domains. It's not logical with the structure of Windows NT security for users to trust resource domains. Resource domains trust[3] account domains, and SQL Server is placed on a Windows NT Server in a resource domain.

A PDC or BDC is by definition a member of an accounts domain (Logons accounts, logon scripts, and so on).

Master Device

Place the SQL Server master device on your most reliable and fastest device. The *master device* is a component of SQL Server and can be found in SQL Server directory <drive:>\SQL60\DATA. *It's wise to mirror the master device.* As you expand the SQL Server database by adding new devices, these devices can exist on different drives that use different file systems.

A reasonable size for the master device is 25 to 35Mb. The default installation is 25Mb. It is a good practice to keep the master device relatively small and to only have the master—tempdb—and model databases on it. It can have only the first portion of the tempdb on it with the rest of the tempdb on another device. Although this isn't critical, a master device with only these three databases makes recovery from a damaged master device easier. You only have to use the *Rebuild Master Database*[4] function from SQL Server Setup to recreate the master device and then load a backup of the master database. If no damage occurs to other devices, you don't need to load any other databases from backup. This is possible since SQL Server saves the files MASTER.DA@ and MASTER.AL@ in \SQL60\INSTALL as prototypes of a new MASTER.DAT.MASTER.DA@. The file MASTER.DAT.MASTERDA@ is used for recovering the master device when the default sort order and character set are used, otherwise it uses MASTER.AL@ when recovering the master device.

SQL Server Version 6 reduces the importance of this initial decision of how large to make the MASTER device compared to earlier releases. It is possible to increase the size of a device using the DISK RESIZE statement.

At installation for both SQL Server and Workstation SQL Server, the dialog box states that 25Mb will be used for the master device. Both servers allocate the disk space indicated in Table 10.2, which is found by selecting *databases* from the SQL Server Enterprise Manager toolbar. Table 10.2 gives the initial default allocations (in MB) established for the different databases by **setup**.

TABLE 10.2 Initial Database Allocations

Database	Used (MB)	Free (MB)	Device	Purpose
tempdb	1	1	master	A temporary database used for intermediate work
pubs	1	2	master	A sample database used for demonstrations and tests
msdb	2	2	MSDBData/ MSDBLog	Bookkeeping for the SQL Enterprise Manager
model	1	0	master	Prototype of all new user databases
master	9	8	master	Controls user databases and SQL Server in general

Service Pack

Service packs are collections of software bug fixes. As of this writing, Service Pack 1 is available for SQL Server 6. It may be downloaded from the CompuServe MSSQL Forum and is also available with a Microsoft Technet of Microsoft MSDN Level II or III subscription.

Sort Orders

The sort order that you specify on installation affects two aspects of the SQL Server:

1. The order that rows are returned in when there is an ORDER BY clause
2. How the server determines when two values are equal

We recommend binary order unless you have a compelling reason to choose one of the others. The binary sort order will maximize performance since it is based on numeric order and no secondary compares are necessary. It also avoids problems inherent in some of the other choices discussed in the next sections.

The following is a sample from the error log for Dictionary order, case-insensitive[5]:

```
95/11/20 09:37:53.41 spid1    SQL Server's default sort order is:
95/11/20 09:37:53.42 spid1          'nocase' (ID = 52)
```

Your choice or sort order is determined by client requirements rather than based on performance issues. All servers and clients should have the same sort order.

All databases on a server must have the same sort order. The requirement for one of your databases and its application may determine the sort order for your server.

Binary Order

With the binary sort order, the collating sequence is based on the numeric value of the character. Two strings are equivalent only when they have identical characters. *AB* is equal only to *AB*. It is not equal to *ab*.

The collating sequence will sort all uppercase characters before any lowercase characters. *Zz* will appear in a sort before *ab*. This does not match what is commonly referred to as *dictionary order*.

Dictionary Order, Case-Insensitive

This is the default sort order for Microsoft SQL Server. In this sort order, upper- and lowercase letters are treated as equivalent. In a comparison (say, in a WHERE clause), *A* is equal to *a*.

The collating sequence reflects the fact that upper- and lowercase characters are treated as equivalent. *AB* will appear after *aa*, but before *ac*.

This sort order seems attractive and is, in fact, used by many installations. It sorts a set of character values much as a dictionary does. It also allows you to use a WHERE clause to look for matches, regardless of the case used to enter values in a table. The following query will find all rows, regardless of the case of the value as it is stored in the database:

```
SELECT * FROM employees WHERE last_name = 'smith'
```

It has been our experience that this leads to laziness when inserting values into the database. You will find that *smith* is sometimes entered as *SMITH*, or *Smith*, and sometimes as *SmItH* (well, not really, but you get the idea). We prefer ensuring that our data is stored appropriately in the application. In some cases we add an extra column called *last_name_upper_case* which includes the last_name forced to upper case using the upper( ) function.

We recently heard of a site that used this case-insensitive order. They unfortunately received a code table from one of their suppliers and discovered that the codes A and a were different. They had to either convert their server or create some new way to manage these codes. This can also be an incompatibility with other servers.

Dictionary Order, Case-Sensitive

Dictionary order provides a dictionary ordering, but is sensitive to case. This means that *AB* will still appear after *aa* but before *ac*. But *AA* is no longer equivalent to *aa*. This does get rid of one of our objections to dictionary order, case-insensitive, but it is still slower than the binary order.

Dictionary Order, Case-Insensitive, Uppercase Preference

Similar to dictionary order, case-sensitive, but in a query with an ORDER BY clause, *AA* will always appear before *aa*.

Dictionary Order, Case-Insensitive, Accent-Insensitive

Similar to dictionary order, case-insensitive, but characters with accents are treated as equivalent to the nonaccented letter.

Alternate Dictionary Orders and Scandinavian Dictionary Orders

The following dictionary orders are only available with code page 850. They offer minor (but for some installations, important) variations in how accented characters are compared to each other, their nonaccented counterparts, and the ordering of certain letters.

- ♦ Version 1.x—Compatible sort order
  This option is included for compatibility with Version 1. The only advantage of this option is strict compatibility with Version 1. Version 1 compatibility is only limited to the first 128 characters and reverts to binary for anything else.
- ♦ Alternate dictionary order, case-insensitive
- ♦ Alternate dictionary order, case-sensitive
- ♦ Alternate dictionary order, case-insensitive, uppercase preference
- ♦ Alternate dictionary order, case-insensitive, accent-insensitive
- ♦ Scandinavian dictionary order, case-sensitive
- ♦ Scandinavian dictionary order, case-insensitive, uppercase preference

Sort Orders and SQL Server Performance

Binary sort order is the fastest. The alternate sort orders provided with SQL Server will result in a slight loss of performance. Only those operations that compare characters, such as building indexes, searching for rows, or sorting rows experience this loss. In general the following rules hold:

- ♦ Binary sort order is always fastest.
- ♦ Any dictionary sort order that is sensitive to accents is about 20 percent slower than binary order.
- ♦ Any sort order that is accent-insensitive will be about 35 percent slower.

Replication

Are you doing replication?[6] If you are, then consider the following items:

- ♦ For replication, the log at the publisher has the added responsibility of being a *temporary holding queue* for transactions not yet distributed. This is not a major issue when the same SQL Server is also the distributor.
- ♦ If you plan to implement a separate distribution server for replication, additional log space will be required at the publisher for situations when

the distribution server is unavailable. This configuration requires two SQL Servers, one for publishing to the distributor and one for distributing to subscribers. Distribution servers must always be recoverable to a point in time *after* the publication server. You may decide that a two-hour buffer with the publisher transaction log is satisfactory for such a situation. This is dependent upon the recovery period for the distribution server.

♦ For SQL Server distribution, the distribution log size is dependent upon subscriber save cycles. If the backup cycle at the subscriber is every 12 hours, then the distribution server must have log space for 24 hours of transactions. Give all subscribers the same backup cycle period so that log requirements at the distribution server are manageable.

♦ If SQL Server is doing publishing and distributing, consider placing the distribution database and its log on a separate disk drive from other databases on the server.

The distribution server for replication server uses Named Pipes or Multi-Protocol for communication with subscription servers. This requires that each subscriber is either a member of the distributor domain or a member of a trusted domain.

When the Installation Fails

Normally SQL Server installations are trouble-free for fresh installations. Listed as follows are some problems you may encounter with an installation:

♦ *You are unable to register a server in Enterprise manager.* At initial installation, you must use Enterprise Manager to register a server. Before using the server registration dialog box of Enterprise Manager, go to SQL Server Setup, choose *Security Options* and select Windows NT *Integrated Security* with **sa** as the login. Enter a meaningful password when prompted and terminate setup normally. Don't lose this password or you will have to reinstall SQL Server.

Use Enterprise Manager and select *Register Server* from the toolbar and the *Server Registration Dialog Box* will be presented. When you register a server in the Enterprise Manager, you must enter the server name if it has never been registered before. This is because the *Server Registration Dialog Box* will not search for a SQL Server installation, since it is the same dialog box used to register remote SQL Servers. Before you select *Register Server,* be sure that you have selected *Integrated Security* since this is the mode we just established in SQL Server Setup. (At some later time, you may use this dialog box to change the security to standard if necessary.)

Selecting *List Servers* from the *Server Registration Dialog Box* and *Refresh* from the resulting dialog box is only meaningful if the server has been registered before. If the server has been registered before and will not start, you'll have to use your own diagnostic procedures. You can investigate the physical data link, you may have a broadcast storm saturating the network, or the remote server may be offline. A good place to start is the network using the Windows NT Performance Monitor.

◆ *You receive a virtual memory error message when upgrading from 4.2x.* SQL Server was overconfigured. In SQL Server 4.2x it was possible to commit more physical memory (RAM) than was available as virtual memory (disk). You need to expand the virtual memory of Windows NT from the *Control Panel, System.*

◆ *You are unable to upgrade from Workstation SQL Server to SQL Server.* Doing an upgrade will fail. You must delete all *MSSQLServer* and *ODBC* entries from the Registry.

Server Management

Devices

Using Files as Database Devices

With SQL Server using Windows NT as a host, SQL Server logical devices are files. Windows NT has three types of file systems, FAT, HPFS, and NTFS.[7] A database may have more than one device and these devices may reside on disks with different file systems.

How Many Devices to Use

If your application is I/O bound, you can increase performance by increasing the number of devices. It is better to have several small devices than a single big device because then the SQL Server spreads the I/O activity among the devices. You can do this by putting different databases on different physical devices, by spreading a database across several devices, or by placing some objects on specific devices. Tables are placed on a segment[8] using the ON clause of the CREATE TABLE statement or sp_placeobject stored procedure. Indexes are placed on a segment using the ON clause of the CREATE INDEX statement or sp_placeobject stored procedure. You can place a text or image column on a segment using the sp_placeobject stored procedure.

If you have a very large table, you may want to consider splitting the table[9] across several devices. This procedure is only recommended for tables that are fairly static or read-only.

Log Device

If possible, reserve the physical device the log is on for only that log. The log device (syslogs table) has a great deal of I/O—it is most efficient if you minimize contention for that device.

At the least, place the log on a separate SQL server device (created using the DISK INIT command). This will improve throughput and allow incremental dumps of the log (DUMP TRANSACTION).

Device Space—sp_devspace

The stored procedure *sp_devspace* will report on all devices on a server and how much space you have allocated to databases on each device.

If you call it without a parameter, it reports on space used and available on each device.

If you call it with the name of a device as a parameter, it reports on that device and the space allocated to that device.

Here is the code for sp_devspace:

```
/***********************************************************************/
PRINT '/***** PROCEDURES                                      *****/'
/***********************************************************************/
go
IF EXISTS (SELECT * FROM sysobjects
    WHERE name = 'sp_devspace'
    AND   uid = user_id('dbo')
    AND   type = 'P')
BEGIN
    DROP PROCEDURE dbo.sp_devspace
END
go
/***********************************************************************/
PRINT '/*****    CREATE PROCEDURE    sp_devspace              *****/'
/***********************************************************************/
go
create procedure sp_devspace @name varchar(30) = null
as
declare      @pgs_per_mb int
/* get the number of pages per Mb */
select @pgs_per_mb = 1048576 / low from master.dbo.spt_values
     where type = 'E' and number = 1
if @name is not null
begin
    /* is @name a database device? */
    if not exists (select * from master.dbo.sysdevices where
        name like @name and cntrltype = 0)
    begin
        declare @msg varchar(80)
        select @msg = "'" + @name + "'" + " is not a database device."

        print @msg
        return
    end
```

```
end
else
    select @name = '%'
    /* get the data for devices that have space allocated to db's */
    select Device = d.name, Capacity_Mb = (d.high - d.low + 1)/@pgs_per_mb,
        Used_Mb = sum(u.size)/@pgs_per_mb
        into #devspace
        from master.dbo.sysdevices d, master.dbo.sysusages u
        where d.name like @name
            and d.cntrltype = 0
            and u.vstart between d.low and d.high
        group by d.name, (d.high - d.low + 1)/@pgs_per_mb
    /* add the data for devices that don't have space allocated to db's */
    insert #devspace select d.name, (d.high - d.low + 1)/@pgs_per_mb, 0
        from master.dbo.sysdevices d, master.dbo.sysusages u
        where d.name like @name
            and d.cntrltype = 0

            and not exists
                (select *
                from master.dbo.sysusages u
                where u.vstart between d.low and d.high)
    /* return the results */
    select distinct Device, Capacity_Mb, Used_Mb, Free_Mb = Capacity_Mb -
    Used_Mb
        from #devspace
        order by Device
        compute sum(Capacity_Mb),
            sum(Used_Mb),
            sum(Capacity_Mb - Used_Mb)
    return
go
```

sp_devspace Output

```
device                    Capacity_Mb Used_Mb Free_Mb
------------------------- ----------- ----------- -----------
MSDBData                            2           2           0
MSDBLog                             2           2           0
master                             25          24           1
                          sum
                          ===========
                          29
                                      sum
                                      ===========
                                      28
                                                  sum
                                                  ===========
                                                  1
```

Configuration

sp_configure

The following are the *sp_configure* values that can be set. The items identified with a * are only displayed when the sp_configure value '*show advanced option*' is set to 1. Dynamic options take effect immediately and are marked with a #. For those options which are not dynamic, SQL Server must be stopped and then restarted for the new value to take effect.

allow updates#	open objects
backup buffer size#	*priority boost
backup threads	procedure cache
*cursor threshold#	*RA cache hit limit#
database size	*RA cache miss limit#
default language	*RA delay#
*default sortorder id	*RA pre-fetches#
fill factor	*RA slots per thread#
*free buffers#	RA worker threads
*hash buckets	recovery flags
language in cache	recovery interval#
LE threshold maximum#	remote access
*LE threshold minimum#	*remote login timeout#
LE threshold percent#	*remote query timeout#
locks	*remote sites#
*logwrite sleep (ms)#	*set working set size
max async IO	show advanced option#
*max lazywrite IO#	*SMP concurrency
max worker threads#	*sort pages#
media retention	*spin counter#
memory	tempdb in ram (Mb)
nested triggers#	*time slice
network packet size#	user connections
open databases	

How to Recover from sp_configure Errors or Insufficient Resources

Occasionally after using sp_configure, SQL Server will not restart since you have overcommitted a resource. To recover from this situation, use from the command line:

```
sqlservr -c -de:\SQL60\DATA\MASTER.DAT -f
```

When this is done, SQL Server starts in the following state:

- Autoexec procedures are not executed.
- If *tempdb in ram* is true, then it is set to 2Mb.
- Remote Access and Read-Ahead are disabled.
- The CHECKPOINT mechanism is disabled.
- Procedure cache is set to 50 percent.

Once SQL Server is started, you can switch immediately to ISQL/w to enter your commands. You know when to switch when following the message below appears:

```
WARNING: OVERRIDE, AUTOEXEC PROCEDURES SKIPPED
```

Don't bother using the Service Manager. Although you can start the SQL Executive, you can't make a connection in Enterprise Manager and your only access to SQL Server is with ISQL/w. *Note that SQL Server is running even though the Service Manager green light is not on. It simply wasn't started in the Service Manager.*

Issue the appropriate *sp_configure* command to correct your problem, terminate SQL Server, then restart it normally. To terminate SQL Server when in the **-f** mode, return to the command line screen and issue a CTL-C. Answer **yes** to the message and SQL Server will be terminated so that it may be restarted normally.

Sample output from *sp_configure* is shown in the next code example when starting SQL Server with the **-f** option. You may compare the *procedure cache* value to a normal start value of SQL Server, which follows. From ISQL/w, the following commands were issued. Note that EXEC is used in each *sp_configure* statement. Although not needed for the first statement of a batch, it is a good habit to always use it. The **go** signifies the end of a batch.

```
EXEC sp_configure 'show advanced option', 1
RECONFIGURE
go
EXEC sp_configure
```

Resultant Output (Started with -f and -c Option)

name	minimum	maximum	config_value	run_value
allow updates	0	1	0	0
backup buffer size	1	10	1	1
backup threads	0	32	5	5
cursor threshold	-1	2147483647	-1	-1
database size	1	10000	2	2
default language	0	9999	0	0

default sortorder id	0	255	52	52
fill factor	0	100	0	0
free buffers	20	524288	204	50
hash buckets	4999	265003	7993	7993
language in cache	3	100	3	3
LE threshold maximum	2	500000	200	200
LE threshold minimum	2	500000	20	20
LE threshold percent	1	100	0	0
locks	5000	2147483647	5000	5000
logwrite sleep (ms)	-1	500	0	0
max async IO	1	255	8	2
max lazywrite IO	1	255	8	2
max worker threads	10	1024	255	255
media retention	0	365	0	0
memory	1000	1048576	4096	1405
nested triggers	0	1	1	1
network packet size	512	32767	4096	4096
open databases	5	32767	20	5
open objects	100	2147483647	500	100
priority boost	0	1	0	0
procedure cache	1	99	30	50
RA cache hit limit	1	255	4	4
RA cache miss limit	1	255	3	3
RA delay	0	500	15	15
RA pre-fetches	1	1000	3	3
RA slots per thread	1	255	5	5
RA worker threads	0	255	3	0
recovery flags	0	1	0	0
recovery interval	1	32767	5	5
remote access	0	1	1	0
remote login timeout	0	2147483647	5	5
remote query timeout	0	2147483647	0	0
resource timeout	5	2147483647	10	10
set working set size	0	1	0	0
show advanced option	0	1	1	1
SMP concurrency	-1	64	0	1
sort pages	64	511	64	64
spin counter	1	2147483647	10000	0
tempdb in ram (MB)	0	2044	0	2
user connections	5	15	15	5

```
(1 row(s) affected)
```

You may wish to keep a hard copy of your configuration parameters for recovery usage. Examples of the normal parameters and advanced parameters with normal SQL Server starts are shown as follows. Both were run from ISQL/w.

```
EXEC sp_configure 'show advanced option', 0
RECONFIGURE
go
EXEC sp_configure
```

Resultant Output (Normal Start, No Advanced Option)

name	minimum	maximum	config_value	run_value
allow updates	0	1	0	0
backup buffer size	1	10	1	1
backup threads	0	32	5	5
database size	1	10000	2	2
default language	0	9999	0	0
fill factor	0	100	0	0
language in cache	3	100	3	3
LE threshold maximum	2	500000	200	200
LE threshold percent	1	100	0	0
locks	5000	2147483647	5000	5000
logwrite sleep (ms)	-1	500	0	0
max async IO	1	255	8	8
max worker threads	10	1024	255	255
media retention	0	365	0	0
memory	1000	1048576	4096	4096
nested triggers	0	1	1	1
network packet size	512	32767	4096	4096
open databases	5	32767	20	20
open objects	100	2147483647	500	500
procedure cache	1	99	30	30
RA worker threads	0	255	3	3
recovery flags	0	1	0	0
recovery interval	1	32767	5	5
remote access	0	1	1	1
show advanced option	0	1	0	0
tempdb in ram (MB)	0	2044	0	0
user connections	5	32767	20	20

```
EXEC sp_configure 'show advanced option', 1
RECONFIGURE
go
EXEC sp_configure
```

Resultant Output (Normal Start, Advanced Option)

name	minimum	maximum	config_value	run_value
allow updates	0	1	0	0
backup buffer size	1	10	1	1
backup threads	0	32	5	5
cursor threshold	-1	2147483647	-1	-1
database size	1	10000	2	2
default language	0	9999	0	0
default sortorder id	0	255	52	52
fill factor	0	100	0	0
free buffers	20	524288	204	204
hash buckets	4999	265003	7993	7993
language in cache	3	100	3	3
LE threshold maximum	2	500000	200	200

LE threshold minimum	2	500000	20	20
LE threshold percent	1	100	0	0
locks	5000	2147483647	5000	5000
logwrite sleep (ms)	-1	500	0	0
max async IO	1	255	8	8
max lazywrite IO	1	255	8	8
max worker threads	10	1024	255	255
media retention	0	365	0	0
memory	1000	1048576	4096	4096
nested triggers	0	1	1	1
network packet size	512	32767	4096	4096
open databases	5	32767	20	20
open objects	100	2147483647	500	500
priority boost	0	1	0	0
procedure cache	1	99	30	30
RA cache hit limit	1	255	4	4
RA cache miss limit	1	255	3	3
RA delay	0	500	15	15
RA pre-fetches	1	1000	3	3
RA slots per thread	1	255	5	5
RA worker threads	0	255	3	3
recovery flags	0	1	0	0
recovery interval	1	32767	5	5
remote access	0	1	1	1
remote login timeout	0	2147483647	5	5
remote query timeout	0	2147483647	0	0
resource timeout	5	2147483647	10	10
set working set size	0	1	0	0
show advanced option	0	1	1	1
SMP concurrency	-1	64	0	1
sort pages	64	511	64	64
spin counter	1	2147483647	10000	0
tempdb in ram (MB)	0	2044	0	0
user connections	5	32767	20	20

All of the advanced parameters are listed in the preceding, but we'll only mention those directly involved with configuration issues. The default[10] values for all *sp_configure* parameters are discussed in the documentation. Some of these parameters such as *time slice* and *SMP concurrency* are issues for the Windows NT system administrator. The *sp_configure* parameters discussed as follows are commonly used for basic configuration issues.

Allow Updates

Some old code is shown in The Procedure which was used in the past to shrink tempdb. This isn't needed anymore with the new Version 6 feature DBCC SHRINKDB; however, it does illustrate the use of BEGIN TRAN, COMMIT TRAN, and ROLLBACK TRAN to protect SQL Server from inadvertent errors. In this mode, set 'allow updates' to 1; we are allowed to update the system tables. This is extremely sensitive and prone to possible problems. This procedure assumes that SQL Server is in single-user mode and the Windows NT Service Control Manager was bypassed with:

```
sqlservr -c -m
```

The following procedure is presented only to show a style of updating system tables. We don't recommend routinely modifying system tables directly. Do not use this procedure to shrink databases other than tempdb (and see notes later in this chapter on other ways to shrink the tempdb). Do not turn on allow updates unless explicitly instructed to do so by a very knowledgeable person. The server that you damage is your own.

The Procedure

```
USE master
go
EXEC sp_configure 'allow updates', 1
RECONFIGURE WITH OVERRIDE
go
BEGIN TRAN
go
DELETE FROM sysusages
     WHERE dbid = db_id('tempdb')
     AND lstart != 0
go
IF 1= (SELECT count(*) FROM sysusages
     WHERE dbid = db_id('tempdb'))
     COMMIT TRAN
ELSE
     ROLLBACK TRAN
go
EXEC sp_configure 'allow updates', 0
RECONFIGURE
go
```

This procedure is rather macho, but it does illustrate a number of important issues for us:

♦ The *sp_configure* option accepts our parameter; however, the RECONFIGURE statement installs the parameter.
♦ The *sp_configure* option 'allow updates', 1 requires the use of RECONFIGURE WITH OVERRIDE to accept user supplied system parameters. Other *sp_configure* parameters may require the use of RECONFIGURE WITH OVERRIDE if SQL Server thinks the value entered is not appropriate. Statements in error will not be accepted. The statement sp_configure 'recovery interval', 120 produced the following message:

```
Msg 5807, Level 16, State 1
Do not recommend recovery intervals above 60 minutes - use override
    option to force this configuration
```

◆ BEGIN TRAN, COMMIT TRAN, and ROLLBACK TRAN can be used to protect SQL Server from invalid updates. When modifying systems tables, place all change operations in a transaction as the example shows.

◆ Always set *allow updates* back to 0 when you are done.

Fill Factor

The *fill factor* is a number used by SQL Server to indicate the fullness of the index page at *index creation*. SQL Server uses *B-tree*[11] technology which will split an index page when it becomes full. By default, the value of *fill factor* is zero (0), which fills the data level pages of a clustered index or leaf level pages for a nonclustered index. All other index pages have room for at least one additional entry with two additional entries reserved for nonunique clustered indexes. Using *fill factor* is only meaningful for existing data and for index creation. After index creation, the *fill factor* is stored in *sysindexes* but is not used.

If you use a number other than zero (0), then all index and data pages will be filled to this percentage level at index creation. This can be valuable for performance tuning on a frequently updated table. To be effective for performance tuning, you must recreate the indexes on a regular basis.

If you do not intend to update the data then the value 100 will completely fill all index pages at initial index creation. The percentage may change after updates have been made, but the *fill factor* isn't considered then.

Max Worker Threads

SQL Server allows you to configure the maximum number of user threads that are made available to the SQL Server process. Each time that a user connection has work to do, it is assigned a user (or worker) thread. If there is not an available user thread, that connection waits until one is available. The maximum value that can be used is 1024. The default value is 255 and you will want to increase this for an enterprise environment. Threads consume resources so allocating too many threads may be self-defeating.

Memory

There is an interplay between SQL Server memory acquired with *sp_configure* and the physical memory of Windows NT. SQL Server manages objects with the data/procedure cache. Making this cache too large will force Windows NT to do excessive paging. SQL Server itself is a Windows NT object, and it will be paged when Windows NT memory resources are low. When excessive paging occurs, your choice is to reduce SQL Server memory, reduce your data/procedure cache, or add physical memory.

Don't let the server page.[12] Nice words, but Windows NT is a *virtual operating system* and will always do some paging. We can, however, calculate what can be considered excessive paging. You can use the Windows NT Performance Monitor and look at *Memory:Pages/sec* and *Logical Disk:Average Disk Sec-*

onds/Transfer for the disk which contains *pagefile.sys,* the Windows NT paging file. If the product of these two numbers over a period of time exceeds 10 percent, then too much paging is occurring and more memory should be added.

The following was captured in *chart* mode from Windows NT Performance Monitor:

```
Reported on \\THOR
Date: 11/21/95
Time: 5:44:21 PM
Data: Current Activity
Interval: 5.000 seconds
Computer: \\THOR
Object: Memory
   Pages/sec      1.198
Object: LogicalDisk
             0
          C:
   Avg. Disk sec/Transfer 0.084
   Disk Transfers/sec     59.425  (Note that this field is scaled 1000)
Object: Process       SQLEXEC  SQLSERVR
   Page Faults/sec               0.0399
```

Using the preceding, we'll do some quick calculations.

```
Avg. Disk sec/Transfer * Pages/sec = Time in ms for paging
                                   = 1.198 * 84 ms
                                   = 100.63 ms
```

If this number is greater than 100 ms or 10 percent, then real memory should be added. These numbers indicate that this system should have more memory and indeed it should since it is only 16Mb. Calculation of this number is more complex if the system has more than one paging file. The numbers will not be accurate unless the system has a separate disk for *pagefile.sys,* the Windows NT paging file.

We already have the value for *Avg. Disk sec/Transfer.* If we add one more parameter, *Disk Transfers/sec,* then we'll use this new parameter to look at our disk load.

```
Avg. Disk sec/Transfer = % Disk Time/Disk Transfers/sec
                       = 1/59.425
                       = 16.82 ms/transfer
```

The actual disk transfer time to the user is 84 ms. Dividing this by the disk transfer time, we get the queue length:

```
84/16.82 = 4.99 average queue length
```

To create the preceding report, use the following procedure while SQL Server is running:

♦ Start SQL Server Performance Monitor.
♦ Select *View* menu bar.
♦ Select *Chart* from the menu.
♦ Select + from the toolbar.

After the Performance Monitor dialog box loads:

♦ In the *Object* combo box, select *Memory.*
♦ In the *Counter* combo box, select *Pages/Sec.*
♦ Press *Add.*
♦ In the *Object* combo box, select *Logical Disk.*
♦ In the *Counter* combo box, select *Avg. Disk sec/Transfer.*
♦ In the *Instance* combo box, select the *pagefile.sys* disk drive.
♦ Press *Add.*
♦ In the *Object* combo box, select *Process.*
♦ In the *Counter* combo box, select *Page Faults/sec.*
♦ In the *Instance* combo box, select *SQLEXEC.*
♦ Press *Add.*
♦ In the *Object* combo box, select *Process.*
♦ In the *Counter* combo box, select *Page Faults/sec.*
♦ In the *Instance* combo box, select *SQLSERVR.*
♦ Press *Add.*

Close the dialog box. Your information will be collecting on the screen. Use the *File* menu to *Export* the report to a .TXT file.

You might not know the actual memory requirements for SQL Server at installation time, but the following can be used as a guideline.[13] The *approximate* column is the suggested value when using the memory option of *sp_configure:*

Machine Memory (Mb)	Approximate Server Memory (Mb)
32	16
48	28
64	40
128	100
256	216
512	464

After the basic memory requirements of SQL Server are satisfied following a *sp_configure<memory, 2k units>*, the remaining memory is divided by default with 30 percent used for procedure cache and the remaining 70 percent used for the data cache.

Network Packet Size

The default packet size is 4096 which is the normal size for *core mode* Server Message Blocks.[14] For Novell networks, you have to set this back to 512 bytes.

Open Databases

The *open databases* setting determines how many databases can be opened. Since the recovery process opens each database in turn, this needs to be as big as the number of databases on your server. In fact, you should allow one or two extra, so that you don't have to reconfigure your server if you create a new database. If this value is too low, some of your databases will not be recovered. In that case you will have to increase the value and reboot your server.

Open Objects

The *open objects* setting determines how many objects (roughly how many tables, stored procedures, views, defaults, and rules) can be accessed at the same time. This should be increased if you get an error message indicating that you have exceeded the number of open objects.

Each open object requires memory that is reserved from the data memory when the SQL Server is booted. You do not want to set the value higher than is needed. A good starting point for this setting is the total number of objects on the server. In each database, execute the following query, then add the resulting values:

```
SELECT count(*) FROM sysobjects
```

Priority Boost

Probably the most misused *sp_configure* parameter. Do not use this parameter. If you boost the priority of SQL Server, and there are intervals where the system is CPU-bound, then not all threads will have an opportunity to execute. Windows NT already provides a priority boost for threads doing I/O.[15] The priority is boosted after completing I/O and then drops with each time slice until it is back to normal.

Set Working Set Size

When adjusting memory, it is recommended that you use the *sp_configure* option *set working set size*. This forces Windows NT to allocate physical memory and virtual pages in your working set for the sum of the *memory* setting and the size of tempdb, if it is in RAM. This is necessary since the *memory* option does not *include memory needs for* tempdb.

tempdb in ram[16]

Use of *tempdb in ram* will certainly help your sorting and improve performance if you use large temporary tables; however, this reduces the memory available for caching with a subsequent lower cache hit ratio. In addition, tempdb will *still be cached* even though it is in RAM. By placing tempdb in RAM, you have reduced the SQL Server available cache *and* increased the cache requirements.

Memory for tempdb is allocated separately from SQL Server memory. Assuming that SQL Server is dedicated and after subtracting the memory for Windows, the remaining memory is divided between tempdb and the *sp_configure memory*. In a 64Mb system with 16Mb reserved for Windows NT, you could have 16Mb for tempdb and the remaining 32Mb for use by *sp_configure memory*. The *working set size* (your allocated virtual pages) will need to be adjusted. To do this, please see *Set Working Set Size*.

For *tempdb in ram* to be beneficial and successful, observe the following guidelines:

♦ The minimum memory configuration for *tempdb in ram* is 64Mb, and preferably should be 128Mb or more.

♦ Use SQL Server Performance Monitor and observe *Object: SQLServr* and *Counter: Cache Hit Ratio*. If your system has a low cache hit ratio, *tempdb in ram* will probably not have any effect.

♦ Even though *tempdb in ram* is intuitively very promising, you need some way to justify the usage of RAM. A very simple approach could use *sp_lock* to observe the lock activity in tempdb. Another approach is to use SQL Server Performance monitor on: *Object:SQL Server-Log, Counter:Log Space Used(%), Instance: tempdb*. Better yet is to use a batch program which runs on a regular basis to sum the *dpage* column of *sysindexes* in the tempdb database. This value is the instantaneous sum of pages allocated to all objects. If none of these approaches is an effective way to measure tempdb utilization for your application, you will probably need to design your own instrumentation. Summing these pages can be accomplished with:

```
select sum(dpages) from tempdb..sysindexes
```

♦ Tempdb operations must be sized so they fit in the tempdb ram configuration.

User Connections

SQL Server Version 6.0 has extended the possible number of user connections. The maximum depends on the version of SQL Server purchased, and may be 25, 128, 256, or 32,767. The value 32,767 is a theoretical limit. You will likely run into other limitations before this is achieved.

Each user connection requires about 40K. This value must be set to at least the maximum number of connections that will ever be established simultaneously. Remember that some applications and tools require more than one connection. There are always several default connections (the number may depend on your configuration options). All applications require at least one connection; however, an application may have more than one connection. The four system processes *mirror handler, lazy writer, checkpoint process,* and *RA manager* each require a connection. The default number of users connections is only 20.

Security

Overview

Security appears complex, but it's not when the architectural issues are identified. SQL Server provides three levels of security which roughly parallel Windows NT architectures:

- *Integrated (trusted connection).* Connection is with Named Pipes or Multi-Protocol and the user Windows NT logon authentication is used.
- *Standard.* Login authentication is established in SQL Server Security Manager independent of the type of connection.
- *Mixed.* Connection may be made with either trusted or untrusted connections. If the connection is from an untrusted link, a user logon ID must be established using SQL Server Security Manager.[17] If the connection is from a trusted link and the login name matches the user network name, apply *Integrated Security* rules. If it doesn't match, then *Standard Security* rules apply.

We see from the preceding that the topology of a SQL Server network parallels that of Windows NT. For small systems, Windows NT systems and SQL Server can function in workgroups with each Windows NT system and SQL Server maintaining its own security. This is equivalent to *Standard Security* for SQL Server where each server maintains separate login information and login IDs may be duplicated. As the enterprise expands, management becomes difficult. This approach does violate a major system management rule: The same user login appears on different servers. If you adopt *Standard Security,* you must develop your own management policies and guidelines. A good starting point is to have them match the user's network name. Users will have one less name to keep track of, and it may allow utilities to verify that the correct user is logged in from a given machine.

With a large enterprise *Integrated Security* may not be practical because of the heterogeneous nature of the network. Access between Windows NT Servers by other Windows NT servers may be with trusted connections using Named Pipes or Multi-Protocol; however, access to other systems will typically be with untrusted connections. For this environment, *Mixed Security* is the best choice.

Security Issues

You may want to establish a security officer login ID for a server. You give the person using this ID the ability to authorize new logins. To do so, you put a new version of *sp_addlogin* on the server that allows the person using this id to add new logins. The version of *sp_addlogin* shipped with the SQL Server verifies (see extract), that the person running it is the system administrator (**sa**).

Stored procedures within SQL Server may be protected with a stored procedure permission test which is just a few lines of code that check for a specific user (for **sa**, *suser_id*( ) = 1). To modify a system stored procedure that modifies system tables, you must execute the following two lines in order to modify the procedure:

```
EXEC sp_configure allow updates,1
RECONFIGURE WITH OVERRIDE
```

Stored Procedure Permission Test

```
If suser_id() <> 1
     begin
            raiserror(15003, -1, -1)
            return(1)
     end
```

The preceding example from *sp_addlogin* is wired to a unique user. To allow another user to execute this procedure, you have to modify the test in the stored procedure.

Using SQL Server configured with *Integrated Security,* a login of **sa** Windows NT workstation, and no password, we were able to connect to SQL Server from ISQL/w by entering *jeddi* (a nonexistent login ID), as the login ID. We were then able to execute the following command in master which added a login account. The top of the screen in ISQL/w indicated that we were connected as **sa** even though we used *jeddi* as the login ID in the ISQL/w dialog box. We were able to do this on both SQL Server and Workstation SQL Server.

```
sp_addlogin Obiwan
```

We also started the server in **-f** mode which is used to recover from configuration errors with:

```
sqlservr -c -de:\sql60\data\master.dat -f
```

We were able to use ISQL/w without a valid login. We then created a new login account using *sp_addlogin.*

You can also view *sp_addlogin* information using DBCC INPUTBUFFER:

```
Input Buffer
sp_addlogin Obiwan, Jeddi
(1 row(s) affected)
DBCC execution completed. If DBCC printed error messages, see your System
    Administrator.
```

sa

The special SQL Server login ID **sa** (System Administrator) lets the user manage the server and any database on the server. This login ID is created by the SQL Server install. This login ID can issue any commands on the server. As a result, it is possible for a user logged in as **sa** to do anything (both good stuff and bad stuff).

Initially, this password is NULL. You must keep the **sa** password tightly controlled. An administrator should only log in as **sa** when performing some activity requiring the privileges provided to an *SA*.

Because of the great deal of power that this login receives, there are a number of good practices that you should follow with respect to this login ID.

First and foremost, change the password for this ID as soon as you complete an install. Then control who gets to know this ID. Many sites think that it is convenient for everyone to know the **sa** password during development. That way, someone who is still around at midnight and runs into a problem can correct it on the spot (dropping databases, authorizing new users, creating objects, and so on). This is indeed convenient—it is also a time bomb. Do set a real password. Do record it someplace where it can be found by another administrator or a manager (if this password is lost, you must reinstall the server!). Give the password out selectively.

Second, don't routinely log in as **sa**, even if you are the system administrator. Your administrator should have a second ID—with far fewer privileges—that can be used to just look around at what is on the server, or do backups, or try out new features. You can do lots of things when logged in as **sa**! You can easily drop databases, drop tables, or perhaps other things that you didn't want to do. When we need to do some serious work as **sa**—we tend to get another cup of coffee, take a deep breath, think about what we are about to do—and then log in as **sa.** If we are about to perform some task that we don't do on a daily basis, we find someone who can look over our shoulder, while we perform the task. We can explain to this person what we are doing. It isn't essential that this person have any idea what we are talking about—the exercise is useful (and we thank our kids for putting up with this from time to time).

Third, periodically use *sp_who* to see who is logged. If you notice that this person named *sa* is logged in many times (or in fact that a number of different people have gotten in the habit of logging in as **sa**), change the **sa** password. From time to time we notice this on our company's servers, and just change the password without telling anyone (except perhaps our general manager) what we are doing. Then we wait for the screams (sometimes we are not very nice). Being logged in as **sa** is really a bad habit.

dbo_database_name

The SA or, preferably, a single *sa_database_name* login name should own each database. Though it may not always be appropriate, you can give this login name and password to more than one person to help administer the database.

You might add a login ID named *dbo_database_name* for each database on the server. You can then make this login be the database owner (special user name dbo) for the database. You set the database owner of a database using the stored procedure *sp_changedbowner.*

A common environment that we find at SQL Server sites is that they have a login *sa,* and all of the databases are owned by this login. This is a reasonable approach, but it means that in order to do certain actions against a particular database an individual must log in as **sa** (and hence must know the **sa** password). Examples of actions requiring this authorization are authorizing new users in the database and loading from a dump. If you have a single server supporting several different development or production groups, you must either have an **sa** who is constantly available (for some fairly mundane activities), or give out the **sa** password to far too many people.

If you create a special database owner login for each database, you can have an administrator for that database. In addition, an administrator who is going to make changes to one database can log in as *dbo_database_name* and be assured of not inadvertently making changes to other databases. The database administrator should log in as *dbo_database_name* only when performing some activity requiring the privileges provided to a dbo in that database.

Error Recovery Issues

Master Database

Full Transaction Log

Normally this doesn't occur since the *Truncate Log on Checkpoint* option is set by default in the *master* database. A separate log backup isn't possible with the *master* database since the log and database exist on the same device in SQL Server. We can use trace flag 3607 to recover the *master* database with the following procedure:

```
sqlservr c:\sql60\data\master.dat -T3607
After SQL Server has started, from ISQL/w do:
DUMP TRANSACTION master WITH NO_LOG
Restart SQL Server normally.
```

Error on Recovery

Automatic recovery occurs every time SQL Server is restarted. Recovery starts with *master, model, pubs, distribution,* and any user databases, in that order, every time SQL Server is restarted. When the *master* database is full the recovery process cannot complete. To recover *master,* you must restart SQL Server with trace flag 3607:

```
sqlservr c:\sql60\data\master.dat -T3607
```

After SQL Server starts, use the previous procedure to recover a full *master* database.

Full Database

Use the DISK RESIZE statement of the Enterprise Manager to increase the size of the *master* database on the MASTER device. This technique is necessary since the *master* database cannot be expanded on any device other then the MASTER device. Be sure that you backup *master* after expanding it. If you find that your master database keeps filling up, even though you enlarged it, look to see what user objects you may have included in this database. Usually you don't want to put any user tables in the master database. Create another database to hold them. Keep your master database small and clean.

Model Database

Tempdb is used during recovery. The *model* database can never be larger than the size of *tempdb*, and if it is, SQL Server will not start. If this occurs, you may use the trace flag 3608 to start recovery:

```
sqlservr c:\sql60\data\master.dat -T3608
```

After recovery has started, use the detailed procedure on recovering the *model* database[18] to truncate the *model* transaction log. After a normal SQL Server recovery, expand tempdb.

Another alternative is to use trace flag 3609, which skips creation of the tempdb database during SQL Server startup. You may want to use this if there are problems with the device or devices for *tempdb* or when problems exist in *model*.

User Database

Full Transaction Log

With Version 6 replication, recovery has become more complex.[19] A transaction log dump will remove published transactions; however, it still must be coordinated with a backup of the distribution database. The distribution database must always have a recovery point in time *after* the publication database. If the distribution server is temporarily unavailable, consider expanding the publisher transaction log.

If the log is full and you don't want to expand it, then you can truncate it with:

```
DUMP TRAN databasename WITH TRUNCATE_ONLY
```

If this fails to truncate the expected number of entries, use *sp_repltrans* and DBCC OPENTRAN to find unpublished and open transactions which cannot be truncated.

The *DUMP* statement creates a CHECKPOINT log entry. When the log is so full that this can't happen then do:

```
DUMP TRAN databasename WITH NO_LOG
```

For more detail on this command, see, *DUMP TRANSACTION, DUMP TRANSACTION command options* (following).

Error on Recovery

User database recovery is automatic at SQL Server startup and occurs after *master, model, pubs,* and the *distribution* databases have been recovered. If this fails and the error is 1105, then SQL Server must be restarted with the trace flag 3608:

```
sqlservr c:\sql60\data\master.dat -T3608
```

There is a detailed procedure (see footnote for recovery of an 1105 error) in the Microsoft documentation. It is too detailed to list here and does involve setting the database status. In the process of recovery you destroy the status, so you capture the status before you start and change it back when you are finished with *sp_dboption.*

Full Database

When a user database is full, a message of the following form is returned:

```
   Can't allocate space for object '%.*s' in database '%.*s' because the
'%.*s' segment is full
```

If the transaction log is full, see *DUMP TRANSACTION* (following). Additional space for the user database can be allocated with the ALTER DATABASE statement. Be certain that you follow this with a backup of the *master* database.

Problem Resolution

Error Log

The error log is an important source of information on errors. Review it daily for error messages and anytime you have a problem on the server. Often there is important information in the error log not displayed on a user's screen.

The error log can be viewed from Enterprise Manager by selecting *Server* from the toolbar and then selecting *Error Log* from the menu. The location of the error log is by default in the directory \SQL60\LOG and the current log is named ERRORLOG.

The location of the error log can be found in the Registry at:

```
HKEY_LOCAL_MACHINE\SOFTWARE\Microsoft\MSSQLServer\MSSQLServer\Parameters.
```

SQL Server Troubleshooting

Your first source of information is *Books OnLine.* Using it is quite simple. Take your error code, such as an 822, open *Books OnLine,* select the *find* icon (binoculars) from the toolbar, enter **822**, and select *find*. Select the topic and then *GoTo* and a complete description of error code 822 is displayed.

In the *SQL Server Administrator's Companion*, refer to the following chapters:

- ♦ Chapter 20—Troubleshooting Overview
- ♦ Chapter 24—Additional Problem-Solving Techniques
- ♦ Chapter 25—Handling Error Messages (Gives procedural solutions to problems encountered)
- ♦ Chapter 26—System Error Messages
- ♦ Chapter 27—DB-Library Error Messages

Another source of information is the CompuServe MSSQL Forum. Although not formally supported by Microsoft, you can find the resolution to your problem simply by reading *old threads*. Posted questions are often answered by users like yourself.

Special Databases

When first installed, SQL Server contains four databases: *master, msdb, model,* and *tempdb*. Every database contains a number of system tables necessary for managing the tables in that database. The *master database* also includes additional system tables necessary for managing the server.

The *msdb database* provides support for SQL Executive and stores scheduling information.

The *model database* is a template for creating any future database. Any object (table, view, and so on) created in the model database will appear in any future database.

The *tempdb database* provides short-term storage needed during the processing of queries or applications. SQL Server drops any temporary table (a table whose name starts with the # character) in the tempdb when the application drops it or when the application disconnects from the server. In addition, SQL Server uses space in the temporary database to satisfy some queries requiring sorting or grouping.

Model

Every database starts out as a copy of the model database. A number of things to create in the model database are the following:

- ♦ Datatypes commonly used in multiple databases
- ♦ Rules or defaults commonly used in multiple databases
- ♦ Standard users you want to have in each database (e.g., a user authorized to do backups)
- ♦ Tables required in each of your databases for documentation purposes

If you have stored procedures you want to access in many databases, consider starting their names with *sp_* and putting them in the master database, not in the model. A user with the appropriate permission can call a stored procedures whose names start with sp_ in the master database from any database.

If you make the model database larger than the default size (2Mb), make sure that *tempdb* is at least as big as the model. If *tempdb* is smaller than the model, the server will not start.

tempdb
Contents

The server uses *tempdb* for all temp tables (tables starting with the character #) and for temporary storage allocation possibly required for joins, sorts (ORDER BY clause) or aggregates (GROUP BY clause).

In addition, you can explicitly create objects in *tempdb*. Avoid doing so, since the server reinitializes the tempdb every time you start the SQL Server.

Expanding

The size for the tempdb depends on the applications you run and how many simultaneous users are accessing the server. If there is not enough space in the tempdb, the user gets the error message 1105, "Can't allocate space for object '%*s' in database *tempdb* . . ." If this occurs, check the application to make sure it is making reasonable use of space. If it is, use **ALTER DATABASE** or the Enterprise Manager to increase the size of the *tempdb*.

Shrinking

Sometimes an SA may enlarge the tempdb in an erroneous attempt to accommodate a particular query.[20] You find your *tempdb* enlarged, and you would like to make it smaller. While discussing the use of *sp_configure*, a macho procedure was listed for shrinking *tempdb*. Don't use it. We need not go to the trouble and the risk that the elaborate procedure entails, since there is a far simpler mechanism. Set *tempdb in ram* true and restart **SQL Server** with the **-f** flag (see earlier, *Recovering from sp_configure Errors*). When SQL Server is restarted, *tempdb* will be 2Mb in RAM.

```
sqlservr -f
```

DBCC SHRINKDB[21] can also be used to reduce the size of *tempdb* if SQL Server is started with the **-m** option. SQL Server can be started in single user mode with:

```
sqlservr -m
```

Starting the Server on System Boot

SQL Server may be started automatically at system boot time. The option to start at boot time can be done from *Setup, Select Server Options,* and then selecting *Auto Start Server at Boot Time* or *Auto Start Executive at Boot Time*.

There is a second choice. From *Control Panel, Services,* double-click MSSQLserver. In the dialog box, change to *automatic* from *manual* and Click *OK*. MSSQLServer will start automatically at the next system boot. The same procedure can be applied to SQL Executive. In the dialog box, change to *automatic* from *manual* and click *OK*.

SQL Server Limits

Table 10.3 illustrates the SQL Server limits.

Database Management

In this section, we present techniques for managing a database. These techniques include loading data, managing users, setting database options (with sp_dboption), and using the database consistency checker commands (DBCC).

Tools for Loading Data

This section describes two techniques for loading data into a table. The first is the SQL Transfer Manager, a Windows-based tool for copying tables from one server to another. The second is bcp, the bulkcopy program.

Transfer Manager

Probably the easiest way to move a database is with *SQL Transfer Manager*. If the transfer is between different platforms such as Intel to Alpha, then Transfer Manager is required. It is ideal for small databases and also useful for large databases.

bcp

bcp is a utility for volume loading data into a table or extracting the data from a table out to a flat file. There are two speeds for bcp in a database: slow and fast. *Slow bcp* is similar in performance to executing a number of INSERT statements to load the data. When using slow bcp, all of the rows are logged as they are inserted. *Fast bcp* is much faster, with the individual inserts not logged. Space allocation is still logged with fast bcp.

Normally, SQL Server will choose to use slow bcp. However, if you use the option

TABLE 10.3 SQL Server Limits

Maximum number of databases	32,767
Size of a database	1 terabyte
Maximum tables in a join	16
Maximum number of tables in a database	2 billion
Maximum number of columns in a table	250
Maximum number of bytes per row in a table	1,962 bytes (*Note:* This includes a minimum of two bytes of overhead in a row.)
Maximum number of nonclustered indexes on a table	249
Maximum number of clustered indexes on a table	1
Maximum number of columns in an index	16
Maximum length of an index (sum of the maximum lengths of all of the columns in the index)	256 bytes
Maximum number of segments in a database	32
Maximum number of disk fragments in a database	32
Maximum number of columns in a primary key constraint	16
Maximum number of columns in a foreign key constraint	16
Maximum nesting level for stored procedures or triggers	16
Maximum number of bytes of text in a stored procedure or trigger	65,025
Maximum number of parameters in a stored procedure	256
Maximum number of database devices	Value specified by sp_configure devices, but no more than 255
Storage	8 terabytes
Maximum user connections	32,767 (15 with workstation version)
Memory	2 gigabytes

```
EXEC sp_dboption 'select into/bulkcopy', TRUE
```

and the table you are bcping into has no indexes, SQL Server will choose to use fast bcp.

With fast bcp, the database *must* be dumped after the bcp operation completes. Recreate the indexes after the database dump. Be sure to reset *Select Into/Bulk Copy* to false.

For either fast or slow operation, defaults defined for columns and datatypes in the target table are observed. *Rules, triggers, and constraints are ignored to load data at maximum speed.* If you want SQL Server to evaluate the rules, triggers, and constraints in your loaded data, take the following steps:

- ♦ Create another table that has the same columns, rules, triggers, and constraints as the original table.
- ♦ Copy the data to this table (possibly with INSERT . . . SELECT)
- ♦ Use an UPDATE that will *set* all of the rows in the table. Use something like:

```
UPDATE tablename SET column1 = column1
```

The last step will evaluate the rules, triggers, and constraints and report any errors.

Using bcp

You can use the bcp utility to load data into a table on the SQL Server. This is often the most convenient way to move volumes of data into the SQL Server. The bcp utility requires a flat file originally generated by some utility. Often, you can extract data from other database management systems in the form of a flat file acceptable to bcp.

With bcp, you can specify the following formats:

1. Native (*/n*), all values written in native datatypes
2. Character (*/c*), all values converted to characters
3. Delimited by a column separator (*/t*)
4. Delimited by a row separator (*/r*)

Another option is to create a format file describing the data's format for each column. The following is a sample bcp format file for the authors table in a pubs database.

```
6.0
9
1 SQLCHAR 0    11    " "    1    au_id
2 SQLCHAR 0    40    " "    2    au_lname
3 SQLCHAR 0    20    " "    3    au_fname
4 SQLCHAR 0    12    " "    4    phone
5 SQLCHAR 0    40    " "    5    address
6 SQLCHAR 0    20    " "    6    city
7 SQLCHAR 0    2     " "    7    state
8 SQLCHAR 0    5     " "    8    zip
9 SQLBIT  0    1     " "    9    contract
```

Using bcp Services of DB-Library

If an application can access the data under program control, an application program may be the most efficient way to load data into a table. It can access data and load the table based on a live feed (e.g., reading data via an RS232 port) or from another server with access via a gateway, open server application, or DB-library calls. The program reads the data and issues bcp service calls in a DB-Library program.

Managing Users with Groups

Managing users within SQL Server requires understanding the Windows NT *group*, which is a logical collection of users. It may be local or global, may have rights and privileges within this domain, and may have rights and privileges in other domains because of *trusts* between domains. In Windows NT, rights and privileges cannot be assigned to accounts but only to groups.

As part of the installation process, you may have created two or more groups: SQLAdmins and one or more SQLUser groups. If you haven't done this yet, go to Enterprise Manager, select your server, and select *Logins,* where you will see the icon for **sa** which we created during installation. Double-click that icon. The security window will be displayed and you will see that **sa** is a member of the group *public*.

The traditional process to give users access to a database is to use *sp_addlogin* to create a login for the user on SQL Server and *sp_adduser* to give a user access to a particular database. A much easier method is to use the Enterprise manager. The real challenge is to *not* rush in and start adding users willy-nilly, but to sit back and design a group structure that accommodates your users. You probably already think of them in different categories, so that can be a first cut at group name definition. When all your groups are named properly, then define them using the Windows NT *User Manager for Domains*. Then use SQL Server Security Manager and give your new groups access to the different databases. Do this with integrated security, and users will be given immediate access to the databases defined by the groups they are members of.

To recapitulate:

◆ Don't enter users using singular *sp_addlogin* and *sp_adduser* commands.
◆ Create groups that categorize your users using *User Manager for Domains*.
◆ Place the users in the proper group using *User Manager for Domains*.
◆ Use SQL Server Security Manager to give the different groups access to different databases. The users will have immediate access to the databases.
◆ If you have followed the preceding steps to create a group named SQLUsers (you may have as many groups as you want), and a user *Obiwan* is a member of that group and you have given that group access to the *pubs* database, then you'll find the *Obiwan* login when you expand the server logins in the Enterprise Manager.

In the previous and following discussions, management of users is discussed in terms of stored procedures such as *sp_adduser, sp_addlogin, sp_droplogin,* and so on. These are used merely to illustrate the point. Actual management of users should be from SQL Server Security Manager. However, if you insist on micromanaging SQL Server, there are two choices from within Enterprise Manager. The first is to select the SQL Server of interest, select

Manage from the toolbar, and *Logins* from the menu. Use the dialog box to add, change, or delete a user login. The second choice is to edit an existing login. Select a server, expand it, expand logins, and then double-click the login of interest for editing. The same dialog box will be displayed that was activated from the toolbar. Edit the current login or select another for editing.

Micromanaging SQL Server is not a good choice. We recommend managing users on a group basis. If you have a large enterprise, things will get out of hand very quickly if you don't use this approach.

Managing Users with Aliases

You can establish aliases within a database. Use the stored procedures *sp_addalias* and *sp_dropalias*. The database owner (dbo) first adds a user (*sp_adduser*) and then aliases one or more additional logins to the same user name (*sp_addalias*). Within the context of this database, the aliased login appears as the original user with all permissions and ownership of objects.

When you alias a login to dbo in a database, that login will appear as the dbo for that database anytime the user logs in. A login aliased as dbo can do almost anything the real dbo can do in that database:

- An aliased dbo can use LOAD DATABASE and LOAD TRANSACTION.
- An aliased dbo can use SETUSER.
- An aliased dbo *cannot* use *sp_dboption* to change an option setting.

Because an aliased dbo cannot use *sp_dboption* and because the user_name for all dbos will say *dbo,* we recommend against aliased dbos. Have the SA log in as **dbo** or set up special dbo users for each database.

Rules of Thumb for User Management

1. dbo should own all tables and production stored procedures.
2. Ensure that users don't have a NULL password.
3. GRANT and REVOKE permissions to groups.
4. Individuals may own stored procedures—some tools may require this.

dbo Should Own All Tables and Production Stored Procedures

Make sure that the dbo owns all tables and procedures in production. This eases the management of the tables, simplifies management of permissions, and avoids difficulties when you remove the user who owns an object from the server with *sp_droplogin*. This also makes permissions more restrictive. If one user owns a stored procedure and the objects that it references, then the owner needs to grant permission to execute the stored procedure. There is no need to grant permission to access the underlying objects. In this way, the user is not allowed direct access to the underlying objects but can access them via the stored procedure.

Whenever multiple users are involved in owning objects, the owners must give out more permissions than is desired.

Ensure that Users Don't Have a NULL Password

All users should have a password. Any user without a password exposes your security. The SA's password, when first installing the SQL Server, is NULL. The SA should change this as soon as installation is complete.

To get a list of all users with a NULL password, **sa** can use the following query:

```
SELECT name FROM master.dbo.syslogins WHERE password IS NULL
```

GRANT and REVOKE Permissions to Groups

You may GRANT and REVOKE permissions from individual users or groups using the GRANT and REVOKE commands. It is much more convenient to do this at the group level. If you establish permissions at the group level, when you add new users you need only add them to the appropriate group and their permissions are established.

Keep the permission structure simple. GRANT and REVOKE either to users or to groups. Don't mix the two. If you GRANT and REVOKE permissions to both users and groups, then the order in which you set up the permissions is critical. If you GRANT a permission to a user and then REVOKE it from the group that user is in, then the user does not have the permission.

Individuals May Own Stored Procedures—Some Tools May Require This

Although it is preferable to have the dbo own all stored procedures, some tools require individual users to CREATE PROCEDUREs. Some tools may also require users to CREATE VIEWs or CREATE TABLEs. When a user other than the dbo owns an object in a database, anyone who wants to access that object must follow this procedure:

1. Specify the owner name (e.g., SELECT * FROM ownerx.object).
2. Receive permission for the access with a GRANT statement.

sp_dboption

The *sp_dboption* stored procedure allows the database owner (dbo) to set certain options for the database. The dbo must run this stored procedure in the master database and then insert a checkpoint in the database. An example is shown following:

```
USE master
go
```

```
EXEC sp_dboption dbname, 'dbo use only',true
go
USE dbname
go
CHECKPOINT
go
```

To unset the option, specify *false* instead of *true*. You cannot set options on the master database.

ANSI Null Default

This is used for nullability control. SQL Server defaults to NOT NULL when you create a table, while the ANSI standard is NULL. If this option is set *true*, then CREATE TABLE and ALTER TABLE will default to allow NULLs on any column not explicitly declared as NOT NULL. Columns with constraints will follow constraint rules independent of the setting of this option. If you want ANSI compatibility, then this option should be set *true*.

dbo Use Only

When the *dbo use only* setting for the *sp_dboption* stored procedure is set to *true*, only the database owner can access the database.

no chkpt on recovery

The *no chkpt on recovery* setting for the *sp_dboption* stored procedure has two uses. One is in a *warm standby* environment. The other is in certain instances when an 1105 error occurs ("Can't allocate space . . .").

The *no chkpt on recovery* setting instructs the server to *not* do a CHECK-POINT at the completion of its recovery operation. Normally, when the server completes recovery (this happens every time you boot the server), the server issues a CHECKPOINT. This forces all dirty pages in cache to disk and writes a CHECKPOINT record in the log. In a warm standby environment or when an 1105 error occurs, you do not want the server to do this. In the warm standby case, this will not allow you to load any subsequent transaction dumps. In the 1105 error case, it may not be possible to issue a CHECKPOINT because the database is full. Issuing the CHECKPOINT in these cases causes the server to mark the database as not recovered.

For more information on warm standby, see Warm Standby in the following.

offline

A database can be marked as *offline*. Databases used with this option are typically on removable media. When a database is placed in this state, all devices of the indicated database are closed and marked as deferred unless they contain space belonging to other databases. *Offline* databases are not recovered automatically at startup. You must mark all databases as offline before removing the media.

The removable media must be installed before a database can be marked as *online*. The devices for the database are opened if they are not already opened and the database is recovered. The database is now ready for use.

published

This does not publish a database but allows the database to be published for replication. When this option is set *true*, the user *repl_subscriber* is added to the database. When set to *false*, the user *repl_subscriber* is dropped, publication is disabled, all publications are dropped, and all transactions marked for publication are unmarked.

read only

The *read only* setting for the *sp_dboption* stored procedure allows users to read from the database but not write to it. This is useful when you plan to use an extracted a copy of a database (using DUMP DATABASE and LOAD DATABASE) for information only (e.g., a copy used by some of your users for decision support systems). A *read only* database will not be recovered automatically at system startup.

select into/bulkcopy

The *select into/bulkcopy* setting for the *sp_dboption* allows the use of WRITETEXT, SELECT INTO a permanent table, or fast bcp.

After you set this option and execute one of the previous statements, you cannot use a DUMP TRAN command to capture an incremental dump of the database because the server does not capture the details of the changes made by those statements in the transaction log. If you subsequently want to recover after a media failure using database and transaction log dumps, you must use a DUMP DATABASE command before you will be able to do a DUMP TRAN.

single user

When you set the *single user* option of the *sp_dboption* stored procedure, only one user at a time can access this database.

subscribed

This allows the database to be subscribed for replication. When *subscribed* is set *true*, the login ID of *repl_publisher* is aliased to dbo. Setting this option *false* removes the alias.

trunc. log on chkpt

When you set the *trunc. log on chkpt* option of the *sp_dboption* stored procedure, the server truncates the transaction log every time the checkpoint process checks this database (usually about once a minute). This may be useful in a development environment or in some instances in production.

When you set this option, you cannot use the DUMP TRAN command to capture an incremental dump of the database. Regular use of the DUMP DATABASE command is the only way to protect the database from loss due to media failure. Still, if there is a media failure on one of the database devices, you can only recover back to the point of the last database dump.

When you issue the CHECKPOINT command and you have set this option, the server does not truncate the transaction log. The truncation of the transaction log only takes place when the server's checkpoint process looks at this database (about once a minute).

If you do not set this option, the DUMP TRAN command is the only way to truncate the transaction log.

DBCC

CHECKALLOC

DBCC CHECKALLOC checks the allocation information contained within the server against the information contained on data pages. The allocation information for both must be consistent.

In a database, we call each set of 256 pages an *allocation unit*. The first page of each allocation unit is an *allocation page*. This page contains (among other things) information about the rest of the allocation unit. Included is whether a given page is in use and what object (table) is on that page. Each page in the database has information indicating whether it is in use and what object (table) is contained on it.

DBCC CHECKALLOC looks at all the allocation units and their pages in a database. It ensures consistency between the information in the allocation page and the information contained on the data pages in that allocation unit.

If you run this command while other users are accessing the database, you may get spurious results.

```
DBCC CHECKALLOC
```

Resultant Output

```
Checking current database.
Database 'master' is not in single user mode - may find spurious
allocation problems due to transactions in progress.
Alloc page 0 (# of extent=32 used pages=93 ref pages=93)
Alloc page 256 (# of extent=32 used pages=152 ref pages=152)
Alloc page 512 (# of extent=32 used pages=240 ref pages=240)
Alloc page 768 (# of extent=32 used pages=242 ref pages=242)
```

```
Alloc page 1024 (# of extent=21 used pages=131 ref pages=131)
Alloc page 1280 (# of extent=17 used pages=133 ref pages=133)
Total (# of extent=166 used pages=991 ref pages=991) in this database.
DBCC execution completed. If DBCC printed error messages, see your
System Administrator.
```

This should be run before any DUMP (like CHECKDB and CHECKCAT-ALOG). Sometimes that is not possible because of time constraints. Then you have to pick and choose—running CHECKDB and CHECKALLOC on different days, or running CHECKTABLE on crucial tables every day, CHECKDB weekly, and CHECKALLOC weekly.

CHECKCATALOG

DBCC *CHECKCATALOG* reads a number of system tables and ensures they are internally consistent. In particular, it reads the *sysobjects, syscolumns, sysprocedures, sysindexes, syssegments,* and *sysusages* tables.

One of the problems caught by DBCC CHECKCATALOG is a usertype (datatype) identified for a column where that datatype does not exist in the *systypes* table. The Microsoft documentation details the steps to correct a SQL Server 2514[22] error. The use of SELECT INTO across databases can lead to this problem. Run DBCC CHECKCATALOG before running any DUMP command for a database.

```
DBCC CHECKCATALOG
```

Resultant Output

```
Checking current database
The following segments have been defined for database 1 (database name master).

virtual start addr     size          segments
       4               1536
                                0
                                   1
                                   2
DBCC execution completed. If DBCC printed error messages, see your
System Administrator.
```

CHECKDB

DBCC *CHECKDB* is equivalent to running DBCC CHECKTABLE on all of the tables in a database. CHECKDB validates the internal integrity of all the tables in a database and their indexes. Fortunately, there are not often problems. However, prior to running any DUMP TRANSACTION or DUMP DATABASE, you should run DBCC CHECKTABLE or DBCC CHECKDB.

Performance for CHECKDB and CHECKTABLE has been improved for scanning nonclustered indexes. SQL Server will spawn multiple threads to scan the indexes in parallel.

```
DBCC CHECKDB
```

Resultant Output (Partial)

```
Checking master
Checking 1
The total number of data pages in this table is 14.
Table has 272 data rows.
Checking 2
The total number of data pages in this table is 5.
Table has 61 data rows.
Checking 3
The total number of data pages in this table is 32.
Table has 926 data rows.
Checking 4
The total number of data pages in this table is 1.
Table has 26 data rows.
Checking 5
The total number of data pages in this table is 3541.
Table has 19523 data rows.
Checking 6
The total number of data pages in this table is 566.
Table has 2970 data rows.
Checking 7
The total number of data pages in this table is 1.
Table has 3 data rows.
Checking 8
The total number of data pages in this table is 1.
The number of data pages in Sysindexes for this table was 16. It has
been corrected to 1.
The number of rows in Sysindexes for this table was 457. It has been
corrected to 10.
*** NOTICE: Notification of log space used/free cannot be reported
because the log segment is not on its own device.
Table has 10 data rows.
Checking 9
The total number of data pages in this table is 2.
Table has 198 data rows.
Checking 10
The total number of data pages in this table is 1.
Table has 5 data rows.
Checking 11
The total number of data pages in this table is 1.
Checking 12
The total number of data pages in this table is 11.
Table has 591 data rows.
Checking 13
The total number of data pages in this table is 1.
...
```

CHECKTABLE

DBCC *CHECKTABLE* validates the internal integrity of a single table and its
indexes. It validates both the internal consistency of the table's data pages and

the pointers from indexes. Fortunately, there are not often problems. However, prior to running any DUMP TRANSACTION or DUMP DATABASE, you should run DBCC CHECKTABLE or, even better, DBCC CHECKDB (against the entire database). The SQL Server is the cause of any problems the system detects—there is nothing you can do to damage a table.

Performance for CHECKDB and CHECKTABLE has been improved for scanning indexes. SQL Server will spawn multiple threads to scan the indexes in parallel.

```
DBCC CHECKTABLE(authors)
```

Resultant Output

```
Checking authors
The total number of data pages in this table is 1.
Table has 23 data rows.
DBCC execution completed. If DBCC printed error messages, see your
System Administrator.
```

NOINDEX

An option which reduces the execution time for CHECKALLOC, CHECKDB, CHECKTABLE, and NEWALLOC. When used on user-defined tables, only the clustered index (the B-tree and the data itself) is checked. When used against system tables, all clustered and nonclustered indexes are checked. An example of the use of this option follows:

```
DBCC CHECKTABLE(authors, NOINDEX)
```

Resultant Output

```
Checking authors
WARNING: NOINDEX option of 'CHECKTABLE' being used, checks on non-
system indexes will be skipped
The total number of data pages in this table is 1.
Table has 23 data rows.
DBCC execution completed. If DBCC printed error messages, see your
System Administrator.
```

DBREPAIR

Use the DBCC DBREPAIR command to drop a damaged database. The DROP DATABASE command does not work on a damaged database. DROP DATA-BASE may be used for normal dropping of a database. DBCC DBREPAIR is historical for backward compatibility and *sp_dbremove* should be used.

dllname (FREE)

This DBCC option unloads a specific dynamic link library (DLL) from SQL Server. Do this on a regular basis. After an extended stored procedure is loaded, it remains loaded until SQL Server is shut down. This feature enables you to remove (unload) a DLL without shutting down SQL Server.

INPUTBUFFER

This returns the first 255 bytes of the current user buffer. The input buffer is the last text sent to SQL Server by the specified process ID. You can use this to monitor what various users are doing. This information is also available from the Enterprise Manager. For viewing from Enterprise Manager, select *Server, Current Activity, Detail Activity* from the menubar and double-click the connection of interest.

Ownership of the buffer is determined by the system process ID found with *sp_who*. If the process does not contain an input stream then an error will be returned. DBCC INPUTBUFFER can only be used by **sa**. Sample output from this command is shown below. The second command below was entered separately after finding the *spid* with *sp_who*.

```
EXEC sp_who
go
DBCC INPUTBUFFER(14)
```

Resultant Output

```
Input Buffer
---------------------------------------------------------------------------
sp_who
(1 row(s) affected)
DBCC execution completed. If DBCC printed error messages, see your System
Administrator.
```

MEMUSAGE

The DBCC *MEMUSAGE* is used to report memory usage in the server. Prior versions of SQL Server required the use of DBCC TRACEON(3604) to send the output to your screen but this is not required with the current version.

The output comes in three sections:

1. The first section shows how the server allocated memory at startup.
2. The second section shows memory usage for the 20 largest objects in the buffer cache.
3. The third section shows memory used by the 12 largest procedures in the procedure cache.

In the third section, it lists some procedures in parsed only trees and lists some as compiled in plans, because when you create a procedure the server places a tree in cache and compiles it and puts a plan in cache when you first execute that procedure.

```
DBCC MEMUSAGE
```

Resultant Output

```
Memory Usage:
                              Meg.       2K Blks        Bytes
        Configured Memory:    8.0000        4096      8388608
               Code size:     1.7166         879      1800000
        Static Structures:    0.2385         123       250064
                   Locks:     0.2480         127       260000
            Open Objects:     0.1068          55       112000
          Open Databases:     0.0031           2         3220
       User Context Areas:    0.8248         423       864824
              Page Cache:     3.3040        1692      3464544
            Proc Headers:     0.0796          41        83448
          Proc Cache Bufs:    1.3379         685      1402880

Buffer Cache, Top 20:
     DB Id    Object Id    Index Id    2K Buffers
        1            1           0         14
        1    640005311           0         11
        5            5           0          7
        1            2           0          5
        1            5           0          4
        1           36           0          4
        1           99           0          4
        1            1           2          3

        5            1           0          3
        5            2           0          3
        5            3           0          3
        5            5           1          3
        1            3           0          2
        1            5           1          2
        1           45         255          2
        2            2           0          2
        2           99           0          2
        3            2           0          2
        4            2           0          2
        1            1           1          1

Procedure Cache, Top 3:

Procedure Name: sp_schedulerrefresh
Database Id: 5
Object Id: 464004684
Version: 1
Uid: 1
Type: stored procedure
Number of trees: 0
Size of trees: 0.000000 Mb, 0.000000 bytes, 0 pages
Number of plans: 1
Size of plans: 0.004690 Mb, 4918.000000 bytes, 3 pages

Procedure Name: sp_server_info
```

```
Database Id: 1
Object Id: 1580532664
Version: 1
Uid: 1
Type: stored procedure
Number of trees: 0
Size of trees: 0.000000 Mb, 0.000000 bytes, 0 pages
Number of plans: 1
Size of plans: 0.002974 Mb, 3118.000000 bytes, 2 pages

Procedure Name: sp_helpalert
Database Id: 5
Object Id: 576005083
Version: 1
Uid: 1
Type: stored procedure
Number of trees: 0
Size of trees: 0.000000 Mb, 0.000000 bytes, 0 pages
Number of plans: 1
Size of plans: 0.003531 Mb, 3702.000000 bytes, 2 pages
DBCC execution completed. If DBCC printed error messages, see your System
  Administrator.
```

NEWALLOC

This returns an allocation list with the number of pages marked and the number of pages actually used by objects. It may return errors if executed while a transaction is progress. Run it only during minimal SQL Server activity.

```
DBCC NEWALLOC
```

Resultant Output (Partial)

```
Checking master
Database 'master' is not in single user mode--may find spurious allocation
  problems due to transactions in progress.
****************************************************************
TABLE:sysobjects           OBJID = 1
INDID=1  FIRST=1 ROOT=8 DPAGES=14          SORT=0
Data level: 1. 14 Data Pages in 4 extents.
Indid    :1. 1 Index Pages in 1 extents.
INDID=2  FIRST=528         ROOT=529        DPAGES=1        SORT=1
Indid    :2. 7 Index Pages in 2 extents.
TOTAL # of extents = 7
****************************************************************
TABLE:sysindexes           OBJID = 2
INDID=1  FIRST=24          ROOT=32         DPAGES=5        SORT=0
Data level: 1. 5 Data Pages in 1 extents.
Indid    :1. 1 Index Pages in 1 extents.
TOTAL # of extents = 2
****************************************************************
```

```
TABLE:syscolumns              OBJID = 3
INDID=1   FIRST=48            ROOT=56        DPAGES=32      SORT=0
Data level: 1. 32 Data Pages in 4 extents.
Indid    :1. 1 Index Pages in 1 extents.
TOTAL # of extents = 5
*******************************************************************
TABLE:systypes                OBJID = 4
INDID=1   FIRST=64            ROOT=72        DPAGES=1       SORT=0
Data level: 1. 1 Data Pages in 1 extents.
Indid    :1. 1 Index Pages in 1 extents.
INDID=2   FIRST=80            ROOT=80        DPAGES=1       SORT=0
Indid    :2. 1 Index Pages in 1 extents.
TOTAL # of extents = 3
*******************************************************************
```

OPENTRAN

This function is very useful to determine whether or not an open transaction exists. The command supplies information on the oldest active transaction and the oldest distributed and nondistributed replicated transaction. You may use the additional parameter WITH TABLERESULTS to capture results formatted for easy readability.

```
DBCC OPENTRAN <database_name> WITH TABLERESULTS
```

OUTPUTBUFFER

This command operates very much like INPUTBUFFER in that the administrator can see the last 255 bytes of data in the user output buffer. In the sample output following, another connection issued a *sp_droplogin* command. You can see that information at the bottom of the buffer. The data is printed in hexadecimal and ASCII for diagnostic reasons. The *sp_who* and DBCC OUTPUTBUFFER commands were entered separately.

```
EXEC sp_who
go
DBCC OUTPUTBUFFER(14)
```

Resultant Output

```
Output Buffer
-------------------------------------------------------------------------
00147ce8:  04 01 00 13 00 00 00 00 00 00 fe 08 00 00 00 01  ................
00147cf8:  00 00 00 73 65 20 63 6f 6e 74 65 78 74 20 74 6f  ....se context to
00147d08:  20 27 70 75 62 73 27 2e 04 54 48 4f 52 00 01 00  'pubs'..THOR...
00147d18:  ff 41 00 00 00 00 00 00 00 00 fe 09 00 00 00 00  A...............
00147d28:  00 00 ff 51 00 00 00 00 00 00 00 00 fe 09 00 00  ..Q.............
00147d38:  00 00 00 00 ff 51 00 00 00 01 00 00 00 ff 41 00  ..Q.......A.
00147d48:  00 00 00 00 00 00 e3 0d 00 01 06 74 65 6d 70 64  ..........tempd
00147d58:  62 04 70 75 62 73 ab 35 00 45 16 00 00 01 00 25  b.pubs.5.E.....%
00147d68:  00 43 68 61 6e 67 65 64 20 64 61 74 61 62 61 73  .Changed databas
```

```
00147d78:   65 20 63 6f 6e 74 65 78 74 20 74 6f 20 27 74 65   e context to 'te
00147d88:   6d 70 64 62 27 2e 04 54 48 4f 52 00 01 00 ff 41   mpdb'..THOR....A
00147d98:   00 00 00 00 00 00 00 fe 09 00 00 00 00 00 00 00   ................
00147da8:   ff 51 00 00 00 00 00 00 00 fe 09 00 00 00 00 00   .Q..............
00147db8:   00 00 ff 51 00 00 00 00 00 00 00 ff 41 00 00 00   ...Q........A...
00147dc8:   00 00 00 00 ff 41 00 00 00 00 00 00 00 e3 0f 00   .....A..........
00147dd8:   01 06 6d 61 73 74 65 72 06 74 65 6d 70 64 62 ab   ..master.tempdb.
00147de8:   35 00 45 16 00 00 01 00 25 00 43 68 61 6e 67 65   5.E.....%.Change
00147df8:   64 20 64 61 74 61 62 61 73 65 20 63 6f 6e 74 65   d database conte
00147e08:   78 74 20 74 6f 20 27 6d 61 73 74 65 72 27 2e 04   xt to 'master'..
00147e18:   54 48 4f 52 00 01 00 ff 41 00 00 00 00 00 00 00   THOR....A.......
00147e68:   41 00 00 00 01 00 00 00 fd 01 00 00 00 01 00 00   A...............
00147e78:   00 fe 09 00 00 00 01 00 00 00 ff 41 00 00 00 00   ...........A....
00147e88:   00 00 00 ff 41 00 00 00 00 00 00 00 ff 51 00 00   ....A........Q..
00147e28:   fe 09 00 00 00 00 00 00 00 ff 41 00 00 00 00 00   ..........A.....
00147e38:   00 00 ff 41 00 00 00 00 00 00 00 ff 41 00 00 00   ...A........A...
00147e48:   00 00 00 00 ff 41 00 00 00 00 00 00 00 ff 51 00   .....A........Q.
00147e58:   00 00 01 00 00 00 fd 01 00 00 00 01 00 00 00 ff   ................
00147e98:   00 01 00 00 00 ff 41 00 00 00 00 00 00 00 ab 2a   ......A........*
00147ea8:   00 00 00 00 00 01 00 0e 00 4c 6f 67 69 6e 20 64   .........Login d
00147eb8:   72 6f 70 70 65 64 2e 04 54 48 4f 52 0c 73 70 5f   ropped..THOR.sp_
00147ec8:   64 72 6f 70 6c 6f 67 69 6e 82 00 ff 41 00 00 00   droplogin...A...
00147ed8:   00 00 00 00 ff 51 00 00 00 01 00 00 00 79 00 00   .....Q.......y..
00147ee8:   G
```

```
(1 row(s) affected)

DBCC execution completed. If DBCC printed error messages, see your System
   Administrator.
```

PAGE

The **sa** can look at information about a database page by using DBCC *PAGE*. This is an undocumented feature of SQL Server. Please do not contact Microsoft if this feature fails to perform properly.

Use DBCC PAGE to determine what object is on a given page, what index for the object is on the page, and how many levels there are in an index. In order to use DBCC PAGE, you must first use DBCC TRACEON(3604). This command will redirect the results to your current session. The syntax for this is illustrated in the example following.

DBCC PAGE requires two parameters. The first is the database name or ID. The second is the page you want to see. The following example shows the information for page 0 of the master database. Note that the objid is 99. This indicates an allocation page.

```
DBCC TRACEON(3604)
DBCC PAGE(master,0)
```

Resultant Output

```
PAGE:
Page found in cache.
```

```
Hex dump of allocation page follows:
BUFFER:
Buffer header for buffer 0xa925a8
  page=0xb0c800 bdnew=0xa925a8 bdold=0xa925a8 bhash=0x0
bnew=0xa90f78
  bold=0xa92558 bvirtpg=4 bdbid=1 bpinproc=0 bkeep=0 bspid=0
  bstat=0x1060 bpageno=0
PAGE HEADER:
Page header for page 0xb0c800
pageno=0 nextpg=7 prevpg=0 objid=99 timestamp=0000 00000001
nextmo=1 level=0 indid=0 freeoff=0 minlen=0
page status bits: 0x0
DATA:
DBCC execution completed. If DBCC printed error messages, see your System
  Administrator.
```

The next example shows page 1 of the master database. Notice that the objid is 1. To find out what object this is, use SELECT object_name(1).

```
DBCC TRACEON(3604)
DBCC PAGE(master,1)
```

Resultant Output

```
PAGE:
Page found in cache.

BUFFER:
Buffer header for buffer 0xa900c8
  page=0xad1800 bdnew=0xa900c8 bdold=0xa900c8 bhash=0x0
bnew=0xa90118
  bold=0xa90078 bvirtpg=5 bdbid=1 bpinproc=0 bkeep=0 bspid=0
  bstat=0x1200 bpageno=1

PAGE HEADER:
Page header for page 0xad1800
pageno=1 nextpg=2 prevpg=0 objid=1 timestamp=0001 08ae6af8
nextrno=18 level=0 indid=0 freeoff=1472 minlen=64
page status bits: 0x1
DBCC execution completed. If DBCC printed error messages, see your System
  Administrator.
```

In order to determine how many levels are in an index for a given table, use

```
SELECT root FROM sysindexes WHERE id = object_name('table_name') AND indid = x,
```

where x is the index id of one of the indexes for the table. An index ID of 1 identifies the entry for a clustered index. Then use DBCC PAGE to look at the page indicated by *root*. The entry identified as *level=* in the output from DBCC PAGE will indicate how many levels are in the index.

PERFMON

A very quick look at the performance statistics for IOSTATS, LRUSTATS, NET-STATS, and RASTATS. This command is shorthand notation for combining SQLPERF(IOSTATS), SQLPERF(LRUSTATS), SQLPERF(NETSTATS), and SQLPERF(RASTATS). Some of the information provided by this command is also available in the SQL Server Performance Monitor by selecting *Object:SQLServer*. All of these parameters are discussed in *SQL Server Books OnLine, DBCC Statement,* or in the parallel written documentation.

Most of the parameters in the sample output following are numbers that indicate your system is working well. If you have a very high number of *Batch Writes* and there is no degradation, there is no cause for worry. The issue is to identify parameters which indicate *waiting for resources.* Under NETSTATS you will find *Command Queue Length* and *Max Command Queue Length. Cache Flushes* from LRUSTATS is another indicator of lack of resources (see LRU-STATS following).

How do you use this information? Watching the output isn't really effective. Watching individual statistics can be misleading sometimes. You may experience temporary exhaustion of a resource with a heavy load, which is normal and something to expect. You want to look at patterns and flows. As traffic increases, so should utilization of resources. *Bytes transferred, frames received,* and *frames transmitted* should always move in the same direction. What you must do to capture this information is establish a *profile* of your system under different conditions. You must also establish *profiles* for your system under the same conditions using SQL Performance Monitor. This assumes that you are running SQL Performance Monitor in Windows NT integrated mode. To check that, go to SQL Server Setup, *Set Server Options,* and verify that *SQLPerfnon Integration* is checked.

Once you have established the profiles, monitor them for changes. Look for either exhaustion of resources or *contrary motion.* An example of *contrary motion* is a defective WAN link where a frame is retransmitted numerous times.

Command Queue Length Is High

Let's assume that you have a problem where *Command Queue Length* fails to meet your *profile* parameters. You might then use SQL Server Performance Monitor to monitor *Object:NetBEUI Resource, Counter:Times Exhausted,* and both *Instance:Receive Buffers* and *Instance:Receive Packets.* Note that we use NetBEUI here because that is our protocol of choice. You will use your particular protocol name and if you have more than one protocol, then you might want to perform the same monitoring operation for each protocol. If this test is negative, then choose other parameters to monitor.

Another reason for the command queue length to be high is that you may not have enough physical memory for network operations. You made a guess of how much memory Windows NT required before using *sp_configure* for

SQL Server memory allocation. Windows NT uses both paged and nonpaged pool. You may be short on one resource while you have an adequate supply of the other resource. The situation to look for is an increase in *Pages/sec* accompanied by a drop in *Total bytes/sec*. One way to look at this problem is to compare *Total Bytes/sec* from the *Redirector* and from your protocol, in our case NetBEUI. As one increases, so should the other. Another way is to monitor *Object:Redirector, Instance:Read Bytes Paging/sec*. This indicates a shortage of memory for paging.

Network Reads Are High, Batch Sizes Are High

The batch sizes over the network are too high and could benefit from stored procedures. You also might want to use **SQL Performance Monitor** and monitor *Object:SQLServer, Instance:Transactions/sec* and *Object:SQLServer, Instance:I/O-Batch Average Size*. This is a cross check on batch sizes being too large. A low transaction rate and a high network I/O rate makes the batch size suspect.

Network Reads High

When your *Network Reads* are high and batch sizes are small or normal, you may simply have a very busy network. If possible, consider upgrading your network interface cards. You may a high volume of traffic which can only be helped by hardware upgrades.

What is discussed here is not exhaustive and may not meet all your needs. Do build profiles. When you have problems, use them as a guide.

```
DBCC PERFMON
```

Resultant Output

```
Statistic                Value
-----------------------  ------------
Log Flush Requests        7.0
Log Logical Page IO       8.0
Log Physical IO          15.0
Log Flush Average         1.13333
Log Logical IO Average    0.533333
Batch Writes             16.0
Batch Average Size        1.77778
Batch Max Size            4.0
Page Reads              183.0
Single Page Writes       74.0
Reads Outstanding         0.0
Writes Outstanding        0.0
Transactions             20.0
Transactions/Log Write    1.33333

(14 row(s) affected)
Statistic                Value
```

```
-------------------------  -------------
Cache Hit Ratio            52.9412
Cache Flushes               0.0
Free Page Scan (Avg)        0.0
Free Page Scan (Max)        0.0
Min Free Buffers          204.0
Cache Size               1670.0
Free Buffers             1495.0

(7 row(s) affected)

Statistic                  Value
-------------------------  -------------
Network Reads               0.0
Network Writes             28.0
Command Queue Length        0.0
Max Command Queue Length    0.0
Worker Threads              4.0
Max Worker Threads          4.0
Network Threads             0.0
Max Network Threads         0.0

(8 row(s) affected)

Statistic                  Value
-------------------------  -------------
RA Pages Found in Cache    41.0
RA Pages Placed in Cache   11.0
RA Physical IO              4.0
Used Slots                  0.0

(4 row(s) affected)
DBCC execution completed. If DBCC printed error messages, see your System
  Administrator.
```

PINTABLE

DBCC *PINTABLE* marks a table so it stays in cache. It does not load the table into cache, but when pages are needed they are loaded and marked as *pinned* and not released from cache. A possible use of this feature is when you have sequential batches, which all use the same table. *Pinned* tables are fully logged and can be recovered. This feature should be used with caution since a large table can consume all the available cache. DBCC UNPINTABLE releases a table from cache but does not unload it.

SHOW_STATISTICS

For a specified table, DBCC *SHOW_STATISTICS* displays the statistical information found in an index page. See Chapter 3, Core Technologies, *USER Tools for Query Plan Maintenance* for details on the usage of this command.

SHOWCONTIG

A tool used to report on table fragmentation. For high levels of fragmentation, a clustered index can be dropped and rebuilt. *Fullness* of the pages is determined by adjusting FILLFACTOR for the index. Items of interest are the space in the pages and the average pages per extent, which is useful for read-ahead.

You use SHOWCONTIG by passing it either a table_id, in which case SHOWCONTIG reports on fragmentation of the data pages; or both a table_id and an index_id, in which case SHOWCONTIG reports on fragmentation of the leaf level of the index.

To get the table_id, use the following command:

```
SELECT object_id('<table name>')
```

To get the index_id, use the following command:

```
SELECT indid from sysindexes WHERE name = '<your-index-name>'
```

The following output was generated with:

```
DBCC SHOWCONTIG(304004114)
```

Resultant Output

```
DBCC SHOWCONTIG scanning 'account_clnum_ncalt' table...
[SHOW_CONTIG - SCAN ANALYSIS]
-----------------------------------------------------------------------
Table:'account_clnum_ncalt'(304004114) Indid: 1 dbid:6
TABLE level scan performed.
- Pages Scanned..............................: 527
- Extent Switches............................: 65
- Avg. Pages per Extent......................: 8.0
- Scan Density [Best Count:Actual Count].....: 100.00%[66:66]
- Avg. Bytes free per page...................: 80.6
- Avg. Page density (full)...................: 96.00%
- Overflow Pages............................: 0
- Disconnected Overflow Pages..................: 0
DBCC execution completed. If DBCC printed error messages, see your System
  Administrator.
```

SHRINKDB

When only a database name is supplied, the system returns the minimum size to which the database can shrink. Databases cannot be shrunk beyond the size of the *model* database or to a size which is not a valid increment of allocation units. This feature can only be used in *single user mode* set with *sp_dboption*. After the database has been shrunk, back up the shrunk database and the *master* database.

SQLPERF(. . . ,CLEAR)

This command is used to clear performance statistics for IOSTATS, LRU-STATS, NETSTATS, and RASTATS.

SQLPERF(IOSTATS)

IOSTATS represent the physical and logical disk I/O performed for SQL Server and are general statistics relating to SQL Server performance. These statistics will not always clearly identify a problem. Consequently, any performance problems may be related to other issues. That is, poor SQL Server performance may be a symptom and the actual problem may be a network issue or an application issue.

SQLPERF(LRUSTATS)

LRUSTATS are statistics on cache management. After your system starts production or a development cycle, build a benchmark that you can use to test the system. Be sure that you don't run it consecutively, since the second time won't be valid. After your benchmark, use the command:

```
DBCC SQLPERF(LRUSTATS).
```

When viewing the SQLPERF(LRUSTATS), you can use the following as a guideline for cache configuration:

1. The Cache Flushes are less than 10.
2. The Average Free-Page Scan is less than 10.

If both these statements are true, then the current cache requirements are satisfactory and cache does not need to be expanded. Over a two-day period, the number of Cache Flushes should be less than 100 and the Average Free-Page Scan should still be less than 10. When these guidelines are exceeded, consider using *sp_configure* to increase your memory setting. Of course, make sure that you have sufficient real memory to support the value you set.

SQLPERF(NETSTATS)

Network Performance statistics were discussed earlier in PERFMON. These statistics are probably the most important system statistics to monitor.

SQLPERF(RASTATS)

RASTATS are the statistics for SQL Server read-ahead. Consider issuing a DBCC SQLPERF(RASTATS, CLEAR) before table scan operations such as SELECT, CHECKDB, CHECKALLOC, or NEWALLOC. Do a DBCC SQLPERF(RASTATS) after the table scans have completed and evaluate the results. This gives you a measure of the effectiveness of read-ahead on table scans. Consider increasing the *read-ahead threads* or the *slots per thread* to see if the performance improves.

SQLPERF(THREADS)

This maps a Windows NT system thread to a SQL Server *spid*. It is useful to monitor a specific user in Performance Monitor.

```
DBCC SQLPERF(THREADS)
```

Resultant Output

```
Spid Thread ID    Status      LoginName        IO         CPU      MemUsage
----- ---------- ----------  ---------------  ---------  -------  -----------
1                  sleeping    (null)            0          0        1
2                  sleeping    (null)            0          0        0
3                  sleeping    (null)            9          0        0
4                  sleeping    (null)            3          0        0
5                  sleeping    (null)            0          0        0
6                  sleeping    (null)            0          0        0
7                  sleeping    (null)            0          0        0
8                  sleeping    (null)            0          0        0
9                  sleeping    (null)            0          0        0
10    116(0x74)    sleeping sa                  20        160        1
11    115(0x73)    sleeping sa                  21       1713        1
12    115(0x73     runnable sa                   0         30        1

(12 row(s) affected)

DBCC execution completed. If DBCC printed error messages, see your System
  Administrator.
```

TEXTALL

Check the allocation chains of *text* or *image* columns in a table. The parameter FAST does not generate a report. The default is the parameter FULL which looks at all tables in the database which have either *text* or *image* columns. The argument may be a database name or database ID. TEXTALL is the same as performing TEXTALLOC for all tables in the database.

TEXTALLOC

Check the allocation chains of *text* or *image* columns in a single table. See the preceding, TEXTALL.

TRACEON

The SQL Server utilizes trace flags for a number of different purposes. Enabling a trace flag provides a way to communicate with the server to change the server's behavior.

Trace flags are turned on dynamically using:

```
DBCC TRACEON(###)
```

Trace flags are turned off dynamically using:

```
DBCC TRACEOFF(###)
```

In addition, some will be turned on when the server is started.
There are three categories of trace flags:

1. Flags that affect the output of certain other DBCC commands. Some DBCC commands will not display any output unless one of the following trace flags is set on for this session:
   DBCC TRACEON(3604)   Sends output to standard output device.
   DBCC TRACEON(3605)   Sends output to error log.
2. Flags that change the behavior of the server. Use of these flags is illustrated in the earlier section above on Error Recovery Issues.[23] These flags are used on the sqlservr command line. For example:
   sqlservr c:\sql60\data\master.dat -T3607
3. Flags that provide additional details of Server activities.
   DBCC TRACEON(302)   The results of this command indicate whether the optimizer considers an index useful or not including costs.
   DBCC TRACEON(310)   The results of this command indicate how a query plan is formed.

UNPINTABLE

This is paired with PINTABLE to release a table from cache. The table remains in cache until flushed. It is not unloaded immediately.

UPDATEUSAGE

This corrects and reports errors in the *sysindexes* table reported by *sp_spaceused*. Be careful in using this since it acquires a shared table lock on the table being processed. This function may take some time to run, so off-hours usage is recommended. The argument may be database name, a database name and table name, or a combination of database name, table name, and index ID.

USEROPTIONS

This returns a list of the SET options that are active for the current connection.

```
DBCC USEROPTIONS
```

Resultant Output

```
Set Option        Value
----------------  ----------------------------------------
textsize          64512
language          us_english
dateformat        mdy
datefirst         7

(4 row(s) affected)

DBCC execution completed. If DBCC printed error messages, see your System
  Administrator.
```

WITH NO_INFOMSGS

This prevents the printing of informational messages which have severity codes 1 to 10 and reduces the verbosity to a manageable level when using DBCC CHECKDB.

Backup and Restore

In this section, we discuss the statements for backup and restore. The DUMP DATABASE and LOAD DATABASE statements are used to back up or restore an entire database. The DUMP TRANSACTION and LOAD TRANSACTION statements are used to perform an incremental dump and to restore from that incremental dump. We also present strategies for using these statements, including a scheme for establishing a warm standby.

We describe various statements that you can use, but you can also use the SQL Enterprise Manager to schedule and execute dumps and restores.

DUMP DATABASE Statement

The *DUMP DATABASE* statement makes a backup copy of a database. This copy captures the state of the database at the beginning of the dump. Other activities can continue in the database while it is being dumped.

The DUMP DATABASE statement writes the contents of all currently written pages in the database to the dump device. The size of a database dump may be significantly less than the size allocated for a database.

Beware of the INIT and NOINIT options on the DUMP DATABASE statement. These options apply to disk dumps as well as tape dumps in this release. The INIT option specifies that any existing dumps on the dump device will be overwritten with this dump. NOINIT specifies that this dump is appended to the dump device.

NOINIT is the default! If you do several DUMPs to the same device and then try to LOAD from that dump file, you will load the first dump (the default on LOAD is the first file in the dump). This may not be what you had in mind.

LOAD DATABASE Statement

The *LOAD DATABASE* statement copies all the pages from the backup copy of the database into the database. To load a database dump, the database must already exist and cannot be in use. (We often find that when we get the message 3101—"Database in use"—the problem is that we are in the database.) If you are replacing an existing database, there is no need to DROP the database first. The LOAD DATABASE statement overwrites the entire database and initializes any unallocated pages.

If the database does not yet exist, you must create it first. The most efficient way is to use CREATE DATABASE FOR LOAD. CREATE DATABASE FOR LOAD is much faster than issuing a CREATE DATABASE statement.

Even though the DUMP DATABASE statement creates a backup copy smaller than the original database, the database you are loading a dump into must be at least as big as space allocated for the original database. Using DUMP DATABASE and LOAD DATABASE together will not reduce the size of a database. Because the LOAD DATABASE statement initializes all unallocated pages, it may take a long time to issue a LOAD DATABASE statement even if the dump is small.

One of the options on the LOAD DATABASE statement is the file number (the syntax is FILE=#). This allows you to pick which dump in a dump file you want to load. See the warning under DUMP DATABASE previously.

You can use the SQL Enterprise Manager to review the contents of a dump file (from the toolbar choose *Tools, Backup/Restore*).

DUMP TRANSACTION Statement

The DUMP TRANSACTION statement copies the transaction log to a backup device and truncates the inactive portion of the log (see Table 10.4). There are also options that allow you to perform one or the other of these two tasks.

TABLE 10.4 DUMP TRANSACTION Statement Options

DUMP TRANSACTION	Copies to log device	Truncates the log
DUMP TRANSACTION . . . WITH TRUNCATE_ONLY		Truncates the log
DUMP TRANSACTION . . . WITH NO_LOG		Truncates the log
DUMP TRANSACTION . . . WITH NO_TRUNCATE	Copies to log device	

In order to issue a DUMP TRANSACTION statement that copies the transaction log to a dump devive, the log must be on a separate SQL Server device. This is not necessary if you are using the WITH TRUNCATE_ONLY or WITH NO_LOG options (which do not copy the transaction log to a dump device).

The WITH TRUNCATE_ONLY option removes the inactive portion of the transaction log. It does not make a copy to a backup device. This is the statement to enter if you get a message that the server is unable to allocate space on the log segment.

The WITH NO_LOG option only removes the inactive portion of the transaction log. Also note the following points:

♦ It does not make a copy to a backup device.
♦ It does not record its activity in the log.
♦ Use this option only if the DUMP TRANSACTION WITH TRUNCATE_ ONLY fails because there is not sufficient log space to log the DUMP TRANSACTION WITH TRUNCATE_ONLY statement.
♦ Back up the database after issuing this statement—use the DUMP DATA- BASE statement.
♦ There is some exposure in the integrity of the database after using this option.

Use the WITH NO_TRUNCATE option for two purposes:

1. For making regular incremental (DUMP TRANSACTION) dumps when you do not want to load a whole series of incremental dumps in case of a failure. This option does not truncate the log with each DUMP TRANSACTION; therefore, by LOADing the original database dump and the latest transaction dump, you restore all transactions up to the point of the last DUMP TRANSACTION. Without this option, you would load each incremental dump taken since the last DUMP DATABASE to recover.
2. For up-to-the-minute recovery after losing a data device. If a data device is lost, you can still issue a DUMP TRANSACTION WITH NO_TRUNCATE statement and capture one last transaction dump that includes all transactions up to the point of data device failure.

The DUMP TRANSACTION statement also supports the INIT and NOINIT options described under DUMP DATABASE.

LOAD TRANSACTION Statement

The LOAD TRANSACTION statement loads a backup copy of the transaction log and applies all the changes reflected to the database's transaction log.

The LOAD TRANSACTION statement also supports the *FILE=#* option described in the LOAD DATABASE section.

DUMP/LOAD Schemes

We discuss several DUMP and LOAD schemes. Choose the most appropriate scheme for your database based on the following criteria:

- ♦ Ease of dumping
- ♦ Ease of loading
- ♦ How much data you are willing to lose in case of a device failure
- ♦ How long you are willing to have the database unavailable

Using Only DUMP DATABASE on a Database

DUMP DATABASE captures a dump of the database at the time of the dump. You can use this dump to recover from damage to the database. If you only use DUMP DATABASE on a database, you can only recover back to the time of the last dump and you lose all transactions since the last dump.

You can also use database dumps to copy a database. The commands to do a database DUMP follow:

```
DUMP TRANSACTION WITH TRUNCATE_ONLY /* truncates the log */
DUMP DATABASE
```

The command to LOAD is:

```
LOAD DATABASE
```

This is the simplest approach. Do a DUMP DATABASE regularly. If you do this once a day, whenever there is a device failure you lose at most one day's worth of data. After the failure, you find new disk space, drop and recreate the database, then LOAD the dump.

Using DUMP DATABASE and Incremental DUMP TRANSACTION

Using a *DUMP DATABASE and Incremental DUMP TRANSACTION* technique minimizes the amount of regular activity needed to maintain all transactions in a transaction dump. You minimize the size of each incremental dump, since the server truncates the transaction log each time you do a DUMP TRANSACTION. It may take quite a while to recover, however, since you must issue a series of LOAD TRANSACTION statements. If these dumps are on tape, each tape needs to be mounted in the correct order in order to recover.

The command to do a full dump is:

```
DUMP DATABASE
```

The command to do an incremental DUMP is:

```
DUMP TRANSACTION
```

The standard sequence to LOAD is:

```
LOAD DATABASE
LOAD TRANSACTION /* load first incremental dump */
LOAD TRANSACTION /* load second incremental dump */
LOAD TRANSACTION /* load third incremental dump, and so on... */
```

With this scheme, there is more work to do for your regular dumps (you are executing DUMP TRANSACTION statements between your regular DUMP DATABASE statements. Your recovery is also more complicated, since you have to load many incremental dumps. When there is a failure, you lose only the changes since your last incremental dump. If you do DUMP DATABASE daily and DUMP TRANSACTION hourly, you will lose at most one hour's worth of transactions.

Using DUMP DATABASE and Accumulating DUMP TRANSACTION

Using a *DUMP DATABASE and accumulating DUMP TRANSACTION* technique requires a larger transaction log. Each incremental dump (DUMP TRANSACTION) takes longer because it contains the entire transaction log since the last DUMP DATABASE. Because you have to issue only one LOAD DATABASE and one LOAD TRANSACTION statement, it reduces recovery time. If a failure happens, you lose all transactions since the last incremental dump.

The command to do a full DUMP is:

```
DUMP DATABASE
```

The command to do an incremental DUMP is:

```
DUMP TRANSACTION WITH NO_TRUNCATE
```

The standard sequence to LOAD is:

```
LOAD DATABASE
LOAD TRANSACTION /* load last incremental dump */
```

The DUMP complexity of this scheme is the same as the previous one. However, loading is simplified, since you need only do two loads (a database dump and one transaction log dump). The potential for lost transactions is also the same.

Up-to-the-Minute Recovery

With an *Up-to-the-Minute Recovery* you also can recover *all* transactions that happened up to the point of a device failure. It minimizes the size of each incremental dump because the server truncates the transaction log each time you do a DUMP TRANSACTION. To recover from a failure you must issue a series of LOAD TRANSACTION statements, so recovery may take quite a while. Also, if these dumps are on tape you must mount each tape in the correct order for recovery.

When a data device fails, you must capture one last transaction log dump using the DUMP TRANSACTION WITH NO_TRUNCATE option. You will not lose transactions; however, while completing the loads the database is unavailable.

The command to do a full DUMP is:

```
DUMP DATABASE
```

The command to do an incremental DUMP is:

```
DUMP TRANSACTION
```

After a device failure occurs on a data device:

```
DUMP TRANSACTION WITH NO_TRUNCATE
```

The standard sequence to LOAD is:

```
LOAD DATABASE
LOAD TRANSACTION /* load first incremental dump */
LOAD TRANSACTION /* load second incremental dump */
LOAD TRANSACTION /* load third incremental dump, and so on... */
LOAD TRANSACTION /* the WITH NO_TRUNCATE dump */
```

We refer to the DUMP TRANSACTION WITH NO_TRUNCATE as a *dying gasp* dump. This dump gives us all of the transactions in the transaction log at the point of failure. Note that we said at the beginning of this section that a *data* device had failed. If the log devices fail, you cannot recover the transaction since the last transaction log dump. This is why it is important to consider mirroring to protect the transaction log. A log device failure is catastrophic. A data device failure is recoverable.

Backing Up Using Operating System Commands

You can back up using operating system commands by first shutting down the server. Once the server is shut down (SHUTDOWN statement) you can use any technique used for Window NT files to copy the files. If you regularly copy all NT files to a backup tape, this may be an attractive approach for SQL Server backup. However, backing up with operating system commands is not always an attractive alternative. For example, striping the backup set is available for backups using SQL Server but not for backups using the Windows NT operating system.

If you have spread a database across multiple SQL Server devices, make sure you copy all the files from all the devices.

Backing Up the Master Database

It is important to back up the master database along with other databases. You need to back up the master database any time there are changes to it.

The following statements and stored procedures make changes to the master database:

ALTER DATABASE, CREATE DATABASE, DISKINIT, DISK MIRROR, DISK UNMIRROR, DISK REMIRROR, DISK RESIZE, DBCC SHRINKDB (and other DBCC options), *sp_addlogin, sp_addremotelogin, sp_addsegment, sp_addserver, sp_addumpdevice, sp_configure, sp_dropdevice, sp_droplogin, sp_dropsegment, sp_dropremotelogin, sp_extendsegment,* and *sp_logdevice.*

Warm Standby

A *warm standby* strategy establishes a second database on the same server or on a different server. The second database matches the primary database through a transaction dump on the primary database. With this warm standby in place, if damage occurs to the primary database, users can easily cut over to a live database as close as possible to the primary. You lose any transaction since the last incremental dump, but you minimize the downtime for users. To set up a warm standby use the following procedure:

On the Primary Database

♦ DUMP DATABASE
♦ DUMP TRANSACTION on a regular basis

On the Secondary Database

♦ CREATE DATABASE (matching the original in size, size of the log, and relative placement of the log)
♦ EXEC sp_dboption dbname, 'no chkpt on recovery', TRUE
♦ EXEC sp_dboption dbname, 'read only', TRUE (you must issue a checkpoint in the database after using sp_dboption)
♦ LOAD DATABASE
♦ LOAD TRANSACTION (on a regular basis—immediately after doing the DUMP DATABASE on the primary database)

A warm standby has other uses as well. You can use it to perform DBCC CHECKALLOC and DBCC CHECKDB commands without impacting your users. In this case you set up the warm standby on another server.

Similarly, you can use this technique to provide a second server that is used by all of your decision support users, so that they don't impact the performance of your online users.

Disk Mirroring

With *Disk Mirroring* the SQL Server maintains a copy of the SQL Server device. All writes go to both devices. If one of the copies has a device failure, the SQL Server proceeds without losing any transactions and without any delay. Disk Mirroring causes writes to take longer because the server must write to both devices. Use Disk Mirroring to improve the reliability of your server. With it, a single device failure will not destroy a database.

At minimum, it is a good idea to mirror the master device. If the master database is ever unavailable, the entire server is unavailable. Next, consider mirroring the log for important databases. Mirroring is done at the SQL Server device level, so place a number of logs on the same device and mirror that.

You can use hardware mirroring or RAID devices. For a discussion of RAID devices, see Chapter 3.

Notes

1. See "SQLMail" in Chapter 5 of this book.
2. See "Network Protocols" in Chapter 9 of this book.
3. See "Managing Windows NT Domains" in Chapter 9 of this book.
4. "Rebuilding the *master* Database," *Microsoft SQL Server Administrator's Companion.*
5. "Sort Order IDs," *Microsoft SQL Server Setup.*
6. See "Replication" in Chapter 5 of this book.
7. See "File Systems" in Chapter 9 of this book.
8. A *segment* is a logical mapping of devices. A segment may exist on only one device. Segments can be extended to other devices. A *table* exists on a segment and the number of physical devices used to represent the table is transparent to the user. A segment is equivalent to a *list of devices* used.
9. "Example of Splitting a Table Across Segments," *Microsoft SQL Server Books OnLine.*
10. "Setting up Replication," *Microsoft SQL Server Administrator's Companion.*
11. See "Clustered Index" in Chapter 3 of this book.
12. "Optimizing Windows NT," *Microsoft Windows NT Resource Kit Version 3.5, Vol. 4.*
13. "Configuring Servers," *Microsoft SQL Server Administrator's Companion.*
14. See "Tuning Replication" in Chapter 5 of this book.
15. "Optimizing Windows NT," Chapter 14, *Microsoft Support Fundamentals for Windows NT 3.5.*
16. "Configuring Servers," *Microsoft SQL Server Administrator's Companion.*
17. For a brief description of security, select *Help* from the toolbar on the Microsoft SQL Server Security Manager.
18. "Error 1105," *Microsoft SQL Server Books OnLine.*
19. "Advanced Replication, Backup Considerations for a Publication Server," Chapter 15, *Microsoft SQL Server Administrator's Companion.*
20. The **sa** may have discovered that the query is a cross product, and the right solution is to rewrite the query—not make the tempdb bigger to accommodate it.
21. "DBCC Statement," *Microsoft SQL Server Administrator's Companion.*
22. Chapter 25, *Microsoft SQL Server Administrator's Companion.*
23. "Trace Flags," *Microsoft SQL Transact-SQL Reference.*

SQL Server 6.5—
New Features

This book was initially written based on the significant new release of SQL Server Version 6.0. Less than six months after the release of that version, Microsoft began beta testing a new version, Version 6.5. This version of SQL Server will be released in mid-1996. It enhances SQL Server in many ways. In this appendix, we will introduce some of the new features and provide advice on what they offer and how you should use them.

We have grouped the new features into the following sections:

- Compatibility
- ANSI support
- Other Transact-SQL enhancements
- New tools
- Administrative enhancements

Compatibility

You can easily upgrade to Version 6.5. The most significant potential problem in upgrading is the introduction of new keywords. The complete list is included later in this appendix. If you have used any of these keywords as object names or column names, you will have to modify them in your database definition and in any application that references the objects before you can upgrade to Version 6.5.

Once you have upgraded to Version 6.5, you can access dumps created on Version 6.0. However, any dumps that you create using Version 6.5 cannot be loaded onto a Version 6.0 SQL Server.

New character sets have been added in Version 6.5, providing support for Japanese, Chinese (both a simplified and a traditional character set), and Korean.

ANSI Support

Microsoft SQL Server Version 6.5 includes support for a number of new SQL language features. Microsoft SQL Server Version 6.5 provides ANSI SQL-92 entry-level compliance. In addition, it supports many of the features required for intermediate or full compliance.

If you want to check conformance of your program to the ANSI SQL-92 entry level, use the SET FIPS_FLAGGER. Many relational database management systems (RDBMSs) conform to the entry level. If you want to write programs that are portable across RDBMSs, you may want to use the FIPS_FLAGGER and stick to this level. On the other hand, many of the important features of SQL Server (such as stored procedures, remote stored procedures, and triggers) are not included in ANSI SQL-92. If you limit yourself to this subset, you will be missing out on much of the power of SQL Server. Make sure you know what your goal is before you decide that certain features are going to be omitted from your applications.

In this section, we describe some of the new Transact-SQL features added to SQL Server Version 6.5 in order to obtain ANSI SQL-92 entry-level compliance. We recommend against using some of these features. Read the following sections to make sure you understand which ones really provide useful new functionality.

CREATE SCHEMA

The CREATE SCHEMA statement allows you to combine multiple CREATE TABLE, CREATE VIEW, and GRANT statements in a single batch. With the CREATE SCHEMA statement, you can specify multiple tables and views, which may have interrelationships. The SQL Server does not try to resolve the interrelationships until all of the statements in the CREATE SCHEMA statements have been processed. In particular, this allows you to create two tables, each of which has a foreign key to the other table. Prior to Version

6.5, you would have to create both tables and then, for the first one, execute an ALTER TABLE statement to add the foreign key constraint to the second table. With the CREATE SCHEMA statement, you specify both tables with CREATE TABLE statements and specify a REFERENCES clause for each. The SQL Server will resolve the references after the tables have both been created.

The following example demonstrates the use of the CREATE SCHEMA statement where you create two tables each of which references the other:

```
CREATE SCHEMA AUTHORIZATION dbo
    CREATE TABLE employees (emp_id int PRIMARY KEY,
        manager_id int NULL REFERENCES managers (manager_id))
    CREATE TABLE managers (manager_id int PRIMARY KEY REFERENCES
        employees (emp_id))
```

The CREATE SCHEMA statement completes at the end of the batch. Note that the manager_id in employees must allow null, or you would not be able to insert a row into the employees table with a manager_id that did not exist in the managers table.

GRANT WITH GRANT and REVOKE GRANT

The GRANT WITH GRANT option allows you to give a user:

♦ Rights to use an object
♦ The ability to pass on those rights to other users

There is a corresponding REVOKE . . . CASCADE statement.

Use these options with caution. They tend to complicate the permission structure and weaken centralized control. We recommend that you not use this new feature.

ANSI Standard Joins

SQL Server Version 6.5 adds support for ANSI-style joins. In some cases, these provide alternative syntax for existing functionality. In other cases, new functionality is provided.

Inner Join

The inner join (commonly referred to as an *equi-join*) allows you to specify the join clause in the FROM clause rather than the WHERE clause. The following statement returns the matching rows from the publishers and titles tables. If the publishers table has 8 rows, and the titles table has 18 rows, the query returns 18 rows (assuming that all titles rows have a matching pub_id).

```
SELECT p.pub_name, t.title_id, t.type
FROM publishers p JOIN titles t
    ON p .pub_id = t.pub_id
```

The advantage of this syntax over putting the join clause in the WHERE clause is that it allows you to separate the join and the restriction. Compare the following two queries which return the same results.

New Join Syntax

```
SELECT p.pub_name, t.title_id, t.type
FROM publishers p JOIN titles t
    ON p.pub_id = t.pub_id
WHERE type = 'business'
```

Existing Join Syntax

```
SELECT p.pub_name, t.title_id, t.type
FROM publishers p,titles t
WHERE type = 'business'
AND p .pub_id = t.pub_id
```

The new syntax is somewhat easier to read (an obvious subjective observation).

Cross Join

The following statement returns the cross product of the publishers and titles table. Every pub_id in the publishers table is returned with every title_id in the titles table. If the publishers table has eight rows and the titles table has eighteen rows, then the cross product has 144 rows.

```
SELECT p.pub_id, t.title_id
FROM publishers p CROSS JOIN titles t
```

This is identical to the existing syntax:

```
SELECT p.pub_id, t.title_id
FROM publishers p, titles t
```

The advantage of the new syntax is that it explicitly declares that you expect a cross product. The existing syntax invites the question: Did I really want a cross product, or did I accidentally leave out the WHERE clause?

I rarely need a cross product, but when it is needed, the new syntax provides better documentation of what I want and conforms to the ANSI standard.

Outer Joins

The new LEFT OUTER JOIN returns all of the specified columns from all of the rows of the left-hand table. If there is a match in the right-hand table, the corresponding columns are also returned. If there is no match in the right-hand table, then the columns that are specified as coming from that table will have the value null. This is identical to the use of the existing *= operator in the second example following.

LEFT OUTER JOIN

```
SELECT DISTINCT p.state, a.state
FROM publishers p LEFT OUTER JOIN authors a
     ON p.state = a.state
```

Existing outer join syntax *=

```
SELECT DISTINCT p.state, a.state
FROM publishers p, authors a
WHERE p.state *= a.state
```

These both yield the following results:

```
state state
----- -----
(null) (null)
CA     CA
DC     (null)
IL     (null)
MA     (null)
NY     (null)
TX     (null)
```

The new RIGHT OUTER JOIN returns all of the specified columns from all of the rows of the right-hand table. If there is a match in the left-hand table, the corresponding columns are also returned. If there is no match in the left-hand table, then the columns that are specified as coming from that table will have the value null. This is identical to the use of the existing =* operator in the second example following.

RIGHT OUTER JOIN

```
SELECT DISTINCT p.state, a.state
FROM publishers p RIGHT OUTER JOIN authors a
     ON p.state = a.state
```

Existing outer join syntax =*

```
SELECT DISTINCT p.state, a.state
FROM publishers p, authors a
     WHERE p.state =* a.state
```

These both yield the following results:

```
state state
----- -----
(null)IN
(null)KS
(null)MD
(null)MI
(null)OR
(null)TN
(null)UT
CA    CA
```

The last example is the FULL OUTER JOIN. This includes all of the rows where the columns specified in the Join clause match, it also returns the left-hand table's rows when there is no match in the right-hand table and returns a NULL for any column in the SELECT list coming from the right-hand table. In addition, it returns the right-hand table's rows when there is no match in the left-hand table and returns a NULL for any column in the SELECT list coming from the left-hand table. This represents new functionality in Version 6.5.

```
SELECT p.state, a.state
FROM publishers p FULL OUTER JOIN authors a
     ON p.state = a.state
```

This yields the following results:

```
state state
------ ------
(null) (null)
(null) IN
(null) KS
(null) MD
(null) MI
(null) OR
(null) TN
(null) UT
CA     CA
DC     (null)
IL     (null)
MA     (null)
NY     (null)
TX     (null)
```

ANSI Standard Defaults

The ANSI standard requires a number of behaviors that are different from those traditionally supported by SQL Server. You should not just turn on the options without evaluating your application to make sure that it will continue to behave as you expect. You turn on all of the options with the following statement:

```
SET ANSI_DEFAULTS ON
```

You should review each of the options to make sure that you understand the implications. The ANSI defaults covered by the preceding statement are:

♦ ANSI_NULLS
♦ ANSI_NULL_DFLT_ON
♦ ANSI_PADDING
♦ ANSI_WARNINGS
♦ ARITHABORT
♦ CURSOR_CLOSE_ON_COMMIT
♦ QUOTED_IDENTIFIER

FIPS Flagger

SQL Server Version 6.5 includes support for a flagger that identifies which statements do not conform to a given standards level. Version 6.5 supports the ANSI SQL-92 entry level. This is the most reasonable level to check with the FIPS flagger. If you try to verify conformance to higher levels, the results may be obscured by the fact that some of the features are not supported by SQL Server Version 6.5.

Enter the following command to turn on FIPS flagging for this connection:

```
SET FIPS_FLAGGER ENTRY
```

If you execute the following statement, you will see the FIPS Warning listed below. The statement is executed and, in this case, the new column is added to the table.

```
ALTER TABLE a ADD b int NULL
FIPS Warning: Line 1: Non ANSI command 'alter table'.
```

Other Transact-SQL Enhancements

SQL Server Version 6.5 includes a number of enhancements to the Transact-SQL language that are not part of the ANSI standard. This section discusses some of the more significant enhancements.

ALTER TABLE Enhancements

The ALTER TABLE statement has been enhanced to allow CHECK and FOR-EIGN KEY constraints to be temporarily disabled. The constraint is still in place and can be enabled again later. This is particularly useful when replicating to a database. Certain constraints may need to be disabled until the replication is complete.

The following ALTER TABLE statement disables all CHECK and FOREIGN KEY constraints on the titles table:

```
ALTER TABLE titles NOCHECK CONSTRAINT ALL
```

The following ALTER TABLE statement turns the constraint checking back on:

```
ALTER TABLE titles CHECK CONSTRAINT ALL
```

There are two other ways to disable constraints in Version 6.5. There is a new option on the SET statement called DISABLE_DEF_CNST_CHK and the NOT FOR REPLICATION clause of the CREATE TABLE and ALTER TABLE statements.

DUMP and LOAD Table

The DUMP and LOAD statements have been enhanced to allow you to DUMP or LOAD individual tables. On the DUMP command, you can specify a single table to be dumped. On the LOAD command, you can specify that a single table is to be loaded from a dump. You can load a single table either from a full database dump or from a dump of that one table.

Usually, you will load a complete database. This is the only way to ensure consistency of all of the tables in your database. In some cases, you will know that you want to restore only a single table. In other cases, you will know that only one table (or a small number of tables) is modified in your application. It may save you system resources to dump only that one table (or small number of tables) on a regular basis.

There are some limitations on the use of LOAD TABLE. You cannot LOAD a table that has text or image columns. You cannot load a table that is published for replication.

It is possible to append to an existing table using LOAD TABLE. If you have two servers which both have the same table, but have different rows, you can dump on one of them and then LOAD TABLE WITH APPEND onto the other server.

Point-in-Time Recovery

The LOAD TRANSACTION statement has been enhanced to provide a STOP-AT clause. In this clause, you can specify a date and time. This specifies that you want the transaction log applied with changes up to the specified date and time.

```
DECLARE @stop datetime
SELECT @stop= '1 jan 1996 11:02am'
LOAD TRANSACTION pubs FROM dumpdevice WITH STOPAT=@stop
```

Point-in-time recovery can be useful where you know that there is some error or corruption that occurred at some specific point in time. As an example, you may have inadvertently truncated an important table, or a user may have deleted a publisher (and its associated titles).

CUBE and ROLLUP

The CUBE and ROLLUP clauses are specified as part of a GROUP BY clause to include additional summary rows.

First, let's look at an example of a SELECT with a GROUP BY. This statement summarizes the total price for each pub_id, type pair:

```
SELECT pub_id, type, sum(price) FROM titles
GROUP BY pub_id, type


0736    business                      2.99
0736    psychology                   45.93
0877    mod_cook                     22.98
0877    psychology                   21.59
0877    trad_cook                    47.89
0877    UNDECIDED                   (null)
1389    business                     51.93
1389    popular_comp                 42.95
```

Next, we use the ROLLUP clause. In this case, we also get an extra summary row for each pub_id. At the end, there is a single summary row which gives the grand total for all pub_ids and titles. On previous releases, you could have obtained a similar result with the COMPUTE BY clause and a COMPUTE clause.

```
SELECT pub_id, type, sum(price) FROM titles
GROUP BY pub_id, type
WITH ROLLUP


0736    business                      2.99
0736    psychology                   45.93
0736    (null)                       48.92
0877    mod_cook                     22.98
0877    psychology                   21.59
0877    trad_cook                    47.89
0877    UNDECIDED                   (null)
0877    (null)                       92.46
1389    business                     51.93
1389    popular_comp                 42.95
1389    (null)                       94.88
(null)  (null)                      236.26
```

Finally, with the WITH CUBE clause, you get all of the rows that we saw in the WITH ROLLUP clause, plus additional summary rows for each of the other GROUP BY columns. In this example, we grouped by type as well as pub_id. In the result set we see a summary row for each type (with the pub_id column set to NULL). On previous releases, this statement would have required multiple statements (and multiple passes through the data).

```
SELECT pub_id, type, sum(price) FROM titles
GROUP BY pub_id, type
WITH CUBE

0736    business                 2.99
0736    psychology              45.93
0736    (null)                  48.92
0877    mod_cook                22.98
0877    psychology              21.59
0877    trad_cook               47.89
0877    UNDECIDED               (null)
0877    (null)                  92.46
1389    business                51.93
1389    popular_comp            42.95
1389    (null)                  94.88
(null)  (null)                 236.26
(null)  business                54.92
(null)  mod_cook                22.98
(null)  popular_comp            42.95
(null)  psychology              67.52
(null)  trad_cook               47.89
(null)  UNDECIDED               (null)
```

INSERT with Stored Procedure Results

The INSERT statement has been enhanced to support inserting rows into a local table with the results of a query in a stored procedure. The stored procedure may be a local stored procedure, a remote stored procedure (a procedure on another server), or an extended procedure call. This allows you to manipulate the results of a stored procedure call on the SQL Server. On previous releases, you had to return the results to the client and manipulate them there.

```
CREATE TABLE #temp
(spid int,
status varchar(10),
loginame varchar(30),
hostname varchar(30),
blk char(3),
dbname varchar(30),
cmd varchar(10))

INSERT INTO #temp EXEC JIMTNT...sp_who
```

The following example inserts the results of the extended stored procedure xp_cmdshell into the temporary table.

```
CREATE TABLE #temp (file varchar(255) NULL)
INSERT INTO #temp EXEC HB2...xp_cmdshell 'dir'
```

Cursor Enhancements

A number of enhancements have been added to cursor support in Version 6.5. These are summarized in the following list:

♦ A cursor can be declared for a table for update, even when that table does not have a unique index.
♦ Cursors can automatically be closed when a transaction commits.
♦ The FETCH statement allows you to fetch the nth row in a result set (with an ABSOLUTE row number).
♦ The FETCH statement allows you to fetch the nth row before or after the current row (with a RELATIVE row number).
♦ There are performance enhancements in the execution of cursors.

DBCC DBREINDEX

The DBCC DBREINDEX statement rebuilds one or more indexes on one table or all of the tables in a database. There are a number of options on this statement. In particular you can specify that you want to reorganize the data or just recreate the index without reorganizing the data.

The reorganization can be important if a table's index has gotten fragmented. The reorganization will reestablish the FILL FACTOR for the index. Use the DBCC SHOWCONTIG statement to determine whether a given table is fragmented.

By default, this statement resorts the data. This can be useful if an index has been corrupted.

This statement is particularly convenient when an index is associated with a PRIMARY KEY or UNIQUE constraint. Without this command, the constraint must be dropped and then re-created.

New Keywords

The following is a list of new keywords included in this version. These keywords may not be used as identifiers. If you have existing databases, you must change any object or column names that match names on this list. Keywords are not case sensitive. Therefore, a table named "work" or "WORK" is not allowed on Version 6.5.

- ◆ AUTHORIZATION
- ◆ CASCADE
- ◆ CROSS
- ◆ ESCAPE
- ◆ FULL
- ◆ INNER
- ◆ JOIN
- ◆ LEFT
- ◆ OUTER
- ◆ PRIVILEGES
- ◆ RESTRICT
- ◆ RIGHT
- ◆ SCHEMA
- ◆ WORK

Distributed Transactions

This is perhaps the most dramatic enhancement to SQL Server Version 6.5. When you begin a transaction, you can specify that you want this transaction to be distributed with the following statement:

```
BEGIN DISTRIBUTED TRANSACTION
```

Once you begin a transaction in this way, all INSERT, UPDATE, and DELETE statements are part of this transaction, as you would expect. In addition, any INSERT, UPDATE, or DELETE statements executed in stored procedures using remote stored procedure calls are also part of this transaction.

For example, if the transaction comprises the following statements:

```
BEGIN DISTRIBUTED TRANSACTION
UPDATE titles SET price = $10.00 WHERE title_id = 'BU1032'
EXEC HB6.pubs.dbo.updateprice 'BU1032',$10.00
COMMIT TRAN
```

Then any INSERT, UPDATE, or DELETE statements executed in the stored procedure updateprice on HB6 is part of this transaction. Either the UPDATE and any changes in updateprice both succeed, or neither succeed (both are rolled back).

On previous releases, you could only accomplish this using a client program utilizing the two-phase commit protocol.

In order to support this capability, Version 6.5 includes a new administration tool, the Microsoft Distributed Transaction Coordinator, described later in this appendix.

Distributed transactions offer an important new capability for managing transactions in an enterprise. Distributed transactions can be used to implement transactions that must span two or more servers. But there is a price. These transactions can succeed only if all of the required servers are currently running, and if the network connections are all in place. For some applications, this will be too restrictive. Other alternatives (such as Replication) may be more appropriate.

Stored Procedure for Dynamic Creation of Web Pages

A new stored procedure is included in Version 6.5 that creates a HyperText Markup Language (HTML) document to display the results of a query. This is used by the Web Page Wizard described later in this appendix, but can also be called directly. The following command generates the HTML document displayed in Figure A.1.

```
EXEC sp_makewebpage 'C:\publishers.html',
    'SELECT * FROM publishers'
```

A number of additional parameters are supported by the sp_makewebpage stored procedure. These allow you to specify a template HTML file that

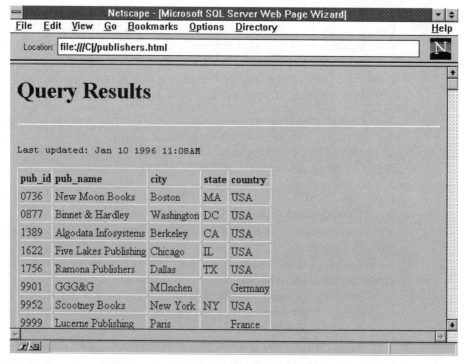

pub_id	pub_name	city	state	country
0736	New Moon Books	Boston	MA	USA
0877	Binnet & Hardley	Washington	DC	USA
1389	Algodata Infosystems	Berkeley	CA	USA
1622	Five Lakes Publishing	Chicago	IL	USA
1756	Ramona Publishers	Dallas	TX	USA
9901	GGG&G	München		Germany
9952	Scootney Books	New York	NY	USA
9999	Lucerne Publishing	Paris		France

FIGURE A.1 Web page created using sp_makewebpage.

should be used to create the HTML document, the title for the page, the title for the query results, a query for other Uniform Resource Locator (URL) jumps that should be included on the page, and a specification of how often the query should be updated (immediately, at some time in the future, or every *n* hours, days, or weeks).

New Tools

Database Maintenance Plan Wizard

The Database Maintenance Plan Wizard creates a set of administrative commands that can be executed periodically using SQL Executive. The wizard collects information from you about the usage of your database and, based on your responses, creates an appropriate plan. It will create a daily and/or a weekly plan.

The Database Maintenance Plan Wizard is part of the Enterprise Manager. You select it from the toolbar (it can also be invoked from a command line on Windows NT). It first asks you to specify a database, then it walks you through screens that solicit the following information (with recommendations in many cases):

- ♦ What percentage of the data do you expect to change each day?
- ♦ What percentage of the data will be new each day?
- ♦ What data verification checks would you like to run (these correspond to DBCC CHECKALLOC, DBCC CHECKDB, etc.)?
- ♦ Would you like these run daily or weekly?
- ♦ Do you want optimizer information updated regularly?
- ♦ Do you want tables reorganized as free space changes?
- ♦ Do you want the database backed up weekly, daily, or not at all?
- ♦ Where would you like the dump to be placed?
- ♦ When would you like the weekly and daily plans executed?

The following is sample output from the execution (in SQL Executive) of a maintenance plan created for a database using the Database Maintenance Plan Wizard:

```
Microsoft (R) SQLMaint Utility, Version 6.50.163
Copyright (C) Microsoft Corporation, 1995 - 1996

Logged on to SQL Server 'JIMTNT' as 'sa' (trusted)
Starting maintenance of database 'music' on Wed Jan 10 11:53:39 1996

[1] Check Data and Index Linkage...

  **Execution Time: 0 hrs, 0 mins, 7 secs**
```

```
[2] Check Data and Index Allocation...

  **Execution Time: 0 hrs, 0 mins, 4 secs**

[3] Check Text/Image Data Allocation...

  **Execution Time: 0 hrs, 0 mins, 3 secs**

[4] Check System Data...

  **Execution Time: 0 hrs, 0 mins, 1 secs**

[5] Update Statistics...

  **Execution Time: 0 hrs, 0 mins, 3 secs**

[6] Index Rebuild (leaving 10% free space)...

  Rebuilding indexes for table 'pbcatcol'
  Rebuilding indexes for table 'pbcatedt'
  Rebuilding indexes for table 'pbcatfmt'
  Rebuilding indexes for table 'pbcattbl'
  Rebuilding indexes for table 'pbcatvld'
  Rebuilding indexes for table 'pieces'

  **Execution Time: 0 hrs, 0 mins, 15 secs**

[7] Database Backup...
  Destination: 'C:\SQL60\backup\music_db_dump.1996110'

  **Execution Time: 0 hrs, 0 mins, 6 secs**

[8] Delete Old Backup Files...
  0 file(s) deleted.

End of maintenance for database 'music' on Wed Jan 10 11:54:18 1996
```

This wizard does not cover all possible maintenance requirements but will do a great job of getting an administrator started. Using this wizard to create a weekly plan is an absolute minimum requirement for all of your databases.

SQLTrace

SQLTrace is a graphical tool that allows an administrator to view activity on the SQL Server. The information can be filtered, allowing you to focus on certain activities of specific users. Figure A.2 shows the filter properties window that allows you to specify what activity you want to monitor. Figure A.3 shows the trace window while it monitors activity on the SQL Server.

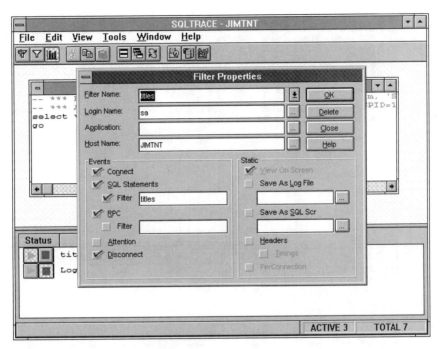

FIGURE A.2 SQLTrace filter properties.

Web Page Wizard

The Web Page Wizard creates an HTML document file based on your specifications. These pages can be created immediately, scheduled to be re-created at regular intervals, or the tool can create triggers to automatically regenerate the HTML document file whenever changes are made to the table the query is based on.

The Web Page Wizard calls the stored procedure sp_makewebpage (see description earlier in this appendix) to create the HTML document file. You are prompted for the database, table, and columns that you want to query. You may also specify a stored procedure to be called or write your own query directly. Next, you are asked whether you want to run it now, later, at regular intervals, or when the underlying data changes. Next, you are asked where you would like it saved, whether you want to use a template for the HTML document, what titles you would like, and to indicate whether you want URL addresses included. Finally, you are given some formatting options.

The following HTML file was created using the Web Page Wizard. Figure A.4 shows the resulting page as displayed using a Web browser.

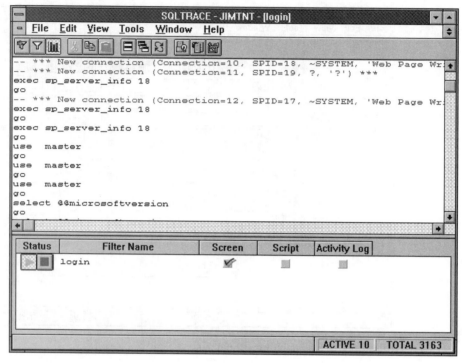

FIGURE A.3 SQLTrace display.

```
<HTML>

<HEAD>

<TITLE>SQL Server Web Page Wizard</TITLE>

<BODY>

<H1>Query Results</H1>
<HR>
<PRE><TT>Last updated: Jan 6 1996 8:02AM</TT></PRE>

<P>

<P><TABLE BORDER>
<TR><TH ALIGN=LEFT>au_lname</TH><TH ALIGN=LEFT>au_fname</TH></TR>
<TR><TD NOWRAP>Bennet</TD><TD NOWRAP>Abraham</TD></TR>
<TR><TD NOWRAP>Blotchet-Halls</TD><TD NOWRAP>Reginald</TD></TR>
<TR><TD NOWRAP>Carson</TD><TD NOWRAP>Cheryl</TD></TR>
<TR><TD NOWRAP>DeFrance</TD><TD NOWRAP>Michel</TD></TR>
<TR><TD NOWRAP>del Castillo</TD><TD NOWRAP>Innes</TD></TR>
<TR><TD NOWRAP>Dull</TD><TD NOWRAP>Ann</TD></TR>
```

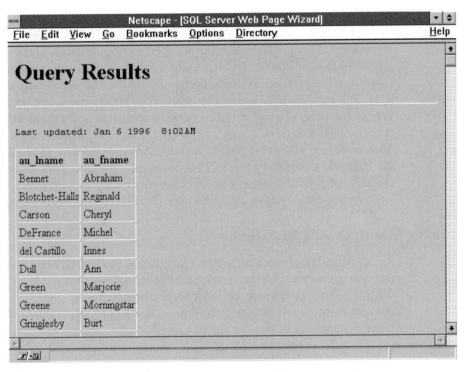

FIGURE A.4 Web page created using Web Page Wizard.

```
<TR><TD NOWRAP>Green</TD><TD NOWRAP>Marjorie</TD></TR>
<TR><TD NOWRAP>Greene</TD><TD NOWRAP>Morningstar</TD></TR>
<TR><TD NOWRAP>Gringlesby</TD><TD NOWRAP>Burt</TD></TR>
<TR><TD NOWRAP>Hunter</TD><TD NOWRAP>Sheryl</TD></TR>
<TR><TD NOWRAP>Karsen</TD><TD NOWRAP>Livia</TD></TR>
<TR><TD NOWRAP>Locksley</TD><TD NOWRAP>Charlene</TD></TR>
<TR><TD NOWRAP>MacFeather</TD><TD NOWRAP>Stearns</TD></TR>
<TR><TD NOWRAP>McBadden</TD><TD NOWRAP>Heather</TD></TR>
<TR><TD NOWRAP>O'Leary</TD><TD NOWRAP>Michael</TD></TR>
<TR><TD NOWRAP>Panteley</TD><TD NOWRAP>Sylvia</TD></TR>
<TR><TD NOWRAP>Ringer</TD><TD NOWRAP>Albert</TD></TR>
<TR><TD NOWRAP>Ringer</TD><TD NOWRAP>Anne</TD></TR>
<TR><TD NOWRAP>Smith</TD><TD NOWRAP>Meander</TD></TR>
<TR><TD NOWRAP>Straight</TD><TD NOWRAP>Dean</TD></TR>
<TR><TD NOWRAP>Stringer</TD><TD NOWRAP>Dirk</TD></TR>
<TR><TD NOWRAP>White</TD><TD NOWRAP>Johnson</TD></TR>
<TR><TD NOWRAP>Yokomoto</TD><TD NOWRAP>Akiko</TD></TR>
</TABLE>

</BODY>

</HTML>
```

Microsoft Query

Microsoft Query is a graphical tool for writing queries. It allows you to select tables using your mouse, and then select columns. From these selections and the tool's knowledge of the database design, it creates your query with a SELECT list, a FROM clause, and, using the referential declarations in your database, a WHERE clause. You can continue to elaborate on your query specifying selection criteria, ORDER BY clauses, and so on. Figure A.5 shows an example using Microsoft Query. After starting Microsoft Query, we chose a database (from a list), selected two tables (and the tool automatically identified the join for those two tables), and finally selected several columns that we wanted to see in the result.

At any time, you can asked to see the SQL code that is being created.

Transfer Management Interface

A new Transfer Management Interface replaces the SQL Transfer Manager of previous versions of SQL Server. This tool allows you to specify the type of object to be transferred; which objects; whether you want the schema, the data, or both; whether you want data replaced or appended; and whether you want the existing objects dropped.

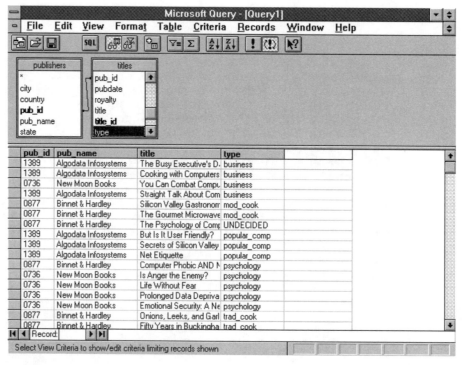

FIGURE A.5 Microsoft Query example.

The destination must be a Version 6.5 server. In the beta version of 6.5, the source can be a Microsoft 4.x or 6.x SQL Server. Sybase source support is expected in the production release.

The default scripting that the Transfer Management Interface uses can be overridden. In addition, there are new SQL Distributed Management Object (SQL-DMO) properties, methods, lists, and collections that can be used to create your own custom transfer programs.

Figure A.6 shows the Transfer Management Interface window. To open this window, select a database in the Enterprise Manager, then select Object, Transfer from the menu.

Administrative Enhancements

Support for SNMP Monitoring of SQL Server

Microsoft SQL Server Version 6.5 includes support for monitoring of SQL Server using a Simple Network Management Protocol (SNMP). With this sup-

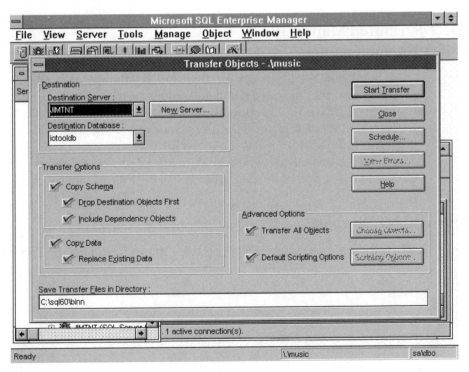

FIGURE A.6 Transfer Management Interface specification window.

port, any SNMP application can monitor configuration parameters, databases, and performance information on the SQL Server.

Replication Enhancements

Microsoft SQL Server Version 6.5 includes support for ODBC subscribers including ORACLE and Microsoft Access. In addition, Version 6.5 includes support for replicating text and image columns.

Distributed Transaction Coordinator

The Distributed Transaction Coordinator is a graphical tool that is part of the Enterprise Manager. It is used to view summary statistics and traces of distributed transactions, to monitor and control individual distributed transactions, and to configure various Distributed Transaction Coordinator options.

This tool is required to resolve uncommitted transactions in the rare instance where at least one of the participants in a distributed transaction has failed before it was informed of the final disposition of the transaction. In these cases, the administrator can evaluate the status of the transaction and manually resolve the transaction at each node.

SQL Distributed Management
Object Enhancements

A large number of new SQL Distributed Management Object (SQL-DMO) properties, methods, lists, and collections have been added in this release. In particular, SQL-DMO support is included for transferring the schema and data for a database and for rebuilding indexes, managing bulkcopy, managing server groups, and registering servers.

With this release, you can write extended stored procedures in Microsoft Visual Basic, and write COM objects will be notified when certain events occur.

PowerPC NT Support

In Microsoft SQL Server Version 6.5, support for NT on the PowerPC is added.

I N D E X

accounts domain, 344
accumulating DUMP TRANSACTION:
 DUMP DATABASE and, 400
ACID properties, 32–33
administration, 23–24, 415, 423–24. *See
 also* Enterprise Manager; SQL
 Executive; System administration
aggregate table, 252
aggregates, 51–52, 212, 370
 adding columns for, 223–24
 using CASE to calculate multiple, 235
 See also GROUP BY clause
Alert Manager, 25–26
alerts:
 administrative, 335
 automated backup using, 180–82
 messaging and, 169
 SNMP, 300
 SQLMail and, 175, 179–80
Alexander Manufacturing Company,
 99–101, 103, 105–10
aliases, 375, 378
allocation chains, TEXTALL and, 394
allocation page, 379, 387
allocation units:
 CHECKALLOC, 379
 NEWALLOC, 385
 SHRINKDB, 392
ALTER DATABASE statement, 215,
 368, 370, 402
ALTER TABLE statement, 144, 214,
 227, 377, 406, 410–11
ANSI, 405–10
 null default, 377
 Transact-SQL features, 13–16
ANSI SQL-92 entry level, 405
APIs (application programming interfaces). *See* DB-Library; MAPI;
 ODBC; ODS; Windows Socket
application architecture, 128–82, 268
 interface, 126–27
 security, 152–53

standards, 113–14
tiered, 128–31
See also client/server architectural
 model; messaging; replication
ARP (address resolution protocol),
 300
attributes, 186–90

backup, 396–404
 automated, 180–82
 DUMP DATABASE statement,
 396–97, 399, 400, 411
 DUMP TRANSACTION statement,
 397–98, 400
 of master database, 402
 using operating system commands,
 401–2
batch, 271–72, 274
 sizes, 390
bcp utility, 371–73
BDC (Backup Domain Controller), 72,
 74, 328, 335, 344
BEGIN TRANSACTION statement, 7,
 33, 62, 269
Berkeley UNIX (BSD) 4.3 release, 312
bill of materials technique, 253–55
binary sort order, 346, 347
black holes, 96
Books OnLine, 368–69
 browsing, 149–50
b-tree structures, 206

C code, using SQL to create, 251–53
cache (caching), 5, 140, 361–62
 flushing, 319
 write-through, 319
calculated data, adding columns for,
 223
calling procedure, output parameters,
 256
careful write file system, 318
cascading delete trigger, 262

CASE expression, 233–35
 with subqueries, 234–35
 in Transact-SQL, 14–15
 use in the SELECT List, 233–34
character sets, 405
 installation issues, 342–43
CHECK constraint, 200, 410–11
CHECKALLOC command, 379–80
CHECKCATALOG command, 380
CHECKDB command, 380–81, 396
CHECKPOINT command, 377, 379
CHECKTABLE command, 380, 381–82
CHKUPG command, 343
classes of locks, 7–8, 34–36
client/server architectural model,
 131–53
 concurrency control, 148–50
 connection management, 132–36
 data access, 139–42
 data validation, 143–45
 distributed processing, 150–51
 error handling, 136–39
 messaging (*see* messaging)
 security, 151–53
 transaction management, 145–48
CLOSE statement, 241
clustered indexes, 38, 45, 46, 206–8,
 210–11, 226
code, formatted or structured, 115,
 117–19, 124
code generation techniques, 250–53
 creating C code, 251–53
 generating SQL statements, 250–51
coding techniques, 228–66
 neat SQL tricks, 243–55
 RAISERROR, 258–59, 264
 simple SQL techniques, 229–43
 stored procedures, 255–59
 triggers, 259–64
collisions, 149–50
columns, 190, 218
 adding, 223–25

columns (*cont'd*)
  constraints on, 15–16, 144, 200
  covering index and, 51
  CREATE INDEX statement, 214
  database design and, 209–12
  density and, 55
  first normal form, 189
  identity and, 14
  names and, 196
  null status and, 155, 191, 197, 198
  OR strategy, 48
  rules and defaults, 144, 196
  table creation and, 194, 195
  text and image, 155, 167
  timestamp and, 149
  update in place and, 21
  user-defined datatype caveat, 145
  vertical splitting, 219–20
Command Queue Length, 389–90
comment header, 115–16, 120
commit service, DB-Library two-phase, 62–63
COMMIT TRANSACTION statement, 6, 7, 33, 62, 269
common joins, 209
communicating with SQL Server, 59–71
  DB-Library, 60–64
  ODBC, 64–67
  ODS, 67–71
CompuServe MSSQL Forum, 369
concurrency control, 148–50
  browsing, 149–50
  preemptive locking, 148–49
  repeatable reads, 150
configuration management, 92, 352–62
  allow updates, 356–58
  fill factor, 358
  max worker threads, 358
  memory, 358–60
  network packet size, 360
  open databases, 361
  open objects, 361
  priority boost, 361
  set working set size, 361
  sp_configure, 352–56
  tempdb in ram, 361–62
  user connections, 362
  See also sp_configure
connect event handler, 69
connection, 132–36
  to ODS, 70–71
constraints, 15–17, 155
  check, 200
  CREATE TABLE statement, 195–96
  default, 199
  foreign key, 16, 201–2, 410–11
  integrity, 201–6
contrary motion, 389
cooperative processing, 87–88
CORBA, 86
Core mode, 168
correlated SELECT, 229–30

CREATE CLUSTERED INDEX statement, 38
CREATE DATABASE FOR LOAD statement, 397
CREATE DATABASE statement, 214, 397
CREATE INDEX statement, 213, 214
CREATE NONCLUSTERED INDEX statement, 39
CREATE PROCEDURE statement, 202–3, 255–57, 376
CREATE SCHEMA statement, 405
CREATE TABLE statement, 195–98, 201, 213
cross joins, 407
cross tabulations, 244–47
CUBE clause, 412, 413
cursors, 15, 141–42, 240–42
  dynamic EXECUTE with, 242–43
  using to create serial numbers, 248
  Version 6.5 enhancements, 414

data access, 139–42
  embedded SQL and DB-Library calls, 141
  set operations and cursors, 141–42
  stored procedures, 140–41
database design, 183–227
  building and tuning (*see* physical database design)
  columns and, 209–12
  identifying needs, 184–85
  logical, 185–93
Database Maintenance Plan Wizard, 417–18
database management, 371–96
  DBCC, 379–96
  loading data, 371–73
  managing users, 374–76
  sp_dboption, 376–79
databases, 369–70
  error recovery issues, 366–68
  open databases setting, 361
  size, 214
  warm standby strategy, 402
  See also master database; model database; Msdb database; relational databases; Tempdb database
data distribution, 153–54. *See also* replication
data loading, 371–73
data management systems, 83–84
data validation, 143–45
  client validation techniques, 145
  SQL Server validation techniques, 143–45
  user-defined datatype caveat, 145
datatypes, 190, 191
  ANSI standard and new, 13–14
  guidelines for, 196–97
  nulls and, 191
  table creation and, 196–98
  user-defined, 144, 145, 191, 197, 198

DBCC statements, 379–96
DB-Library, 1, 8, 60–64
  calls, 141
  connection management, 133–34
  using bcp services of, 373
dbo use only setting, 377
dbo_database_name, 365–66
DBREINDEX statement, 414
DBREPAIR statement, 382
deadlocks, 36–37
DEALLOCATE statement, 241
DEC Open VMS operating system, 328
DECLARE statement, 117, 240
defaults, 191, 198–99
DELETE statement, 231, 262
  triggers for, 259–61
deleted tables, 204–5, 260
denormalization, 217–25
density, 54–55
deployment phase of project life cycle, 108–9
design, database. *See* database design
design phase of project life cycle, 104–6
destination database table, 160
development. *See* software development
development methodologies, 90–91
device failure
  disk mirroring, 3, 324, 325, 403
  DUMP TRANSACTION WITH NO_TRUNCATE, 398, 401
  RAID 1 and, 325
  up-to-the-minute recovery, 400–1
devices, 349–51
  log device, 163, 397, 401
  sp_devscpace, 350–51
  using files as database, 349
DHCP (Domain Host Control Protocol), 279, 297, 301–2
diagrams, entity-relationship, 187–88
dictionary order, 346–47
difference operations, 243–44
Digital Equipment Corporation (DEC), 72
Direct-Hosting, 283, 284, 291
disciplines, 78–94
  infrastructure arena, 79, 82–83, 93
  roles and responsibilities, 93–94
  software development arena, 80–81, 83–89, 94
  support and control arena, 81, 89–94
Disk Mirroring, 3, 324, 325, 403
DISK RESIZE statement, 21–22, 366–67
distributed data, 153–54. *See also* replication
Distributed Management Objects. *See* SQL-DMO
distributed processing, 150–51
Distributed Transaction Coordinator, 424
distributed transactions, 62, 154, 415–16

distribution database, 26, 367–68
replication and, 155, 160, 161, 163–67, 348
distribution page, 51, 53–55, 59
distribution server, 27, 74, 367
replication and, 155, 156, 159–68, 347–48
SMS and, 336–38
distributor, 155
DLC (Data Link Control), 285
dllname (FREE), 382–83
DLLs (Dynamic Link Libraries), 8
used by DB-Library, 60
DNS (domain naming service), 302
documentation, 91–92, 116, 120–23
domains, 302, 328, 333–34, 374
constraints, 16, 17
global groups in, 331
installation and, 344
server manager and, 334–36
User Manager for, 331–33
DROP DATABASE command, 382
DSS (decision support systems), 71, 192–93, 216–17
DUMP DATABASE statement, 325–26, 367, 396–97
using only on database, 399
Version 6.5 enhancements, 411
DUMP TRANSACTION statement, 367, 368, 378, 379, 397–98
accumulating, 400
incremental, 399–400
WITH NO_TRUNCATE, 398, 401
duplicates:
adding columns for, 222–23
checking for, 233
dynamic EXECUTE:
with cursor, 242–43
in a stored procedure, 242
dynamic transaction, 271

e-mail, 179–80
automated backup using, 180–82
embedded SQL, 141
encryption:
RAS and, 315–16
of stored procedure text, 18–19
enterprise database product, 12–13, 22–30
centralized administration, 22–26
messaging, 27–30
replication, 26–27
Enterprise Manager, 2, 10, 24–25, 374–75
backup and restore, 396, 397
Database Maintenance Plan Wizard, 417–18
DISK RESIZE statement, 366–67
Distributed Transaction Coordinator, 424
error log, 368
input buffer, 383
managing users, 374
MAPI and, 27

OLE Automation and, 28
Register Server, 348
SQL-DMO and, 11
tempdb size and, 370
updating of statistics, 59
viewing locks, 40
entities, 186–90
constraints, 16, 17
entity-relationship (E-R) diagram, 185
equi-joins, 406–7
error handling, 136–39
RAISERROR, 137–38
techniques, 138–39
transaction logic and, 147–48, 258–59
error log, 137, 342, 345, 368
error recovery. *See* recovery
Ethernet networks, 279, 284, 285, 292
event handlers, 69
Event Manager, 25
events, 179
exclusive locks, 7, 35, 36
EXECUTE statement, 18, 242–43, 271
existence checks, 223–24
extended stored procedures, 1, 9, 131, 177, 178, 428
ODS and, 10, 67–68, 70
extents, 35, 36

fast bcp, 371, 372
FAT (file allocation table), 319–21, 327
fault tolerance, 324–26
FETCH statement, 15, 241, 414
file systems, 318–28, 349
FAT, 319–21
fault tolerance, 324–26
HPFS, 320, 321
NTFS, 320–21
RAID 5, 326–27
security, 321–24
selecting, 327–28
fill factor, 358
FILLFACTOR parameter, 227
FIPS flagger, 405, 410
first normal form (1NF), 189
float datatype, 13
force index, 20
FORCEPLAN ON, 20, 50–51
foreign keys, 208
constraints, 16, 201–2, 410–11
formatted code, 115, 117–19, 124
frame types, 284, 292
frameworks, reusable, 127
FROM clause, 232
full database, 366–68
FULL OUTER JOIN, 409
Full Transaction Log, 366, 367

global groups, 329–31
global temporary tables, 16–17
GRANT statement, 375, 376, 405
GRANT WITH GRANT option, 406
GROUP BY clause, 52–53, 235–39
CUBE and ROLLUP, 412–13

dangerous, 238–39
HAVING clause and, 237
groups, 328–31
managing users with, 374–76
GUIs (Graphical User Interfaces), 84–86

hardware, 82
HAVING clause, GROUP BY clause and, 237
HOLDLOCK, 34, 35, 38, 142, 148–50
horizontal splitting, 218–19
host name resolution, 302–4
hotspots, 211, 226
HPFS (high performance file system), 320, 321, 327
HTML (HyperText Markup Language), 316, 416, 419

ICMP (Internet Control Message Protocol), 300
IDENTITY property, creating serial numbers using, 249
IEEE Project 802, 280, 284
IF EXISTS test, 262, 263
IF UPDATE clause, 260
ImpersonateNamedPipeClient, 71
impersonation, 71, 323–24
incremental DUMP TRANSACTION, 399–400
index creation, 206–14, 358
clustered or nonclustered, 210–12
planning indexes, 213
syntax, 213–14
types of indexes, 206–7
indexes:
analysis, 47–48
covering, 51
selection, 45–46
size, 215
statistics, 20, 47
tuning, 226–27
indirect relationship queries, 225
infrastructure, 79, 82–83, 93
file systems, 318–28
interprocess communication, 309–12
network models, 279–84
network protocols, 285–309
project management sequencing and, 99, 100, 102, 104, 106, 108
INIT options, 396
inner join, 406–7
INPUTBUFFER, 383, 386
INSERT statement
INSERT . . . VALUES, 230
simplest form of, 230
with stored procedure results, 413–14
triggers for, 259–61
using a SELECT clause, 230–31
inserted tables, 204–5, 260
installation, 341–49
accounts, 341
character sets, 342–43

installation (*cont'd*)
    CHKUPG, 343
    environment, 343–45
    problems with, 348–49
    replication and, 347–48
    service packs, 345
    sort orders, 345–47
integrated security, 153, 161, 348, 363, 365, 374
integrity constraints, 15–16, 201–6
interface models, 280–82
Internet, RAS and, 316–18
interprocess communication, 309–12
    RPC, 311–12
    SMBs, 310
    Windows Socket, 312
IOSTATS, 389, 393
IP (Internet protocol), 300
IPX/SPX (Internetwork Packet Exchange), 281
ISO 8859-1, 342
isolation levels, locking, 33–34
ISQL/W feature, 59
iterative development, 96–97

join selection index, 46
joins (join order), 48–51, 100, 101, 222
    ANSI standard, 407–9
    columns and, 222, 224, 239
    database design and, 209, 211, 216, 217
    density and, 54
    GROUP BY, 236
    IF EXISTS test, 263
    indirect relationship queries, 225
    join clauses, 43, 46
    JOIN reformatting strategy, 49–51
    joint nested iteration strategy, 49
    nested SELECT, 230
    nulls and, 220
    referential integrity checks, 193
    relational solution to, 275, 277
    SELECT, 246
    user-defined datatypes, 145, 197
    views and, 53
    WHERE clause, 119, 208, 244, 406–7
    workstation to domain, 330
    See also outer joins

keywords, 404–5, 414–15

language event handler, 69
lazy write file system, 318, 319
LEFT OUTER JOIN, 407–8
librarianship, 92
LOAD DATABASE statement, 396, 397
LOAD TABLE statement, 411
LOAD TABLE WITH APPEND, 411
LOAD TRANSACTION statement, 398, 411
    STOP-AT clause, 411–12
loading data, 371–73
local groups, 329–31
local pipe, 70–71

local temporary tables, 16–17
locks (locking), 7–8, 31–41
    basic principles, 32–33
    concurrency and, 148–49
    transaction design and, 268–70
    VLDB, 75–76
log device, 163, 349–50, 397
    failure, 401
LOG ON option, 215
log reader task failure, 166
log size, 214
logical database design, 185–93
logical unit of work, 267–68
login, 363–66
    account locked out flag and, 332
    aliased, 375, 378
    dbo_database_name, 365–66
    establishing a connection, 133
    query tools and, 152
    replication and, 163–65
    sa (system administrator) and, 3, 162, 348, 363, 364–66, 374–75
    sp_addlogin, 162, 363, 364, 374
    sp_droplogin, 375, 386
    SQLMail and, 176, 341
logon, unified, 29–30
LRUSTATS, 389, 393

Mail Slots, 310, 312, 313
maintenance and support, 109–10
management issues, 110–13
management tools, 23–24, 417–23. *See also* Enterprise Manager; SQL Executive
managing a database. *See* database management
managing users, 328–33, 374–76
managing Windows NT, 333–39
MAPI (Messaging Application Programming Interface), 27–28, 169–71
mapping of logical to physical layout, 3–4
master database, 366–67, 369, 370
    backing up, 402
master device, SQL Server, 344
max worker threads, 358
memory:
    cache, 5, 140, 319, 361–62
    Command Queue Length, 389–90
    connection resources and, 134
    MEMUSAGE, 383–85
    Named Pipes and, 311
    NBF and, 287, 309
    RAID 5 and, 326
    set working set size, 361
    sp_configure, 358–62, 389–90, 393
    stored procedures in, 140
    system management server and, 338, 339
    TCP/IP and, 306
    tempdb in ram, 361–62
    upgrades from 4.2x and, 349
MEMUSAGE, 383–85

merging tables, 221
messaging, 27–30, 169–82
    automated backup, 180–82
    MAPI, 27–28, 169–71
    OLE Automation, 28
    removable media, 29
    unifed logon, 29–30
    Windows NT Mail, 169, 171–75
messaging protocols, 87
methodologies, 90–91
Microsoft Access, 424
Microsoft Query, 422
Microsoft Systems Management server, 336, 338–39
mixed security, 363
model database, 367, 369–70
MRP (Multiple Provider Router), 282
msdb database, 369
MSSQLServer, 176
multiple aggregates, 235
Multiple Provider Router (MRP), 282
multiple publishers–multiple subscribers model, 157–58
multiple publishers–single subscriber model, 156, 157
multitiered architectures, 129–30
MUP (Multiple UNC Provider), 282

Named Pipes, 9, 70, 310–11
    distribution server and, 161
    replication and, 164, 168
    SQL Bridge and, 298
    VREDIR.386 and, 282
    Windows for Workgroups and, 290
name resolution, 283
naming conventions, 115, 119–20, 124–25
NCP, 282
NDIS (Network Device Interface Specification), 280–81
nested cursors, 277
nested SELECT, 230
NetBEUI Frame (NBF), 286–91, 309
    issues, 290–91
    resolving problems, 291
    tuning, 287–90
NetBIOS, 293–95, 311
    name resolution, 304–5
    RAS and, 314–15
    tuning for, 307
Net-Library, 8–9
netlogon Service, 333
NETSTATS, 389, 393
NetWare, 284
network(s):
    file systems, 282
    installation, 343
    operating systems (NOS), 83
    packet size, 360
    reads, 390
    support with RAS, 312–18
network models, 279–84
    IEEE Models, 280
    interface models, 280–82

OSI, 279–81
routing models, 282–85
network protocols, 285–309
choosing, 309
DLC, 285
NBF, 286–91
NWLink, 291–97
TCP/IP, 297–309
NEWALLOC, 385–86
NFS, 282
NICs (network interface cards), 282–83
no chkpt on recovery, 377
NOINDEX, 382
NOINIT options, 396, 397
nonclustered indexes, 45, 47, 206–8, 211–12, 226
normalization, 188–90, 218
denormalization, 217–25
queries, 41–42
NOT NULL, 377
Novell IPX/SPX protocols, 292, 295–97, 309
NTFS (new technology file system), 320–21, 327
NULL password, 172, 365, 375, 376
null status, 198
nullability control, 377
nulls, 191
NWLink protocol, 281, 291–97, 309
NWLinkIPX, 295–97
NWLnkSPX, 292–93
NWNBLink, 291, 293–95

object-oriented technology, 82, 86–87, 89
ODBC (Open Database Connectivity), 1, 9, 64–67
implementation considerations, 65–66
performance issues, 66–67
typical usage, 65
ODS (Open Data Services), 1, 9–10, 67–71
offline databases, 377–78
OLAP (Online Analytical Processing), 71
old threads, 369
OLE 2.0, 86
OLE Automation, 28
OLTP (online transaction processing), 71, 113–14, 153, 154, 192–93, 216, 217
Open Data Services, 130–31
open databases setting, 361
open interoperability, 87
open objects setting, 361
open servers, 130–31
Open System Interconnect (OSI) Model, 279–81
OpenVMS, 72
OPENTRAN, 386
operating systems, 83
optimistic concurrency control, 149

optimizer, query. *See* query optimizer (query optimization)
OR clauses, 45, 48
OR processing strategy, 48
ORACLE, 424
ORDER BY clause, 20, 52, 117, 345, 346, 370, 425
order table, 245
OSI Model, 279–81
outer joins, 244–46, 277, 407–9
OUTPUTBUFFER, 386–87
output parameters, 256

packet size, 134, 168, 293, 360
PAGE, 387–88
pager-provider, 27
paging, 358–59
parallel development, 97–98
parallel processing, 74–75
parallelization, 19
parsing:
application logic and processing, 128
queries, 41
Transact-SQL, 5
passwords:
creating trusts and, 333
encryption schemes and, 315
NULL, 172, 365, 375, 376
replication and, 164, 165
security issues and, 152, 348, 364, 365–66
SQL Executive and, 341
SQLMail and, 175–77
Windows NT administrator, 29
PDC (Primary Domain Controller), 72, 74, 328, 330, 335, 337, 344
PERFMON, 389, 393
performance:
database design and, 192–93
enhancements, 12, 19–22
with ODBC usage, 66–67
sort orders and, 347
statistics, 389, 393–94
physical database design, 193–216
planning capacity, 214–16
translation from logical to, 193–94
tuning (*see* tuning phase of database design)
physical disk storage, 3
pinned tables, 391
PINTABLE, 391, 395
placing objects, 227
planning capacity, of physical database design, 214–16
Point-in-time recovery, 411–12
POSIX, 320
postmaster, SQLMail, 177–78
postoffice, Windows NT, 172–75
PowerPC, 424
PPP (Point-to-Point Protocol), 313
preemptive locking, 148–49
primary database:
security, 152
warm standby, 402

primary identifier, 187
primary keys, 208, 209, 211
changing the trigger, 263–64
constraints, 16
priority boost parameter, 361
problem resolution, 368–69
procedural processing, 272, 273–75
procedure event handler, 69
profiles, 389
programming, 89
standards, 114–27
project control, 90
project design, 89
project life cycle, 77–127
disciplines (*see* disciplines)
management issues, 110–13
standards, 113–27
timing, 94–110
iterative and parallel development, 96–98
project management, 89–90
sequencing, 98–110
protocol drivers, 279–81
protocol stacks, 283–84
publication database tables, 161, 162, 166
publication server, 155, 156, 163, 165, 166–67, 352
published option, 378
publisher, 26–27, 154–58, 160
publisher transaction log, 160, 163
pull subscription, 27, 155
push subscription, 27, 155

queries, 422
query coverage, 226
query optimizer (query optimization), 42–46
enhancements to, 19–21
phases of, 42–46
processing strategies, 47–53
stored procedure caveat and, 140–41
tools, statistics, and the distribution page, 53–55
tuning, 20–21
query plan maintenance, 55–59
query processing, 41–55
translating the query, 41–42
user tools, query plan maintenance, 55–59

RAID (redundant arrays of inexpensive disks), 324–27
RAISERROR statement, 17–18, 137–39, 258–59, 264
with the sysmessages Table, 264–65
rapid application development (RAD), 95
RAS, 312–18
Internet and, 316–18
as a NetBIOS gateway, 314–15
security, 315–16
as a SLIP client, 313
as a software router, 313–14

RASTATS, 389, 393–94
ratio table, 252
Raw mode, 168, 169
Read Access, 323
READ COMMITTED, 33, 34
read locks, 7–8
read only setting, 378
READ UNCOMMITTED, 33, 34
read-ahead, 74–75
recovery:
    point-in-time recovery, 411–12
    Up-to-the-Minute Recovery, 400–401
    See also restore
reference constraints, 16, 201–2
referential constraints, 16, 17
reformatting strategy, 49–51
Regedt32, 173, 288–90, 292–93
relational databases, 83, 272–77
    mentoring and rules of thumb,
      276–77
    relational versus procedural process-
      ing, 273–76
relational processing techniques, 267
relationships, 186–90
Remote Access Server. *See* RAS
Remote Procedure Calls (RPC),
    311–12
remote stored procedures, ODS and,
    68–69
removable media, 29
REPEATABLE READS, 33, 34
repeatable reads, 150
replication, 24, 26–27, 153–69
    installation issues and, 347–48
    Version 6.5 enhancements, 424
    Replication Manager, 25
replication_cleanup task, 159–60
repl_publisher, 378
repl_subscriber, 378
resource domains, 333, 344
resource usage, 134–35
response time, connection performance
    and, 135–36
restore. *See also* recovery
    LOAD DATABASE statement, 397
    LOAD TRANSACTION statement,
      398
    Up-to-the-Minute Recovery, 400–401
restricted publication, 155
reusable frameworks, 127
REVOKE command, 376
REVOKE . . . CASCADE statement,
    406
RIGHT OUTER JOIN, 408–9
roles, 93–94
ROLLBACK, 147
ROLLBACK TRANSACTION state-
    ment, 6, 7, 33, 269
ROLLUP clause, 412
Routing Models, 282–85
RPC (Remote Procedure Calls), 311–12
rule creation, 199–200
rules, database design and, 190–92

sa (system administrator), login3, 3,
    162, 348, 363, 364–66, 374–75
    DBCC PAGE, 387–88
    See also system administration
scalability, 71–73, 276
search arguments, 43–45
second normal form (2NF), 189–90
secondary database, warm standby,
    402
security, 151–53, 363–66
    for ad hoc tools, 152
    control and, 152–53
    dbo_database_name, 365–66
    file systems, 321–24
    integrated, for application compo-
      nents, 153, 161, 348, 363, 374
    login ID sa, 363–66
    ODS, 71
    overview of, 363
    primary database, 152
    RAS, 315–16
    stored procedure permission test,
      363–64
segments, placing objects on, 227
SELECT clause, INSERT statement
    using, 230–31
select into/bulkcopy setting, 378
SELECT List, use of CASE expression
    in, 233–34
SELECT statement, 117, 148–50,
    229–30
    GROUP BY clause in a, 235–39
    locking and, 37–38
    nested, 230
    simplest form of, 229
selectivity, 140
serial numbers:
    creating in existing tables, 247–49
    managing, 249–50
SERIALIZABLE, 34
Server Engine. *See* SQL Server Engine
server management, 349–71
    configuration, 352–62
    devices, 349–51
    error recovery issues, 366–68
    problem resolution, 368–69
    security, 363–66
    special databases, 369–70
server manager, 334–36
server message blocks (SMBs), 168,
    169, 282, 310
server-based cursors, 141
servers, 278–79, 328. *See also* SQL
    Server
service packs, 345
SET FIPS_FLAGGER, 405, 410
SET FORCEPLAN ON, 20, 50–51
set operations, 141, 142
SET options, 395–96
    connection, 133–34
SET ROW COUNT, 277
SET statement, 58
set working set size option, 361

shared locks, 35, 36
Show Query Plan (ISQL/W), 59
SHOW_CONTIG, 21, 392, 414
SHOW_STATISTICS, 55–56, 391
SHRINKDB, 21, 392
SHUTDOWN statement, 401
single processor, SQL Server on,
    343–44
single publisher-multiple subscribers
    model, 156
single publisher/single subscriber
    model, 158
single user option, 378, 392
SLIP (Serial Line Internet Protocol),
    313
slow bcp, 371, 372
SMBs (Server Message Blocks), 168,
    169, 282, 310
SMS (System Management Server),
    336–38
SMS Despooler, 338
SMS Logon Server, 337
SMS Site Server, 337
SMSLS (System Management Server
    Logon Script), 337
snapshot, 158, 162
SNMP (Simple Network Management
    Protocol), 300–301, 423–24
sockets, 70, 312
software development, 80–81, 83–89,
    94, 110
    changing styles of management in,
      94–95
    methodologies, 90–91
    project management sequencing
      and, 99, 100, 102, 104–8
software distribution, 337–38
software inventory, 337
sorts (sort orders):
    dictionary orders and, 346–47
    installation issues and, 345–47
    OR processing strategy, 48
    range retrievals based on price and,
      213
    reformatting strategy, 49
    SQL Server performance and, 347
    tempdb in ram and, 361–62
    tempdb table and, 361, 370
space, device, 350–51
sp_addalias, 375
sp_addlogin, 162, 363, 364, 374
sp_addmessage, 264–65
sp_adduser, 374
sp_configure, 75, 352, 370
    allow updates, 356–58
    memory, 358–60
    priority boost, 361
    recovery from errors or insufficient
      resources, 352–56
    set working set size, 361
sp_dboption, 368, 376–79
sp_dbremove, 382
sp_devscpace, 350–51

sp_dropalias, 375
sp_droplogin, 375, 386
specification phase, 99–100
spiral technologies, 94–95
splitting tables, 218–21
sp_lock stored procedure, 39–40
sp_makewebpage, 416–17, 419
sp_processmail, 177–78
sp_remotelogin, 162
sp_repltrans, 367
sp_updatealert, 182
sp_who, 386
SQLAdmins, 374
SQL Bridge, 297, 298
SQLColumns, 67
SQL-DMO (SQL Distributed Manage-
    ment Objects), 11, 24–26
    Version 6.5 enhancements, 424
SQL Executive, 2, 10, 24
    installation, 341
SQLMail, 169, 171, 172, 175–80
    installation, 341
SQL Server:
    communicating with, 59–71
        ODBC, 64–67
        ODS, 67–71
        using DB-Library, 60–64
    limits, 371, 372
    new features in Version 6, 12–30
    overall architecture, 1–11
    simple techniques, 228–43
    starting on system boot, 371
    troubleshooting, 368–69
SQL Server Administrator's Companion,
    369
SQL Server Distributed Management
    Objects, 2
SQL Server Engine, 1, 2–8
    locking pages and tables, 7–8
    logging changes, 6–7
    maintaining logical object design, 4
    managing multiple users, 4–5
    managing network connections, 5
    mapping of logical to physical lay-
        out, 3–4
    optimization of queries, 5–6
    parsing of Transact-SQL, 5
    physical disk storage, 3
    transaction management, 7
    transmitting data to the client, 6
SQL Server Enterprise Manager. *See*
    Enterprise Manager
SQL Server Performance Monitor, 389,
    390
SQL Server Security Manager, 374
SQLTrace, 418–19
SQL Transfer Manager, 371, 422
SQLUser groups, 374
standards, 113–27
standard security, 363
statistics, 53–55
Stats_Date(), 59
STOP_AT clause, 411–12

stored procedures, 202–3, 255–59
    accessing in many databases, 370
    advantage over Transact-SQL state-
        ments, 255
    comment header, 123
    data access and, 140–41
    dbo ownership and, 375–76
    defined, 140, 192, 202
    documentation and, 120, 121, 123
    for dynamic creation of Web pages,
        416–17, 419–21
    dynamic EXECUTE in, 242
    encryption of text, 18–19
    giving help for, 256
    individual ownership and, 376
    INSERT statement with, 413–14
    output parameters, 256
    permission test, 363–64
    for SQLMail, 177–78
    syntax, 255–56
    table creation and, 202–3
    transaction error handling, 258–59
    transaction management and, 271,
        272
    using temporary tables in, 256–57
    See also extended stored procedures;
        triggers
striping, 74
structured code, 115, 117–19, 124
stubs, 70
subqueries, 20
    CASE with, 234–35
subscribed option, 378
subscribers, 26–27, 155, 156–58, 162,
    165–67, 348
subscription, 155
subscription server, 27, 155, 159–65,
    167, 168, 352
subtraction operations, 243–44
subtypes, 220–22
supertypes, 220–22
support and control, 81, 89–94
    project management sequencing
        and, 99, 100–101, 103, 105, 107,
        108
symmetric server architecture, 72–74
synchronization, 162, 167, 168
    of a new subscriber, 27
syslogs, 6
sysmessages table, RAISERROR with,
    264–65
system administration, 12–13, 22–30.
    See also sa (system administrator)
system catalog, 4
System Management Server, 336–38
system procedures. *See* stored proce-
    dures

table_id, 392
tables:
    constraints, 15–16, 144
    creating serial numbers in existing,
        247–49

creation of, 194–206
    integrity constraints, 15–16, 201–6
    fragmentation, SHOWCONTIG and,
        21, 392
    loading data into, 371–73
    merging, 221
    scans, 45, 47–48, 206
    size, 215
    splits, 218–21
    SQL Server locks, 35–37
Tabular Data Stream (TDS), 8
Task Manager, 25, 26
tasks, 81–82, 89–96
    automated backup using, 180–82
    detailed list for, 98–99
TCP/IP, 297–309
    architecture, 298–301
    diagnosing connection problems,
        308–9
    diagnostic utilities, 307–8
    Domain Host Control Protocol,
        301–2
    Host and NetBIOS Name Resolution,
        302–5
    tuning for NetBIOS activity, 307
    tuning for performance, 305–6
TDI-NDIS model, 282
TDS (Tabular Data Stream), 8, 60, 69,
    132
technical review, 93, 277
technology issues:
    communicating with SQL server,
        59–71
    locking, 31–41
    query processing, 41–59
    VLDB (very large database), 22,
        71–76
tempdb database, 367, 369, 370
    contents, 370
    expanding, 370
    shrinking, 370
tempdb in ram, 361–62
templates. *See* Model database
temporary tables, 16–17
    using in a stored procedure, 256–57
testing, 88, 92–93
    and deployment, 108–9
TEXTALL, 394
TEXTALLOC, 394
threads, 394
    max worker, 358
    SSA and, 73
tiered architecture, 128–31
timeboxing, 95
timestamp, 149, 167
timing, 94–110
    iterative and parallel development,
        96–98
    project management sequencing. *See*
        project management, sequenc-
        ing
TNEF (Transport Neutral Encapsula-
    tion Format), 171

TPC (Transaction Processing Council), 72

trace flags, 394–95

transaction dumps, 7

transaction log:
  dumps, 6, 160, 367
  sizing, 215–16

transaction management, 7, 145–48, 267–72
  BEGIN TRANSACTION statement, 7, 33, 62, 269
  COMMIT TRANSACTION, 6, 7, 33, 62, 269
  error handling and, 147–48, 258–59
  implementation issues, 268–70
  logical unit of work, 267–68
  ROLLBACK TRANSACTION, 6, 7, 33, 269

transaction rollback, 7

transactions, distributed, 62, 154, 415–16

Transact-SQL, 12–19, 24, 116–23
  ANSI standard features, 13–16, 116
    CASE expression, 14–15
    cursor support, 15
    identity, 14
    integrity enhancement feature, 15–16
    new datatypes, 13–14
  connection management, 133
  documentation, 120–23
  enhancements, 16–19
  formatting and structuring code, 117–19
  naming conventions, 119–20
  parsing of, 5
  SQL Server Version 6.5 enhancements, 410–17
  Transfer Management Interface, 422–23

transmission control protocol/Internet protocol (TCP/IP). *See* TCP/IP

triggers, 259–64
  business rules and, 192, 259
  cascading delete, 262
  changing the primary key, 263–64
  defined, 259
  documentation and, 116, 120, 121, 123
  errors and messages, 138, 147
  guidelines, 260–61
  headers and comments, 120, 121, 123

for INSERT, UPDATE, or DELETE, 259–63
  MAPI and, 27
  referential integrity and, 15, 16, 259
  subscribers and, 155
  syntax, 260
  table creation and, 201, 203–6
  validation technologies and, 144

trusted connections. *See* integrated security

trusted domains, 333

trusts, 344, 374

tuning phase of database design, 216–27
  denormalization, 217–25
  modifying design, 216–17
  placing objects, 227
  tuning indexes, 226–27

two-tiered architecture, 128–29

UDP (user datagram protocol), 299

UNC (Universal Naming Convention), 282, 283

unified logon, 29–30

unique constraint, 16

unique index, 191

Unix, 64, 302–4, 307, 312, 313

UNPINNABLE, 391

UNPINTABLE, 395

unrestricted publication, 155

update locks, 35, 36

UPDATE statement, 19, 149, 232, 263
  triggers for, 259–61

UPDATE STATISTICS statement, 18, 53–54, 59, 226
  locks and, 39

UPDATEUSAGE statement, 21, 395

Up-to-the-Minute Recovery, 400–401

user connections, 362

user database, 367–68

user documentation, 91–92

user login ID, 363–65

user management, 328–33, 374–76

User Manager for Domains, 331–33

user review, 88

user tools, 55–59

user-defined datatypes, 144, 145, 191, 197, 198

user-interface standards, 125–27

USEROPTIONS, 395–96

validating data. *See* data validation

variable scope conventions, 125

version control, 92

vertical splitting, 219–21

VINES, 282

Visual Basic, DB-Library with, 63–64

Visual Basic for Applications (VBA), 28

VLDBs (very large databases), 22, 71–76
  distributed operating system, 73–74
  lock management, 75–76
  parallel processing, 74–75
  RAID0, RAID1, and RAID5, 74
  scalability of hardware, 71–72
  symmetric server architecture, 72–73

VREDIR386, 292

VREDIR.386, 281–82

warm standby, 402

Web Page Wizard, 416–17, 419–21

Web Servers, 316–17

WHERE clause, 208, 212, 231, 232, 244

Windows for Workgroups, 282–83

Windows NT, 2
  architecture, 278–79
  DB-Library for C with, 60–61
  as distributed operating system, 73–74
  file systems, 318–28, 349
  network protocols, 285–309
  Performance Monitor, 168, 287, 349, 358–60
  RAS and. *See* RAS
  SMBs and, 168
  System Management Server, 336–38
  unified logon, 29–30
  User Manager for Domains, 164, 331, 333, 341, 374

Windows NT Mail, 169, 171–76
  creating the postoffice, 172–73
  recreating the postoffice, 173–75
  SQLMail password, 175

Windows Sockets, 312

WINS (Windows Internet naming service), 73, 278, 297–98, 302, 304–5

WITH CUBE clause, 413

WITH NO_INFOMSGS, 396

WITH NO_LOG, 398

WITH RECOMPILE, 140, 203, 257

WITH TRUNCATE_ONLY, 398

Wnet API, 282

World Wide Web, 316–17
  Web Page Wizard, 416–17, 419–21

Write Access, 323